Interfaces in Linguistics

OXFORD STUDIES IN THEORETICAL LINGUISTICS

GENERAL EDITORS: David Adger, Queen Mary University of London; Hagit Borer, University of Southern California

ADVISORY EDITORS: Stephen Anderson, Yale University; Daniel Büring, University of California, Los Angeles; Nomi Erteschik-Shir, Ben-Gurion University; Donka Farkas, University of California, Santa Cruz; Angelika Kratzer, University of Massachusetts, Amherst; Andrew Nevins, University College London; Christopher Potts, University of Massachusetts, Amherst; Barry Schein, University of Southern California; Peter Svenonius, University of Tromsø; Moira Yip, University College London

RECENT TITLES

For a complete list of titles published and in preparation for the series, see pp. 436.

Interfaces in Linguistics

New Research Perspectives

Edited by
RAFFAELLA FOLLI AND CHRISTIANE ULBRICH

OXFORD
UNIVERSITY PRESS

OXFORD

UNIVERSITY PRESS

Great Clarendon Street, Oxford OX2 6DP

Oxford University Press is a department of the University of Oxford.

It furthers the University's objective of excellence in research, scholarship, and education by publishing worldwide in

Oxford New York

Auckland Cape Town Dar es Salaam Hong Kong Karachi
Kuala Lumpur Madrid Melbourne Mexico City Nairobi
New Delhi Shanghai Taipei Toronto

With offices in

Argentina Austria Brazil Chile Czech Republic France Greece
Guatemala Hungary Italy Japan Poland Portugal Singapore
South Korea Switzerland Thailand Turkey Ukraine Vietnam

Oxford is a registered trade mark of Oxford University Press
in the UK and in certain other countries

Published in the United States
by Oxford University Press Inc., New York

British Library Cataloguing in Publication Data

Data available

Library of Congress Cataloging in Publication Data

Library of Congress Control Number: 2010930307

Typeset by SPI Publisher Services, Pondicherry, India
Printed in Great Britain on acid-free paper by
MPG Books Group, Bodmin and King's Lynn

ISBN 978–0–19–956723–2 (Hbk)
      978–0–19–956724–9 (Pbk)

1 3 5 7 9 10 8 6 4 2

Contents

General Preface

The theoretical focus of this series is on the interfaces between subcomponents of the human grammatical system and the closely related area of the interfaces between the different subdisciplines of linguistics. The notion of 'interface' has become central in grammatical theory (for instance, in Chomsky's recent Minimalist Program) and in linguistic practice: work on the interfaces between syntax and semantics, syntax and morphology, phonology and phonetics etc. has led to a deeper understanding of particular linguistic phenomena and of the architecture of the linguistic component of the mind/brain.

The series covers interfaces between core components of grammar, including syntax/morphology, syntax/semantics, syntax/phonology, syntax/pragmatics, morphology/phonology, phonology/phonetics, phonetics/speech processing, semantics/pragmatics, intonation/discourse structure as well as issues in the way that the systems of grammar involving these interface areas are acquired and deployed in use (including language acquisition, language dysfunction, and language processing). It demonstrates, we hope, that proper understandings of particular linguistic phenomena, languages, language groups, or inter-language variations all require reference to interfaces.

The series is open to work by linguists of all theoretical persuasions and schools of thought. A main requirement is that authors should write so as to be understood by colleagues in related subfields of linguistics and by scholars in cognate disciplines.

The current volume provides a snapshot survey of the kind of empirical and explanatory success that an interface-based approach to the analysis of linguistic phenomena brings. It spans the field, crossing boundaries between lexical semantics, syntax, compositional semantics, morphology, phonology, phonetics, and discourse. The chapters employ cross-linguistic methodologies, insights from acquisition, processing, and psychology, as well as careful linguistic analyses within single languages. The book as a whole highlights the explanatory success that may arise from bringing to bear, upon the problem at hand, generalizations and technologies developed independently in theories of radically different kinds of linguistic phenomena.

David Adger
Hagit Borer

List of Contributors

Peter Ackema is Reader in Linguistics at the University of Edinburgh. He has worked extensively on issues regarding the morphology-syntax interface, on which he has published two books, *Issues in Morphosyntax* (John Benjamins, 1999), and *Beyond Morphology* (OUP 2004, with Ad Neeleman). He has also published a number of articles on morphological and syntactic topics in such journals as *Linguistic Inquiry*, *Natural Language and Linguistic Theory*, and *Yearbook of Morphology*.

Sang-Cheol Ahn is Professor of English at Kyung Hee University. He received BA (in 1977) and MA (in 1981) degrees in English Language at Yonsei University (Seoul, Korea) and a Ph.D. (in 1985) in Linguistics at the University of Illinois at Urbana-Champaign (USA). He has been teaching at Kyung Hee University in Seoul since 1986. His current research interests include issues of phonological representation, especially lexical phonology, and the historical and synchronic phonology of various languages, including Korean, English, French, Russian, and Japanese. He has published various books on Korean phonology, morphology, and Optimality Theory. He is on the editorial boards of *Language Research* and the *Korean Journal of Linguistics*. He also serves on the advisory board of the Phonology Circle of Korea.

Artemis Alexiadou is Professor of Theoretical and English Linguistics at the Universitaet Stuttgart. Her research interests lie in theoretical and comparative syntax, with special focus on the interfaces between syntax and morphology and syntax and the lexicon. She is currently working on nominal structure and verbal alternations. She has published work in *Linguistic Inquiry*, *Natural Language and Linguistic Theory*, and *Studia Linguistica* among others.

Ute Bohnacker is Reader in Scandinavian Languages at the University of Lund and Senior Lecturer of Linguistics at the University of Uppsala. Before moving to Sweden, she taught German and studied linguistics at the Polytechnic of Central London, at Tübingen University, and at the University of Durham, England, where she completed her Ph.D. in 1999 with a thesis on Icelandic-English child bilingualism. Her research focuses on Scandinavian languages, child language, and second language acquisition.

Nigel Duffield is currently Professor of Linguistics and Language Acquisition at the University of Sheffield. Prior to returning to the UK in 2005, he held posts at McGill University, Montreal and Heinrich Heine University, Düsseldorf, as well as guest positions at Radboud University and the Max Planck Institute for Psycholinguistics, Nijmegen. His research interests include theoretical syntax, with a focus on syntactic variation, experimental approaches to first and second language acquisition, and the competence-performance distinction. In the former area, his work has focused on the comparative syntax of Modern Irish, and, more recently on the grammar of Vietnamese: he is the Director of the Vietnamese (Online) Grammar Project, <http://vietnamese-grammar.group.shef.ac.uk>. Nigel's recent publications include articles in *Linguistics, Theoretical Linguistics, Studies in Second Language Acquisition,* and *Second Language Research*: he is perhaps best known for his 1995 monograph *Particles and Projections in Irish Syntax* (Kluwer).

Andrea Gualmini received his Ph.D. in linguistics from the University of Maryland in 2003 with a dissertation on children's knowledge of polarity phenomena. He is currently Senior Research Associate at Utrecht Institute of Linguistics (Uil-OTS). The focus of his research is on the development of semantic and pragmatic competence in children, with particular reference to the role of contextual information. Andrea Gualmini has published in journals such as *Journal of Semantics, Linguistic Inquiry,* and *Natural Language Semantics.*

Heidi Harley is Associate Professor of Linguistics at the University of Arizona. She received her doctorate in 1995 from MIT under the supervision of Prof. Alec Marantz, and worked at the University of Lille III and the University of Pennsylvania before taking up her position at the University of Arizona in 1999. She has published in morphology, syntax, and lexical semantics in several journals, including *Linguistic Inquiry, Lingua,* and *Language,* and is the author of the textbook *English Words: A Linguistic Introduction,* from Wiley.

Jonathan Howell received his Ph.D. in linguistics from Cornell University in 2010 with a dissertation entitled 'Empirical Approaches to Focus' which uses web-harvested speech data in the investigation of meaning and prosody. Jonathan has also taught at Syracuse University in Syracuse, NY, USA, and in Fall 2010, he will begin a post-doctoral research position at McGill University in Montreal, Canada.

Kyle Johnson is Professor of Linguistics at the University of Massachusetts at Amherst. He has held appointments at the University of California, McGill University, and the University of Wisconsin-Madison. His 1985 dissertation from the Massachusetts Institute of Technology was on the locality conditions that govern 'rightward' movement, and much of his early work in theoretical syntax was on the conditions on movement operations. For the past ten years, his focus has been on the syntax-semantics interface, with special attention to phenomena that arise in coordinations (gapping, right node raising, asymmetric coordinations) and ellipsis.

Arsalan Kahnemuyipour is an Assistant Professor of Linguistics at Syracuse University. His areas of expertise are syntax and the syntax-phonology interface. His monograph *The Syntax of Sentential Stress* was published by Oxford University Press in 2009. His other published work includes articles in *Natural Language and Linguistic Theory* and the *Canadian Journal of Linguistics*.

Elsi Kaiser is an Assistant Professor of Linguistics at the University of Southern California. She received her Ph.D. from the University of Pennsylvania in 2003. Her current research focuses on the comprehension of various referential forms (including pronouns, reflexives, and demonstratives) in different languages, which she investigates using tools from both psycholinguistics and linguistic theory.

Jaklin Kornfilt is a Professor of Linguistics at the Department of Languages, Literatures and Linguistics, Syracuse University. Her main research interests are theoretical syntax, theoretically informed typology, and diachronic linguistics. She has written *Turkish*, a descriptive grammar, published by Routledge in 1997. She is also the author of a number of articles on Turkish and other Turkic languages, and she has some publications on German, as well. She is currently working on projects concerning syntactic nominalization, relative clauses (including their acquisition by children), and on syntax-phonology interface issues.

Juhee Lee's areas of specialization are phonology and its interface with phonetics and morphology, with a special focus on Korean. Her current research focuses on the sound patterns of Korean and Japanese loanwords into Korean; specifically she is investigating the role of detailed phonetics in explaining the patterns of transformation undergone by borrowed words, and the phonological and morphological changes that arise in internet and mobile texting. Lee is an assistant professor in the Department of Korean Language and Literature at Kyung Hee University in Seoul. Previously, she taught at Sungshin Women's University. She holds a BA in Korean Language and Literature from Sungshin Women's University and a Ph.D. in Linguistics from the University of Essex.

Chien-Jer Charles Lin is Assistant Professor of Chinese Linguistics at Indiana University. Prior to his appointment at Indiana, he taught in the Department of English at National Taiwan Normal University from 2006 to 2009, where he founded the Language and Cognition Lab. He received his Ph.D. from the University of Arizona with a specialization in experimental syntax and sentence processing. His research interests include the processing of head-final relative clauses, processing issues in syntactic theorization, mass/count distinction in classifier languages, the representation and processing of lexical ambiguity, and Taiwanese tone sandhi.

Jamal Ouhalla is a Professor of Linguistics at University College Dublin with research interests in syntax, morphology, and the lexicon. He is the author of several publications, including *Functional Categories and Parametric Variation* (1991) and the co-editor of *Themes in Arabic and Hebrew Syntax* (2002).

Christina Rosén was educated at Växjö University and at the Teacher Training College in Malmö (Sweden). Since 1992 she has taught German linguistics and didactics at Växjö University. In 2006, she completed her Ph.D. at Lund University and is now a Senior Lecturer at Linnaeus University Växjö. Her research focuses on second language acquisition.

Jeffrey T. Runner is Associate Professor of Linguistics and Brain & Cognitive Sciences, and Director of the Center for Language Sciences at the University of Rochester. He has worked extensively on issues relating to the syntax-semantics interface and has published in journals such as *Linguistic Inquiry, Syntax, Cognition,* and *Cognitive Science.* He is the author of the book *Noun Phrase Licensing* and his current research focuses on the interaction of structural and non-structural constraints on binding and ellipsis.

Professor James M. Scobbie is director of the Speech Science Research Centre at Queen Margaret University, Edinburgh. His Ph.D. was in constraint-based theoretical phonology, and he now concentrates mostly on empirical research into phenomena that illuminate the phonetics-phonology interface, combining methodological approaches from phonology, experimental phonetics, and sociolinguistics. He has investigated a variety of topics in adult variation, child language acquisition, and speech pathology.

Koen Sebregts is Lecturer in Linguistics at the Department of English at the University of Leiden, Netherlands. He was a Ph.D. student at Utrecht University, Netherlands, and his Ph.D. thesis, to be published in 2010, is entitled 'The sociophonetics and phonology of Dutch r'. Main interests are the phonetics-phonology interface and the impact of sociophonetic variation on phonological theory.

Rachel Sussman was most recently a Postdoctoral Fellow in the Department of Psychology at the University of Wisconsin-Madison. Her work focused on the lexical semantics of verbs where she investigated the connections between real-world events, their conceptualization, and the linguistic forms used to express them. Her work has been published in journals such as *Language and Cognitive Processes* and *Cognition*. She now works in industry and keeps the verbs (and other parts of speech) of the financial sector of Boston in line.

Michael K. Tanenhaus is the Beverly Petterson Bishop and Charles W. Bishop Professor of Brain and Cognitive Sciences and Linguistics at the University of Rochester. His research focuses on real-time spoken language comprehension, where his publications span a wide range of issues from topics in speech perception to topics in interactive conversation.

Naoko Tomioka received her Ph.D. in linguistics from McGill University in 2006. She then worked as a post-doctoral researcher as part of the Natural Language Interface Assymetry Research Project at Université du Québec à Montréal until December 2008. Her research interests include structure of VP, resultative constructions, causative constructions, morphology, and research methodology.

Lisa Travis obtained her Ph.D. from MIT in 1984 with a dissertation entitled *Parameters and Effects of Word Order Variation*. She is currently an Associate Professor in the Linguistics Department at McGill University in Montreal, Quebec, Canada where she has been teaching since 1984. Her research has consistently returned to the issue of word order variation and the system of phrase structure and movement that underlies its permutations. Recent research has focused on two areas. One explores a language typology characterized by the interaction of head movement and phrasal movement. The other investigates what the syntax-phonology interface can reveal about head movement and phases.

Robert Truswell is British Academy Postdoctoral Fellow at the University of Edinburgh. He received his Ph.D. from University College London in 2007 and subsequently worked at Tufts University. He works on many aspects of syntax, semantics, and their interface, particularly with reference to locality and scope. He has a monograph on event semantics and locality forthcoming with OUP.

Reiko Vermeulen received her Ph.D. in 2005 from University College London with a dissertation on external possession in Japanese and Korean. She spent a further three years at University College London as a post-doctoral researcher in a project on information structure. Her main research interests include the interaction between syntactic operations and information structure, particularly in Japanese and Korean. Since 2009 she has been a researcher at the University of Ghent in a project on comparative syntax and cartography.

Matthew Whelpton is Associate Professor of English Linguistics at the University of Iceland, where he teaches English linguistics, semantics, and syntax in the Faculty of Foreign Languages, Literature, and Linguistics and researches the argument structure of English and Icelandic in the Institute of Linguistics. He received his doctorate in 1995 from the University of Oxford under the supervision of Prof. James Higginbotham. He has published in several journals, including the *Journal of Linguistics* and *Natural Language Semantics*; his earlier work focused on the syntax and semantics of teleological infinitival modifiers in English; his more recent work addresses secondary predication and the resultative with a focus on Icelandic.

Suwon Yoon is currently a Ph.D. candidate of linguistics at the University of Chicago. Her research interests lie at the intersection of the fields of theoretical syntax, semantics, pragmatics and experimental linguistics. The main thrust of her research is the uncovering of cross-linguistic variation, while also establishing the underlying systematic unity of apparently diverse syntactic and semantic phenomena. She has worked on various topics including, among others, argument-adjunct asymmetry in intervention effects, scrambling, case marking, negative concord, specificity and polarity, and more recently, scope diagnostics of negation, expletive negation, mood and modality, expressivity in metalinguistic comparatives, NPI-licensing, and rhetorical force.

List of Abbreviations

1	1st person
2	2nd person
3	3rd person
ACC/acc	accusative
act	active
ADV	adverbial
Agr	agreement
AOR	aorist
Asp	aspect
Asr/asr	assertion
AsrP	assertion phrase
AT	Actor Topic
B	bunched post-alveolar approximant
BEI	passive marker in Mandarin
BPPA	Bare Present Participial Adjuncts
C	complement
CAUS	causative
CL/cls	classifier
cl	clitic
Comp	complement
COND	conditional
COP	copula
CP	complementizer phrase
DAT	dative
DEC	declarative marker
DEIC	deictic
dem	demonstrative
DiscAnaP	discourse anaphoricity phrase

DIST-PL	distributive plural
D-OBJ	direct object
DOC	double-object construction
DP	determiner phrase
DR	definite restriction
DRS	Discourse Representation Structure
EP	event phrase
EPP	Extended Projection Principle
F/f	feminine
Foc	focus
FOF	first occurrence focus
FREQ	frequentative
FSV	focus semantic value
FUT	future
GEN/gen	genitive
imperf/Imp	imperfect
IE	intervention effect
IP	inflection phrase
ITER	iterative
JNDs	just noticeable differences
L1	native language
L2	second language
LF	logical form
LOC	locality
MNSC	Minimal Negative Structure Constraint
M/m	masculine
MUA	Merger Under Adjacency
NEG/neg	negation
NIB	Negation Induced Barrier
NOM/nom	nominative
NP	noun phrase
NPI	negative polarity item

O	object
OP	operator phrase
part	participle
pass	passive
PAST	definite past
perf	perfect
pers	person
PF	phonetic form
PL/pl	plural
PNP	picture noun phrase
pol	politeness marker
PossP	possessive phrase
PP	preposition phrase
PRES	present
PRON/prn	pronoun
PROG	progressive
PRT	particle
PST/pst	past
Q	question
R	retroflex alveolar approximant
REFL	reflexive
REL	relativizer
RMS	root mean squared
RP	reported past
S/s/SBJ	subject
SCL	subject clitic
SD	linguistic expression
SEC	Single Event Condition
SG/sg/Sg	Singular
SOF	second occurrence focus
Spec	specifier
t	trace

T	tense
TOP	topic
TP	tense phrase
TRNS	transitivity
U	uvular trill
UG	Universal Grammar
unF	unfocused
V	verb
V2	verb second
voiceP	voice phrase
VOT	Verb Onset Time
vP	'little v' verb phrase
VP	verb phrase
XP	X phrase

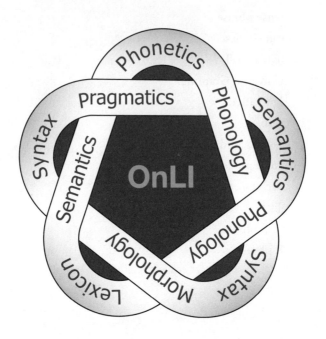

1

Understanding Grammar at the Interfaces: An Inevitable Development

RAFFAELLA FOLLI AND CHRISTIANE ULBRICH

1.1 Introduction

In recent years, the study of the interaction between different levels of linguistic knowledge has attracted increasing interest. In order to speak or understand a language we need to access different mechanisms whose interaction cannot be fully appreciated through a non-integrated approach. Following several decades of research within individual components of the language faculty, the field has shown itself increasingly ready to develop integrated theories of how language works and, to a certain extent, this type of study is dominating current linguistic research. Many of the chapters in the present volume deal with issues that more than half a century of linguistic research has progressively proven to require just such an approach.

In response to this, in June 2007 we (Raffaella Folli and Christiane Ulbrich) hosted a conference on linguistic interfaces (OnLI) at the University of Ulster. The conference brought together scholars working in different fields of linguistics, focusing on problems occurring at the interface of the various components of the language faculty. The conference was very successful in that it triggered an impressive level of discussion, and a very fruitful exchange between participants. It ended with the proposal for a follow-up or indeed the possibility of turning OnLI into a series of conferences which we feel highlights the consideration that researchers in linguistics now have for interface approaches. Considering linguistic problems within a single and crystallized component of linguistic analysis is less and less possible and hence less satisfactory, and this we think is a sign of the development of the theory and the field more generally.

The book that developed from this conference presents cutting-edge research into the interaction between the components of our knowledge of language. The individual chapters address problems at the cross-section of one or more interfaces in a number of languages. The chapters consider interface issues from various different perspectives and use data gathered with several methodologies, including standard grammatical elicitation and judgements, experimentally gathered data, and corpus-based methods. Crucially, the approach adopted by the various contributors shows how interface tools can be used to provide novel and more effective analyses to issues that have been in most cases long studied in the literature and that appear to reveal an impossibility of being fully understood by more traditional approaches.

Below we begin with short summaries of the chapters included in this volume and the rationale for the structure we have given it. We then conclude with some considerations regarding the status of current work on interface issues, the development of the field, and its manners of investigation.

1.2 The Book's Structure

The book consists of four parts: the first three present chapters on the interface between one or more levels of grammar, while the last contains experimental approaches to interface issues.

Part I, 'The structural properties of sentences interfacing with meaning and the lexicon', deals generally with issues portraying the interrelation of syntactic phenomena with the lexical component, the semantic component, and discourse. In particular, the section contains chapters on movement (*Johnson, Truswell*), on argument structure issues (*Alexiadou, Duffield, Whelpton*), on parts of speech categorization (*Ouhalla*), and on topicalization (*Vermeulen*).

Part II, 'The morphological properties of words interfacing with syntax and phonology', focuses on word-internal structure and the effect it has on the syntactic and the phonological component, using data from various languages, namely Japanese, Cupeño, Navajo, Turkish, and English. In particular, this section contains a chapter on adverbial modification and word-internal structure (*Tomioka*), two chapters on the Mirror Principle (*Harley, Travis*), and a contribution on syntactic cues to stress assignment (*Kahnemuyipour and Kornfilt*).

Part III, 'Sound interfacing with structure', addresses issues related to the syntax-phonology interface on the one hand, and the phonetics-phonology interface on the other. The syntax-phonology interface is investigated through the study of three different phenomena: wh-subject extraction from embedded clauses and its relation to prosodic phrasing (*Ackema*), intervention effect asymmetries and prosodic repair strategies (*Yoon*), and second occurrence focus and its acoustic properties (*Howell*). The phonetics-phonology interface is discussed in relation to the issue of intra- and inter-speaker variation (*Scobbie and Sebregts*) and articulatory phonetic properties in loanword adaptation *(Ahn and Lee)*.

Finally, Part IV, 'Experimental work on interface issues', presents a variety of studies which try to pinpoint the effect of various interfaces on certain aspects of language acquisition and language processing. In particular, the section contains two chapters on language acquisition, one dealing with the resolution of scopal ambiguity in child language (*Gualmini*), and one considering transfer effects on word order in second language learning (*Bohnacker and Rosén*). The final two chapters present current research on processing issues. More specifically, the chapters investigate the processing of inalienable nouns (*Lin*), as well as the processing of pronouns and anaphors in 'picture NPs' (*Kaiser, Runner, Sussman, and Tenenhaus*).

1.2.1 *Part I: The Structural Properties of Sentences Interfacing with Meaning and the Lexicon*

This section of the book contains two chapters that relate to the interface between syntax and semantics. The first chapter is Truswell's *Cyclic interaction of event structure and A′ locality* which discusses cases where a restriction on the formation of an A′ dependency is due to event structure properties of the predicates involved in a complex sentence. In particular, the chapter analyses examples of wh-extraction out of *Bare Present Participial Adjuncts* such as 'What did John drive Mary crazy [working on __]?' This grammatical example is contrasted to ungrammatical sentences such as '*What does John drink coffee [working on __]? The analysis developed by Truswell is that the formation of an A′ dependency is regulated by the *Single Event Condition* according to which A′-movement is allowed only if the head and the foot of the chain of the dependency describe a single event, while in the ungrammatical example above the two events of *John drinking coffee* and *John working on something* are simply happening at the same time. This is an extremely interesting and novel data set that allows the author to propose that in the study of A′ dependency, a field that has traditionally been seen as a purely syntactic, cyclicity-driven area of grammar, event structure relations and more generally semantic representations play a crucial role.

Johnson's *Determiners and movement* addresses issues that constitute traditional examples of the interface nature of certain syntactic phenomena, namely the analysis of determiners and the nature of movement rules and in particular the hypothesis that took root in the mid-Nineties according to which movement is a copying mechanism which does not delete an element from its base position, but rather replaces it with a copy. The chapter develops a novel account, based on previous literature, of two fundamental issues that the copy theory of movement has to address: namely why only one copy is pronounced, and secondly what mechanism is in place to explain the interpretation of copies where one binds the other.

Following this, the section contains four chapters that relate to the syntax-lexicon interface. Alexiadou's *Post-verbal nominatives: an unaccusativity diagnostic under scrutiny* is a perfect example of how current syntactic theorizing needs to relate to the workings of grammar at the interface between levels. Her chapter discusses the distribution of VS order with bare nominative subjects in Greek and Hebrew. It addresses two crucial issues, one relating to the interface between syntax and the lexical semantics of verbs, and one relating to the syntax-discourse interface, since VS order is typically connected with new information focus. The first issue is that it is certain semantically defined classes of unaccusatives (verbs of appearance and existence, verbs of inherently directed motion, and 'break' verbs in the disappearance interpretation) and some classes of unergatives (verbs of emissions, agentive manner of motion, and activity verbs) which occur in this construction. In other words, not all unaccusatives can give rise to these structures; but some unergatives can also do it, pointing therefore to another case of *unaccusativity mismatch* and therefore once again raising the question of whether the syntax of unaccusatives/unergatives is uniform. The second issue relates to the specific discourse function of VS order and the fact that it is normally used with unaccusative verbs, but that again not all types of unaccusatives are equally possible with this word order (for example change of state verbs). Alexiadou's hypothesis is that it is at the syntax-discourse interface that certain derivations are filtered out.

Duffield's *Unaccusativity in Vietnamese and the structural consequences of inadvertent cause* presents two independent sets of arguments from Vietnamese which bring support to Travis's and many others' proposals in the literature that the structure of the VP is complex and that the internal articulation of the verb phrase is a direct reflection of the sub-evental structure of verbal predicates. The first problem is the formation of causatives. Vietnamese is another excellent test case for the little v hypothesis since causatives are formed analytically by means of the verb *làm*. Interestingly also, their external argument typically receives an indirect or inadvertent cause interpretation. Duffield provides an analysis for the types of verbs that can and cannot occur under this type of causative, offering support for a fundamental idea in syntax-based approaches to argument realisation, namely that the thematic realisation of arguments is dependent and determined by syntactic position. The second phenomenon discussed in the chapter is the structure of Vietnamese responsives introduced by the assertion morpheme *có* which seems to be realised only in the presence of an eventive predicate, hence providing support for an Assertion projection between the TP and vP.

Whelpton's *Building resultatives in Icelandic* starts with an extremely lucid and profound discussion of the various issues that are at stake in the formation of resultatives, paired with an impressive review of the way the literature has dealt with them. It then concentrates on the formation of resultatives in Icelandic and in particular on Kratzer's (2005) proposal according to which adjectival resultatives are the only true resultatives and that they are derived through a process of causativization of the AP: a zero morpheme affixing to an AP such as 'the metal flat' and turning into a causative verb which can then be serialized with the main verb. Whelpton shows that this kind of analysis has serious problems when applied to the formation of resultatives in Icelandic since in this language predicational adjectives are inflected, while Kratzer's analysis heavily relies on the fact that the zero affix that attaches to the AP blocks agreement on the adjective. Also contrary to what is argued by Kratzer, Icelandic has both unaccusative and unergative verbs in AP resultatives. Whelpton's conclusion is that previous analyses that took for granted the equivalence of PP and AP resultatives might be mistaken and that indeed the consideration of the types of verb classes that enter the constructions coupled with the analysis of the language-specific properties regarding the lexicalization of functional structure might give us a better insight into the formation of these structures cross-linguistically.

Finally the syntax-lexicon interface is at the centre of Ouhalla's chapter entitled *Categorization and the interface levels* which is concerned with the problem of parts of speech categorizations and previous approaches to this issue. The author reviews and discusses two main takes on what drives categorization, namely the approach that sees meaning, and in particular semantic features, as the crucial factor in the determining parts of speech categorization, and the other view which holds that formal, morphosyntactic features drive the process. The goal of the chapter is to use data from Arabic to show how an approach that reconciles both positions and argues for the need to consider both semantic and morphosyntactic features is possible and indeed offers a better solution to the question of how language categorizes roots.

The last chapter in Part I addresses syntax-information structure issues. Vermeulen's *Non-topical* wa-*phrases in Japanese* analyses the distribution of *wa* phrases in Japanese and argues that previous analyses that have claimed that *wa* is a topic marker are mistaken since *wa* phrases can also be non-topic. This consideration comes from the discussion of examples where *wa* phrases can follow a fronted focused element which is in stark contradiction to traditional articulation of the information structure of the sentence and cross-linguistic evidence that confirms the impossibility for topics to follow foci. Vermeulen convincingly shows that in fact this kind of *wa* phrase marks discourse anaphoric items. The conclusion she reaches is that topic *wa* phrases must occur in clause-initial position, while *wa* phrases that function as discourse anaphoric elements can occur in other positions. The ultimate consequence of this analysis is that the identification of topics in Japanese cannot be simply reduced to the presence of a topic marker, but rather is related to more complex discourse-motivated conditions. This in turn represents a problem for rigid syntax-driven approaches to information structure accounts such as the cartographic approach.

1.2.2 *Part II: The Morphological Properties of Words Interfacing with Syntax and Phonology*

Tomioka's *Word-internal modification without the syntax-morphology interface* discusses the phenomenon of internal modification of morphologically complex predicates in Japanese. The specific constructions under scrutiny are the modification of complex predicates, in particular causative constructions formed with *sase,* by the adverbial modifiers such as *again,* and by locative PPs. The crucial hypothesis that Tomioka wants to challenge is the 'Word-Effect hypothesis' according to which the internal structure of words is unavailable for the purpose of syntactic and semantic operations, such as that of modification, and that this principle by itself provides a simple and general explanation for the types of modifications that grammar does not allow. Her analysis and discussion of the data instead show that there are cases where word-internal modification is possible, and that more generally where modification is not possible the reason has to be found elsewhere, namely in syntax-based, language-specific structural properties of complex predicates. The ultimate conclusion is that the Word-Effect hypothesis which seems to require an interaction between PF and LF is incompatible with the current model of grammar.

The next two chapters discuss issues that deal with apparent violations of the Mirror Principle in two polysynthetic languages, Navajo and Cupeño. Baker (1985, 2002) argues that the parallel consideration of morphological and syntactic structure seems to point towards the existence of a general principle according to which 'the order of morphemes in a complex word reflects the

natural syntactic embedding of the heads that correspond to those morphemes' (Baker 2002: 326). Both chapters show that the problematic data
which would seem to challenge the Mirror Principle can in fact be reconciled
with it if an interface approach that allows for the intervention of subsystems
of the syntax module were to be adopted.

The first chapter is Harley's *Affixation and the Mirror Principle* where two
apparent violations of the Mirror Principle in Cupeño and Navajo are discussed. These cases are effectively showcases for Harley's strong thesis that the
derivation of morphologically complex words is determined by three mechanisms, namely head movement which allows separate morphemes to combine under a single mother node in the syntax, affix-specific linearization
requirement, and Merger Under Adjacency which combines morphemes that
are adjacent post-syntactically. This is the operation that Bobalijk (1994)
proposes to account for the famous puzzle of English verbal morphology
where the verb does not raise to T but is affixed with verbal inflection. Harley's
conclusion is that intricate morphological patterns like the ones presented by
the two polysynthetic languages she discusses might suggest that the Mirror
Principle does not hold quite as generally as we may think. In reality, a strong
syntactocentric approach which adopts tools that have been independently
motivated can account for the data.

The second chapter, Travis's *Phases and Navajo verbal morphology*, discusses
an old and very complex problem with Navajo verbal morphology. Navajo
verbal morphology is described, following previous literature, as being composed of a template containing nine morphemes plus the root. Travis notices
that in fact many generalizations about the grammar of Navajo and relating
different modules of grammar stem from this templatic structure. The problem is that a number of 'apparent contradictions' can be identified when
considering the groupings that different modules of grammar determine:
phonology, syntax, and semantics each requires the morpheme in the template
to be organized in separate ways. Further, Travis identifies a Mirror Principle
violation because the morphemes that are related to the subject are closer to
the root than those related to the object and also the morphemes for tense are
closer to the root than those for aspect. Travis does an outstanding job in
illustrating and describing these facts with data and accounting for these
patterns by resorting to a large set of independently motivated mechanisms
and tools that minimalism and DM have long argued to be needed to describe
the working of grammar at the interface.

The section concludes with Kahnemuyipour and Kornfilt's *The Syntax and
Prosody of Turkish 'Pre-stressing' Suffixes*. This chapter provides an alternative
approach for a set of suffixes in Turkish that trigger stress placement on the

preceding syllable, i.e. pre-stressing suffixes that have previously been dealt with from a purely phonological perspective. Those previous accounts treated suffixes in Turkish as a homogeneous group of morphemes and attributed their stress behaviour to a lexically pre-specified property, thereby failing to explain their irregular pattern. Contrary to these analyses, Kahnemuyipour and Kornfilt argue for a solution that ties the prosodic properties of pre-stressing suffixes to their syntactic behaviour in order to provide a principled reason that explains why clausal and verbal suffixes trigger irregular stress patterns while other suffixes do not. The solution offered by the authors is multi-fold. They argue that the subset of 'pre-stressing' suffixes cannot be treated as a homogeneous class and that the similarity of the stress pattern has to be interpreted as an epiphenomenon. The analysis shows that complementizers and agreement suffixes result in what looks like pre-stressing behaviour due to their affixation to a phonologically null copula that introduces its own stress domain. The prosodic prominence patterns observed in negation suffixes and question markers on the other hand are the result of their appearance as head of a focus projection that attracts a focused constituent to their specifier position.

1.2.3 *Part III: Sound Interfacing with Structure*

Ackema's *Restrictions on subject extraction: a PF account* provides an interface account for restrictions on subject extraction out of embedded clauses that are most commonly referred to as the complementizer-trace effect. While the effect has previously and extensively been discussed from a purely syntactic perspective, his analysis suggests that the implementation of the prosodic phrase level can account for a number of movement operations such as the 'adverb effect', subextraction out of a subject, in-situ wh-phrase, extraction out of complementizer-final clauses, and extraction out of complementizer-less clauses. Ackema's proposal that feature checking is not limited to local syntactic domains but depends on the alignment between syntactic and prosodic domains provides a more straightforward account for those syntactic operations and is supported by numerous examples from a wide variety of languages.

Yoon's *An experimental approach to the interpretation of wh-phrases: processing and syntax-prosody interface* provides an account for a dichotomy between argument wh-phrases and adjunct wh-phrases, that has not been addressed in previous accounts dealing with intervention effects in wh-phrases. Yoon presents data from Korean, Japanese, and Turkish and shows that previous uniform analyses of wh-phrases are not tenable. Instead the data clearly points to the existence of an asymmetry in the existence of intervention effects between argument and adjunct wh-phrases. Based on empirical data from acceptability judgements in the processing between argument and adjunct intervention stimuli, Yoon establishes her proposal that intervention effects—only triggered by argument wh-phrases but not by adjunct wh-phrases—must be analysed as syntactic LF constraints. The phonetic analysis of prosodic cues, namely pitch and pause duration, and the consideration of inherently different properties between argument and adjunct wh-phrases pertaining to their semantic ambiguity, lead her to the conclusion that the syntactic-semantic location between the two types of wh-phrase differs thus consolidating the novel division of wh-phrases.

In the third chapter of this section, *Second occurrence focus and the acoustics of prominence*, Howell addresses phonological prominence in repeated occurrences of focus associates and its relation to language modules. The chapter is based on the acoustic analysis of prosodic cues in the realization of potential focus associates to test the validity of contradicting predictions that arise from non-integrated approaches. While syntactic and semantic theories predict a grammatically mediated association between first and second focus elements, pragmatic theories do not. The chapter also aims to contribute to the debate concerning the modelling of focus and given-ness as a single notational category or as two distinct mechanisms. The chapter reports the results of two production studies and one perception experiment. The acoustic analysis of prosodic cues including fo measurements, syllable duration, RMS intensity, energy, power, and spectral balance reveal only quantitative differences between second focus and non-focused elements which are subsequently attributed to rhythm effects in the analysis of the following second production data. Additionally, the perception results suggest that despite a significant contribution of duration to the acoustic demarcation of second focus elements in the production data, these cues are not exploited by listeners in order to identify focus associates correctly. As a result Howell concludes that a theory allowing for a multifaceted notion of focus can best account for the reported data.

The two remaining chapters in Part III address issues pertaining to spoken language and thereby investigate the interface between phonetics and phonology. While Scobbie and Sebregts's *Acoustic, articulatory, and phonological perspectives on allophonic variation of /r/ in Dutch* questions the existence of a categorical distinction between the two modules, Ahn and Lee's *Loan adaptation of laryngeal features* illustrates how the use of acoustic phonetic data aids in the explanation of typological facts in the phonology of loanwords.

Scobbie and Segbregts's contribution critically debates a polarization between theoretical frameworks that adopt a more phonological view in favour of categorical and abstract systematization of fine phonetic detail versus a more phonetic-oriented view exploring and modelling the function of phonetic specification and quantification. Focusing on an element of spoken language that is known for its complex and wide variation—Dutch /r/—enables Scobbie and Sebregts to investigate concrete aspects of the interplay between the two domains of spoken language, between phonetic detail and phonological abstraction. The chapter is based on acoustic and articulatory data to illustrate its main argument, namely that the nature of the interface is multidimensional. Although the authors do not question the existence of either of the two domains, a strong methodological proposal is made encouraging research in the area regarding a strict commitment to large-scale studies that allow for a thorough investigation and modulation of cross-speaker and within-speaker variation over various periods of time.

Ahn and Lee's *Loan adaptation of laryngeal features* discusses previous approaches to borrowing processes from one language to another which have argued for either perceptually driven mechanisms, and thereby an automatic phonetic input, or a more phonologically operative level of loanword phonology. The chapter presents data resulting from an acoustic analysis of phonetic realizations of laryngeal features such as voice onset time, closure durations and fo. The authors show that the representation of these phonetic factors depends on typological differences and similarities between the source language and the borrowing language. Subsequently they argue that the understanding of loanword phonology gives insight into native phonology. The examination of adaptation patterns for laryngeal features from English loanwords in Thai and Korean and their comparison to adaptation patterns between Thai and Korean lead the authors to the conclusion that the typological categorization of languages determines the strategy for loanword adaptation and that this strategy can be based on either phonemic or phonetic mapping of laryngeal features.

1.2.4 *Part IV: Experimental Work on Interface Issues*

The final section of the volume begins with Gualmini's contribution *Scope ambiguity in child language: old and new problems*, which discusses children's performance in the interpretation of quantified sentences with inverse scope. The first part of the chapter reviews the development in the literature regarding the analysis of this problem. Early analyses attributed children's failure in inverse scope interpretations to a syntactic problem, while more recent approaches, where a paradigm change from UG-based parameters towards more pragmatically based inferences to parsing mechanisms has taken place, contend that children's mistakes are due to frequency effects in the input. The author stresses the fact that, although interactions on different levels of linguistic representation are taken into consideration in previous analyses to account for observable ambiguities in the resolution of scope, they have so far failed to isolate and explain the relative contribution of the interacting modules in a systematic fashion. The second part of the chapter provides a solution that has wide-reaching methodological implications. The proposal is that the main factor affecting their behaviour in inverse scope interpretations is children's inability to compute scalar implicatures; this, in turn, leads the author to the conclusion that in addition to bootstrapping mechanisms at the syntax-semantic interface, pragmatic information needs to be considered. This implies that it is important for research at the interface between two modules of the grammar to consider intersecting information from several levels of analysis.

The following contribution in this section also draws on language acquisition data at the syntax-discourse interface, but in the acquisition of a second language. Bohnacker and Rosen's *Interaction of syntax and discourse pragmatics in closely related languages: how native Swedes, native Germans, and Swedish-speaking learners of German start their sentences* investigates properties of sentence-initial elements in second language acquisition data with focus on the syntax-discourse interface. The analysis is based on the Swedish and German produced by L1 speakers of Swedish. The corpus they use includes a variety of spoken and written data gathered through several elicitation tasks such as rewriting and rating which allow the authors to draw conclusions on the basis of comparisons across a number of data sets. The acquisition data of the two closely related languages show that L1 Swedish speakers are successful in using V2 word order in German, but that they transfer the discourse functions of the pre-field element from Swedish to German. The results thereby provide evidence for different frequency distributions of pre-field constituents whereby new information is realized further to the right in Swedish clauses, compared to a strong preference in German for new information to be placed in clause-initial position. These differences are traced back to discourse-pragmatic differences in the functions of V2 declaratives. Although syntactic characteristics are transferred from Swedish into German yielding a correct V2 word order, L2 speakers of German are found to underuse the pre-field position in German which is less constrained to informationally given elements and expletives. These results highlight the fact that the achievement of native-like L2 depends on the mastery of interfacing modules, i.e. the appropriate discourse-pragmatic use of syntax.

Lin's *Processing (in)alienable possessions at the syntax-semantics interface* discusses the syntax, semantics, and processing of (in)alienable possession noun phrases in Chinese. The chapter presents both theoretical arguments and processing evidence for a structural distinction between alienable and inalienable nouns. In particular, Lin proposes that inalienable nouns subcategorize for a possessor in the specifier position and this gives rise to a narrow possessive interpretation. Alienable nouns on the other hand take a possessor via the presence of a functional phrase which has the external possessor in the specifier position and the possessed alienable noun in the complement position. The functional phrase expresses a generic relation and inherits specific meanings depending on the context. A self-paced reading experiment with possessive relative clauses in Chinese shows that sentences with inalienable nouns are read faster than those with alienable nouns on the possessor region (the head noun). Reaction time differences in fact show up only on the head noun (the possessee) and no other regions, suggesting that possessive relations are more easily formed by the comprehension system when the possessor is an inalienable noun since the possessor in this case directly fills an argument slot of the head noun.

Kaiser, Runner, Sussman, and Tanenhaus's chapter *Picturing the syntax-semantics interface: online interpretation of pronouns and reflexives in picture NPs* investigates the contribution of syntactic and semantic information to anaphor resolution in real-time language comprehension. The chapter discusses shortcomings in previous accounts of anaphor resolution that have resorted to adoption of binding principles from a purely syntactic perspective. Contrary to a two-stage, syntax-first processing theory, the results of two eye-tracking experiments suggest that in addition to syntactic knowledge source/ perceiver information is also accessed to guide the resolution of pronouns and reflexives. Furthermore, the authors argue that differences between the effects of structural and semantic constraints on the final interpretation of pronouns or reflexives are not systematic in relative strength or in timing during real-time processing, therefore suggesting a complex interaction of the constraints. The chapter concludes with an indication of the need for future research addressing issues arising from the gradient nature found in the data. The solutions could either assume a gradient core grammar or a non-gradient grammar whereby gradience would have to be attributed to the processing system. The authors propose that the effects of syntactic and semantic constraints differ in that syntactic constraints have more categorical effects compared to more gradient effects of semantic constraints

1.3 Conclusions

Linguistics as the scientific study of human language, the study of what makes up our linguistic knowledge, rests on the assumption that there exists a complex set of modules or components that interact to 'produce' language. The study of the various components of our knowledge of language, or what we can refer to as 'grammar', has at its base an explicit and thorough description of what language involves. For example, Hockett (1942) claims that 'linguistics is a classificatory science'. With the Chomskian revolution, we see a crucial shift in this perspective as linguistics is now involved in explaining why languages are what they are, rather than just describing what they are. In a sense the move from description to explanation can be seen as a natural development.

This book presents current research on the interaction of components of the language faculty which in recent times have become an extremely prominent topic in linguistic research. Considering how language works at the interface is a dominant issue and this new perspective is to a certain extent a second development of the field and has arisen, in our view, from two fundamental events. The first is a natural result of time: over half a century of linguistic research has led individual fields of linguistic analysis to develop descriptions and explanations that are sophisticated enough to lend themselves to be taken to the next step, that of the consideration of complex interrelations of components in the workings of grammar. The second event is the move in the early Nineties from Principle and Parameters to Minimalism and the consequences that this development has on the architecture of grammar, and the prominent role of interfaces in this new view. Chomsky's 'inaugural' paper on Minimalism, 'A Minimalist program for linguistic theory' (1993) contains two important considerations which we think the research presented in this volume stems from and clearly develops as fundamental to current methods of investigation:

A standard assumption is that UG specifies certain linguistic levels, each a symbolic system, often called a 'representational system.' Each linguistic level provides the means for presenting certain systematic information about linguistic expressions. Each linguistic expression (SD) is a sequence of representations, one at each linguistic level.... Some basic properties of language are unusual among biological systems, notably the property of discrete infinity. A working hypothesis in generative grammar has been that languages are based on simple principles that interact to form often intricate structures, and that the language faculty is nonredundant, in that particular phenomena are not 'overdetermined' by principles of language. These too are unexpected features of complex biological systems, more like what one expects to find (for unexplained reasons) in the study of the inorganic world. The approach has, nevertheless, proven to be a successful one, suggesting the hypotheses are more than just an artefact reflecting a mode of inquiry. Another recurrent theme has been the role of 'principles of economy' in determining the computations and the SDs they generate. Such considerations have arisen in various forms and guises as theoretical perspectives have changed. There is, I think, good reason to believe that they are fundamental to the design of language, if properly understood. (1993: 1–2)

This short quotation highlights two issues that this book presents as crucial to the field of linguistics. The first one is the underlying fact about language and its biological substance: it must be regulated by simple principles, but it contains intricate structures. The data discussed by Travis and Harley is in this respect a perfect example. The complexity of word structure in polysynthetic languages like Navajo could be seen as requiring very complex, language-specific and module-specific mechanisms to be understood, but they don't. If their analysis is tackled from an integrated approach, the data becomes more understandable and ultimately analysable by means of tools that are independently recognized as needed for the task at hand.

The second issue is perhaps the most important guiding principle in generative linguistics since Minimalism, namely 'the role of principles of economy'. That together with the assumption that language is non-redundant means that it is less and less conceivable to analyse linguistic phenomena as pertaining to one and only one level of grammar. In this perspective, the discussion of determiners and movement operations that applies to this category and the copy theory of movement in Johnson's contribution is a particularly relevant example of how current theorizing is able to provide analyses that are sensitive to several levels of grammar.

These are only two examples of how the research presented in this volume has taken these two issues seriously. The essential fact that this book highlights is that interface approaches are now fast developing, they are informing and being informed by applied research, and they are a very important, inevitable development of the field and its goals.

Part I
The Structural Properties of Sentences Interfacing with Meaning and the Lexicon

2

Cyclic Interaction of Event Structure and A′ Locality[*]

ROBERT TRUSWELL

2.1 Introduction

Davidson (1967) introduced the hypothesis that sentences correspond to descriptions of events, much as noun phrases correspond to descriptions of individuals. This provides the basis for accounts of many natural language phenomena. For example, pronouns in English can refer anaphorically to events as well as ordinary individuals, as in (1).

(1)   a. It happened last night [*It* = event]
      b. It went thataway [*It* = individual]

Research building on Davidson's original insight (particularly Higginbotham 1985 and Parsons 1990) has taken this to indicate that events are just another variety of first-order discourse referent, treated by the compositional semantics in much the same way as ordinary individuals. More specifically, a verbal head generally denotes a property of events, just as a nominal head generally denotes a property of individuals. Regular semantic composition normally then leads to a semantic representation of a sentence as an assertion of the existence of a particular event: just as a determiner typically binds the individual variable introduced by a noun, the tense head binds, and existentially quantifies, the event variable introduced by a verb.

    This analysis is complemented by a line of research, stemming ultimately from the Generative Semantics program (see Lakoff 1970 and McCawley 1968, as well as later seminal work by Dowty 1979), into *lexical decomposition*.

[*] This research was carried out at University College London, and supported by a Wingate scholarship. Thanks to Klaus Abels, Ad Neeleman, two reviewers, and audiences at MIT, UMass Amherst, and OnLI itself for helpful comments.

Particularly within the verbal domain, this aimed to break verb meanings down into combinations of recurring, primitive elements such as causation. For example, the alternations in (2) are seen by decompositionists as resulting from the addition, in (2b), of a primitive corresponding to inchoation, or becoming, to the state description in (2a), and then the addition, in (2c), of a second primitive corresponding to causation of the change of state described in (2b).

(2)   a. The glass is broken: broken(g)
       b. The glass broke: BECOME (broken(g))
       c. John broke the glass: CAUSE (P(j), BECOME (broken(g)))[1]

Combining lexical decomposition with a Davidsonian event semantics gives us a theory, as in Parsons (1990), in which an event can consist of multiple subevents standing in relations such as causation and inchoation. This, in turn, has led to a very productive line of research, growing out of Hale and Keyser (1993) and Kratzer (1996), in which such relations between subevents are reflected directly in the syntactic phrase structure. More recent major works in this field include Travis (2000a), Borer (2005b), and Ramchand (2008), each of which elaborate in different ways upon this foundational hypothesis.

   Although these proposals differ substantially in their details, one idea, most explicit in Hale and Keyser (1993) and Ramchand (2008), is that if a constituent XP describes an event e_1, and if e_1 contains e_2 as a subevent, then XP contains a phrase YP, which describes e_2, as a complement of X. Moreover, because each maximal projection contains a single specifier position, each additional subevent potentially licenses one additional argument position. This gives us at least a hope of finding a principled explanation for alternations in argument structure (and, in some cases, morphology), like those in (2).[2] (3) shows the general pattern: the heads X and Y introduce variables corresponding to events

---

[1] This departs from Lakoff (1970) and many other researchers in seeing CAUSE as a relation between two events, rather than between an individual and an event. This seems to me to be the most natural way of proceeding: individuals do not bring about changes of state except through some action of their own. This assumption is also required as part of the theory to be developed below. However, both positions have plenty of adherents, and the issue is not resolved.

[2] Ramchand (2008), in particular, defends a uniform analysis of causative-inchoative pairs, among other alternations, based on the hypothesis that each projection in the lowest portion of the tree (her 'first phase') introduces an event-describing head, along with a slot (in specifier position) for a 'subject' of that head. Each of these positions can be filled either by movement from a lower projection, or by first Merge of a lexical item. Moreover, relations between these eventive heads and their complements correspond to semantic relations of causation. A more complex event structure is therefore optionally accompanied by an expansion of the argument structure, and/or extra morphology. The major hurdle for this hypothesis to overcome is that it predicts that causatives are always

(e_1 and e_2), which will eventually be existentially quantified, but also variables corresponding to individuals (x, y, and z), which can be saturated by arguments in their specifier and complement positions.

(3)

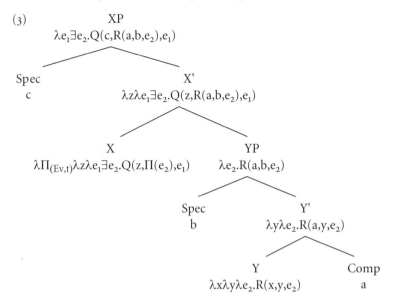

Two striking properties of this tree should be noted. Firstly, the semantic representation of XP contains both an extra individual argument and an extra event argument compared to the more deeply embedded YP. This gives the broad outline of an explanation for the rough correspondence between more complex event structures and more complex argument structures illustrated in (2). Secondly, binary branching syntactic combination corresponds uniformly to function application in the semantics, giving a direct mapping between the two levels of representation.

One question I want to ask in this paper is whether the mapping between event structure and phrase structure is always so close. I will argue that, in fact, it isn't (a claim traditionally associated with lexicalist theories such as Jackendoff 1990a and Pustejovsky 1991). I show that causal relations apparently identical to those which correspond to complementation in the tree in (3) can be found in other syntactic configurations. Hopefully, though, this argument can be made without damaging the real empirical results in the line of research growing out of Hale and Keyser's paper, for a simple reason: that

derived from inchoatives, and not vice versa. In contrast, the morphological and other evidence (Haspelmath 1993; Levin and Rappaport-Hovav 1999; Reinhart 2002) suggests that both causativization and anticausativization are attested.

research deals overwhelmingly with the syntactic instantiation of the event variable in constructions with a single verb, while I will be concerned with constructions with multiple verbs in non-c-commanding configurations.

Once we have the argument for a less uniform syntax-semantics mapping in place, things get more interesting from the point of view of the interface between those two modules. If we allow a slightly looser relation between phrase structure and event structure, we can start to ask which structure is most suitable for describing certain empirical phenomena, and also about the determination of the relation between the different structures. These are huge, open-ended questions, and I have no good general answer to them. My more modest aim here is to show the following: a phenomenon traditionally considered as syntactic (locality of A′-movement) is best described in terms making reference to events, rather than just phrases, as units, and so should be represented in partially event-structural, rather than wholly phrase-structural, terms. However, event-structural well-formedness conditions on the phenomenon in question must be checked cyclically, at points determined by the phrase structure. We therefore end up with a novel argument for a familiar type of cyclic architecture, broadly along the lines of phase theory (Chomsky 2000 *et seq.*) or the parallel architecture of Jackendoff (2002): the interface between the syntactic representation of phrase structure and the semantic representation of event structure is not wholly determined post-syntactically, but rather at multiple points during the syntactic derivation.

The rest of the paper is structured as follows. Section 2.2 gives some evidence for a degree of independence of event structure from phrase structure. This evidence is inextricably intertwined with an event-structural constraint on the locality of A′-movement, which I call the Single Event Condition, or SEC, so I introduce that condition there, too. Section 2.3 shows how this condition, initially motivated by patterns of extraction from adjuncts, extends to do empirical work in extraction from complements. However, section 2.4 shows that, if checking of the semantically based SEC is allowed to operate in a global, post-syntactic fashion, as we might expect on an EST-era Y-model, the model overgenerates. This motivates an architecture in which the SEC interacts cyclically with A′-movement.

2.2 The Single Event Condition

One potential empirical argument in favour of the syntactic decompositional approach sketched above with regard to (3) is that it gives us a possible way to explain an observation concerning the interpretation of lexical and periphrastic causatives, due to Fodor (1970), and subsequently developed in various directions by Shibatani (1976), Dowty (1979), Kamp (1979, 1981a), Levin and Rappaport-Hovav (1994), Bittner (1999), and Wolff (2003), among many others. Fodor noticed that the available interpretations of a lexical causative like *melt* are a proper subset of those of periphrastic causatives like *cause to melt* or *make melt*. A variety of different types of causation can be described by verbs like *cause* or *make*, while the causation expressed synthetically in a lexical causative is specifically *direct causation*. Recent research (see in particular Wolff 2003) has begun to converge on a precise, falsifiable characterization of this notion of direct causation, making reference to force-dynamic configurations of participants (Talmy 1976, 1988), and volitional properties of the causer, as well as basic relations among events, but for our purposes, we can make do with a simplified characterization, as follows:

(4)   Given a set $E = \{e_1, e_2, \ldots, e_n\}$ of events and a transitive, irreflexive relation $\subset$ over E, e_i *causes* e_j iff $e_i \subset e_j$, and e_i *directly causes* e_j iff $e_i \subset e_j$ and there is no e_k such that $e_i \subset e_k \subset e_j$.

In other words, one event causes another iff, at the appropriate level of granularity, there are no intermediate events in the causal chain linking them.[3]

Now, coming back to Fodor's claim regarding lexical and periphrastic causatives, this characterization of direct causation predicts the degradation of (5a), relative to (5b): the lexical causative in (5a) implies that Floyd heating the glass directly caused it to melt, but that leaves us without an explanation for the fact that the heating (on Saturday) happened some time before the melting (on Sunday). The periphrastic causative in (5b), encoding a more general, possibly indirect type of causation, has no such clash.[4]

---

[3] A causal chain is a series of causally related events linking the initial cause and ultimate effect, as in Lewis (1973). Of course, the definition of direct causation in the main text is only as good as our characterization of the set of events it applies over, and this is where a lot of work (in particular Kamp 1979, 1981a, and Bittner 1999) has been focused. The most important consideration is that not every conceivable event is included in the pragmatically determined set of events E in (4), but only relevant events of roughly the same 'size' (so we don't simultaneously consider huge events like wars, medium-size events like killings, and tiny events like muscle movements leading to the pulling of a trigger).

[4] I am aware of only one serious challenge to Fodor's generalization concerning direct causation and lexical causatives. This comes from Hindi, which has two causative suffixes, *-aa* and *–vaa*, corresponding to what has traditionally been termed 'direct' and 'indirect' causation, respectively (Saksena 1982; Ramchand 2008: ch. 6). Despite this distinction in directness of causation, both suffixes show the same degree of morphological idiosyncrasy, and the two suffixes cannot co-occur. In other words, Hindi respects the distinction between direct and indirect causation, but does not map it onto the distinction between lexical and productive causatives in the expected way. There is more empirical work to be done here, and cross-linguistically in general, for sure.

(5)   a. #Floyd melted the glass on Sunday by heating it on Saturday.
       b. Floyd caused the glass to melt on Sunday by heating it on Saturday.

(Fodor 1970: 432–3)

This could be taken, *contra* Fodor, as support for syntactic decomposition, because syntactic decomposition offers the possibility of explaining restrictions on the class of possible lexical meanings in terms of, firstly, a restricted set of functional elements which make the same semantic contribution across lexical items; and secondly, constraints on the relationship between syntactic and semantic combination. Certainly, this is an attractive position, and I don't want to quarrel with it here.

Rather, the interest of this position for my purposes is the following: the authors cited in the introduction see a verb phrase as denoting a property of a single event, even if the event in question may have proper subparts that are events in their own right. And (5) shows us that there are restrictions on the types of event that a single verb phrase can describe. As things stand, these restrictions could either build on facts about syntax (the inventory of available null heads, for example, or constraints on possible interpretations of relations between a head and the material it c-commands), or they could be due to facts about conceptual semantics (there are certain non-linguistic restrictions on what we can consider as a single event, and if syntactic decomposition is on the right track, these are reflected in phrase structure). There has been a large amount of research in cognitive science which suggests language-independent restrictions on the ways in which we chunk the flow of stuff that happens into discrete units that we might call 'events' (see, for example, Zacks and Tversky 2001, Baldwin *et al.* 2001, Gergely and Csibra 2003, Wolff 2003, and Jackendoff 2007: ch. 4, as well as earlier work on related structures by Miller, Galanter, and Pribram 1960, and Schank and Abelson 1977). This research shows that the notion of a non-linguistic constraint on the set of possible events is a viable one. The argument to be made here is that, to the extent that the same restrictions show up in unrelated syntactic configurations, it is more likely that the restrictions in question are conceptual, rather than phrase-structural, in origin.

To make this argument, I will look at a second construction. This involves A'-movement out of a class of constituents that I shall call *Bare Present Participial Adjuncts* (BPPAs), as in (6).

(6)   a. What did John drive Mary crazy [working on __]?
       b. What did John die [working on __]?
       c. *What does John drink coffee [working on __]?

The most salient difference between extraction from BPPAs and the lexical causatives discussed above is that BPPA constructions contain two verbs, standing in an adjunction relation.[5] This means that the syntactic configuration purported to map directly onto relations among subevents such as CAUSE and BECOME is not present in these constructions. However, we can argue that the same constraints on the internal structure of events are active here as in lexical causatives. I will discuss two such constraints here.

The first involves the relationship between aspectual classes, as in Vendler (1957), and the contribution of the subject's actions. In both (6a) and (6b), the BPPA describes what the subject was doing immediately before the culmination described by the matrix verb: the matrix verb specifies that there *is* such a preceding process, but does not attach any descriptive content to it, and the BPPA fills in that blank. However, the two differ in how that action relates to the culmination. John's work in (6a), where the matrix VP describes an accomplishment, describes the cause of Mary's craziness, while there is no necessary causal link between John's work and his death in (6b), where the matrix VP describes an achievement.

This distinction is inherited directly from the event structure and argument structure of accomplishments and achievements (see also Pustejovsky 1991). In accomplishment predicates, like transitive *melt* in (5a), the actions of the agent bring about the result state of the glass being molten. No such relation holds in the case of achievement predicates like intransitive *melt* in *The glass melted*. In those cases, the melting is understood to happen spontaneously. The interpretations of BPPAs are parallel to those of the aspectual classes, then, despite the fact that the syntax of BPPA constructions is quite different from the syntax of regular single-verb sentences.

The second similarity involves the directness of the relations involved. In (6a), what drove Mary crazy was John's work, and that relation has to be immediate: (6a) is unacceptable in a situation in which John's work sets off a long chain of causally related events which eventually lead to Mary going crazy. For instance, if John's work made him late for another date with Mary, and his lateness was the immediate cause of her craziness, we couldn't

---

[5] A reviewer suggests assimilating the possibility of extraction out of BPPAs to the adjunct-complement distinction: when the BPPA and the matrix VP can jointly describe a single event, the BPPA is a complement of the matrix verb; otherwise, it is an adjunct. Although I have no argument against this, it represents a higher degree of semantic determination of phrase-structural relations than is usually countenanced, and I don't see any independent reason to weaken the autonomy of these two modules to this extent. Note that the alternative of treating BPPAs under the single-event reading as *specifiers* is problematic for different reasons: (i) it would require a baroque set of movements to accommodate basic word-order facts, as BPPAs certainly appear to be right-adjoined on the surface; (ii) many specifiers disallow subextraction in English in any case.

felicitously ask (6a). Similar arguments can be made for (6b), although the relation there is purely temporal rather than causal: the question is felicitous if John was working on something immediately before he died, but not if there is a significant gap between the end of the working and the time of death. This parallels Fodor's observation that the causation in (5a) must be direct.

So far, this looks like a condition on the interpretation of BPPAs: the matrix VP asserts the existence of a number of related subevents, but leaves the nature of one of those subevents unspecified. In the case of both (6a) and (6b), this is the subevent which immediately precedes the beginning of the result state—in the case of (6a), we also infer that whatever John was doing immediately before Mary went crazy is the direct cause of that craziness. In both cases, the BPPA tells us that this immediately preceding subevent was one of John working on something. In the case of (6c), where there is no such complex subevent structure, and so no underspecified subevent to which the descriptive content of the BPPA could be attached, the structure is ill-formed.

However, there is a further twist. The range of interpretive options for BPPAs in non-A′-movement contexts is wider than in cases like the interrogatives in (6). For example, a declarative counterpart of (6a) like (7a) allows much more readily for an interpretation, such as the one given above, in which trying to fix the radiator wasn't the immediate cause of Mary's anger.[6] Equally, (7b) is quite acceptable, despite the fact that the corresponding interrogative (6c) was degraded.

(7) a. John drove Mary crazy [working on the radiator].
     b. John drinks coffee [working on his thesis].

This leads to the conclusion that the interpretive effects are not common to all BPPAs, but rather only to extraction out of BPPAs. This can be captured by the following condition, described more fully in Truswell (2007):

(8) **The Single Event Condition:**
     An A′-dependency is legitimate only if the minimal constituent containing the head and foot of the chain describes a single event.

How this works is as follows: we assume a set of well-formed event structures, along the familiar decompositional lines. Specifically, I assume that two subevents can form a single event if they stand in a relation of direct causation or

---

[6] For some speakers, including a reviewer, this contrast between the interpretation of declarative and interrogative examples is not clear. Such idiolects are unproblematic for this theory—they just reflect grammars in which a BPPA and the VP it modifies must *always* jointly describe a single event, regardless of the presence or absence of A′-movement. For our present purposes, though, this is less revealing than those idiolects where there is an interpretive difference between the declarative and interrogative cases.

immediate temporal precedence (corresponding broadly to the CAUSE and BECOME operators of Dowty 1979, or the event structures of Pustejovsky 1991), but other relations like 'going on at the same time' are not sufficient to allow formation of a single event from multiple subevents. When the events described by the matrix VP and the BPPA jointly form a single complex event description in accordance with well-formedness conditions on event structure, as in (6a) and (6b), extraction out of the BPPA is possible, according to the SEC. When this cannot be done, as in (6c), which describes two events going on at the same time, extraction out of the BPPA is ruled out by the SEC, although the structure remains legitimate in declarative cases with no A′-dependency, as in (7b).

The striking architectural implication of this condition is that the constraints on event structure are formulated in terms independent of phrase structure. Rather, well-formed event structures may correspond to several different phrase-structural configurations, going beyond the chains of head–complement relations which are the bread and butter of the syntactic decompositional approach.[7] The SEC then acts as a constraint on the interface between one aspect of the transformational syntax and an independent level of event structure, with its own primitives and relations.

2.3 Extraction from Complement Clauses

On the assumption that every verb introduces its own event variable, it is natural to ask how the SEC handles extraction from complement clauses, the classic case of successive-cyclic movement. Given that we have a verb in each clause, and therefore two event descriptions, we may ask whether such configurations satisfy the SEC.

In fact, I want to say that extraction from complement clauses sometimes satisfies the SEC, and sometimes doesn't. This correlates with a difference in acceptability of such extractions, explored by Kiparsky and Kiparsky (1970) and Erteschik-Shir (1973), and illustrated in (9).

(9)   a.   Who does John think [__ that Mary kissed __]?
      b.   ??Who does John regret [__ that Mary kissed __]?

The basic observation is that certain classes of verbs act as 'bridges', allowing constituents to get out of subordinate clauses, while others don't. Moreover, as originally reported by Ross (1967), and Kiparsky and Kiparsky (1970), these classes have something in common semantically. One class (not the only one)

---

[7] Of course, I haven't shown that there is no way of expanding the syntactic decompositional approach to cover these additional phrase-structural configurations. However, no natural expansion suggests itself to me.

that doesn't allow extraction out of complements is the class of *factive* verbs, as in (9b).[8] What these have in common, unlike (9a), is that they presuppose the truth of their complement clause: (9a) does not imply that Mary kissed someone, whereas (9b) does.

This means that the speaker is committed to the occurrence of two events in (9b): an event of Mary kissing someone and an event of John regretting the fact that the previous event occurred. On the other hand, in (9a), the speaker is committed to the occurrence of only a single event: an event of John thinking that Mary kissed someone. We can represent this difference perspicuously in Discourse Representation Theory (Kamp 1981b; Kamp and Reyle 1993) by using the approach to presupposition resolution from Van der Sandt (1992). The major properties of that approach are, firstly, that presupposed content generally comes to take wider scope than asserted content would in parallel syntactic configurations; and secondly, after the resolution of presuppositions, presupposed content comes to be indistinguishable from asserted content in a Discourse Representation Structure.[9] This means that the DRSs for the two sentences in (9) look as follows.

(10)   a.

j m x e_1
john(j)
mary(m)
x = ?
$e_1 = \text{think}\left(j, \begin{array}{\|c\|} \hline e_2 \\ \hline e_2 = \text{kiss(m,x)} \\ \hline \end{array} \right)$

   b.

j m x e_1 e_2 f
john(j)
mary(m)
x = ?
$e_1 = \text{kiss(m,x)}$
$f \approx \begin{array}{\|c\|} \hline e_1' \\ \hline e_1' = \text{kiss(m,x)} \\ \hline \end{array}$
$e_2 = \text{regret(j,f)}$

[8] There is substantial disagreement in the literature about the strength of the degradation induced by extraction out of a factive complement. It is clear that extraction of anything except an argumental DP is completely impossible, and that extraction of an argumental DP is somewhat better. This has led many people to classify factive complements as weak islands. However, it is often felt that extraction from factive complements is worse than extraction from typical weak islands like *wh*-islands (typical judgements are ?? for factives and OK or ? for *wh*-islands). Also Erteschik-Shir (1973: 90) found that the degree of ungrammaticality of extraction from a factive complement was gradient, depending on the choice of embedding verb. This is not typical behaviour for other classes of weak islands. I will idealize away from these serious empirical issues here, and instead treat extraction from factive complements as substantially degraded across the board.

[9] The first of these properties is noted already in Kiparsky and Kiparsky (1970), and Langendoen and Savin (1971), who claimed that presuppositions always took maximally wide scope. The DRT approach also accounts for some exceptions to this claim, but those exceptions are tangential to our interests here.

Several details are glossed over in these representations—I refer the interested reader to Van der Sandt (1992) for a DRT treatment of presupposition; Asher (1993) for a detailed theory of the representation of abstract objects, including events, facts, and propositions; and Geurts (1998) for a suggestive discussion of the interaction of presupposition and propositional attitude verbs (albeit one that doesn't say much explicitly about factives). However, hopefully the point is clear. If we look at the universe of the outer DRS in each case, which shows the entities that the utterance claims to exist in the actual world, we see that the non-factive (10a) includes only a single event variable, e_1 (the second event variable, e_2, is buried inside a subordinate DRS, and so the utterance doesn't make any claims about its existence in the actual world). However, the outer DRS in the factive (10b) has two event variables, e_1 and e_2. This full DRS should be read roughly as follows: there are three individuals: John, Mary, and a third whose identity we are asking about. There is an event of Mary kissing that third individual, and the occurrence of that event corresponds to a fact, f. There is also a second event of John regretting that fact.

Of course, this extra event variable means that the representation in (10b) falls foul of the SEC, while that in (10a) does not. This, then, is what the SEC has to say about extraction from complement clauses. It is possible, but only when the content of the complement clause is not presupposed.

2.4 Cyclicity

The account of extraction from complement clauses and of factive islands in the previous section made crucial use of presupposition. But presuppositions have a habit of disappearing when embedded in certain contexts. For example, propositional attitude verbs such as *believe* and *hope* tend to block any presuppositions that their complements carry (they are what Karttunen 1973 calls *plugs*). So most people find that (11b) does not carry the same presupposition as (11a), that John was a smoker (see Karttunen 1973: section 11, for some discussion of the variability of this judgement).

(11)   a. John has stopped smoking.
       b. Bill believes that John has stopped smoking.

In conjunction with the SEC, this could lead to a very strong prediction. This is that, because embedding under a presupposition plug blocks any presuppositions and so frequently yields a description of a single event, as in (9a), such embedding should ameliorate any of the degraded sentences ruled out by the SEC. This prediction is clearly false. (12) reproduces the paradigm from (6), with each example embedded under a presupposition plug, and (13) does the same for (9). The judgements are just as before.

(12) a.   What did Bill say [__that John drove Mary crazy [working on__]]?
      b.   What did Bill say [__that John died [working on__]]?
      c.   *What did Bill say [__that John drinks coffee [working on__]]?

(13) a.   Who did Bill say [__that John thinks [__that Mary kissed__]]?
      b.   ??Who did Bill say [__that John regrets [__that Mary kissed__]]?

However, we only predict this if we check the SEC in a global, post-syntactic fashion. That is, the problem only arises if we wait until we have our final syntactic representation, and only then check if the SEC is satisfied. The alternative is to check the SEC at some intermediate point, plausibly after movement to the intermediate landing site in embedded [Spec,C]. At this point, the SEC is violated in a degraded case like (12c) in just the same way as it was in (6c) above.

(14)   *What that John drinks coffee [working on__]?

This leads us to the following conclusion.

(15)   The Single Event Condition is checked cyclically.

In other words, the event-structural approach to extraction from adjuncts and complements requires a model of the grammar which allows the semantic SEC to influence syntactic operations cyclically. Although the final output in examples like (12) and (13) satisfies the SEC, an ill-formed intermediate stage still suffices to rule out the degraded examples.

2.5 Conclusion

This chapter has made two major claims with respect to linguistic interfaces. The first is that if we adopt a model of event structure which stands in a looser correspondence to phrase structure than is often assumed, we see that certain conditions on locality of A'-movement which are generally handled by conditions on phrase-structural representations should instead be handled in terms of conditions on the mapping between phrase structure and event structure. Secondly, the interaction of these two structures is determined cyclically, rather than globally. Although the size of the cycles in question was left open here (is the SEC checked at every phrase? At every phase?

At every clause? At every movement step?), it is clear that such cyclic interactions of different levels of representation are incompatible with the classical Y-model of the Extended Standard Theory, but resonate well with phase theory, initiated by Chomsky (2000), as well as more radical departures such as the parallel architecture of Jackendoff (2002).

3

Determiners and Movement*

KYLE JOHNSON

A commonplace treatment of determiners has it that they name relations between predicates of individuals. In (1), for example, *every* says that the set of students is included in the set of things that ran.[1]

(1) Every student ran.

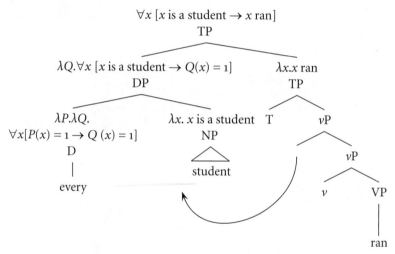

There are two kinds of modifications to this view that are required. One is made necessary by the discovery that predicates are not simple descriptions of

* My thanks to Satoshi Tomioka, Jan Anderssen, Shoichi Takahashi, Angelika Kratzer, Emily Elfner, Margaret Grant, Jesse Harris, Misato Hiraga, Wendell Kimper, Pasha Siraj, Martin Walkow, Yoko Hattori, Yumi Kawamoto, and the participants of the conference.

[1] See Barwise and Cooper (1981). I will give TP and *v*P the same denotations in this paper. This seriously misrepresents things, but it also greatly simplifies matters in a way that allows us to concentrate on the quantification introduced by determiners. I will also systematically obscure the independent contributions of the lexical verbs and voice, represented here with *v*.

individuals, but instead describe events.[2] Instead of (1) we require something along the lines of (2).

(2)   Every student ran.

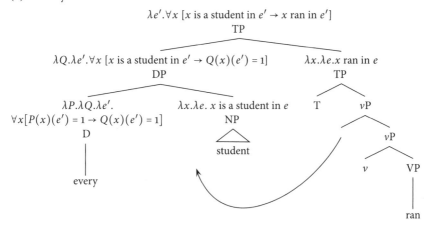

$\lambda e'.\forall x\ [x$ is a student in $e' \to x$ ran in $e']$
TP

$\lambda Q.\lambda e'.\forall x\ [x$ is a student in $e' \to Q(x)(e') = 1]$ $\lambda x.\lambda e.x$ ran in e
DP   TP

$\lambda P.\lambda Q.\lambda e'.$
$\forall x[P(x)(e') = 1 \to Q(x)(e') = 1]$ $\lambda x.\lambda e.\ x$ is a student in e T vP
D   NP

every   student vP

                                                                                                      v VP

                                                                                                                  ran

The other comes from the study of reconstruction effects, in which a moved DP seems to be interpreted in two positions. (3) illustrates such an example. Under treatments of constituent questions that claim that the interrogative phrase is semantically interpreted in its surface position,[3] the disjoint reference effect between *John* and *he* in (3) indicates that the moved phrase is interpreted in the position it moved from as well.

(3)   *Whose kissing John₁ does he₁ object to?

Chomsky (1993) suggested that these effects arise because movement produces 'copies' of the phrase being moved and that certain of these copies are interpreted semantically. On this view, the representation that (3) would get is (4), and the principles of semantics require that all of the lower copy be interpreted.

---

  [2] See Davidson (1967), Parsons (1990), Higginbotham (1983), Schein (1993), Kratzer (1996), Harley (1995), Rothstein (2004) and many others.

  [3] And this is indicated by the ability of examples such as *They asked which pictures of each other she liked* to meet the locality requirements that hold between reciprocals and their antecedents. See Barss (1986) and Fox and Nissenbaum (2004).

(4)

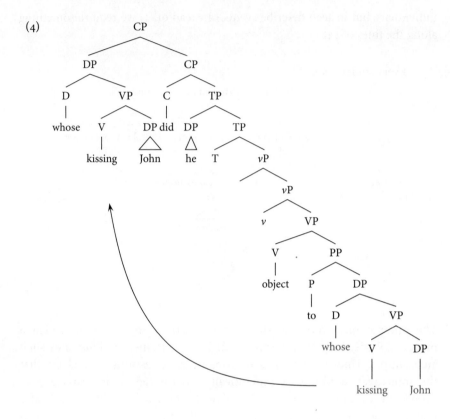

I adopt here the convention of indicating that a copy is unspoken by putting it into a shaded font. The disjoint reference effect arises in (3), then, because one copy of *John* is c-commanded by *he* in (4) and this is the configuration that triggers disjoint reference effects. This 'copy theory' of movement appears to be the most successful account of such phenomena, so I will adopt it.

But it raises some questions. There are two I will try to answer in this paper, and they are:

(5)   Why is only one of the copies pronounced?

(6)   How are the two copies interpreted so that one binds the other?

The present answer to (6) is in Fox (1999, 2002, 2003) (see also Sauerland 1998) and it has the consequences for the treatment of determiners that I am interested in. It is expressed in terms of a semantics like that in (1) which treats determiners as relations between predicates of individuals. I'll begin by reviewing Fox's proposal, modifying it slightly so that we get an answer to (5). Then I will translate it into an event-based semantics that makes use of an approach to quantification in Elbourne (2005). The result is a view that splits up the meaning of determiners, and in this respect has elements in common with the papers in Szabolcsi (1997), and also Williams (1986, 1988), Beghelli (1993, 1995), Sportiche (2003), Hallman (2000), Butler (2004), and Kratzer (2005). It's different in its details, however, and I think better equipped to make sense of the 'apparent' resumptive pronouns discussed in Aoun, Choueiri, and Hornstein (2001) (see section 3.5) as well as the cases in which copies are claimed to be doubled. We'll begin by considering how to interpret copies so that reconstruction effects are captured.

3.1 Trace Conversion

Another context where the sort of reconstruction displayed in (3) is found are cases of Quantifier Raising, like that in (7).

(7)   *A different student told her$_1$ every story about Diana$_1$'s parents.

The *every story* DP can have the subject in its c-command domain. We know that because the subject in (7) can get an interpretation that's only available when *different* is c-commanded by the universally quantified DP, as (8) shows.

(8)   a.   Every woman talked to a different student.
      b.   *[Her visit to every woman] disturbed a different student.
      c.   *A different student cried after every woman left yesterday.

But at the same time, the *every story*-DP must be within the c-command domain of *her*; that we know because there is a disjoint reference effect between *Diana* and *her*. We must therefore let movement create a representation for (7) like that in (9).

(9)

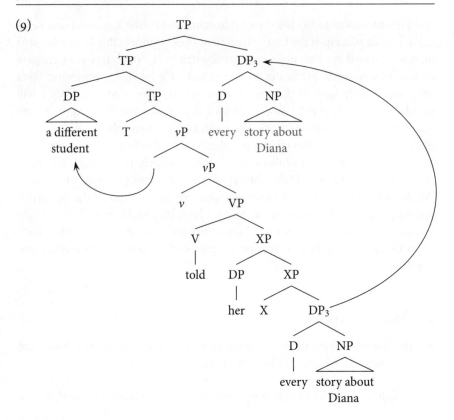

As in (3), this representation places one copy of *Diana* within the c-command domain of *her*, and therefore correctly produces the environment for disjoint reference. The only difference between (3) and (9) is which copy gets pronounced. In (9) it is the lower copy, while in (3) it is the higher one. Throughout the rest of this paper, I will focus on cases like (9), ones in which Quantifier Raising occurs.

A feature of this representation that will be important for what follows is that the higher, unspoken, copy contains the NP that we see in the lower, spoken, copy. On some accounts of these cases, the higher copy contains only the quantifier and not the NP. I will therefore report the argument from Fox (2002) for this feature of the proposal.

Fox's argument comes from a phenomenon discovered by Fiengo and May (1994). There are situations where the disjoint reference effect that (7) illustrates are overcome. If the name is within a relative clause that is forced by ellipsis to be interpreted outside the phrase that contains the coreferent pronoun, as in (10), then the disjoint reference effect is modulated.

(10)   ? I told her₁ every story that Diana₁ asked me to △.
        △ = tell her *x*

The ellipsis in (10) appears to lie within the VP that serves as its antecedent, and this produces well-known problems. Thus, both the disjoint reference effects and the presence of ellipsis indicate that the copy theory of movement cannot have its normal outcome in this case:

(11)

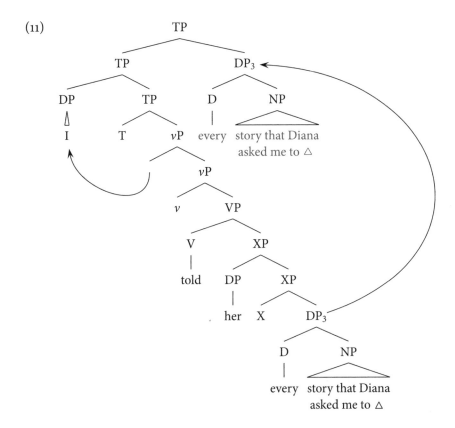

There is a parallel phenomenon in cases of movement that form questions. Unlike (3), where a name inside a moved *wh*-phrase is interpreted in its lower position, examples where a name is within a relative clause in a moved *wh*-phrase do not trigger parallel disjoint reference effects; (12) is such a case.

(12)   Which story that Diana₁ told does she₁ now regret?

Without modification, the copy theory of movement would also wrongly give this sentence a representation in which a *Diana* falls within the

c-command domain of *she* and a disjoint reference effect should consequently arise.

(13)

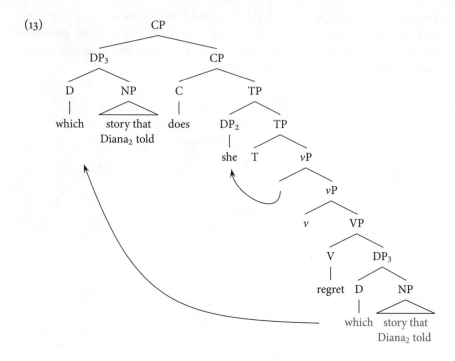

The solution to both cases is to allow for a derivation that involves the
following steps.

(14)   Late Merger
   a. Build the D+NP phrase that will move
   b. Move that D+NP
   c. Build and attach the relative clause to the higher copy only.

This is David Lebeaux's solution,[4] and it is adopted by Fox. These derivations
would give to (10) and (12) the representations in (15).

As (15) indicates, this account claims that in (10) the relative clause is not in
the spoken copy of the object, but is instead part of the higher, unspoken,
copy. It's this part of the account that serves as evidence that the higher,
unspoken, copy in such cases contains the NP part of the object. That is
necessary because under standard assumptions, a restrictive relative clause of

---

[4] See Lebeaux (1988), and also Freidin (1986).

(15) a.

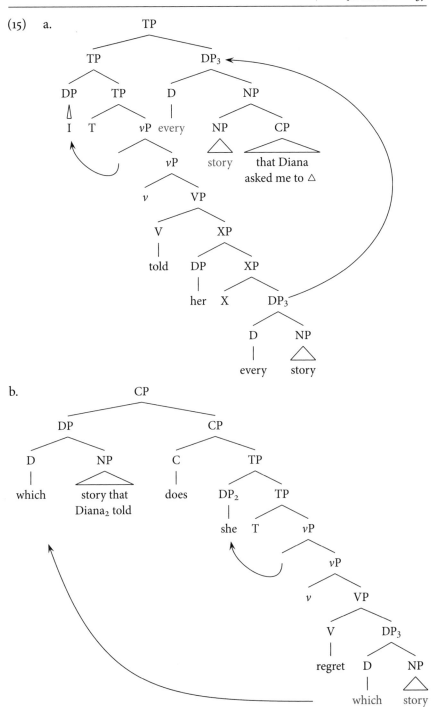

b.

this kind must attach to an NP to produce the right meaning. Fox (2002) produces a variety of arguments that the relative clause in such examples is indeed not in the spoken copy of the DP.[5] One of these is based on the contrast in (16), from Tiedeman (1995).

(16)   a.   *I said that everyone you did △ arrived.
                    △ = say that *x* arrived

        b.   I said that everyone arrived that you did △.
                    △ = say that *x* arrived

(Fox 2002: 77, (35b), (36b))

Just as this proposal predicts, the relative clause containing an elided VP cannot be spoken within the antecedent VP: that's what makes (16a) ungrammatical. Instead, that relative clause must be spoken in a position outside the antecedent VP and, more particularly, as part of the material that determines the scope of the quantificational DP the relative clause modifies. That's what's happened in (16b), which has the representation in (17).

(17)

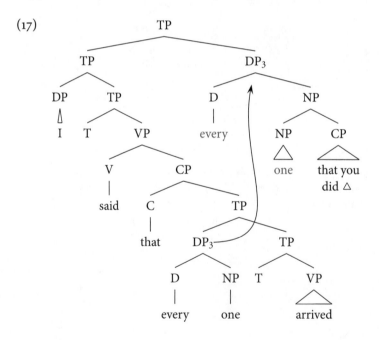

For this account to be complete, it requires an explanation for when late merger derivations are possible and when they are not, for otherwise all of the effects gained by the copy theory of movement will be lost. See Takahashi (2006) for many steps in this direction.[6]

We're now ready to see Fox's proposal for interpreting copies. He suggests that movement creates not only copies of the phrase that is moved, but also that it appends the same index on all of them. He then devises the following rule for interpreting structures with movement indices in them.[7]

(18)   TRACE CONVERSION

In ϕ',   interpret ϕ as a function that maps an individual, x, to the meaning of $\phi[x/n]$. $\phi[x/n]$ is the result of replacing the head of every constituent with the index n in ϕ with the head *the*$_x$, whose interpretation, $\lVert the_x \rVert$, is: $\lambda P. \lVert the \rVert [P \cap \lambda y.y = x]$.

(slightly modified from Fox 2003: 111, (52))

We can think of this rule has having two parts. One part expresses the standard method of interpreting a binder.[8] It gives the phrase that the binder combines with the denotation of a lambda-abstract. That part of the rule could be expressed with (19).

(19)   In ϕ',   change the denotation of ϕ to $\lambda n.\phi$.

The other part rewrites the meaning of the copies inside ϕ. The new meaning is one that is like a definite description, but with a variable bound by the lambda-operator introduced in the other part of the rule. It has the effect of turning a lower copy of '[$_{DP_3}$ every story]', for example, into:

(20)   [$_{DP_3}$ every story] $\rightarrow$ the story that is 3.

With Trace Conversion, a simple example like (21) will get an interpretation like that shown.

---

[6] The account reviewed here for Extraposition from NP is argued in Fox and Nissenbaum (1999) to only arise when the term extraposed is an adjunct. When a PP or clause that is an argument of the NP appears in extraposed position, they argue that the clause itself has moved.

[7] See also Sauerland (2004) for an examination of alternative ways of formulating this rule.

[8] See, for example, Heim and Kratzer (1998).

(21)   She told every story.

$$\forall x[x \text{ is a story} \rightarrow [\![\text{she}]\!] \text{ told } [\![\text{the}]\!][\lambda z. z \text{ is a story} \cap \lambda y.y = x]]$$

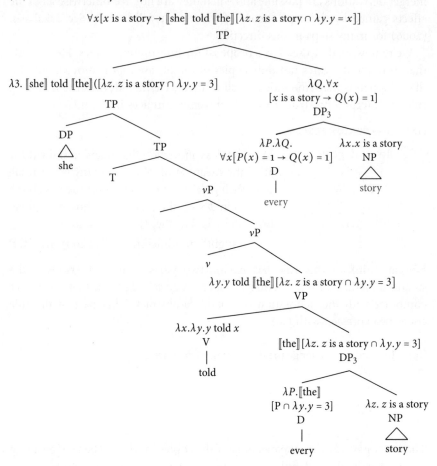

A clumsy paraphrase for the denotation of this sentence is:

(22)   For all x, if x is a story, then she told the thing that is a story and x.

Trace Conversion turns determiners of lower copies into kinds of restricted variables, then. It works for all of the cases we've viewed so far, and it arguably extends correctly to all cases in which a DP has moved. As noted at the outset, it's built upon a view of determiner quantification that has them relate properties of individuals. It still requires translation into a framework in which predicates describe events. But before we do that, let's take a closer look at it and the notion of 'copies' that it relies on.

3.2 Trace Conversion

The second part of Fox's Trace Conversion has the undesirable property of letting a whole class of lexical items be ambiguous. In the cases we're examining, those lexical items are determiners. It resolves that ambiguity by syntactic rule. It claims that the meanings of determiners are not fixed, but change according to their position. It gives syntax the power to change lexical content. That's more than syntax should be allowed. So let me offer a variant of Fox's proposal that avoids these consequences.

This variant builds on ideas many have had about the syntax of quantification.[9] Imagine, as in Matthewson (2001), that quantified nominals make use of two functional heads. One has the denotation of quantifiers, and the other is something with the meaning given to determiners by Fox's Trace Conversion rule. Unlike Matthewson, but like those cited above, let's separate these two functional heads, putting the term that expresses the quantification in the position where its scope is computed, while the definite determiner part is in construction with the NP. The morphological form of the definite determiner varies depending on the quantificational term. Let's follow Kratzer (2005) and Adger and Ramchand (2005) and let this dependency be mediated by AGREE. AGREE will determine the morphological form of the term in the lower position, and make both heads share an index. On this view, then, there is only one determiner—the one that Fox's Trace Conversion creates—with a morphological form that is fixed by AGREEing with a silent quantifier.

(23)   The only (quantificational) determiner is $\lfloor$the$_x\rfloor$. Its morphological form is determined by the silent Q it agrees with.

This proposal would give to (24) the derivation indicated. (I will use '∀' to represent the silent universal quantifier that AGREES with *every*.)

---

[9] See, e.g., Williams (1986, 1988), the papers in Szabolcsi (1997), Giannakidou and Merchant (2002), and Hallman (2000). Perhaps it's closest to ideas in Beghelli (1993, 1995), Sauerland (1998), Sportiche (2003), Butler (2004), Kratzer (2005), and Adger and Ramchand (2005).

(24)   She told every story.

a.

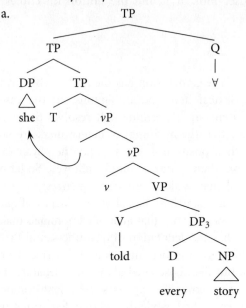

b.

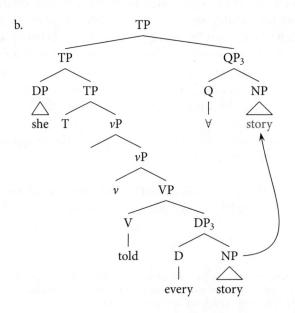

On this view then, there is no rule of Trace Conversion, and we can rely on the plainer binding rule in (19) to express configurations created by movement. The part that Fox credited to a special rule that rewrites the denotation of a quantificational determiner is now taken up by a more complex syntactic theory about how quantificational determiners are represented. It requires one part of quantificational determiners to stand in the scope position, and the other to stand in the variable position, where Fox's rule created a new denotation for a determiner. This isn't a small rethinking. It requires a complete overhaul of the syntax, and semantics, of quantificational DPs. We need to understand, among other things, the conditions that determine how far apart the two parts can be, and how the rules of Spell Out determine which component is pronounced and how. I can't do that overhaul here, and not just for reasons of space. Nonetheless, I hope it strikes the reader as an appealing alternative to Fox's rule.

3.3 Multidominance

Let's now consider what the copies are in the copy theory of movement. There are two criteria that any successful characterization of copies must meet.

(25) a. Only one copy should be able to be pronounced.
      b. Every copy must be identical.

One proposal that achieves both these goals is (26).

(26) Copies of α are one and the same α in different syntactic positions.

A simple implementation of this idea is to let phrase markers allow for multidominance, i.e., relax the requirement that a term have no more than one mother (see Nunes (2001), Starke (2001), Frampton (2004), and Fitzpatrick and Groat (2005) for recent proposals along these lines, and Citko (2005) for an application of the idea to across-the-board movement). This would give to (24) the representation in (27).

(27)

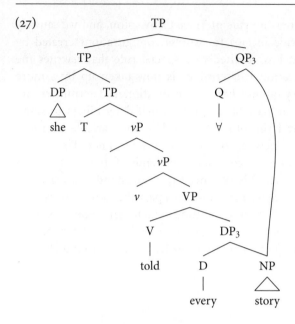

An example involving late merger, such as (15a), will get a representation like (28).[10]

These representations ensure that every copy has exactly the same material in it, and that the semantic contribution it makes is precisely the same in each position.

It also provides a way of deriving that only one copy may be pronounced, along the lines described in Nunes (1995, 1996, 1999).[11] The procedure that

[10] Heidi Harley asks by what derivation a representation like that in (28) could be manufactured. If we assume that the basic tree-building operation is MERGE, as in Chomsky (1995), then we seek a derivation that involves nothing more than bringing two terms together to form a larger term. I suggest that (28) is achieved by way of a derivation in which at one point *story* has two mothers: one containing *every* as well as *story*, and another that contains the relative clause as well as *story*. It's this second phrase that will merge with ∀ to form the QP in the higher position. The derivation I've just described is in all relevant respects equivalent to derivations that involve 'Sideward Movement' in Nunes (2001, 2004). The difference between Nunes's representations and mine are that the terms which MERGE forms under Nunes's scheme are sets, whereas they are mereologies in my representations.

[11] Nunes does not have representations that involve multidominance. Instead, copies are represented as more than one phrase occupying different positions. He then stipulates that the linearization algorithm treats these phrases as one and the same item, with the consequences that will be described in a moment. I am merely removing this stipulation through a multidominant definition of 'copy'. The technique of using ill-formed linearizations that result from multidominant representations to produce some effect has a precedent in Citko (2005), which examines cases of across-the-board movement. In her work, multidominant relationships arise in co-ordinations of certain sorts, and the linearization problems they create are alleviated by movement.

maps syntactic structures onto strings will (sometimes) get conflicting information from phrases that have more than one mother, and this leads to conflicts that Nunes argues are resolved by failing to linearize the copy in all of its positions. For instance, consider how a representation like (29) might get linearized.

(28)

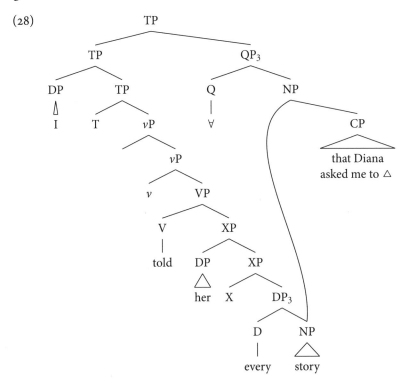

Nunes adopts the linearization procedure in Kayne (1994) which involves certain complexities that are better dodged here. So, for illustrative purposes, I'll adopt an algorithm that incorporates some of the cyclic nature of procedures described in Epstein and Seely (2002) and Fox and Pesetsky (2004), and expresses linear information in terms of strings.

(30) Let γ be a node in a phrase marker projected from α, and β be an immediate daughter of γ. Map each γ to a string that is formed from the strings associated with α and β, so that:

  a. If γ is an X^0, then the string associated with γ is the terminal γ dominates, and

(29)

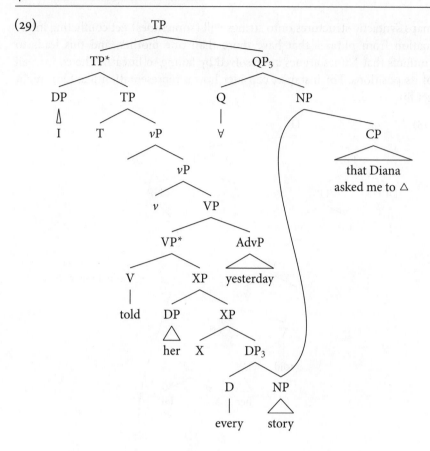

b. If γ has only one daughter, α, then the string associated with γ is the string associated with α, and

c. The string associated with γ is formed by concatenating the string associated with β to the left of the string associated with α when β is in Specifier of γ, otherwise

d. The string associated with γ is formed by concatenating the string associated with α to the left of the string associated with β.

A proper understanding of (30) would require unpacking what is meant by 'specifier'. This is one of the foundational problems for linearization theories, and not usefully engaged here. I'll stipulate that the DPs *I* and *her* are in Specifier positions in (29).

When (30) interprets (29), it will require that *story* precede *yesterday* (because VP* $= \alpha$ and AdvP $= \beta$ for VP) and it will require that *yesterday* precede *story* (because TP* $= \alpha$ and QP $= \beta$ for TP). This, Nunes assumes, is an illicit result as it disobeys the well-formedness constraint on linearizations in (31).

(31)   Consistency
        If α precedes β, then β cannot precede α.

Representations that have multiply dominated phrases in them will (often) violate (31) in just the way that (30) does. If these phrase markers are to have licit linearizations, (30) must be modified.

As it stands, (30) achieves the goal of making sure that every terminal in a phrase marker is part of the resulting string by requiring that the string associated with every daughter phrase is part of the string associated with the phrase immediately dominating. If that requirement were replaced with something else that ensured every terminal gets into the linearization, it would be possible to avoid producing an output that violates Consistency in situations where something is multiply dominated. Lifting that requirement would allow the linearization scheme to ignore those phrases that lead to violations of Consistency. That will also have the effect of (usually)[12] ensuring that a multiply dominated phrase be linearized in only one of the positions it occupies.

I'll demonstrate that by adding to the set of well-formedness constraints on a linearization something that ensures that every terminal finds itself in the resulting string (=(32)) and changing (30) to (33).

(32)   Totality
        Every terminal in a root node, ρ, must be present in the string associated with ρ.

(33)   Let γ be a node in a phrase marker projected from α, and β be an immediate daughter of γ. Map each γ to a string that is formed from the strings associated with α and β, so that:
        a. The string associated with γ is the terminal γ immediately dominates, or
        b. The string associated with γ is the string associated with one of its immediate daughters, or
        c. The string associated with γ is formed by concatenating the string associated with β to the left of the string associated with α when β is in Specifier of γ, otherwise
        d. The string associated with γ is formed by concatenating the string associated with α to the left of the string associated with β.

---

[12] In situations where a phrase's two mothers put it in positions that are linearly adjacent (as in cases of 'string vacuous movement'), linearizing that phrase in both positions does not produce a violation of Consistency.

Consider how this revised linearization procedure will apply to (29). In order to meet Totality, enough phrases will have to contribute the strings they are associated with to the strings of phrases dominating them for every terminal to end up with a position. But in order to meet Consistency, not every phrase can submit the string it is associated with to the strings associated with phrases that dominate them. There are just two ways that (33) can meet those goals. In one, the string associated with [NP *story*] is made part of the string associated with [DP *every story*] but not the string associated with [NP *story that Diana asked me to*]. On that linearization, (29) gets mapped onto the string in (34).

(34)   I told her every story yesterday that Diana asked me to.

In the other linearization, the string associated with [NP *story*] is made part of the string associated with [NP *story that Diana asked me to*] but not the string associated with [DP *every story*]. On that linearization, (29) gets mapped onto the string in (35).

(35)   I told her yesterday every story that Diana asked me to.

In this example, both linearizations arise. In other cases, we will want to allow only one of the feasible linearizations. In simple constituent questions in English, for instance, a multidominant representation would allow for two linearizations parallel to the ones we've seen for (29): one where the moved phrase is linearized according to its higher position and another where the moved phrase is linearized according to its lower position. English, however, only permits the linearization that follows the higher position, i.e., *wh*-movement is 'overt' in English. Whatever is responsible for this effect will not be part of what I offer. The syntactic representations I am suggesting we adopt will provide several positions in which moved phrases can be spelled out, but which of these positions are actually available will have to come from factors independent of the syntax of movement.

This, then, is the syntax I suggest we adopt for movement. It requires disassembling determiners into two parts that provide the effects of Fox's Trace Conversion rule. And it requires modelling copies as phrases in more than one position. This second assumption can be wedded to a linearization scheme that derives the fact that moved phrases get pronounced in only one of their positions, along lines sketched by Nunes. We are now ready to turn to the task of beefing up the semantics of determiners so that they involve events.

3.4 Events

There is now considerable evidence that predicates like *ran* do not describe properties of individuals, as in (36), but instead relate individuals to events, as in (37).

(36)   ⟦she⟧ told ⟦it⟧

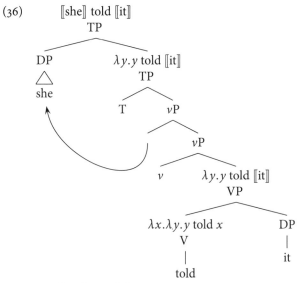

(37)   λe. ⟦she⟧ told ⟦it⟧ in *e*

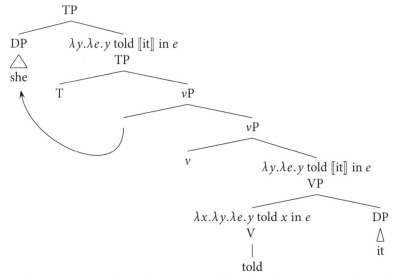

On this view, sentences refer to the events in which the relations named by their predicates hold of the arguments those predicates combine with. The account sketched in the previous two sections is built upon a non-event view of sentence meanings and won't work with an event-based semantics as it stands.

It's not hard to modify what we've got so that it fits a event-based semantics. Elbourne (2005) incorporates Fox's Trace Conversion rule to his event-based study of quantification. He provides a comprehensive semantics for definite determiners that allows them to have the very meaning that Fox suggests as a special case. On his view, as on Fox's, the movement operation will involve not only producing copies—multidominated NPs, if I am correct—but also cause the index on the lower copy to be the same as the index on the higher copy. The semantics associated with the Trace Conversion rule will then apply giving the correct interpretations.

I want to explore a different possibility here. I will use Elbourne (2005) as my model, but focus on his account of definite descriptions that, though not bound, nonetheless behave like variables related to an antecedent. One example of this sort is (38).

(38)   Every man who owns a donkey beats the donkey.

In (38), *the donkey* is anaphoric on the donkeys described in the subject: the donkey each man beats is the donkey that he owns. This can be achieved by letting the universal quantifier associated with *every* quantify over the events that *man who owns a donkey* and *beats the donkey* describe. Simplifying somewhat, Elbourne's proposal is that $\forall$ has the denotation in (39).

(39) $[\![\forall]\!] = \lambda f_{<e,<s,t>>}.\lambda g_{<e,<s,t>>}.\lambda s.$ for every x and every minimal s' such that $s' \leq s$ and $f(x)(s') = 1$, there is a minimal s'' such that $s' \leq s''$ $\leq s$ and $g(x)(s'') = 1$.

(compare: Elbourne 2005: section 2.2.4)

The variables s, s', and s'' range over 'situations', which we can equate with events, and '$\leq$' is the reflexive part-of relation. (39) says that $\forall$ takes two relations between individuals and situations (*qua* events), f and g, and describes those situations, s, in which, for every x, all of the smallest sub-situations of s that contain x and make f true are part of the smallest sub-situations of s that contains x and makes g true. What this will do in the case of (38) is give it a meaning that can be paraphrased with (40).

(40)   There is a situation, s, such that for every x and every minimal situation s' in s such that x is a man who owns a donkey in s', there is a larger minimal situation, s'' in s that contains s' such that x beats the donkey in s''.

A looser, but perhaps more revealing, paraphrase is (41).

(41)   For every x, all of the minimal situations of a man, x, owning a donkey are part of a larger minimal situation in which x beats the donkey.

The notion of 'minimal situation' does the work of getting the donkeys that are beaten to be the donkeys that are owned in (38). Think of a situation as being made up of individuals, relations, and properties. A minimal situation can be informally described as one which is made up of only those individuals, relations, and properties necessary to make some proposition true. (See Berman 1987, Schein 1993, Elbourne 2005, and especially Kratzer 1989, 1990, 2002, forthcoming.)

(42) A situation, s, is a minimal situation in which $P(s) = 1$ iff there is no s'
      $< s$ such that $P(s') = 1$.

Therefore, a situation that makes 'a man, x, owns a donkey' true will be a
minimal situation just in case it contains only that man and one donkey and
the 'own' relation between them. A situation that makes 'x beats the donkey'
true will be a minimal situation just in case it contains only x and the donkey
and the 'beats' relation between them. If the 'owns' situation is a part of the
'beats' situation, then, because they are each allowed only one donkey, the
donkey in both situations will be the same.

This treatment of (38) extends to cases like (43).[13]

(43) Every man who owns a donkey beats it.

The *it* in (43) is anaphoric to *a donkey* in the very same way that *the donkey* is in
(38). Elbourne (2005) argues that this is because *it* is, in fact, *the donkey* with the
NP containing *donkey* elided. His proposal, following Postal (1969), is that
pronouns are how definite determiners are pronounced when the NP they are
in construction with is elided. The transformations in (44) are all on a par.

(44) a. She saw some books and he read some books. → She saw some
          books and he read some △.
      b. She wrote no books and he read no books. → She wrote no books
          and he read none △.
      c. She wrote the book and he read the book → She wrote the book and
          he read it △.

Thus, (43) is actually (45), where *it* has the meaning of *the*, and the semantics
has the same consequences for (45) that it does for (38).

(45) Every man who owns a donkey beats [$_{DP}$ it [$_{NP}$ ~~donkey~~]].

The work done by minimal situations in guaranteeing that *the donkey* in (38),
or *it* in (43), are anaphoric to the descriptive content of the preceding
quantified expression mimics the work done by indices in Fox's Trace Conversion rule. In translating Fox's system into an event-based semantics, I
propose that we dispense with the indices in his rule and exploit the minimal
situation technique. Because Elbourne's system is built on quantificational
expressions binding indexed variables, I will have to change his denotation for
$\forall$ as well. I propose changing it to (46).

(46) $[\![\forall]\!] = \lambda f_{<e, <s,t>>} \cdot \lambda g_{<s,t>} \cdot \lambda s$. for every minimal s' such that $s' \leq s$ and
      $\exists x f(x)(s') = 1$, there is a minimal s'' such that $s' \leq s'' \leq s$ and $g(s'') = 1$.

---

[13] See Geach (1962), Evans (1977), Cooper (1979), Heim (1990).

This assumes that NPs are functions from individuals to predicates of situations (or events).

(47) $[\text{story}] = \lambda x.\lambda s.\ x$ is a story in s.

Not only will this proposal dispense with the indices in Fox's Trace Conversion rule, it will dispense with Fox's Trace Conversion rule entirely. Here's an illustration.[14]

(48)

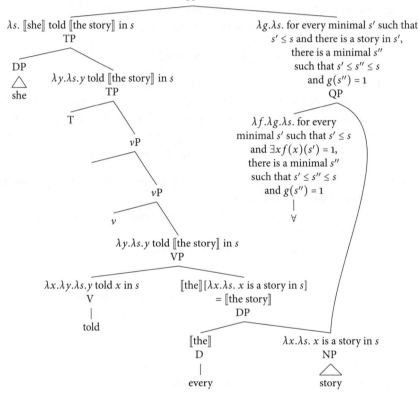

$\lambda s.$ for every minimal s' such that $s' \le s$ and s' is a story, there is a minimal s'' such that $s' \le s'' \le s$ and $[\text{she}]$ told $[\text{the story}]$ in s''

My proposal, then, is that lower copies are plain definite descriptions—or the pronoun version of them—which share an NP with a higher quantificational expression. The connection between the higher quantifier and the lower definite description comes by way of quantifying over situations.

Under this proposal, then, 'traces' of QR are kinds of donkey pronouns.[15] They are entirely parallel to the pronoun in (45), but whereas the pronoun in

---

[14] My proposal has certain features in common with the 'choice function' version of the Trace Conversion rule that Sauerland (2004) argues for. On Sauerland's view, the definite determiner in the lower copy is a variable over choice functions that is quantified over by the higher copy. As he shows in Sauerland (1998), this approach gives an interesting explanation of certain crossover phenomena. My proposal does not obviously extend to these cases.

[15] Compare Boeckx (2003), who attempts to reduce donkey anaphora to movement.

(45) is missing its NP by way of deletion, traces share their NPs with a higher quantificational term. This achieves Chomsky's (1993) goal of reducing the movement relation entirely to structure building; it does so in a way that is close in spirit to Starke (2001). It raises a raft of questions, of course, including how to model the familiar island conditions characteristic of movement, as well as how to distinguish pronominal binding, donkey anaphora, and traces.

3.5 Open Questions

The account given in section 3.3 for why only one copy is pronounced is not complete. To see this, consider a case of *wh*-movement in which, unlike the cases of quantifier raising I have concentrated on, the moved phrase is allowed to be linearized in only one of its two positions. A case like (49), for example, gets a representation like (50) under the proposals here.

(49) Which story did she tell?

(50)

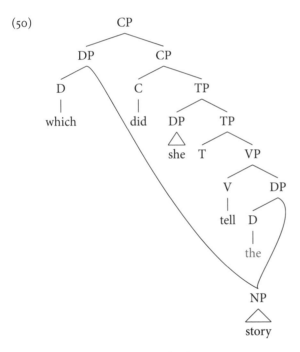

The lower copy of the *wh*-phrase is not pronounced in (50) for the following two reasons. First: the shared NP can be pronounced in only one of its positions, and something independent of our story determines in this case that it will be the higher position. Second: the determiner in this example is silent. For both these reasons, then, the lower, 'trace', position of *wh*-movement has nothing in it that is pronounced. But these two reasons are only accidentally combined. It does not seem accidental that the position in which the NP cannot be pronounced is always the position in which the determiner happens to be silent. My proposal does not connect these two facts.

This is a problem. But I am encouraged by the existence of cases that are just what would be expected if the determiner were pronounced in cases like (50). If Elbourne's analysis of pronouns as determiners is correct, we should expect a determiner that is in construction with a silent NP to have the form of a pronoun. Therefore if (50) were to arise with an overt determiner, it should look like a resumptive pronoun but with the reconstruction effects characteristic of movement. As Elbourne (2005: section 3.5.3) notes, this is just what we find. Aoun, Choueiri, and Hornstein (2001) report such cases for Lebanese Arabic. An illustrative example from their paper is (51).

(51) təlmiiz-a₁   lkəsleen ma   baddna nχabbi [wala mʕallme]₁ ʔənno
       student-her₁ the-bad NEG want.1P tell.1P [no teacher]₁   that
       huwwe zaʕbar   b-l-faħṣ
       he   cheated.3SM in-the-exam
       'her bad student, we don't want to tell any teacher that he cheated on the exam.'

(Aoun, Choueiri, and Hornstein 2001: 381, (25b))

The phrase 'tə lmiiz-a₁ lkəsleen' (*her bad student*) contains a pronoun that is bound to a lower quantifier ('wala mʕallme', *no teacher*). This is made possible by the phrase 'tə lmiiz-a₁ lkəsleen' (*her bad student*) being related to the resumptive pronoun 'huwwe' (*he*) through movement. These cases, then, suggest that the two ingredients my proposal uses to make 'traces' silent do, indeed, sometimes come separately. If these two ingredients are truly independent, or are interdependent in some way, is an open question.

Another open question, and one that is very likely to harbour problems for the proposal made here, concerns the class of things that move. All the cases examined in this paper involve movement of DPs, and the account is especially designed for the reconstruction effects that arise when DPs move. But it appears that many other sorts of things can move: heads of certain sorts, PPs, VPs, APs, and, perhaps, clauses. The reconstruction effects that arise when these other sorts of things move are frequently different from what is found with DPs. Reconstruction effects are largely manufactured by the syntactic representations movement generates, if the conclusions reached here are correct, and yet it's syntactic representations that are also responsible for the fact that a moved term can be pronounced in only one of its positions. For the most part, this latter constraint on movement holds irrespective of the kind of thing that moves, and yet the reconstruction effects vary considerably. That's a puzzle that gets no easier as a result of this chapter. Indeed, because my redoing of Fox's Trace Conversion rule would only apply to cases where a determiner is involved in what moves, there is no straightforward way of extending this system to phrases of other types.

3.6 Conclusion

We have looked at a narrow range of cases, but if the conclusions reached here can be extended to all examples of movement, then we have the following results.

(52)   Results
   • There is only one determiner, pronounced many ways, and it is *the*.
   • Indices are not part of what relates a moved phrase with its 'trace'.
   • (Phrasal) Movement arises when one term has more than one position in a phrase marker, and nothing more.

4

Post-verbal Nominatives: An Unaccusativity Diagnostic Under Scrutiny*

ARTEMIS ALEXIADOU

4.1 Introduction

Verbs as argument-taking elements show very complex sets of properties. A particularly interesting illustration of the complex properties of verbs is the phenomenon of unaccusativity. The *unaccusativity hypothesis*, as formulated by Perlmutter (1978) and later adapted by Burzio (1981), suggests that the class of intransitive verbs consists of two subclasses, the class of unergative and the class of unaccusative verbs, each associated with a distinct syntactic configuration. From a Government and Binding perspective (Chomsky 1981 and subsequent work), an unergative verb takes a theta-marked deep-structure subject and no object, whereas an unaccusative verb takes a deep-structure theta-marked object, as in (1):

(1) a. $[_{IP}$ NP $[_{VP}$ V$]]$ *unergative*   John sings
     b. $[_{VP}$ V NP $]$ *unaccusative*   John came

Several aspects of unaccusativity are best characterized as interface phenomena. First, it has been pointed out that the classification of intransitive verbs into the one or the other class is not accidental. Rather there appear to be striking semantic regularities in the composition of the two classes, regularities that are manifested across languages. For this reason, the unaccusativity

* Many thanks to Terje Lohndal, Susanne Lohrmann, Florian Schäfer, two anonymous reviewers, and the editors of this volume for their comments and suggestions. My research was partially supported by a DFG grant to the SFB 732 *Incremental Specification in Context* at the Universität Stuttgart.

hypothesis has established itself as a fertile ground for the investigation of the relationship between lexical semantics and syntax (see in particular Levin and Rappaport Hovav 1995): it is seen as a means of indentifying aspects of verb meaning that are relevant for syntax.

The second aspect concerns the syntax-discourse interface. This is so, as several presentational focus constructions have been linked with unaccusativity, e.g. locative inversion being one such case (cf. Bresnan and Kanerva 1989).

In the centre of this twofold interface discussion are unaccusativity diagnostics, i.e. phenomena that are sensitive to unaccusativity and classify intransitive verbs as unaccusatives or unergatives. Such diagnostics primarily focus on the fact that the single argument of unaccusatives behaves like an object despite being expressed as a grammatical subject. Not all of these are available in every language, rather different criteria are linked to unaccusativity in different languages.

This chapter discusses one unaccusativity diagnostic that has been proposed for pro-drop languages such as Italian, Hebrew, Greek, Spanish, and Catalan. The phenomenon at hand is the distribution of bare post-verbal nominatives, and, as we will see, it bears direct relevance to both interface aspects (see e.g. Borer 1980, 2005; Shlonsky 1987 for Hebrew; Belletti 1988 for Italian; Torrego 1989 for Spanish; Alexiadou 1996; Alexiadou and Anagnostopoulou 1998a for Greek; Rigau 1997 for Catalan). The distribution is as follows: unaccusatives tolerate bare/mass nouns in free inversion contexts (2a, 3a, 4a), while unergatives do not (2b, 3b, 4b). As has also been noted, the bare noun receives an existential interpretation:

(2) a. irthan pedia   *Greek*
         came children-NOM
         'Children came'
     b. *epezan   pedhia
         were playing children-NOM
         'Children were playing'

(3) a. llegaron livors   *Spanish* (Ortega-Santos 2005)
         arrived books
     b. ??corren chicos
         run   boys

(4) a. hitxilu hapganot   *Hebrew* (Borer 2005)
         started demonstrations
     b. *nazlu   mayim
         dripped.m.pl water.m.pl

The standard explanation for (2)-(4) has been as follows: arguments of unaccusatives are generated as complements of V (cf. 1b). In VS orders, they remain in their base position and are close to the verb. Similarly to *there* sentences in English, an expletive *pro* occurs in Spec,IP. On the other hand, arguments of unergatives are generated outside the VP (cf. 1a). On this view, the behaviour of bare nouns in pro-drop languages can be understood: since these are licensed under head government, they can only be licit in the complement position of a verb. Thus, arguments of unaccusatives pattern like the internal argument of transitives, as shown by the Greek example in (5a). This also explains the fact that bare nouns are out in subject position, see the Greek example in (5b):[1]

(5)   a.   i Maria   efage psaria
           the-Mary-NOM ate   fish-ACC
           'Mary ate fish'

      b   *Pedhia   efagan to psari
          children ate   the fish
          'Children ate fish'

In all the (a) examples in (2)-(4), the presence of expletive *pro* offered an explanation for the satisfaction of the Extended Projection Principle (EPP) and nominative case was assigned from I° under government to the post-verbal noun phrases.

  However, this picture is no longer maintainable in light of recent developments in syntactic theory, including e.g. dispensing with the notion of government (Chomsky 1995), and the introduction of alternative ways of achieving nominative case and EPP checking. Moreover, Alexiadou and Anagnostopoulou (1998b), Manzini and Savoia (2002), McCloskey (1996) and more recently Kucerova (2009) among others provided a series of arguments suggesting that expletive *pro* is not part of the grammar inventory.[2]

---

[1] Subjects in Greek generally cannot appear as bare indefinites (see Roussou and Tsimpli 1993). They have to be preceded by the definite article, a quantifier, or to bear focus. This is not the case in Hebrew, where, as Borer (2005) notes, pre-verbal subject bare nouns are licit also without focus and receive a generic interpretation. Note that Greek, as Roussou and Tsimpli (op. cit.) discuss, also allows for object bare indefinites to appear in clause-initial position (i) under topicalization.

(i)   Piimata diavasa
       poems read-1sg
       'Poems, I read'

These authors argue that such noun phrases have an empty D head which is lexically governed by the verb.

[2] But see Alboiu (2005, 2007), Cardinaletti (2004), Rezac (2004), Rizzi and Shlonski (2007) among others for arguments in favour of expletive *pro*.

A different set of developments affected our understanding of the projections of arguments. Under current assumptions, it is not clear how to account for the ungrammaticality of unergatives in VS contexts. One could structurally express the difference between the single argument of unergatives and that of unaccusatives through the postulation of an asymmetry in terms of semi-functional heads, e.g. voice as in Kratzer (1994). On this view, the subject of an unergative is introduced by a semi-functional head Voice, while unaccusatives lack a voice layer (cf. Chomsky 1995, Hale and Keyser 1993, and others).

(6)   a. [$_{VoiceP}$ unergative argument [$_{vP}$]]
       b. [$_{vP}$ unaccusative argument]

Assuming, however, that VS orders arise through V-movement to T, as it has been argued to be the case for Greek, Hebrew, and Spanish independently (see e.g. Alexiadou and Anagnostopoulou 1998b, Borer 1995, Zubizarreta 1998, and references therein), it is not clear how the above paradigm can be explained.

       c. [$_{T}$ T-Voice/v [$_{VoiceP/vP}$ NP]]

Two facets of the distribution of post-verbal nominatives are the main concern of this contribution. Both of them touch upon the issue of the syntactic representation of unaccusativity and are not easily amenable to an account under the standard approach to the syntax of unaccusativity. The first one relates to the fact that only certain unaccusative verbs are permitted in VS orders and moreover, unergative predicates are also licit, under very specific conditions, which involve the presence of a locative. This behaviour is an unaccusativity mismatch. As we will see, the verbs that can occur in VS orders belong to specific semantic classes, hence the distribution of post-verbal subjects will be revealing as far as the relationship between lexical semantics and syntax is concerned. The question here is whether the unaccusativity mismatch points to a syntactic difference between the two classes of unaccusatives in the former case and/or an unaccusative analysis of unergatives in the latter one.

The second fact concerns the very specific discourse function which VS orders display. VS orders generally bring about presentational/informational/new information focus, and as such, and as already mentioned, they belong to the larger set of presentational focus constructions which are linked with unaccusativity (cf. Bresnan and Kanerva 1989). The question here is whether there is something special about the argument structure of (unaccusative) predicates that predetermines them to be connected with the presentational focus, or whether the core ingredient of presentational focus subsumes some (unaccusative) structures.

The chapter focuses on the distribution of VS orders in Greek and Hebrew, which I compare to English *there* insertion and locative inversion environments. The English constructions have been widely discussed in recent literature, and Borer (2005, 2006) offers a comprehensive discussion of the Hebrew data on which my discussion here is based. As will become clear, Greek and Hebrew provide an interesting minimal pair with respect to the distribution of post-verbal nominatives for the following reasons. First, they differ as far as the nature (strong vs weak) of the post-verbal noun phrase is concerned and second, they provide an interesting comparison to the two English constructions that is directly linked with the syntactic representation of locatives. I argue that the distribution of post-verbal nominatives can be explained, if we pay particular attention to the presence of locatives, which are taken to be the core ingredient in presentational focus constructions (see Bentley 2004, 2006; Kayne 2008). This is the unifying factor behind unergatives and unaccusatives that are allowed in inversion. I will argue that in Greek the locative is in the CP layer and it functions as a discourse/perspective marker. In Hebrew, on the other hand, the locative will have an analysis similar to English *there*: its primary function is to check EPP (in line with Borer 2005) and then to act as a discourse marker. In other words, the Greek VS pattern including a locative is more similar to English locative inversion, while the Hebrew one to English *there* constructions. The difference in the analysis of the locative in the two languages will account for the presence of definiteness restriction (DR) effects in Hebrew and the absence thereof in Greek. The presentational focus associated with both VS orders is related to the fact that such sentences are interpreted as taking a location as the discourse perspective of the utterance. Since only a limited class of verbs is compatible with such a perspective, the restrictions/mismatches observed can be accounted for.

This chapter is structured as follows. In section 4.2, I examine the distribution of VS orders in Greek and Hebrew in some detail. In section 4.3, I deal with the question of whether an unaccusative analysis of unergatives should be pursued or not and address the issue of the two classes of unaccusatives. In section 4.4, I discuss the syntax of locatives. In section 4.5, I discuss the syntax-discourse interface issue that arises with VS orders. In section 4.6, I turn to the distribution of DR effects and the differences between Hebrew and Greek. Finally, in section 4.7, I offer some brief conclusions.

4.2 The Fine-grained Distribution of Post-verbal Nominatives

4.2.1 *VS Orders and Two Classes of Unaccusatives*

The picture suggested by (2)–(4) needs to be refined. It has been pointed out in the literature that the distribution of post-verbal nominatives exhibits a number of restrictions. First of all, if we compare the (2a, 3a, 4a) above to the examples in (7) and (8) below, we note that not all unaccusative predicates can appear in VS orders. The same holds for the single argument of passives: certain passives are in, while others are out—(7d) vs (7e); (see Alexiadou and Anagnostopoulou 1998a, and Borer 2006 reports similar restrictions on Hebrew):

(7) a. ??pagosan   potamia   *Greek*
            froze   rivers

     b. ??kokinisan fila
            turned red leaves

     c. ??vromisan spitia
            got dirty houses
            'Houses got dirty'

     d. * thavmastikan pinakes
            were admired paintings

     e. htistikan   spitia
            built.pass houses
            'Houses were built'

(8) a. * qap'u mayim   *Hebrew*
            froze water

     b. * hibšilu šlošet tapuxim
            ripened three   apples

     c. * hitmotetu qirot (be-šabat)
            collapsed   walls (on Saturday)

     d. * culma   zebra
            photographed.pass zebra

     e. * putru   šloša yobdim
            fired.pass three workers

This is reminiscent of the restrictions that have been observed in *there*-insertion contexts (see Levin 1993; Deal 2009) and locative inversion in English (Levin and Rappaport Hovav 1995: 246f.):

(9) a. There arrived a man (in the garden)
     b. *There broke a glass (in the kitchen)
     c. Out of the house came a tiny old lady
     d. *Out of the house broke a tiny old lady
     e. *In the kitchen were chopped pounds and pounds of mushrooms
     f. ... and from under it was thrust forth a narrow snake-like head ...

The important generalization that emerges is that for all three languages, inversion is deviant with verbs of change of state and passives of verbs that are not verbs of causing something to exist or appear.

   On the other hand, in Hebrew and Greek, the verb classes that can be identified as being acceptable in VS orders include primarily verbs of appearance or existence, verbs of inherently directed motion, and 'break' verbs in a so-called 'disappearance' interpretation. This is exemplified below for Greek, and see Borer (2005) for Hebrew and cf. (2)-(4) above. Similar restrictions hold for English *there* insertion and locative inversion contexts; see Deal (2009) and Levin and Rappaport Hovav (1995).

(10) a. irthan pedia   *Greek*
          came   children
          'Children came'

      b. sinevisan   thavmata
          happened miracles
          'Miracles happened'

      c. espasan piata
          broke   dishes
          'Dishes broke'

4.2.2 *VS Orders and Unergatives*

An interesting fact that has been noted is that in languages like Greek and Hebrew, VS orders with certain unergative predicates become acceptable when a locative adverbial is added to the sentence (Torrego 1989; Rigau 1997; Alexiadou and Anagnostopoulou 1998a; Borer 2005):

(11) **edo** pezun   pedia   *Greek*
      here   play-3pl children
      'There are children playing here'

(12) yabad   **kan**   gaman   *Hebrew*
      worked there gardener

In addition, in Greek, choice of a particular aspect shows a similar effect. VS orders with imperfective aspect are marked, while VS orders with perfective aspect are much better:

(13) a.   dulepsan   kseni   ergates
           worked-<u>perf</u>-3pl foreign workers
           'Foreign workers worked'

     b. (??)dulevan   kseni   ergates
           worked-3pl foreign workers

The group of unergatives that becomes completely acceptable when a locative is present includes verbs of emission, agentive verbs of manner of motion, and activity verbs such as *work, chatter, sing,* and *doze.* Again, the same class is identified as being acceptable in English locative inversion by Levin and Rappaport Hovav (1995); see (14):

(14)   In crude banks slept John and Harry

A reasonable question to ask concerning the acceptance of unergatives is whether the above behaviour leads to an unaccusative analysis of these verbs. In line with Levin and Rappaport Hovav (1995) and Borer (2005), I argue in section 4.3 that this is not the case. This in turn suggests that the appearance of nominatives in inversion is not an unaccusativity diagnostic, strictly speaking, as it is not even possible with all unaccusative verbs, as was shown in the previous section. Rather, the appearance of nominatives in inversion is a reflex of a specific structural representation that can be linked, but is not necessarily linked, with unaccusative syntax.

4.2.3 *VS Orders and Presentational Focus*[3]

As is well known, subject inversion is generally used as a focalization device in languages such as Greek, Spanish, and Italian (e.g. Zubizarreta 1998, Pinto 1997, Alexiadou 2000, Belletti 2004, among many others). Specifically, post-verbal subjects are used for presentational focus and express new

---

[3] The presentational focus effects are primarily discussed for English *there* constructions. According to Bresnan (1993), in inversion, the referent of the NP is introduced on the scene. The post-verbal NP is not shared knowledge, rather it is a hearer-new entity (Ward and Birner 1995; Prince 1992). Birner (1994) claims that inversion introduces rather unfamiliar information to the discourse. Lambrecht (2000) uses the term *sentence focus* and suggests that we no longer have a topic-focus structure, but rather the whole proposition is in focus. This is achieved by de-topicalizing the subject. See Landau (2009) for a recent discussion.

information, while pre-verbal subjects are topic/given information. When all information is new, verb choice (i.e. properties of the lexicon-syntax interface) may determine word order: SV is favoured for unergatives and VS for unaccusatives and is subject to the restrictions mentioned in the previous sections. By contrast, VS is preferred to SV with both unaccusatives and unergatives in special focus contexts (syntax-discourse interface), e.g. when only the subject is new information. The latter pattern is illustrated below for Greek, and Borer (2005) notes similar constraints about Hebrew, where post-verbal nominatives are very restricted with unergatives, acceptable only under very specific stress and information structure related patterns:

(15) Q: a. pios fonakse   b. pios irthe
            who   shouted   who came

      A: a. fonakse o   Janis   b. irthe o   Janis
            shouted the John   came the John
            'John shouted'   'John came'

The examples that interest us here are NOT of the type in (15), since they are sensitive to the type of predicate involved in VS orders.

4.2.4 *VS Orders and Weak vs Strong Nominatives*

Finally, one difference can be observed between Hebrew and Greek VS orders. In Hebrew, post-verbal nominatives are necessarily weak subjects. While weak subjects are certainly possible in this position in Greek, definite/strong subjects are fine too:

(16) a. arhisan   i   diadilosis   *Greek*
         began-3pl the demonstrations
         'The demonstrations began'

      b. irthe kathe anthropos edo
         came every person   here
         'Every person came   here'

      c. *hitxilu   kol ha. hapganot   *Hebrew*
         started.m.pl all the demonstrations

As the English examples in (9) and (14) suggest, the same difference is found with *there* insertion (only weak subjects allowed), as opposed to locative inversion (strong subjects allowed).

    In the next section, I turn to the issue raised by the behaviour of unergative predicates.

4.3 Against an Unaccusative Analysis of Unergatives

4.3.1 *Position and Status of the Locative*

To begin with, in both Hebrew and Greek, unergatives occur in inversion but only if the adverbial is a locative; a temporal expression does not yield grammatical results:

(17)   a.   *rac gata yeled   *Hebrew*
           run now boy
       b.   ??tote dulevan   kipuri   *Greek*
           then worked-3pl gardeners

In both languages, the locative necessarily needs to be close to the verb, and not in any other sentence position. The two languages seem to differ, however, as to the phrasal status of the locative. In Hebrew, according to Borer (2005), the locative is a clitic adjacent to the verb, the order being V-clitic. In Greek the order is locative-V and the locative is an XP. The phrasal status of the Greek locative can be seen in that, unlike its Hebrew counterpart in (18b), it can be substituted by a PP, as in (18e):

(18)   a.   *^{c}abdu   gananim   kan   *Hebrew*
           worked   gardeners   there
       b.   *^{c}abdu   kan   vs   šám   gananim
           worked   here   and   there   gardeners
       c.   edo   pezun   pedia   *Greek*
           here   play-3pl   children
           'Children play here'
       d.   ??pezun   pedia   edo
           play-3pl   children   here
       e.   sto parko   pezun   pedia
           in the park   play-3pl   children
           'Children play in the park'

Since the locative precedes the verb in Greek, and assuming that V raises to T°, we can conclude that the adverbial is located higher than T. For Hebrew, Borer argued that the clitic is merged together with the verb and moves to T°. As a first approximation, one can offer the structures in (19a) and (19b) for Greek and Hebrew respectively. These will be updated in sections 4.4 and 4.6:

(19)   a.   [$_{XP}$ Locative [$_T$ T- Voice ... [$_{VoiceP}$ DP]]]
       b.   [$_T$ T- Voice-locative clitic ... [$_{VoiceP}$ DP]]]

4.3.2 *The Locative is not an External Argument*

A possible analysis is to view the locative as the realization of the spatio-temporal argument of eventive verbs, which can take the function of an external argument. All structures with bare nouns and unergative verbs would thus be unaccusatives in that they contain a single DP argument, which is then realized as a VP-internal one. In fact, Torrego (1989) explicitly proposes this analysis for Spanish VS orders, as in this language *en*-cliticization, which is normally out with unergatives, is possible in these structures, see also Mendikoetxea (2006).[4]

But, if the former external argument of the unergative predicate were projected as an internal one, we would expect it to behave as an object of the verb with respect to other phenomena (e.g. lose agentivity), contrary to fact. The following pieces of evidence point to this conclusion. First, in both Hebrew, as argued by Borer (2005), and Greek, the DP argument is within the VoiceP, as it follows aspectual adverbs located in AspectP (the order of projections being TP > AspectP > VoiceP), but precedes VP-internal adjuncts:

(20) edo   pezun   sihna   pedia   ta proina   *Greek*
      here   play-3pl often   children in the mornings
      'Children often play here in the morning'

(21) ʿabad   šam   ganan   be-mešek kol ha.yom   *Hebrew*
      worked   here gardener during all-the day
      'A gardener worked here during all day'

Assuming that in (20) the aspectual adverb is an indicator that V has raised out of VoiceP, the fact that the nominative follows the adverb suggests that the DP remains within this domain. Since it precedes VP internal adjuncts in (21), it must be within VoiceP, as shown by Borer (2005).

Second, the predicate retains its agentive characteristics, so it is compatible with agentive/instrumental adverbials just like any other unergative predicate. The same holds for the sentences with perfective Aspect in Greek (22c):[5]

---

[4] Bentley (2004) argued for Italian that *ne*-cliticization is also possible with unergatives under similar conditions.

[5] Bentley (2006) argues that the function of these constructions is to turn the predicate into a stage-level predicate. Rigau (1997) argues that the locative turns the unergative verb into a stative one. On this view, the presence of agent-oriented adverbs in (22) cannot be explained.

(22) a. edo epezan   pedia
      here played-3pl children
      prosektika/me ti hrisi bala/epitides   *Greek*
      carefully/with the golden ball/on purpose
      'Children play here carefully/with the golden ball/on purpose'

    b. hištolelu   šam eyze yeladim be-toqpanut   *Hebrew*
      made. noise there some children aggressively
      'Some children made noise aggressively'

    c. tragudisan pedia   me kefi/me dio mikrofona sto heri *Greek*
      sang-perf children with lust/with two microphones at hand
      'Children sang with lust/with two microphones'

Third, we can combine, following Borer (2005), the presence of the locative with the licensing of another unaccusativity diagnostic, e.g. *possessive datives*. Borer and Grodzinsky (1986) argued that in Hebrew possessive datives can be used as an unaccusativity diagnostic because they can only be construed with a DP in a properly governed position. This also holds for Greek (Alexiadou and Anagnostopoulou 1999). In (23a-b) the dative clitic can be understood as the possessor of the subject, while in (23c) it cannot:

(23) a. mu   skotosan to pedi
      cl-gen killed   the child
      'They killed my child'

    b. mu   espase to potiri
      cl-gen broke the glass
      'My glass broke'

    c. *Tis   tragudise i   mitera
      cl-gen sang   the mother
      '*Her mother sang'

In both languages possessor datives are out with unergatives in the presence of the locative, see (Borer 2005: 281) for Hebrew. This is also true for perfective aspect in Greek:

(24) *ᶜabad šam le rani-'eyze ganan   kol la boqer   *Hebrew*
      worked here to Rani some gardener all morning
      'A gardener of Rani's worked here all morning'

(25) a. *edo tu   tragudusan pedia   *Greek*
      here cl-gen sang   children
      '*Here were singing his children'

b. *edo   tu   tragudisan pedia
   here   cl-gen   sang-perf   children
   '*Here sang his children'

Finally, if unaccusative predicates are generally telic, we note that in our examples the event type of the predicate does not change, i.e. the predicate remains atelic:[6]

(26) a. racu kan yeladim   be mešek kol ha.yom/*tok šaloš ša yot *Hebrew*
        ran there gardeners during all the day/inside three hours
        'Garderners were running during the whole day'

     b. edo dulevan   ergates ja ores/*se 3 ores   *Greek*
        here worked-3pl workers for hours/in 3 hours
        'Workers were working here for hours'

Note that no change in event type takes place with perfective aspect in Greek either:

(27) dulepsan   ergates ja ores/*se 3 ores
      worked-perf-3pl workers for hours/in 3 hours
      'Workers worked here for hours/*in 3 hours'

This is expected, as perfective aspect in Greek does not change the event type of the predicate, see Horrocks and Stavrou (2003) and Sioupi (2002); see also Verkuyl (1993), but cf. Chila-Markopoulou and Mozer (2001). Choice of aspect has been described as follows: with intrinsically terminative verbs such as *ljono* 'melt', perfective aspect means that the verbal action is viewed as complete (28a). Imperfective aspect means that the action is viewed as continuous/progressive (28b):

(28) a. o iljos eljose   tin asfalto *ja mia ora   /se mia ora
        'the sun (completely) melted the tarmac *'for one hour /in one hour'

     b. o iljos eljone   tin asfalto ja mia ora
        'the sun (progressively) melted the tarmac for one hour
        /*se mia ora
        /* in one hour'

With basically non-terminative verbs like *hti'po* 'beat', perfective aspect introduces a bounded, in fact a punctual interpretation, as shown in (29a). Imperfective aspect in (29b), by contrast, presents the action as performed continuously or randomly, but without specification of any external bound.

---

[6] The telicity issue is a problem for Borer's (2005) framework, noted by the author herself: with unaccusatives the predicate is interpreted as telic, in spite of the presence of a 'weak' subject. But in her system, only quantized arguments lead to telic interpretation. I will not discuss this here.

(29) a. htipise   ta avga ja   mia ora /   *se mia ora
          'He gave-a-beating-to the eggs for one hour/ * in one hour'

      b. htipuse   ta avga ja   'mia ora /   *se mia ora
          'He was-beating the eggs   for one hour/ * in one hour'

The contribution of perfective aspect to the interpretation of unergatives is thus punctuality and not telicity.

To conclude, the locative is not an external argument and thus unergatives with a locative do not become unaccusatives, if by that we mean that the former external argument of the verb is projected as its internal argument. This raises the question whether it is a second external argument or an external argument at some point in the derivation. In order to determine this, we need to have a closer look at the syntax of locatives and the syntax of expletives. This is discussed in the next section, where English will be the point of departure.

4.4 The Syntax of Locatives

4.4.1 *Locative Inversion*

The syntax of locative inversion has been controversially discussed in the literature (see Hoekstra and Mulder 1990, Levin and Rappaport Hovav 1995, Branigan 1992, Bresnan 1993, Landau 2009 among many others). On Hoekstra and Mulder's analysis, the locative phrase forms a small clause together with the DP argument, as in (30):

(30)   [V [$_{SC}$ NP PP]]

The two possible surface word orders that emerge out of this basic structure involve either DP fronting or predicate fronting (see den Dikken 1995, Collins 1997, and others). Branigan (1992) explicitly argues that in the latter case the locative undergoes A'-movement to the CP area.

4.4.2 *The Syntax of* There

Hoekstra and Mulder (1990) make a similar proposal for *there*, which they treat as a locative. However, in Chomsky (1981), Chomsky (1995), and subsequent work, *there* is an expletive which is externally merged in the derived subject position Spec,TP to satisfy the EPP. The standard analysis of *there* insertion has recently been challenged (Richards and Biberauer 2005, Richards 2007; cf. also Deal 2009, Moro 1997, Sabel 2000, and Kayne 2008), as it faces a number of problems, which I will not discuss here. The analysis proposed by Richards (2007), is that expletives are externally merged either in Spec,CP or in Spec,vP. If an expletive occurs in Spec,TP, as in English, it must have moved there (on this view, EPP is checked only via *MOVE*). I will assume here the low *there* hypothesis, but I will not analyse *there* as a locative, as Hoekstra and Mulder and more recently Kayne do, for reasons that become clear below.

The low *there* hypothesis offers a way to explain the mismatches observed with unaccusative predicates in English. In a recent treatment of the mismatch concerning *there*, Deal (2009) proposes that *there* is inserted at the edge of a vP that lacks an external argument, i.e. into a non-thematic Spec,vP position. Unaccusatives rejecting *there* have Spec,vP already occupied by a causative event.[7]

Hale and Keyser (2000) propose that with verbs such as *arrive and occur* the theme is introduced within the complement of the verb, in the specifier of a small clause headed by a (potentially covert) P-projection. With other unaccusatives, the theme is introduced in the specifier of the verb that takes an adjective as its complement (31b):

(31)   a. [$_V$ arrive [$_{PP}$ many guests pro/at the party]]
        b. [$_{vP}$ the sky [$_{v'v}$ clear]]

Alexiadou and Schäfer (2009), adopting Deal's insights, show that the theme argument of these two classes of unaccusatives occupies different structural positions within the vP. Combining Hale and Keyser's proposal with Richards's low *there* hypothesis, the authors identify Spec,vP and Spec, ResultP/PP in (32) as the positions in question. Insertion of *there* is blocked, if the theme obligatorily occupies Spec,vP:

(32)   a. [$_{vP}$ ***there*** [$_{ResultP/PP}$ *theme*]]   *arrive*
        b. [$_{vP}$ ***theme/*there*** [$_{ResultP/PP}$]]   *redden*

This suggests that the two classes of unaccusative verbs do not have a uniform syntax, and crucially only one group, the *arrive* group, involves a locative structure. Does the above account extend to our data? As already mentioned in the introduction, VS orders were seen as the counterpart of *there* constructions in English. But as already pointed out, it has also been argued that expletive *pro* does not exist. Hence, we do not have a structure comparable to (32a), with an expletive projected in Spec,vP. In English,

---

[7] In Deal's (op. cit.) analysis, a causative event is situated in Spec,vP in the case of *melt*-type unaccusative verbs. Alexiadou and Schäfer (2009) argue against this view, pointing out, among other things, that a Spec position is typically a DP/NP position. Specifiers need a category; but the term 'event' is not a category. 'Event' is a semantic, not a syntactic notion. This corresponds to a v-category in the syntax, but v does not merge in Spec.

locality would force movement of *there* to Spec,TP; in pro-drop languages V-movement to T° would satisfy the EPP.

If we look carefully at the original structures proposed by Hale and Keyser (2000) in (31), we note that another difference between the two classes of unaccusatives is the presence of a locative. *Arrive*-type verbs contain a covert (or overt) locative, which is independent of the expletive *there*. On this view, predicates of the type in (31b) lack a locative, verbs of existence or appearance contain a locative as part of their lexical semantics (31a). When this locative is implicit, these verbs receive a deictic interpretation, i.e. they are 'speaker-oriented' (see Beninca 1988, Pinto 1997, Tortora 1991, Kayne 2008). Thus, for instance, as argued in Pinto (1997), a sentence like (33) means that Gigi arrived here, i.e. at the place where the speaker is located:

(33)   e   arrivato   Gigi
       is arrived   Gigi

But sometimes this locative can also be overt, as is shown by examples from Borgomanerese, a Piemontese dialect discussed in Tortora (2001: 317), see also Kayne (2008):

(34)   ngh è   rivà-**gghi**   na fjola
       scl be.3sg arrive PP.cl a girl
       'A girl has arrived here'

As pointed out by Tortora, *ghi* figures obligatorily in the perfect of constructions with verbs of inherently directed motion such as *arrivare* 'arrive', *entrare* 'come in', *tornare* 'return', *venire* 'come', when the subject is post-verbal. These constructions entail a location which corresponds to the location of the speaker ('here'). The lack of such marking with other unaccusatives suggests that *ghi* spells out the locational goal that is part of the semantics of verbs of inherently directed motion.

What the above data suggest is that the locative simply does not have the same function as English expletive *there*; the locative is a referential/deictic element and contributes to the interpretation of the clause. Rather the locative identified in the above data is similar to the patterns of English locative inversion, and hence amenable to a small clause analysis of the type in (31a).

Assuming this to be the case, we can then argue that all inversion orders involve a locative; this locative has a specific discourse perspective, is a *stage topic* in Cohen and Erteschik-Shir's (2002) terms, cf. also Beninca (1988), and for this reason must surface in the CP domain, the area in the clause structure that is responsible for discourse features (see Rizzi 1997). The presence of a locative in the CP area leads to a focus interpretation of the elements following it. Now if this is the correct analysis for the locative, then this should be uniform for unergatives and unaccusatives, as already suggested by Beninca (op. cit.).

The structures in (31) can be straightforwardly extended to the Greek and Hebrew unaccusatives, and thus explain the mismatches observed with this class of predicates (though more needs to be said about the nature of the post-verbal nominative, see section 4.6). But what about unergatives? Since the locative behaves in a similar manner as in the case of unaccusatives, it should be inserted in the structure in a similar way. This would mean that unergatives with a locative have a structure similar to unaccusatives of the type (31a). Since, however, in such sentences the DP argument is agentive (see section 4.3), the DP must move to Spec,VoiceP to receive an agent theta-role (cf. Ramchand 2008); subsequently, in Greek, V-movement checks the EPP (Alexiadou and Anagnostopoulou 1998b), and the locative moves to Spec,CP. Support for the view that the locative in Greek is in the C domain comes from the fact that the locative bears special stress, a property also associated with the C domain (see Tsimpli 1995). Thus the structure proposed for Greek in (19a) can be updated as follows (the difference being that (19′) is not to be interpreted as a telic structure):

(19′)   [$_{CP}$ Locative [$_T$ ... [$_{VoiceP}$ DP$_i$ [$_{PP}$ DP$_i$ P]]]]   *Greek*

For Hebrew, in principle a similar analysis could be proposed, but again something more needs to be said in view of the restrictions on the interpretation of post-verbal nominatives in this language (only weak subjects allowed). I come back to this in section 4.6.

Note here that Borer (2005: 282) explicitly argues against an analysis like the one illustrated in (19′), as it leaves unexplained the behaviour of possessive datives. As we saw in section 4.3, the possessive dative is ungrammatical with the unergative argument in the presence of a locative; the structure in (19′), however, would predict that the argument is within the scope of the possessive. But if we assume an analysis of possessives in terms of low applicatives (see Anagnostopoulou 2003, Cuervo 2003 and references therein), possession is captured in terms of an applicative head that licenses the possessor argument semantically and syntactically, and relates it to the theme DP. In the above examples, the DP argument is in Spec,PP, which would suggest that it is not in the right configuration to be embedded in a possessive relation.[8]

---

[8] This correctly predicts that possessive datives are out with all predicates of type (31a), but does not offer an immediate account of the reason why possessive datives are in with type (31b). It seems that the presence of a PP is the crucial factor here, suggesting that the right configuration for the low applicative should not involve intervention of a phase head, and P is such a head (cf. Chomsky 2001).

4.5 VS Orders, the Interpretation of Bare Nouns and the Syntax-Discourse Interface

4.5.1 *Locatives and Weak Subjects*

As is well known, locatives bring existential force and this property goes hand in hand with their ability to license post-verbal subjects and bring about presentational focus (Freeze 1992, Borer 2005, Bentley 2004, and many others).

In the cases under discussion, bare nouns are interpreted existentially as only localizable predicates give rise to existential interpretations, i.e. the existence relevant to these sentences is always existence relevant to a given location (cf. Dobrovie-Sorin and Laka 1996).[9] Borer (2005) derives the obligatory presence of weak subjects in Hebrew from this specific function of the locative. She argues that the locative existentially binds the event, the domain of existential closure being the c-command domain of the verb, which moves to T, following Benedicto (1997). The bare DP is existentially bound by (specifier-head) agreement. This correctly predicts why the subject argument has an existential interpretation. In other words, in Hebrew the locative affects the interpretation of the noun in ways that a true locative does not: namely, it rules out strong DPs. This is expected under Borer's analysis. However, this leaves us with no explanation as to why definite subjects are possible in post-verbal position in Greek but not in Hebrew. As already mentioned, I come back to this in section 4.6.

4.5.2 *Perfective Aspect and Post-verbal Nominatives*

Similarly to locatives, perfective aspect can also act as an event-binder. Giannakidou and Merchant (1998) argue that perfective aspect in Greek is interpreted as episodic. Episodic sentences describe single, delimited events (see section 4.3.2). They express existential quantification over eventualities, i.e. perfective aspect involves existential event closure. On this view, the existential interpretation of bare nouns is accounted for, assuming again some version of Benedicto's analysis. This means that in the presence of perfective aspect bare nouns will be interpreted as existential, and the interpretation of strong subjects will not be affected.

Standardly, the position in which perfective/imperfective aspect is evaluated is Aspect° (36); naturally, since verbs move to T, ultimately the c-command domain of the verb will be the complement of T.

---

[9] Several researchers have suggested that the notion of location is relevant for the interpretation of bare nouns, see e.g. Higginbotham and Ramchand (1997).

(36)   [$_{CP}$ [$_{TP}$ [$_{AspectP}$ *Perf* [$_{VoiceP}$]]]]

The question that arises is why perfective aspect should have a similar effect to locatives, i.e. making VS orders licit with unergatives.

4.5.3 *Perfective Aspect and Locatives*

As suggested above, both perfective aspect and *there* introduce existential event closure. But they share another common property. Both are involved in changing the speaker's perspective on the situation in Partee and Borschev's (2005) terms, as in (37), a notion perhaps reducible to that of information/ focus structure:

(37)   Perspectival Center Presupposition
        Any Perspectival Center must be normally presupposed to exist.

In the case of the locative, when we choose the location as what the authors call the Perspectival Center, the sentence speaks about what things there are or are not in that situation and potentially about what is happening in the situation. In the case of perfective aspect (Klein 1994; Smith 1991), the speaker chooses the perspective in which to present the situation, namely in its totality. This suggests that VS orders require a discourse perspective to be interpreted. This is provided either by the locative or by perfective aspect, in languages that make this distinction.

   This leads us to the following observation concerning the syntax-discourse interface. We have established that VS orders with verbs of appearance have a locative in the CP. We have also seen that VS orders are out with certain unaccusatives. While the syntax of these verbs in languages such as Greek/ Hebrew would not automatically rule these out, the syntax-discourse interface does filter them out. Verbs of changes of state receive the structure in (31/32b), but after verb movement to T, a VS order should in principle be possible. But it is not, as a certain clash arises. In other words, a kind of an interface filtering emerges. Since no locative is in Spec,CP, and thus a discourse perspective is absent, the orders are deviant due to the very specific semantic and discourse properties associated with inversion (see also Landau 2009).[10] This also explains the ameliorating effect on such orders the introduction of a locative can have both in Greek and in Hebrew with this class of unaccusatives.

---

[10] Judgements improve if the subject is heavy. Long and complex constituents carry new information; see Lozano and Mendikoetxea (2005) for discussion and references:

(i)   kokinisan   ta   fila   tu   dendru   pu   fitepse   o   papus   persi to kalokeri
       reddened-3pl the   leaves the   tree-gen   that   planted   the   grandfather   last summer

4.6 Weak vs Definite Subjects

Let me now turn to the question why definite subjects are out in Hebrew, but not in Greek VS orders and how this can be captured by the analysis put forth here. The relevant contrast is repeated below:

(38) a. arhisan   i   diadilosis   *Greek*
          began-3pl the demonstrations
          'The demonstrations began'

     b. irthe kathe anthropos edo
          came every person   here
          'Every person came here'

     c. *hitxilu   kol ha. hapganot   *Hebrew*
          started.m.pl all the   demonstrations

In order to make sense of the restriction on Hebrew post-verbal subjects, it is important to see some details of Borer's (2005) analysis. Borer makes the point that Hebrew VS orders are the counterpart of Icelandic existential constructions. Evidence for this comes from the observation that, like Icelandic, Hebrew permits transitive expletive constructions.

(39) a. hipcic   šam matos 'et   ha. ⁶ir
          bombed there plane OM   the town
          'There bombed a plane the town'

     b. *hipci   šam ha. matos 'et   ha. ⁶ir
          bombed there the plane OM   the town

Thus, in order to understand the difference between Greek and Hebrew, we need to examine the factors that permit transitive expletive constructions and are responsible for DR effects under the low *there* hypothesis. If the Hebrew locative is like English *there*, we could follow Richards (2007), who argues that in languages such as Icelandic, the expletive is merged in the outer specifier of thematic v/Voice. Reconciling this analysis with Borer's insights, we could argue that prior to moving to CP, the locative moves to T to check its EPP features. Hence, the Hebrew locative, like English *there* in Barbiers and Roryck (1998), primarily checks the EPP features in T, it then further moves to CP to check discourse features. Nominative assignment to the post-verbal subject in Hebrew takes place in the same manner as it does in Icelandic and DR effects are expected to arise much like they do in Icelandic.[11]

If Greek and Hebrew differ as far as the analysis of the locative is concerned, then we expect to find differences in the distribution of weak and strong nominatives, as we can relate them to the differences between Greek and Icelandic. Alexiadou and Anagnostopoulou (1998b) have argued that languages split into two groups with respect to the mode of EPP checking. Updating also this analysis in the light of what has been said up to now, Icelandic/Hebrew move an XP (=an expletive) to the specifier of the EPP-related projection; Greek, on the other hand, satisfies the EPP via V-raising. This explains why VS(O) orders in Greek, but not in the other languages, are never associated with DR effects. V in T checks the EPP in all VS examples, while the DP is in its internal position.[12] In sum, there is a clear syntactic effect in free inversion linked with the presence of DR effects, and this has to do with the ways languages choose to satisfy the EPP.

4.7 Conclusions

The patterns described in this chapter are reminiscent of other unaccusativity mismatches that have been pointed out in the literature, for example the Russian genitive of negation (Pesetsky 1982; Babby 1980, 2001; Harves 2002; Babyonyshev forthcoming), and *ne*-cliticization in Italian (Lonzi 1986; Bentley 2004). In Levin and Rappaport Hovav (1995), cases that trigger such unaccusativity mismatches are taken to be diagnostics of surface unaccusativity, which are not regarded as real unaccusativity diagnostics (cf. also Mendikoetxea forthcoming).

What remains then of the unaccusativity hypothesis? What this chapter showed is that importantly unaccusative syntax is not uniform (see Borer 1991; Alexiadou and Anagnostopoulou 2004): not all verbs that behave as unaccusatives on the basis of other diagnostics should receive a uniform syntactic treatment and this explains the mismatches within the unaccusative

[11] An alternative would be to say that in Hebrew the locative and the DP begin as a unit and the locative moves away, as has been recently proposed for English *there* (see Kayne 2008; Hornstein 2009). On this view, the Hebrew locative is a D-like element that requires an NP complement (Chomsky 1995; Alexiadou and Anagnostopoulou 1998b). The locative moves then to TP to satisfy the EPP. But this doubling alternative does seem to be able to account for the restrictions on the types of predicates that are licit in inversion.

[12] To account for the assignment of nominative within the vP in VS orders, the proposal was made that they are actually clitic-doubling configurations, where pronominal agreement doubles the S which is located in the vP. The availability of V [$_{vP}$ S] and the availability of clitic doubling are interlinked. Greek has extensive clitic doubling of objects and the clitic agrees in all features with the doubled object (see Anagnostopoulou 1994, 2003 for extensive discussion).

class. The relevant mismatch is the presence of a locative component, as already proposed by Hale and Keyser (2000). Second, when it comes to the syntax of unergatives again there is a certain flexibility with a subclass of these verbs that relates to the availability of introducing a location component. Now, if there is no uniform syntax for unaccusatives/unergatives, one needs to go back to the other diagnostics and see how far the different structures proposed here can take us. The result might well be that unaccusativity is actually an epiphenomenon in the sense that it refers to structures where the argument entering an Agree relationship with Tense is not the one projected/located in VoiceP, but an argument further down in the structure.

A further related point that was made here concerns the discourse function of inversion, associated with presentational/sentence focus. As we have seen, presentational focus constructions are not to be equated with unaccusative structures. Rather some unaccusative verbs can happily co-occur in presentational constructions. As we have seen, those structures that contain a locative are most easily accommodated in orders which introduce presentational focus, since location is the key to understand these constructions to begin with. Because of this, inversion patterns cannot be used as a real test for the unaccusativity hypothesis.

In addition, the chapter showed that there is a significant interplay between syntactic operations and interface filtering. To the extent that the results of this chapter are valid, we need to investigate further test cases that will enable us to distinguish between derivations that are filtered by the interfaces and others that are strictly determined by the syntactic computation (see Frampton and Gutmann 2000 and subsequent work).

Interestingly, while the discourse function of inversion is not subject to variation, at least in the group of languages discussed here, real differences can nevertheless be detected. A case in point is the distribution of Hebrew vs Greek strong subjects. This was shown to relate to modes of EPP checking, and the syntax of expletives and thus to be the result of a different syntactic parameter setting. Specifically, languages differ as to what can satisfy the EPP, and that seems to be a true parametric difference, as has recently also been stressed by Richards and Biberauer (2005).

5

Unaccusativity in Vietnamese and the Structural Consequences of Inadvertent Cause*

NIGEL DUFFIELD

5.1 Introduction

Developing ideas about the lexicon-syntax interface originally due to Hale and Keyser (1993), Travis (1991, 1992, 2000, forthcoming) articulates a specific structural proposal for the l-syntax/s-syntax divide, schematized in (1), according to which verbal properties traditionally viewed as syntactically inert are associated with autonomous structural projections. Among other claims, Travis's proposal distinguishes the base position of Agents/Intentional Causers ([Spec,V1]) from those of arguments interpreted as non-volitional or 'inadvertent' Causes ([Spec,InnerAsp]). In the more recent work just cited, Travis also syntactically represents the event structure of a clause through the projection of an independent EVENT PHRASE (EP), located immediately above VP1 (vP, in many other analyses).[1] Empirical support for both of these claims—relating to specifier and head positions, respectively—comes mainly from Malagasy (to a lesser extent from Tagalog). The purpose of the

* Acknowledgement: This work was partially supported during 2009 by an AHRC Research Leave Extension Award. I should like to thank Tue Trinh and Trang Phan for invaluable comments and judgements on various aspects of this chapter, as well as the reviewers whose suggestions have helped me to clarify the presentation and improve the analyses. As ever, I am solely responsible for all remaining errors. The initial data collection for this work was undertaken in the context of the Vietnamese Grammar Project, <http://vietnamese-grammar.group.shef.ac.uk> . I am grateful to all those Vietnamese speakers who provided relevant judgements.

[1] Travis's articulated phrase structure further distinguishes the projection of EP from that of a super-ordinate functional projection that she labels Outer Aspect. These syntactic labels correspond to the distinction between Viewpoint and Situation Aspect made in Smith (1991). Vietnamese also provides direct evidence for this Aspect projection, in the shape (and interpretation) of the 'anterior' marker đã. Space constraints preclude discussion of this topic here: see Duffield and Phan (in prep.); Duffield (in prep.).

present paper is to show how Travis's proposal offers a natural account of certain structural effects in a genetically and typologically unrelated language, namely, Vietnamese.[2]

(1)   [EP [E' **E** [VP1 (*Agent*) [V1' **v1** [InnerAspP (*Inadvertent Cause*) [IAsp' **IAsp** [VP2 [V' **v2**]]]]]]]]]

With respect to the overarching theme of this volume, it is hoped to demonstrate that, largely in virtue of its radically isolating morphology, Vietnamese effectively has no l-syntax/s-syntax interface: everything that must be inferred from other languages' internal lexical structure is left exposed. In other words, it's s-syntax 'all the way down'. This feature of the language makes Vietnamese especially valuable for our understanding of a different interface relation, namely, the mapping between thematic relations and syntactic structure (Baker 1997).

5.2 Intentional vs Inadvertent Cause

5.2.1 *Previous Work*

The first idea considered here is that a structural distinction exists between the canonical position of two types of cause argument, such that DPs interpreted as non-agentive, unintentional, or (as they are termed here) INADVERTENT CAUSES originate in [Spec,Asp] position, lower in the extended VP-shell than DPs interpreted as intentional/volitional/agentive causers. The key piece of morphosyntactic evidence that Travis offers for this claim involves the 'telic' prefix (*ma*)*ha* in Malagasy. Travis observes that the addition of this morpheme to intransitive predicates has a causativizing function: compare (2a) vs (2b).

(2)   a.   Tsara   ny   trano.   [Malagasy, from Travis (2000)]
              beautiful   the   house
              'The house is beautiful.'

       b.   Maha-tsara   ny   trano   ny   voninkano.
              PRES.a.ha.beautiful   the   house   the flowers
              'The flowers make the house beautiful.'

       c.   *Maha-tsara   ny   trano   Rabe.
              PRES.a.ha.beautiful   the   house   Rabe
              'Rabe makes the house beautiful.'

---

[2] See also Duffield (2005, 2007a, submitted) for additional supporting arguments from English participial constructions.

The crucial point about these examples is that this prefix only licenses an additional argument expressing *inadvertent* cause: this is evidenced by the prohibition of Agent arguments, such as *Rabe* in (2c). Travis accounts for this restriction in terms of [Spec,Head] relations: *ha*, as the morphological realization of Inner Asp(ect), is only able to license an additional argument that is initially generated in/merged to its Spec position; by hypothesis, it is unable to license agents because the point of initial merger of such arguments—[Spec,V1]—is too high in the structure.

Asymmetric constraints on one or other of these thematic relations are observable in other languages also, including English. The sentences in (3) and (4) illustrate thematic parallels between periphrastic *make*-causatives and Object Experiencer predicates: in both cases backwards binding is permitted where the subject expresses inadvertent cause, but blocked where the surface subject anaphor must be interpreted agentively: see Pesetsky (1995), Harley (1995), Fujita (1996).

(3)   a. ?Each other's remarks made Bill and Mary laugh.
       b. *Each other's friends (intentionally) made Bill and Mary laugh.

(4)   a. ?Each other's pictures annoyed Sue and Mary.
       b. *Each other's friends (intentionally) annoyed Sue and Mary.

The examples in (5) show that double-object constructions (DOCs) exhibit the same asymmetry as psychological predicates with respect to backwards binding, while the contrast between DOCs and prepositional datives in (6) further distinguishes these two thematic relations, this time to the disadvantage of inadvertent cause arguments: whereas agentive causes may freely appear in the surface subject position of *either* DOCs or prepositional datives, inadvertent cause subjects are excluded from the prepositional dative constructions. For discussion and analyses of such cases, see Fujita (1996), Barss and Lasnik (1986), Larson (1988), Burzio (1986), Pesetsky (1995), and Zubizarreta (1992).

(5)   a. ?Each other's pictures gave Bill and Mary (an idea for) a book.
       b. *Each other's friends (intentionally) gave Bill and Mary a book.

(6)   a. Interviewing Nixon gave Mailer a book.
       b. *Interviewing Nixon gave a book to Mailer.
       c. The exam gave Mary a headache.
       d. *The exam gave a headache to Mary.

These parallels between Malagasy and English go beyond demonstrating that the thematic distinction between intentional and advertent causes may have syntactic consequences: they also suggest the same relative structural position of the two thematic relations. Specifically, it is clear that cases in which inadvertent cause subjects are permitted (and agentive subjects are blocked) are all 'derived subject' constructions,[3] where it is plausible to suppose that the surface subject is syntactically linked to an initial position that is comparatively low in the VP-shell relative to the experiencer/goal argument, as schematized in (7) below.[4] Conversely, those constructions where the inadvertent cause argument may not be realized as a surface subject are all 'canonical transitive' constructions, where the predicate denotes an intentional/volitional action: it seems plausible to analyse these latter constructions as involving the obligatory projection of the higher segment of the VP-shell (VP1). If this the correct way of viewing the problem, then the exclusion of inadvertent cause arguments from the surface subject position in (6) should be made to follow from the interaction between the Thematic Hierarchy and Economy considerations.

(7)

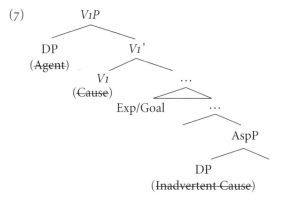

Beyond what is sketched in (7), I will not offer an analysis of these English facts, since the main goal at this point is only to suggest that Travis's proposal has wider application than one might otherwise suppose. In any case, analyses

---

[3] In the older—pre-VP-internal subject hypothesis—sense of the term. Even if one assumes that all surface subjects are derived, the notional contrast between grammatical subjects derived from underlying 'thematic subject' positions, and those from derived from 'thematic *non*-subject' positions remains.

[4] This, for example, seems to be the simplest structural explanation for the backwards binding facts in (3)-(4), namely, that these are not cases of backwards binding at all, but instead of quite standard forwards binding, where the goal/experiencer antecedents properly c-command the silent copy of the reflexive: see Belletti and Rizzi (1988), Fujita (1996), and especially Pesetsky (1995). Of course, this does not preclude non-syntactic accounts, in particular, accounts in terms of thematic hierarchies—see Wilkins (1988), Reinhart and Reuland (1993)—or in terms of other relative prominence relations at a level of conceptual structure: see, for example, Jackendoff (1992), Culicover and Jackendoff (1995).

along these lines have already been developed by others; see especially Pesetsky (1995), Fujita (1996), also Duffield (2007a, in prep.).

Setting the English facts aside, then, the remainder of this article is concerned with some previously unremarked contrasts in a much less familiar language. A member of the South East Asian linguistic area, Vietnamese shares most of its better known grammatical features—its radically isolating morphology, relatively rigid word order, and tonology—with its much better studied neighbour, Chinese. Ironically, historical comparison with other Vietic languages provides grounds for thinking that these seemingly emblematic features of Vietnamese are not archetypal, but are instead the result of shared areal developments and/ or borrowing from genetically unrelated *Sprachbund* varieties (though not necessarily from Chinese in all cases: see Alves (1999) for further discussion). Indeed, it happens to be just those structural properties that distinguish Vietnamese and Chinese from each other—in particular, strict head-initiality, availability of overt TAM markers as free morphemes, and absence of V-V incorporation—that are most relevant to the issues at hand.

5.2.2 *Vietnamese Causatives and the Unaccusative-Unergative Distinction*

First, let us consider Vietnamese causative constructions. As might be expected of a strictly isolating language, there are no synthetic causatives in Vietnamese, nor do bare verb-stems permit transitivity alternations of the kind observed in English, as demonstrated by the unacceptability of (8b):[5]

(8)   a. Cái đèn   vỡ.
          cls lamp break
          'The lamp broke.'

       b. *Tôi vỡ   cái đèn.
            I   break cls lamp
            'I broke the lamp.'

Instead, causativization is invariably expressed analytically: the presence of an additional subject argument (DP_1) must be licensed by a higher causative predicate (V_1), typically the verb *làm*, sometimes by *cho*, sometimes, as we shall see, both predicates are required.[6] The examples in (9) represent typical

---

[5] Vietnamese passive constructions give the appearance of permitting such alternations; however, in such cases there is reasonable evidence that no de-transitivization is involved (see Duffield 2009; Simpson 2009) and that passive involves theme topics (rather than subjects), with A'-binding of an *in-situ* theme argument (see Thomas 1988; Duffield in prep.)

[6] Both of these predicates also occur as independent lexical verbs: *làm* is usually glossed as 'make, do', *cho* as 'let, give, to/for' depending on its distribution (it can function as a simple matrix predicate, as a preposition, or—as here—as a type of prepositional complementizer; compare English *for*).

Duffield   83

instances of simple *làm* causatives involving monovalent base predicates, with
DP₁ V₁ DP₂ V₂ order:

(9)   a. (?)Tôi làm   cái que   gãy.
          I   make cls stick break
          'I broke the stick.'

      b. (?)Tôi làm   tờ   giấy   rách.
          I   make sheet paper torn
          'I tore the sheet of paper.'

Sentences involving core unaccusative predicates such as those in (9) also
permit the alternative word order shown in (10), in which the lower predicate
and its subject (DP₂) are inverted. Indeed, as indicated by the question marks
in (9), the inverted word order is clearly preferred where it is available:

(10) a. Tôi làm   gãy   cái que.
          I   make break cls stick
          'I broke the stick.'

      b. Tôi làm   rách tờ   giấy.
          I   make torn cls paper
          'I tore the sheet of paper.'

Thus far, the Vietnamese facts might seem little different from those observable in Mandarin Chinese, which also allows inversion in certain resultative
contexts (though not with the bare causative *shi*). However, Vietnamese
causatives exhibit important distributional and interpretive restrictions that
distinguish them from those in Chinese. The first of these constraints relates
to the interpretation of the higher subject argument: in all cases—irrespective
of the thematic properties of V₂—Vietnamese causatives with simple *làm*
receive a default *indirect* interpretation: that is to say, the clausal subject is
normally interpreted as an 'inadvertent cause' of the event—a participant,
rather than an agent. Notice that in contrast to the English periphrastic
causative this does not imply that the subject has any less involvement in
the core event, just that there is less intentionality on the subject's part. Thus,
a better translation for (10a), for example, might be through the 'ethical
dative' construction: 'The stick broke on me'.[7] The interpretive parallels
with the Malagasy paradigm in (2) above should be clear, except that Vietnamese, unlike Malagasy, has a simple remedy for making such causatives
intentional, namely, by embedding them under intentional predicates, such as
cõ ý ('intend'), as in (11):

---

[7] This is also the case for Thai causatives, as discussed by Vichit-Vadakan (1976).

(11) a. Tôi cõ ý   làm *gẫy*   cái que.
          I   intend make break cls stick
          'I (intentionally) broke the stick.'

      b. Tôi cõ ý   làm *rách* tờ giấy.
          I   want   make torn   cls paper
          'I (intentionally) tore the sheet of paper.'

In spite of this difference, however, the clear implication is that *làm,* like Malagasy *ha,* is preferentially associated with inadvertent cause subjects.

The second point to observe about simple *làm* causatives is that they cannot normally embed transitive predicates, nor typically unergative predicates denoting controlled actions, such as *nhảy* ('dance') or *hát* ('laugh').[8] This is shown by the unacceptability of the examples in (12) and (13) below, which also show a gradient of unacceptability: while some speakers marginally accept *làm* + unergative V$_2$ in uninverted order (12), no speakers permit the inverted order with such predicates (13), in direct contrast to the situation with respect to core unaccusatives (cf. 9 vs 10).

(12) a. ??Tôi làm   [đứa con gái *giúp* anh ấy]
             I   make cls cls girl *help* prn dem
             'I make the girl help him.'

      b. ??Tôi làm   [đứa con gái *nhảy/hát/ngủ.*]
             I   make cls cls girl *dance/sing/sleep*
             'I make the girl dance/sing/sleep.'

(13) a. *Tôi làm   [*giúp*   con gái anh ấy.]
            I   make *help* cls cls girl prn dem

      b. *Tôi làm   *nhảy/hát/ngủ*   đứa con gái.
            I   make *dance/sing/sleep* cls cls girl

Here again, it is not the case that such causativization is impossible, but it *does* require recourse to a different kind of complement structure: the examples in (12) become completely acceptable where the prepositional complementizer *cho*—see fn. 13—is added following *làm,* as in (13):

(14) a. Tôi làm   [cho [đứa con gái *giúp* anh ấy]]
             I   make give cls cls girl *help* prn dem
             'I make the girl help him.'

---

[8] In this respect, Vietnamese diverges from all of its near neighbours: Chinese shows no unergative-unaccusative split, while Thai, Lao, Khmer, and Burmese seem to disallow inversion quite generally.

b. Tôi làm   [*cho* [đứa con gái nhảy.]]
   I   make give cls cls girl dance
   'I make the girl dance.'

Aside from this thematic effect, there are various reasons to believe that *làm* and *làm cho* admit of separate syntactic analyses, and that the former is typically monoclausal, the latter bi-clausal. The most significant, and immediately relevant, evidence comes from sentences involving the reciprocal anaphor *nhau* ('each other'): as the examples in (15) show, with V₂ predicates that admit either complement, *nhau* is accessible to a subject antecedent across *làm*, but not across *làm cho*:[9]

(15)   a. Họ [làm *nhau*   khóc].
           they made each other cry
           'They made each other cry.'

       b. *Họ làm [cho [*nhau* khóc]].
           they make give e.o.   cry
           'They made each other cry.'

As important as the binding contrast that holds between (15a) and (15b) is the third effect of interest here: the contrast in acceptability between (15a) and (12b) above. The examples show that whereas simple *làm* causatives may not embed unergative predicates denoting controlled actions, *làm* may freely combine with unergatives denoting *uncontrolled* actions—the same speakers who reject example (12b) find those in (15a) and (16) perfectly acceptable.

(16)   a. Tôi làm đứa con trai khóc.
           I   make cls cls male cry
           'I made the boy cry.'

       b. Tôi làm đứa con trai cười.
           I   make cls cls male laugh
           I made the boy laugh.'

---

[9] Kwon (2004) discusses a series of arguments for and against a monoclausal analysis of Vietnamese causatives: all of the standard syntactic diagnostics (including negative polarity licensing and anaphor binding) argue in favour of a monoclausal analysis, whereas other tests seem to implicate a bi-clausal structure. Arguably, one of the reasons for the equivocal results in Kwon's study is precisely that she does not distinguish between *làm* and *làm cho* constructions: had she done so, the evidence for a monoclausal analysis of (unaccusative) *làm* causatives would have been much clearer.

Moreover, in special contexts, the predicates *nhảy* ('dance') and *hát* ('sing') *may* combine with *làm* for all speakers, as exemplified in (17) below. The crucial difference between these examples and those in (12) is the degree of autonomous control ascribed to the causee (DP$_2$): simple causativisation with these predicates is permitted just in case the causee is interpreted as having no control over the action denoted by the predicate: in this example, the puppet is operated by pulling strings or other remote control).

(17) ?Tôi làm   con búp-bê nhảy/hát.
      I   make cls puppet dance/sing
      'I make the puppet dance/sing.'

Taken together, what these examples seem to show is unergative predicates may be embedded under *làm* just as long as they're not really unergative! To express this slightly more formally, a predicate may combine with *làm* just as long as its sole argument (DP$_2$) is interpreted as lacking intentionality. This looks very much as if what would be an l-syntax effect in other languages is expressed in Vietnamese as a regular piece of s-syntax. It also suggests—consistent with the spirit of l-syntax proposals—that the terms 'unergative' and 'unaccusative' do not denote inherent properties of lexical stems/roots, but refer instead to different patterns of syntactic projection, whether this is represented covertly in l-syntax, or overtly, as is the case in Vietnamese.

The fourth and final complicating factor with respect to causativization is internal to the set of unaccusative predicates. It turns out that for some predicates, such as those in (9) and (10) above, the inverted order is strongly preferred, whereas for others, such as those in (18), the uninverted order is considered more acceptable. Once again, this split is thematically determined: inversion is preferred in cases where the causee undergoes a radical and permanent change of state—for example, where the causee is torn, shredded, smashed, or killed—but dispreferred where the causee is merely the 'key participant' in the event, as in (18):

(18) a. Tôi làm   (?*ngã*) thang-be (*ngã*).
        I   make fall   boy   fall
        'I made the boy fall.'

      b. Tôi làm   (?*biến-mất*) thang-be (*biến-mất*).
        I   make disappear   boy   disappear
        'I made the boy disappear.'

TABLE 1. Position of causee (DP$_2$) *in làm* causatives by thematic relation.

Standard Classification	Thematic Relation DP$_2$	*làm* DP$_2$ V$_2$ 'No Inversion'	*làm* V$_2$ DP$_2$ 'Inversion'	Examples
Unergative	Causer (volitional)	??	*	(12, 13)
Unergative	Inadvertent Cause	ok	*	(15–17)
Unaccusative	Participant	ok	?*	(18)
Unaccusative	Theme (undergoes Change of State)	?*	ok	(10)

5.2.3 *Analysis*

Table 1 provides a summary of the effects just discussed: it also immediately suggests an analysis. Up to this point, I have used the term 'inversion' to describe the non-canonical (VS) order in (10). Inversion clearly implies movement (of V$_2$); indeed, treatments of Asian causativization often invoke head-movement ('V-V incorporation') to account for this non-canonical word order: see, for example, Li (1990). Yet Table 1 points to the opposite conclusion: it is not the verb that occurs in a different position, but the lower argument. And no movement is necessarily involved.

Considering first only the position and interpretation of DP$_2$, the following analysis suggests itself. If one assumes that *làm* is the realization of V1, and that *làm* causatives have a monoclausal structure, then the varying distribution of DP$_2$ in pre-verbal or post-verbal position—as well as the total exclusion of 'controlled' unergatives from the construction—becomes immediately predictable from their thematic relations. All that is required is a pre-verbal syntactic position for inadvertent causes in (16) and (17); this is, of course, just what Travis's phrase structure offers us. The tree in (19) spells this out:[10]

---

[10] It should be clear that the data presented in this paper are consistent with two analyses of the position of the root predicate and of the Theme DP within the tree in (19): the alternative analysis would have the root verb move to Asp, and the Theme DP in {Spec, VP2}. In fact, evidence from the behaviour of aspectual/modal morpheme được ('can') provides support for the latter analysis, at least in certain contexts. Since space constraints preclude further discussion here, I leave the matter open: for preliminary discussion, see Duffield (1999), Kwon (2004); for a more complete treatment, Duffield (in prep.).

(19)

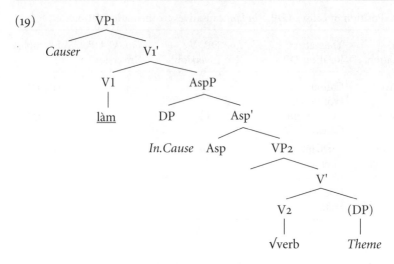

So, in (19), *làm* cannot take a uncontrolled unergative predicate as a complement (*12), since its sole argument (prior to causativization) is normally
projected to a position *above* that of *làm*, i.e., [Spec,VP1]. This means that
the only way for such an argument to be embedded under *làm* is by selecting a
separate VP1 contained within a clausal complement; this is just the alternative *làm cho* construction (14). However, unergatives are permitted where
their sole argument is interpreted as controlled, since these DP$_2$ subjects
(17)—as well as 'key participant' subjects of unaccusative predicates (18)—
are merged instead to [Spec,Asp]. In all of these cases, pre-verbal order is
required, or strongly preferred. True Themes, by contrast, must appear post-
verbally (12), hence the apparent inversion effect.

If this analysis is correct, then it lends significant support to the (pre-
Minimalist) idea that phrase structure does more than merely combine
and express pre-specified lexical features: thematic relations are function-
ally determined by structural configurations. More specifically, it re-
inforces the point made earlier, namely, that there is no inherent lexical
difference—in Vietnamese, at least—between certain unaccusative and
unergative predicates: if it is in fact the case that 'non-radical unaccusatives' project identically to 'uncontrolled unergatives' then the standard
lexicalist view of the distinction is unhelpful at best.

5.2.4 *Predictions and Extensions*

As Gillian Ramchand was quick to observe at the oral presentation of an
earlier version of this chapter, the analysis presented in (20), in which
non-volitional unaccusatives and uncontrolled unergatives compete for

the same syntactic slot, seems to make a clear prediction, namely, that it should be impossible to have a *làm* causative involving an inadvertent cause DP_1 and a non-volitional DP_2. That is to say, the analysis predicts a minimal contrast between the grammaticality of the sentences in (16) and (17) above, and those in (20):

(20)   a. Con gió'   làm   thang-be   ngã.
            cls   wind make cls   boy fall
            'The wind blew the boy over.'

       b. Cái chuyện đó   làm   thang-be cười
            cls story   dem make boy   laugh
            'The story made the boy laugh.'

Were this prediction borne out, it would provide clear confirmation of the analysis in (19).[11] However, the facts are different: for native speakers, the sentences in (20) are perfectly natural. Though disappointing, it should be noted the acceptability of these sentences only constitutes a problem if one can exclude in such cases the alternative bi-clausal analysis with *cho* unexpressed, i.e., (20) as the silent counterpart of (21). Yet this bi-clausal alternative always seems to be available: indeed, it is the most likely analysis assigned by speakers who accept the examples in (12) above. Thus, it remains unclear whether the results in (20) are really problematic.

(21)   a. Con gió'   làm   [(cho) thang-be   ngã].
            cls   wind make give   cls   boy fall
            'The wind blew the boy over.'

       b. Cái chuyện đó   làm   [cho thang-be cười].
            cls story   dem make give boy   laugh
            'The story made the boy laugh.'

That said, there is something *ad hoc* about this response: given this, it seems proper to consider alternative analyses. One such option would be to invoke an additional intermediate specifier position, as in (22):

---

[11] It could also offer an alternative approach to deriving 'animacy hierarchy effects' observed in many other languages. Recent structural explanations of person hierarchy and animacy hierarchy effects—especially in languages where 'inverse' affixes are employed to prevent inanimate arguments outranking animate ones (Aissen 1997)—generally assume a common initial position for both types of argument, and account for the effects in terms of the (phi-)features of the attracting head ([Spec,TP] or some intermediate attractor): see, for example, Bianchi (2006), Bruening (2001), Nichols (2001). The alternative offered by the splitting of thematic positions presented here is that animates outrank inanimate arguments because they start off higher in the first place. Without further modification, this would not of course replace these other explanations—it offers no account of *person*-hierarchy effects, for example—but it could nevertheless explain part of the story.

(22)

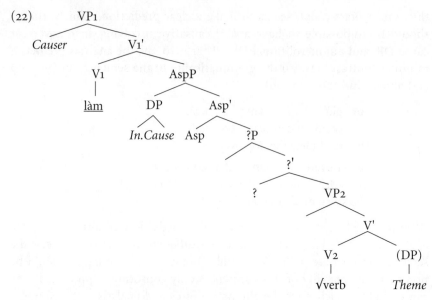

Although this additional projection produces a less constrained and less elegant analysis, it would certainly solve the problem at hand, and may turn out to be necessary for empirical reasons beyond Vietnamese, as observed by Lisa Travis (personal communication).

Finally, it should not have escaped notice that this analysis—by focusing on the thematic properties of DP_2—fails to explain the interpretive parallels between Vietnamese and Malagasy with respect to the inadvertent cause reading for DP_1, which was the point of departure for this section: if anything, the initial position of *làm* in (19) implies that Vietnamese *làm* causatives should be preferentially interpreted as direct, rather than indirect. The revised tree in (22), with its extra specifier position, immediately offers a solution: Vietnamese *làm* is not projected under V1, but, like Malagasy *ha*, under Asp. Thus, this revision simultaneously accommodates the present data, including the facts in (20), while drawing out cross-linguistic parallels.[12]

5.3 Functional Heads: Outer Aspect and Event Phrase

5.3.1 *Background*

I turn now to the second of Travis's structural claims, for which Vietnamese provides relevant data, namely, that clausal architecture below Tense and

---

[12] Conceivably, this would also permit a monoclausal analysis of the intentional cause construction in (12), with the modal element *cốý* inserted under V1. Binding evidence should be able to refute or confirm this: unfortunately, it is not clear at this stage what the relevant facts are: see Duffield (in prep).

above VP1 includes a functional projection EP, the syntactic realization of event structure (see fn. 2 above). As Travis points out, the more general idea that events should be treated as grammatical objects—just as, for example, the *participants* of an event are treated in terms of thematic relations/theta roles—is not a proprietary one: other recent articulations of event structure in syntax and semantics include Parsons (1990), Pustejovsky (1991), and Klein (n.d.), amongst others. Independently of this question, it is worth noting that there is general consensus in the literature on functional categories in favour of a functional head between T and VP (even though there is much less agreement on the correct label or functional role for this syntactic position; cf. Pollock (1989), Chomsky (1989), McCloskey (2001), amongst many others).

What is original to Travis's proposal is the particular synthesis of these two current ideas, by which this intermediate projection is directly identified with the notion 'event'. The label spells out the purported primary interpretive function of E, namely, 'to theta-bind...[in the sense of Higginbotham (1985)]...the E theta-role in V' (Travis forthcoming). Travis further proposes that this E head is the initial host of infinitival and subjunctive morphology, and suggests that E should be equated with Mood. This functional head, then, serves an important interpretive function in the grammar: it is not simply there for formal feature checking (cf. AgrO).

5.3.2 *Vietnamese Responsives*

In this final section, I will claim that Vietnamese also provides illuminating evidence for a syntactic projection with the right semantic properties in just the right position to confirm this part of Travis's proposal.[13] In Duffield (2007b), I present a detailed analysis of the Vietnamese pre-verbal 'assertion morpheme' *có*, which functions like *do*-support in English, appearing in the same range of negative, emphatic, and interrogative contexts, and giving rise to a parallel set of interpretive effects.[14] This evidence, as well as that presented immediately below, provided support for the proposal that *có* is the realization of a putatively universal functional projection—Assertion Phrase—situated immediately above VP and below Tense, as schematized in (23):

---

[13] Space constraints preclude any detailed substantiation of this claim: for more extensive discussion, see Duffield (2007b).

[14] Except that, unlike *do*, *có* never raises to any higher functional head position; here once again, morphemes in Vietnamese have an attractive habit of staying put.

(23)

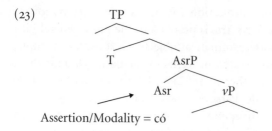

Assertion/Modality = có

The parallels with Travis's EP should be clear. It could be claimed, of course, that such an analysis is simply coincidental with Travis's proposal, or—at best—that the Vietnamese facts only provide more evidence for *some* type of functional category in this position, not necessarily one relating to events. This may yet turn out to be correct. Nevertheless, several other pieces of evidence motivate a merger of the two analyses. The first of these is purely interpretive. In affirmative sentences, the appearance of *có* before the main verb signals not only emphasis (typically milder than the corresponding effect of emphatic *do* in present-day English), but also encourages what is usually referred to as a 'past-tense' interpretation for the sentence, as indicated by the translations in (24).

(24) a. Anh ấy   có đi Luân Đon.
         prn dem co go London
         'He went/did go to London.'

Now, since tense is always only optionally realized in Vietnamese, it is often the case that *có* is the only functional category in the sentence, and it might therefore be concluded from this that *có* is itself a tense marker. However, the positioning of these elements with respect to the negation morpheme *không* allows us to reject this possibility: the examples in (25) and (26) shows that the future tense morpheme *sẽ* invariably precedes negation, whereas *có* must follow this element:[15]

(25) a. Anh ấy   sẽ   không đi Luân Đon.
         prn dem fut   neg   go London
         'He *will* not go to London.'

---

[15] The other tense-related morpheme, which also precedes negation, is the anterior morpheme (đã): this element, which normally has an aspectual interpretation, is interpreted as a preterite marker in negative contexts. See Duffield (submitted), Duffield and Phan (in prep.), for arguments that this element is not a tense element underlyingly, but is normally the realization of Outer Aspect. Also, rather unexpectedly, there is an antagonism between the future morpheme *sẽ* and (assertion) *có* such that for most speakers the two may not co-occur, in spite of the fact that they do not compete for the same syntactic position. See Duffield and Phan (in prep.) for discussion.

b. *Anh ấy   không sẽ   đi Luân   Đon.
   prn dem   fut   neg go London
   'He *will* not go to London.'

(26) a. *Anh ấy   không đi   Luân Đon.
     prn dem   neg   go   London
     'He *did not* go to London.'

b. ??Anh ấy   không có   đi Luân Đon.
   prn dem   neg   asr go London
   'He *did not* not go to London.'

This contrast offers *prima facie* evidence that *có* is not itself a tense morpheme. So where does the past-tense effect come from? Arguably, from the (asserted) events theta-bound by *có*, and from the fact that definite events typically take place in the past. The second piece of evidence, offered by responsives, supports this interpretation.

Responsives are (minimal) answers to yes-no questions.[16] In common with many languages, Vietnamese has no separate words for *yes* and *no*: rather, yes/no-questions are responded to affirmatively either by *có* or by repetition of the predicate. As the following examples reveal, which of these options is selected depends on whether or not an actual prior event is being referred to. As a consequence, typically active predicates in neutral contexts strongly favour a *có* response over predicate repetition (27a), whereas the opposite is true of stative predicates (27b). (These examples also indicate that it is more common to omit *có* in the question if a stative predicate is involved).[17]

(27) a. Chị Phường có mua nhà   không?   Answer: Dạ có!/??*Dạ mua.
        Phuong   co buy house neg   pol co/ pol buy
        'Did Phuong buy a house?'   'Yes! (she did.)'

b. Anh Tân (có) thích Luân Đon không?   Answer: Dạ, thích lắm!/??Dạ, có!
   prn Tan co like London neg   pol like very/pol co
   'Does Tan like London?'   'Yes, he does.'

---

[16] For an analysis of yes-no questions in Vietnamese, see Duffield (submitted, b).

[17] Contrary to what is implied in Duffield (2007b), the contrast between individual vs stage-level predicates is not entirely parallel to that of active vs stative predicates: though broadly congruent with what is presented above—as predicted, individual-level predicates (e.g. *đẹp* 'beautiful', *lười* 'lazy') tend to prefer predicate repetition, stage-level predicates preferring *có*—nevertheless, speakers' judgements are more mixed about this contrast, according to Trang Phan (personal communication).

(28) a. người Nhất (có) ăn cá không?   Answer: ?Dạ, có./Da, ăn.
          person Japan co eat fish neg   pol co/pol eat
          'Do Japanese people eat fish?'   'Yes, they do.'

      b. Anh có sửa   mảy.ảnh không?   Answer: ?Dạ, có./Da, sửa.
          prn co repair camera neg   pol co/pol repair
          'Do you repair cameras?   'Yes, I do.'

However, alternative uses of the active predicates show fairly clearly that the
correlation between predicate and responsive type is not an inherent one.
Comparing the examples in (28) with those in (29), it can be seen that in
generic contexts, where no specific eventuality is involved, the preferred
responsive is predicate repetition, but where specific eventualities are referred
to, responsive *có* is once again strongly preferred over predicate repetition.

(29) a. Tuần trước trong nhà hàng của anh người Nhất   có ăn
          last week   in   restaurant poss prn people Japanese co eat
          cá không?
          fish neg
          'Last week in your restaurant did Japanese people eat fish?'
          — A: Dạ, có/ *Dạ, ăn.

      b. Hôm qua khi   máy.ảnh của   chúng tôi bị   hư,   anh
          Yesterday when camera poss plural I   pass break, prn
          có sửa   không?
          co repair   neg
          'Yesterday when our cameras broke did you fix the cameras?'
          — A: Dạ, có/ *Dạ, sửa.

This is reinforced by the observation, due to Trang Phan (personal communication), that *có* does not occur either when the eventuality is hypothetical or
counterfactual: compare, finally, the example in (29b) with that in (30):

(30) Giả sử   hôm qua máy ảnh của   chúng tôi bị   hư,   anh có
      Suppose yesterday camera poss plural I   pass break, prn co
      sửa   không?
      repair   neg
      'Suppose that yesterday our camera had broken would you have fixed it?'
      —A: *Dạ, có/ Dạ, sửa.

In short, no real event = no *có*. It should be clear that these contrasts are not
only consistent with Travis's proposal, but that they speak directly in favour
of her semantic claims. Furthermore, they seem to show once again that
what are traditionally viewed as inherent properties of a verbal root—in

this case, the active-stative distinction—are better understood as emergent properties of particular syntactic configurations: in Vietnamese, these are regular s-syntax projections; in other languages, these effects are better disguised (in l-syntax).

5.4 Conclusion

In this paper, I have presented two types of distributional contrast in Viet-namese, a language that hitherto has been neglected by Western linguistics, at least by comparison with its dominant South East Asian neighbours. I have argued that both contrasts provide direct support for a highly articulated VP-structure that differentiates subtle thematic relations, as well as encoding some syntactic representation of eventualities. Both sets of facts immediately support the theoretical proposals put forward by Travis (2000, forthcoming), which are based on a quite distinct range of languages. The special virtue of Vietnamese in this regard is to offer a maximally transparent phrase structure: the near-total absence of any bound morphology means that l-syntactic operations—especially VP-internal verb movement operations—are kept to a minimum, with the result that internal VP-structure is laid bare. From a more general perspective, the facts presented here provide support for what I take to be one of the main conceptual goals of the l-syntax/s-syntax project, namely, to show that what are usually taken to be classificatory dichotomous labels for inherent lexical properties—'unaccusative/unergative', 'active/sta-tive', etc.—are in fact relational notions, derivative of particular syntactic structures.

6

Building Resultatives in Icelandic*

MATTHEW WHELPTON

6.1 Introduction

(1) is an example of a resultative (Halliday 1967).

(1)   The blacksmith hammered the metal flat.

The sentence describes an event (the blacksmith hammering the metal) with a specific result (the metal is flat). What is special about this construction is that the final result is specified not by the main verb ('hammer') but by a secondary predicate ('flat'). Given its explicitly compositional nature, the construction promises insights into the nature of argument structure composition and hence the interfaces between syntax, semantics, and morphology.

  The specific focus of this paper is the resultative in Icelandic and its implications for the account of the resultative in German and English offered by Kratzer (2005b). Section 6.2 introduces four questions which provide a context for Kratzer's account and the debates to which it makes a contribution, including a brief overview of Kratzer's analysis (section 6.2.5). The implications of data from Icelandic are then considered (section 6.3), in particular for two major claims in her analysis: that adjectival resultatives are in fact causativized verbs involving compounding (section 6.3.1); and that all verbs with adjectival resultatives are used unergatively (section 6.3.2).

* This chapter was supported by the sabbatical fund of the University of Iceland; data was contributed by the projects 'Sagnflokkar og táknun rökliða' (RANNÍS 2007) and 'Tilbrigði í setningagerð' (RANNÍS Grant of Excellence 2005) and by my invaluable assistant Theódóra A. Torfadóttir. I thank participants in the OnLI conference (Ulster 2007) and members of the Icelandic Grammar Society for their feedback. A special word of thanks goes to Angelika Kratzer for patience and insight in discussing this material with me. Needless to say all errors and misunderstandings remain mine solely.

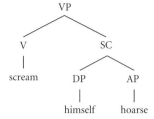

FIGURE 1. A small clause representation of the resultative.

6.2 Four Questions Concerning the Resultative

6.2.1 *Question 1—Object Selection*

The question which has dominated discussion of the resultative (especially early discussion) concerns semantic selection of the object.

Q1   What is the semantic relation of the object in (1) to the main predicate 'hammer' and the secondary predicate 'flat', as it clearly bears some interpretive relation to both?

Small-clause approaches (cf. Hoekstra 1988) treat the relation of the object to the secondary predicate as transparent (simple subject-predicate relation); it is this small clause that merges with the main verb (cf. Figure 1). Carrier and Randall (1992) also assume direct predication of the secondary predicate's subject argument to the verbal object, though without the syntactic scaffolding of a small clause.

Complex predicate approaches (cf. Larson 1991) argue that the main verb and the secondary predicate merge first to produce a complex predicate which then takes the object as co-argument, introducing a potential opacity in the relation between secondary predicate and verbal object (cf. Figure 2).

Borer (2005b) explicitly treats the verb-predicate pair as an opaque lexical unit, with argument interpretation assigned exclusively by higher functional structure. Ramchand's (2008) constructivist model preserves more transparency,

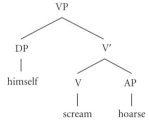

FIGURE 2. A complex predicate representation of the resultative.

arguing for a series of functional heads forming complex predicates with their complements which co-assign interpretation to their specifiers, under a uniform semantic mapping.

The main controversy concerns the relation of the main verb to the verbal object. One influential (and early) view (cf. Simpson 1983; Carrier and Randall 1992; Levin and Rappaport Hovav 1995) is that the semantic relation of the verb to the object is the same with or without the resultative predicate. Following Simpson's (1983) classic paper, this claim is linked to the Unaccusative Hypothesis (Perlmutter 1978) and used to explain the distinct behaviour of transitive, unaccusative, and unergative verbs in the resultative.

(2)   a.   The blacksmith hammered the metal.
       b.   The blacksmith hammered the metal flat.

(3)   a.   _____ froze the juice.
       b.   _____ froze the juice solid.
       c.   the juice froze *t* solid.

(4)   a.   John screamed.
       b.   John screamed himself hoarse.
       c.   *John screamed himself.

The transitive verb in (2a) allows the simple addition of a resultative predicate, as in (2b). The unaccusative verb in (3a) has an underlying object and no subject; to this a resultative predicate can be added, as in (3b); the object raises to subject, yielding (3c). The unergative verb in (4a) has a subject but no object; a resultative can be formed, as in (4b), where the unergative now appears to be transitive; however, this verb cannot be used transitively, as in (4c). Simpson (1983) suggests that the resultative is therefore tied to the direct object, occurring naturally with transitives and unaccusatives but occurring with unergatives only if an unselected object is inserted. This restriction to direct object has been enshrined in Levin and Rappaport Hovav's (1995) Direct Object Restriction (DOR) and challenged in various studies (cf. Verspoor 1997; Wechsler 1997, 2005a; Rappaport Hovav and Levin 2001; Van Valin 1990). Figure 3 illustrates an account which preserves verb argument structure in the resultative and adopts a small clause representation of the resultative predicate.

An alternative view is that the (apparent) object of the verb in the resultative bears no formal semantic relation to the verb at all but is exclusively the argument of the resultative predicate (cf. Kayne 1985; Hoekstra 1988; Kratzer 2005b; Harley 2007b). Hoekstra (1988) provides the classic statement of this view in his rebuttal of Simpson (1983). He argues that the Direct Object Restriction in Simpson's (1983) view is unmotivated and rather mysterious in that it is not

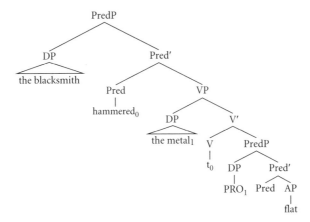

FIGURE 3. Resultatives, based on Bowers (1997).

clear why and how it would force the presence of an object with unergatives (Hoekstra 1988: 120). He suggests that the fundamental pattern is the one we see with unergatives: an intransitive verb followed by a small-clause predication, as in (5a).

(5) a. John snored [Bill awake].
     b. *John snored Bill.

Verbs such as 'hammer' which are cited as transitive verbs can usually also be used intransitively, as in (6b).

(6) a. The blacksmith hammered the metal for hours.
     b. The blacksmith hammered away for hours.

In the resultative they can also appear with unselected objects.

(7) a. The blacksmith hammered his arm sore.
     b. *The blacksmith hammered his arm.

He therefore suggests that it is always the intransive use that we find in the resultative, with any apparent argument-like interpretation simply being an inferential effect, as we get in (8) (cf. Kayne 1985).

(8) John hammered away for hours but the padlock would not break.
     Inference: John hammered the padlock.

The appropriate structure is therefore as in Figure 4.

Carrier and Randall (1992) present sophisticated evidence against Hoekstra (1988) and in favour of Simpson (1983) to the effect that the objects of

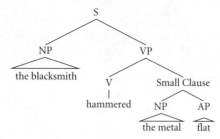

FIGURE 4. Resultatives, based on Hoekstra (1988).

transitives in the resultative do not behave like the objects of unergatives. To give one example, they show that middle formation is sensitive to argument selection of the object but that passive formation is not. Under Hoekstra's (1988) account, neither transitive nor unergative resultatives should appear with the middle but both should appear with the passive; under Simpson's (1983) account, transitive but not unergative resultatives should appear in the middle and both should appear in the passive.

(9)   a.   My socks won't scrub clean easily.
       b.   The socks have finally been scrubbed clean.

(10)   a.   *Competition Nikes run threadbare easily.
       b.   Her Nikes have been run threadbare.

As Carrier and Randall (1992) predict, transitives (9) behave differently to unergatives (10), suggesting that transitive resultatives cannot be simply reduced to unergative resultatives.

6.2.2 *Question 2—Result Interpretation*

Q2   What is the nature of the result interpretation in (1) and where does it come from?

One approach is simply to use a lexical rule to add a result interpretation to the verb, as in Simpson's (1983) Lexical-Functional Grammar account, Wechsler's (1997, 2005a) Head-Driven Phrase Structure Grammar account, and Carrier and Randall's (1992) Government-Binding account.

Probably the most influential approach is to link resultative formation to verb aspectual structure, the idea being that merging an activity predicate like 'hammer' with a state predicate like 'flat' conforms to the aspectual structure of accomplishments (activity leading to final state). In Levin and Rappaport Hovav (1995), this is treated as aspectual coercion: the language faculty prescribes a limited number of event types for VP denotation and given an activity-denoting verb and a state-denoting secondary predicate there is no semantic choice but to interpret the result as an accomplishment, introducing the implication of a causal relation between the activity and the state. A similar line is adopted in Hoekstra (1988), who suggests that small-clause complements of activity verbs are freely interpreted as denoting the final state of the activity.

Williams (2005, 2008) and Lidz and Williams (2002) distinguish between the causal predicate, which introduces the result meaning, and the two overt ingredients of the construction: the means predicate (the verb) and the result predicate. Williams argues that the construction, and especially its cross-linguistic variation, can only be understood if this distinct head predicate is recognized and the verbal object is represented as the argument of this causal predicate. Higginbotham (1999) also introduces a result predicate to account for the result reading but in this case it is an accomplishment preposition, 'to', which relates a pair of events, where the first event leads to the second. Ramchand (2008) introduces a result head *res* which can be identified either by change-of-state verbs or the preposition *to*. The issue of resultative meaning may therefore be implicated not only in verb aspectual structure but also in properties of the resultative predicate itself.

6.2.3 *Question 3—The Result Predicate*

Q3   Are the properties of the resultative largely independent of the grammatical properties of the resultative predicate?

Halliday's (1967) original observation was that resultatives can occur with AP, NP, or PP predicates.

(11)   John painted his car pink/a screaming pink/in a bright shade of pink.

It is therefore common to generalize across predicate types (XP) in the analysis of resultatives (cf. Levin and Rappaport Hovav 1995). As Son (2007) observes, many scholars (cf. Beck and Snyder 2001; Mateu and Rigau 2001, 2002; McIntyre 2004; Beavers *et al.* 2004) have also generalized across change-of-state resultatives and directed motion constructions; for instance, English allows both and Spanish neither.

(12)   a.   Mary ran/walked/crawled to the store.
             (Son 2007: 127, her ex. 1b)
        b.   The blacksmith hammered the metal flat.

(13)   a.   Juan ??corrio/ *anduvo/ *gateo a la tienda.
             (Son 2007: 127, her ex. 4a)
        b.   *El herrero martilleó el metal liso.

Son (2007) challenges this correlation, showing that some languages (Korean and Japanese) have adjectival resultatives but not manner-of-motion PP-goal constructions, whereas others (Hebrew, Indonesian, and Czech) have manner-of-motion PP-goal constructions but not adjectival resultatives. In English, the constructions differ with respect to the Direct Object Condition.

(14)   a.   He danced into the room.
        b.   *He danced into a frenzy.
        c.   He danced himself into a frenzy.

The goal-of-motion construction in (14a) displays the unaccusative pattern but the change-of-state resultative does not, as in (14b), requiring the unergative pattern with object, as in (14c).

   Just within the resultative, there is evidence of a significant interaction between the properties of the resultative predicate and the properties of the verbal predicate (cf. Ramchand 2008; Wechsler 1997, 2005a; Beavers 2008). Wechsler (2005a: 267, his ex. 26) observes for instance that that the AP 'dead' tends to be used with punctual predicates like 'shoot' rather than durative predicates like 'batter', whereas the PP 'to death' favours durative predicates (but can be used with either).

(15)   a.   The rabbits had apparently been battered {*dead/to death}.
        b.   He and a confederate shot the miller {dead/to death}.

Ramchand (2008) and Folli and Ramchand (2005) also note a significant interaction between verb aspectual properties and preposition path properties. Result-entailing predicates like 'break' can take stative PP results but non-result-entailing predicates like 'pound' cannot; both are compatible with path PPs.

(16)   a.   Katherine broke the stick in pieces.
             (Ramchand 2008: 75, her ex. 30a)
        b.   *Kayleigh pounded the metal in pieces.
        c.   Kayleigh pounded the metal into pieces.
             (Ramchand 2008: 76, her ex. 31a-b)
        d.   Katherine broke the stick into pieces.

Ramchand (2008) proposes that, as well as the more familiar *v* and V (*init* 'initiation' and *proc* 'process' in her system), there is a third verbal head *res* 'result' which specifies the result state of an activity. Change-of-state *break* licenses *res* and activity *pound* does not. Crucially, the preposition *to* also licenses *res* (see also Beavers (2008) for the special status of *to*). *Pound* therefore requires *to* for a PP resultative but *break* already licenses result semantics and so can take a stative PP complement. Germanic languages like English and Icelandic also have a null *res* with the semantics 'x have the property y', where the semantics of *y* can be supplied by an AP. Romance languages lack this item. Therefore Germanic languages have adjectival resultatives with activity verbs and Romance languages do not.

These interactions have important implications for the approach to parametric variation.

6.2.4 *Question 4—Macro- Versus Microparameters*

Q4   Does the availability of the resultative in a language reflect the setting of a general parameter (macroparametric) or the specific pattern of functional lexicalization in the language (microparametric)?

As is well known, there appear to be significant typological constraints on the distribution of resultatives cross-linguistically. For instance, adjectival resultatives are generally grammatical in Germanic languages and generally ungrammatical in Romance languages. Some approaches relate this difference to a broad parametric pattern, where a single parameter relates to the occurrence of a number of constructions, for instance Snyder's (2001) suggestion that a cluster of constructions, including *make*-causatives, double-object datives, and resultatives, are related to a parameter allowing compounding. This is the macroparametric approach (cf. Chomsky 1981). Others (cf. Ramchand 2008; Son and Svenonius 2008; Son 2007) challenge this approach, arguing that the typological distribution is much more complex and that this can be explained in an approach that relates variation to the different lexicalization of functional structure, allowing fine-grained variation according to the functional properties of particular lexical items. This is the microparametric approach (cf. Kayne 1984; Rizzi 1982).

This in fact is part of a far broader debate concerning the fundamental organization of the language faculty. As well as approaches exploiting macroparameters and microparameters, there is a rich Construction Grammar literature (cf. Goldberg 1995; Boas 2003; Iwata 2006); one important discussion (Goldberg and Jackendoff 2004, 2005; Boas, 2003, 2005) in this area concerns the extent to which resultatives reflect the analogical generalization of individual lexical collocations as opposed to the conflation of more general constructional templates.

Kratzer's account provides support for the macroparametric approach but data from Icelandic suggests that a microparametric approach may be better suited to addressing the range of variation.

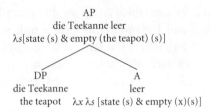

FIGURE 5. Step 1 - Merge A with DP in Hoekstra's account.

6.2.5 *Kratzer's Proposal*

Kratzer's proposal draws on Hoekstra's (1988) uniform unergative analysis of resultatives, Bittner's (1999) analysis of concealed causatives, and Snyder's (2001) compounding macroparameter hypothesis. She assumes that only adjectival resultatives are true resultatives and makes a novel proposal for the lack of predicational agreement on resultative adjectives in German (and English). Consider Kratzer's analysis of *die Teekanne leer trinken* 'drink the teapot empty'.

The first step is shown in Figure 5. The DP *die Teekanne* 'the teapot' is merged with the adjective *leer* 'empty'; the DP is interpreted as the holder of the state denoted by the adjective. The resulting AP is a property of states. Within Kratzer's compositional semantics this is the equivalent of a small clause.

Merging AP with V at this point however will produce a semantic problem, as shown in Figure 6.

The AP *die Teekanne leer* 'the teapot empty' is a property of states; the V *trinken* 'drink' is a property of actions. An attempt to combine these by identifying s with e will produce as a denotation the empty set (nothing is both a state and an event). To solve the problem, the AP denotation must be converted to an event property denotation exactly like that of V.

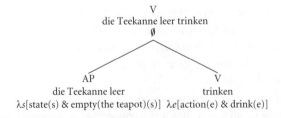

FIGURE 6. Step 2 - Merge of AP and V fails.

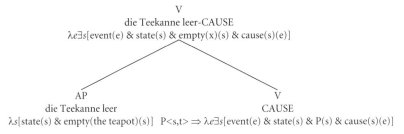

V
die Teekanne leer-CAUSE
$\lambda e \exists s$[event(e) & state(s) & empty(x)(s) & cause(s)(e)]

AP
die Teekanne leer
λs[state(s) & empty(the teapot)(s)]

V
CAUSE
P<s,t> $\Rightarrow \lambda e \exists s$[event(e) & state(s) & P(s) & cause(s)(e)]

FIGURE 7. Step 2 Take 2 - Merge AP with CAUSE.

Kratzer follows Bittner (1999) in assuming that this conversion occurs by a process of causativization but rejects Bittner's purely compositional type-shift rule on the grounds that rules of composition should be content-neutral and only individual formatives should be allowed to introduce 'lexical' content (such as a description of causation). Instead, she argues that the causativization rule is triggered by a zero affix which merges with the AP and which attracts and compounds with the adjectival head. This is shown in Figure 7.

The zero affix converts the AP into a causative verb which can be serialized with the main verb. This involves simple unification of the two predicates by identification of variables and conjunction. The AP argument can then raise to receive case from the main verb. This is shown in Figure 8.

This account therefore provides the following answers to the Questions identified in the Introduction.

A1   The object is purely the argument of the adjectival predicate and bears no direct semantic relation to the main verb. The grammatical object relation is established by raising for case.
A2   The result interpretation is a reflex of causativization, introduced by a verbalizing causative zero morpheme, compounded with the adjective. As a consequence of compounding, adjectives must be bare.

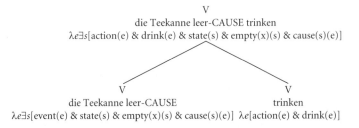

V
die Teekanne leer-CAUSE trinken
$\lambda e \exists s$[action(e) & drink(e) & state(s) & empty(x)(s) & cause(s)(e)]

V
die Teekanne leer-CAUSE
$\lambda e \exists s$[event(e) & state(s) & empty(x)(s) & cause(s)(e)]

V
trinken
λe[action(e) & drink(e)]

FIGURE 8. Step 3 - Serialize verbs.

A3   The properties of the resultative are dependent on the grammatical properties of the resultative predicate in the sense that only adjectives can form true resultatives.

A4   The availability of (true adjectival) resultatives is a consequence of setting a macroparameter to allow compounding, one reflex of which is allowing the causativization of bare adjectives.

Data from Icelandic presents challenges for Kratzer's proposal concerning compounding and for the uniform unergative hypothesis. It supports her distinction between adjectival and prepositional 'resultatives' but in doing so it also suggests that a microparametric approach might be better suited to understanding variation in this area.

6.3 Kratzer (2005b) and the Resultative in Icelandic

6.3.1 *Compounding Blocks Agreement*

Kratzer cites Fabricius Hansen (p.c.) for pointing out problems with the hypothesis that resultative adjectives are uninflected, as Norwegian resultative adjectives can bear an inflectional affix (neuter agreement). This paper elaborates that challenge with data from Icelandic where predicational adjectives inflect richly, agreeing with nouns in number, gender, and case. This is seen with all three major verb classes, transitive, unergative, and unaccusative.

(17)   Járnsmiðurinn   hamraði   málminn
     blacksmith=the hammered metal.M.ACC.SG=the.M.ACC.SG
     flatan.
     flat.M.ACC.SG
     'the blacksmith hammered the metal flat'

(18)   Dóra æpti   sig   hása.
     Dóra screamed herself.F.ACC.SG hoarse.F.ACC.SG
     'Dóra screamed herself hoarse'

(19)   Hann   fraus fastur   í   ísnum.
     he.M.NOM.SG froze fast.M.NOM.SG in ice=the
     'he froze fast in the ice'

This would appear to provide strong evidence against the claim that zero compounding blocks adjectival agreement in the process of syntactic resultative formation. This evidence is strengthened by the contrast with overt compounding of adjectives, when the adjective must indeed be in root form.

(20) hreinskrúbbuðu   pönnurnar
     clean-scrubbed.F.NOM.PL pan.F.NOM.PL=the.F.NOM.PL

Here the participle but not the adjective bears agreement inflection. This suggests that compounded resultative adjectives and free resultative adjectives are not formed by the same process in Icelandic—the compounded version must have bare roots and the free version must have full inflection. Whelpton (2006, 2007) further elaborates this constrast with evidence showing much greater lexical idiosyncracy with overt compounds than with free resultatives.

Kratzer argues that several counterexamples to her proposal are in fact adverbials and not true resultatives. Icelandic does indeed make adverbial use of adjectives with resultative-like readings, typically those involving what Geuder (2000) calls 'resultant individuals' (i.e. a specified portion or configuration of the object resulting from the action described by the verb); however, in such cases, the adverbial function triggers a default agreement form (neuter accusative singular) rather than a full predicational agreement form (though most speakers do find the agreeing form marginally acceptable).

(21) Hann muldi piparkornin   fínt.
     he   ground peppercorns.N.ACC.PL=the.N.ACC.PL fine.N.ACC.SG
     'he ground the peppercorns finely'

The examples in (17–19) bear full predicational agreement, not default adverbial agreement. The formation of free resultatives in Icelandic cannot therefore involve compounding as Kratzer argues.

6.3.2 *All Resultatives Involve Unergatives*

The implications of Icelandic data for a Hoekstra-style analysis of the resultative is much more complex. In section 6.3.2.1, I consider the use of unaccusative verbs with adjectival resultatives. In section 6.3.2.2, I contrast the use of unergative verbs and transitive verbs with adjectival resultatives.

6.3.2.1 *Unaccusative Resultatives* At first sight, Icelandic, like English, appears to provide clear evidence against Hoekstra's account in that unaccusatives do appear with adjectival resultatives.

(22) Hann   fraus fastur   í   ísnum.
     he.M.NOM.SG froze fast.M.NOM.SG in ice=the
     'he froze fast in the ice'

Various scholars have argued that such examples in English are not true resultatives but rather result adverbs, further specifying the verbally entailed result state
(Mateu 2005; Iwata 2006; Rapoport 1999). Such an approach cannot be applied
straightforwardly to Icelandic, as we have seen, because adverbial resultatives in
Icelandic bear default agreement inflection. In (22), the adjective bears full
agreement inflection; adverbial agreement is sharply ungrammatical here.

(23)   *Hann   fraus fast   í   ísnum.
        he.M.NOM.SG froze fast.N.ACC.SG in ice=the
        'he froze fast in the ice'

However, it turns out that (22) is the exception rather than the rule. Most
examples of adjectival resultatives with unaccusative verbs are ungrammatical.

(24)   *Safinn   fraus gegnheill.
        juice.M.NOM.SG=the.M.NOM.SG froze solid.M.NOM.SG
        'the juice froze solid'

(25)   *Ísinn   fraus svo harður
        ice cream.M.NOM.SG=the.M.NOM.SG froze so   hard.M.NOM.SG
        að   við gátum ekki tekið hann upp með skeiðinni.
        that we could not take it   up   with spoon=the
        'The ice cream froze so hard that we couldn't scoop it out with the spoon'

(26)   *Pakkinn   rifnaði opinn
        package.N.NOM.SG=the.N.NOM.SG tore   open.N.NOM.SG
        á   hornunum.
        at corners=the
        'the package tore open at the corners'

In most cases, the transitive-causative equivalents of these sentences are also
ill-formed.

(27)   ?*Hann frysti safann   gegnheilan.
        he   froze juice.M.ACC.SG=the.M.ACC.SG solid.M.ACC.SG
        'he froze the juice solid'

(28)   ?*Hann frysti ísinn   svo
        he   froze ice cream.M.ACC.SG=the.M.ACC.SG so
        harðan   að   við gátum ekki tekið hann
        hard.M.ACC.SG that we could not take it
        upp með skeiðinni.
        up   with spoon=the
        'he froze the ice cream so hard that we couldn't scoop it out with the spoon'

(29)   *Barnið   reif pakkana   opna.
       child=the tore packages.M.ACC.PL=the.M.ACC.PL open.M.ACC.PL
       'the child tore the packages open'

Fastur 'fast' is therefore the exception rather than the rule in allowing resultative use with unaccusatives. I suggest in section 6.3.3 that this relates to a
critical distinction between adjectives expressing qualities (*gegnheill* 'solid';
harður 'hard') and those expressing relative locations (*fastur* 'fast'), which
itself relates to a broader contrast between adjectives on the one hand and
prepositions and particles on the other.

     Setting aside examples with *fastur* 'fast', we seem to have evidence supporting Hoekstra's hypothesis: i.e. unaccusatives do not occur with adjectival
resultatives. However, it turns out that unaccusativity and in particular
participation in the causative-transitive alternation is not the factor which
blocks these resultatives. Rather it is the specific class of causative-inchoative
change-of-state verbs which fail to appear with qualitative adjectival resultatives in Icelandic. Contact-by-impact verbs also undergo the causative-
transitive alternation in Icelandic, yet both the transitive and intransitive
variants are compatible with adjectival resultatives.

(30)   Hann skellti   Guðmundi   flötum   á
       he   slammed   Guðmundur.M.DAT.SG   flat.M.DAT.SG   on
       fyrstu mínútunni
       first   minute=the
       'he slammed Guðmundur flat in the first minute'

(31)   Hún   skall   flöt   í   hálkunni
       she.F.NOM.SG   slammed   flat.F.NOM.SG   on   slippy-ice=the
       og   lærbrotnaði
       and   leg-broke
       'She slammed down flat on the slippy ice and broke her leg.'

The critical factor is therefore not whether the verb introduces an object (as
skella does) but rather whether it lexically specifies a result state (as *frjósa*
'freeze' does but *skella* 'slam' does not). This suggests that Rapoport (1999)
and Tenny (1994) are on the right track in focusing on the lexical specification
of a result state rather than selection of an object.

     A proposal in Folli and Ramchand (2005) offers a promising way of
accounting for this data: result semantics is introduced by the result head
res; *res* can take a PP complement which further specifies the result but which
is independent in its argument structure from *res* because P can project a
specifier; *res* can also in principle take an AP complement (cf the null *res*

meaning 'x have the property y' in section 6.2.3) but A does not project a specifier and can only merge with a *res* which licenses a specifier for it: only null *res* does this. Icelandic therefore has no AP complements with inchoative verbs.

This raises the important question of the generality of this analysis, given that English precisely allows inchoative verbs with adjectival resultatives. There is not space here to explore this question in detail but it is worth pointing out that Icelandic appears to be fairly representative of the situation in Germanic. *freeze* plus *hard/solid* is at best marginal in several other Germanic languages.

(32)   a. ?Juicen frös hard. (Norwegian)
      b. ?Juicen frös hårt. (Swedish)
      c. *Der Saft ist solid gefroren. (German)

I conclude that evidence from unaccusative verbs with adjectival resultatives in Icelandic does not support Hoekstra's claim that selected objects are excluded from the resultatives. Rather it supports the claim that verbs specifying a resultant state exclude (true) adjectival resultatives. We return to this issue in section 6.3.3.

6.3.2.2 *Transitives, Unergatives, and 'Fake' Reflexives*   Further evidence that selected direct objects can occur in the resultative comes from a contrast between transitives and unergatives in Icelandic which goes back to Simpson's (1983) original observation concerning 'fake' reflexives.

Unergative verbs with adjectival resultatives are common in Icelandic, e.g. (33), and sufficiently productive to occur in novel rhetorical uses, e.g. (34).

(33)   að öskra,   tromma,   klappa   og   stappa   sig
      to   scream   drum   clap   and   stamp   oneself.M.ACC.SG
      brjálaðan
      crazy.M.ACC.SG
      'to scream, drum, clap and stamp yourself crazy'

(34)   Síminn   getur bara hringt sig   hásan.
      phone=the can   just   ring   itself.M.ACC.SG hoarse.M.ACC.SG
      'the phone can just ring itself hoarse'

However, the restriction to reflexive object is extremely strong in Icelandic. None of the standard examples in the literature of unergatives with disjoint reference objects (cf. (35) and (36)) translate naturally into Icelandic.

(35)   *Hundurinn gelti   hann   vakinn/vakandi.
       dog=the   barked   him.M.ACC.SG awoken.M.ACC.SG /awake
       'the dog barked him awake'

(36)   *Háværa klukkan   tifaði barnið
       noisy   clock=the ticked child.N.ACC.SG=the.N.ACC.SG
       vakið/vakandi.
       woken.N.ACC.SG /awake
       'The noisy clock ticked the child awake'

Whelpton (2006) does offer an example of an adjectival resultative with an unergative verb and a pronoun referring to a body part.

(37)   Ég svaf hana   [öxlina]   flata   í
       I   slept it.F.ACC.SG [shoulder=the] flat.F.ACC.SG in
       fyrrinótt
       night-before-last
       'I slept it [my shoulder] flat the night before last'

However, this is the exception which proves the rule as body-part reference is not truly disjoint. Whelpton (2006) also footnotes a crude sexual example taken from the internet which has a true disjoint reference object.

(38)   Geir þoldi ekki lengi   við   og   brundaði rassinn   hennar fullan.
       Geir bore   not longer with and ejaculated arse=the her   full.
       'Geir could not bear it any longer and ejaculated her arse full.'

This is the only example I am aware of with a disjoint reference object and even here the context implies, shall we say, a merger of individuals. The general pattern therefore seems to be that with an unergative verb and an adjectival resultative, the object cannot refer to an entirely distinct participant. The key point for us here is that this restriction does not apply to transitive verbs.

(39)   að nudda þá   slétta
       to rub   them.M.ACC.PL smooth.M.ACC.PL
       'to rub them smooth'

(40)   Hann skrúbbaði pönnurnar   hreinar.
       he   scrubbed   pan.F.ACC.PL=the.F.ACC.PL clean.F.ACC.PL
       'he scrubbed the pans clean'

If all verbs appearing in resultatives are really unergatives in disguise, this contrast is mysterious.

Pseudo-transitives add an interesting wrinkle here in that they behave like transitives rather than unergatives, even though their objects are unselected.

(41)   Hann reif hurðina   opna
      he   tore door.F.ACC.SG=the.F.ACC.SG open.F.ACC.SG
      'he tore the door open'

(42)   Þeir dældu   hana   fulla   af lyfjum
      they pumped her.F.ACC.SG full.F.ACC.SG of drugs
      'They pumped her full of drugs'

This suggests, once again, that the issue at stake is not object selection. For some reason it appears to be enough that transitive verbs are associated with a transitive structure ($v + V$), even if the object that appears is not selected by V.

With unergative verbs, the issue is therefore (potential) transitivity rather than object selection *per se*; with unaccusative verbs, it is inchoativity (specification of a final state; selection of *res*) rather than the presence of an internal argument. Data from Icelandic therefore undermines Hoekstra's unergative generalization, as adopted by Kratzer.

6.3.3 *Resultative Predicates and Parameters*

Kratzer (2005) assumes that only adjectives and not prepositions form true resultatives. Evidence from Icelandic strongly supports a distinction between the properties of adjectival and prepositional resultatives. However, the contrast is not simply between adjectival change-of-state resultatives and prepositional goal-of-motion constructions. Rather, PP change-of-state resultatives differ systematically from AP change-of-state resultatives; and relative-location AP resultatives differ from AP change-of-state resultatives.

All the differences between Icelandic and English resultatives with unaccusatives and unergatives discussed above disappear when the resultative predicate is a PP. So, PP resultatives co-occur freely with inchoative unaccusatives in Icelandic.

(43)   Tjörnin fraus í   gegn.
      lake-the froze in through
      'the lake froze through'

(44)   Pakkinn   rifnaði upp á   hornunum.
      package.M.NOM.SG=the.M.NOM.SG tore   up   at corners=the
      'the package tore open at the corners'

Recall Folli and Ramchand's (2005) proposal that P projects its own specifier and so is independent of the *res* which introduces it, whereas A cannot project a specifier on its own and is dependent on a specific *res* head to do this work for it. The suggestion was that only null *res* 'x have property y' is able to co-project a specifier in this way. It is therefore not surprising that PPs and particles appear as the complements of inchoative *res* but that APs appear as the complements only of null *res* with activity verbs.

Why then do inchoatives appear with *fastur* 'stuck'? *Fastur* may be an adjective but it shares with prepositions the fact that it does not express a simple quality of an entity but rather a locational relation between two entities (the two entities are fixed in contact with each other). It may be that this relational property of prepositions is precisely what allows them to project their own specifier but prevents qualitative adjectives from doing so. As *fastur* has the relevant relational semantics it can project its own specifier and is hence independent of the *res* which introduces it, just as PPs are. It can therefore occur with inchoative *res*. Once again, this is not an isolated property of Icelandic. We have already seen that German, like Icelandic, does not form natural resultatives of the form 'freeze solid'; cf. (32c). However, relational *fest* does occur, just as in Icelandic, as shown in the internet example in (45).

(45)   ... dass die gekühlte Katheterspitze so im Wasser fest gefroren ist,
       that the chilled   catheter-rod so in water   fast frozen   is,
       dass man das Glas mit   dem Katheterschaft anheben kann.
       that one the glass with the   catheter-shaft pick-up can.
       '...that the chilled catheter rod has frozen so fast in the water that
       you can pick up the glass by the shaft of the catheter.'

Even in English, which appears to be exceptional in allowing AP resultatives with inchoatives, it is striking that the two examples of adjectival resultatives which are frequently cited as violating the Direct Object Restriction are also relative-location adjectives, 'clear' and 'free', in the sense of 'away from/away from contact with'.

(46)   a. The sailors managed to catch a breeze and ride it clear of the rocks.
          (Wechsler 1997: 313, ex.15)
       b. She danced/swam free of her captors.
          (Levin and Rappaport Hovav 1995: 186)

Unlike the Icelandic and German examples, these are however direct motion and not change-of-state constructions. The adjectives *clear* and *free* are here describing a path of motion, like typical prepositions. This suggests the

TABLE 1. Typology of motion verbs in resultative and directed motion constructions.

Manner of motion verbs	Change-of-state (Unergative)	Goal-of-motion (Unaccusative)
AP	He danced himself dizzy	He danced free of his captors
PP	He danced himself into a frenzy	He danced into the room

following four-way typology with change-of-state constructions obeying the Direct Object Restriction and goal-of-motion constructions not.

This leaves a final contrast between PP and AP resultatives. Unergative verbs with PP resultatives allow disjoint reference objects (where AP resultatives do not).

(47)   Kisan   malaði mig í   svefn
       cat=the purred me to sleep
       'the cat purred me to sleep'

(48)   Við hlupum sólana   af skónum
       we ran   soles=the off shoes=the
       'we ran the soles off our shoes'

Why this should be remains an unsolved problem but it is not explained by Hoekstra's unergative-only hypothesis (which indeed predicts that there should be no such effect). Nor is the contrast explained in an obvious way by Ramchand's *res*. However, the fine-grained distinctions allowed in Ramchand's system, as well as the space provided for interactions between verbal and prepositional functions, suggests that this may be a fruitful framework for exploring this curious interpretive constraint. It remains a matter for future research.

6.4 Conclusions

Evidence from Icelandic therefore undermines two central claims of Krazter's account, that covert compounding of resultative adjectives blocks agreement inflection and that verbs used in resultatives necessarily behave as unergatives. The distinction between adjectival and prepositional resultatives is strongly supported but clearly must be extended to recognize the semantic distinction between qualities and relative locations. This semantic distinction in turn appears to have implications for the projection of functional structure in the syntax. Given the subtle interactions between functional properties of the verb and of the resultative predicate, a microparametric approach which considers the fine-grained lexicalization of functional structure offers the most promising way forward in understanding this construction and its cross-linguistic variation.

7

Categorization and the Interface Levels

JAMAL OUHALLA

7.1 Introduction

Parts-of-speech categorization seems to be a basic and necessary property of language, yet there are radically divergent views about it in the main linguistic traditions. According to a mainstream view in the functionalist tradition (Hopper and Thompson 1984; Givón 1984; Croft 1991), category distinctions are rooted in meaning (semantics, pragmatics) and operate on the basis of relevant prototypical distinctions with fluid boundaries that yield categories with overlapping properties.[1] In the generative tradition, category distinctions were initially based on the lexically specified specialized features $[\pm V]$ and $[\pm N]$, combinations of which were thought to account for categories with mixed properties, e.g. adjectives (Chomsky 1970, 1981; Bresnan 1982). These features were later concluded by some linguists to be inadequate and consequently supplemented with other features, some contextual (Jackendoff 1977; Hale and Keyser 1993) and others semantic in nature that make reference to concepts such as predication and referentiality (Déchaine 1993; Baker 2003).[2]

The debate concerning parts-of-speech categorization within the generative tradition acquired a new dimension in Minimalism and Distributed

---

[1] Newmeyer (1998: ch. 4) includes an evaluation of the functionalist approach to categorization, which casts doubt on the relevance of the notion of prototype to grammar, although it concedes that it may play a role in the acquisition of vocabulary.

[2] Baker (2003) does away with category features and replaces them with properties that appear to be syntactic-semantic in nature. Verbs are defined by their unique ability to license a subject that they typically theta-mark and therefore are true predicates. Nouns are defined by their equally unique ability to bear an index, and therefore are true arguments, referential expressions. Adjectives are defined relative to verbs and nouns by not having any of the defining properties of verbs and nouns. They are neither verbs nor nouns.

Morphology. In Minimalism, lexically valued features are expected to be interpretable at the LF/Meaning Interface (have relevance to meaning), but it is not clear that specialized category features have this property. This led Chomsky (2001: 7) to conclude that category features reduce to independently needed features. This development coincided with the claim in Distributed Morphology (Halle and Marantz 1993) that the lexicon consists of category-neutral roots and that categorization results from the combination of roots with certain functional heads in syntax such that $[\sqrt{}\text{-}v] = $ Verb, $[\sqrt{}\text{-}n] = $ Noun and so on. Two main views have emerged concerning the nature of the relevant features of the functional heads responsible for categorization. According to Marantz (1997), the features are essentially semantic in nature as they interact with the semantic features of roots to determine, among other things, whether a lexical category has an agent/causer. On the other hand, Embick (2000) and Ouhalla (2005) argue that the features are morphosyntactic in nature such that lexical categories are essentially morphosyntactic objects rather than semantic-syntactic objects. More detailed summaries of these two main views are given in sections 7.2 and 7.3 of this chapter.

Details apart, it is possible to discern three different views in the main linguistic traditions concerning parts-of-speech categorization, with roots that go back in history to include the old Greek and Semitic linguistic traditions. One view holds that categorization operates on the basis of semantic features and therefore is necessarily related to meaning. The other view holds that categorization operates on the basis of formal, morphosyntactic features, specialized or otherwise, and is not necessarily related to meaning. The third view argues that both types of features are necessary for an adequate theory of categorization. One of the main objectives of this chapter is to show that these views are not necessarily in competition with each other and that they are a function of the design of language, namely the interface levels Syntax-LF/Semantics and Syntax-PF/Morphology in addition to the internal interface level Lexicon-Syntax.

The discussion will assume the model in (1), which incorporates Distributed Morphology's view of the lexicon as consisting of three lists, two of which are of concern here. One list, called '(narrow) lexicon' consists of category-neutral roots in the form of semantic features and functional heads in the form of bundles of semantic and morphosyntactic features. This list precedes syntax as it includes the objects that syntax makes use of. Another list, called vocabulary, consists of morphemes with phonological features inserted under appropriate terminal nodes at PF (vocabulary insertion).

(1)   Vocabulary   →   PF/Morphology   LF/Meaning

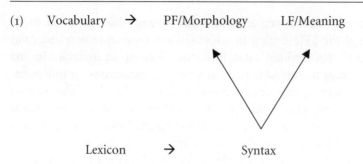

Lexicon   →   Syntax

To the extent that categorization necessarily involves functional heads, inevitable on the view that roots are acategorial, and to the extent that functional heads are bundles of semantic and morphosyntactic features, it follows that lexical categories can be defined either in terms of the semantic (or semantic-syntactic) features of the relevant functional heads or their morphosyntactic features or both. However, this is expected to be true only of syntax, where both types of features are present. It is not expected to be necessarily true of the interface levels, where categories are defined in terms of either semantic-syntactic features (LF/Meaning) or morphosyntactic features (PF/Morphology). A basic tenet of Minimalism is that uninterpretable features such as the agreement features of verbs, participles, adjectives, and derived nouns, delete before the derivation reaches the LF/Meaning interface. Another main objective of this chapter is to show that categorization in terms of these different types of features yields different classes with different membership patterns. Categorization in terms of semantic-syntactic features yields at least four classes (verbs, participles, adjectives, and derived nouns) with overlapping membership such that a given category can be partly verbal and adjectival. Moreover, the classes are broadly similar across languages. In contrast, categorization in terms of morphosyntactic features is language-specific, a by-product of the morphological peculiarities of languages and their vocabulary. In the case of Standard Arabic discussed here, it yields a strict binary distinction that opposes verbs to non-verbs (participles, adjectives, and derived nouns).

7.2 Categorization and the Syntax-LF/Meaning Interface

This section includes a presentation of the approach to categorization outlined in Marantz (1997) based on lexical semantic features (section 7.2.1) and a demonstration of the type of category distinctions it yields when applied to data from Standard Arabic (section 7.2.2). Both presentations are brief and sketchy in parts.

7.2.1 *Semantic-Syntactic Categorization*

Marantz (1997) outlines an approach to categorization which takes the form of associating category-neutral roots with designated functional heads understood as 'semantic categories' or bundles of syntactic-semantic features. Roots come in different semantic classes depending, in the case of those that denote change of state, on whether the change is internally or externally caused. The examples repeated in (2a–c) are used to illustrate some of the relevant classes of roots.

(2)   a. $\sqrt{\text{DESTROY}}$:   change of state, not internally caused (so implies external cause or agent)
       b. $\sqrt{\text{GROW}}$:   change of state, internally caused
       c. $\sqrt{\text{BREAK}}$:   result (of change of state)

The functional heads responsible for categorization also come in different classes or 'flavours' that seem to reflect corresponding properties of roots. The functional head responsible for deriving verbs can either be of the type that projects an agent (*v-1*) or the type that does not project an agent (*v-2*), where *v* is understood to be 'aspectual in some sense'. The second type is incompatible with roots that imply an agent such as $\sqrt{\text{DESTROY}}$. The verb based on this root includes *v-1* instead (3a and b).

(3)   a. John destroyed the city.
       b. [v-1 [$\sqrt{\text{DESTROY}}$]]

The corresponding -*ing*-nominalization also co-occurs with *v-1*, its external nominal property being the consequence of embedding [*v-1* [$\sqrt{\text{DESTROY}}$]] under D (4a and b). According to this analysis, -*ing*-nominalizations are essentially 'nouns made from verbs'. In contrast, the nominalization in (5a) does not include *v-1*. The agentive reading of *John* in (5a), rather than implying *v-1*, is the manifestation of the property of the root as implying an external agent or cause. Unlike -*ing*-nominalizations, nominalizations of the type in (5a) are not 'nouns made from verbs'. They have the representation shown in (5b), where the root is nominalized in the context of D.

(4)   a. John's destroying the city
       b. [D [*v-1* [$\sqrt{\text{DESTROY}}$]]]

(5)   a. John's destruction of the city, the destruction of the city
       b. [D [$\sqrt{\text{DESTROY}}$]]

Unlike $\sqrt{\text{DESTROY}}$, the root $\sqrt{\text{GROW}}$ is non-agentive and therefore co-occurs with *v-2* in sentences such as (6a). Its causative-transitive use in contexts such as (7a) involves addition of *v-1* in syntax, possibly along the lines shown in (7b).

(6)   a. Tomatoes are growing.
      b. [*v-2* [$\sqrt{\text{GROW}}$]]

(7)   a. John grows tomatoes.
      b. [*v-1* [*v-2* [$\sqrt{\text{GROW}}$]]]

The remaining details are not of major concern to the purposes of this article. The main point is that the functional heads responsible for categorization, in particular *v*, have semantic features that interact with similar features of roots to yield verbs and nominalizations that are internally verbal. Although this is not explicitly stated, *v* has morphosyntactic syntactic features as well, including those that determine the case form of the internal argument. The presence of *v-1* correlates with accusative case for the internal argument (verbs and *-ing*-nominalizations) and its absence correlates with the absence of accusative case for the internal argument (*destruction*-type of nominalizations) (Burzio's Generalization). A version of this approach is applied to data from Standard Arabic in the remainder of this section.

7.2.2 *Voice-Aspect*

The Standard Arabic paradigm in (8a–f) includes the trilateral root $\sqrt{KTB}$ 'to do with writing' and the various lexical categories derived from it. The derived noun form is not included in the paradigm as its internal structure and derivation raise issues that cannot be reasonably be dealt with in this chapter (see below).

(8) $\sqrt{KTB}$ 'to do with writing'
      a. KaTaB   'active perfective verb'
      b. KuTiB   'passive perfective verb'
      c. KTuB   'active imperfective verb'
      d. uKTaB   'passive imperfective verb'
      e. KaaTiB   'active participle'
      f. ma-KTuuB   'passive participle'

The first point to notice in relation to (8a–f) is that categorization results from the mapping of the root onto specific vocalic patterns (and a prefix in the case of passive participles), which broadly correspond to a category that can be described as Voice-Aspect (Fassi Fehri 1993). In view of this, it makes little sense to assign a category identity to the root. Moreover, to the extent that the vocalic patterns correspond to independent functional heads in syntactic structures, categorization takes place in syntax and results from the association of the root with the functional heads corresponding to the vocalic patterns. These conclusions are reached in Ouhalla (1988) on the basis of an interpretation of ideas from the old Semitic tradition in linguistics.

Starting with verbs, the root in (8a–f) is of the type that selects *v-1*, which projects an agent/causer. This type of *v* can either have an active value [act] or a passive value [pass], which accounts for the fact that the verbs in the paradigm show an active-passive distinction. The active value correlates with accusative case for the internal argument (9a), while the passive value does not (9b). In the latter case, the internal argument appears in the nominative form in the subject position. The exact status of the (implicit) agent/causer argument in the passive form is left open as it is not crucially relevant to the purposes of discussion here.

(9) a. katab-a   al-walad-u   al-dars-a.
        write.act.perf-3.m.s   the-boy-nom   the-lesson-acc
        'The boy wrote the (class) lesson.'

    b. kutib-a   al-dars-u.
        write.pass.perf-3ms   the-lesson-nom
        'The (class) lesson was written.'

While the active-passive voice distinction is associated with *v-1*, the perfective-imperfective aspectual distinction is associated with the functional head Asp (Fassi Fehri 1993; Ouhalla 1988, 1990, 1991). The type of aspect that yields the perfective-imperfective distinction is understood here, following standard ideas (Comrie 1976; Smith 1991; Klein 1995; Demirdache and Etxebarria 2000), to be concerned with the temporal structure of situations, whether they are viewed from the outside as a whole with a beginning and an end or from inside as in progress. This type of aspect interacts closely with the other temporal category Tense, which is deictic in nature and locates situations relative to utterance time. We will see below that the close connection between the two types of temporal categories is often reflected in head-raising of Asp to T that yield forms whereby the aspectual form implicitly conveys tense distinctions.[3]

---

[3] This type of aspect is to be kept separate from another type variously called inner aspect (Borer 2005; Travis 2000; Verkuyl 1993) and situation aspect (Smith 1991), which interacts with argument structure. Whether this particular aspect too corresponds to an inner Asp node or is encoded in *v* as suggested by its description in Marantz (1997) as being 'aspectual in some sense' is left open here.

(10) a. yaktubu   al-walad-u   al-dars-a.
         write.act.imperf.3.m.s   the-boy-nom   the-lesson-acc
         'The boy writes the (class) lesson.'

      b. yuktabu   al-dars-u.
         write.pass.imperf-3ms   the-lesson-nom
         'The (class) lesson is written.'

Accordingly, sentences with the active form of verbs can be assigned the syntactic representation shown in (11a) and sentences with the passive form the structure shown in (11b). The various verb forms are derived by head-raising of $\sqrt{}$ to v[act/pass] followed by raising of this complex to Asp[(im) perf]. Further raising to T is discussed in section 7.3. Accusative case is assigned by v[act] but not v[pass], and nominative case is assigned by T. The representation in (11b) does not show raising of DP-nom to the grammatical subject position, which is irrelevant to the purposes of discussion.

(11) a. [$_{TP}$ T [$_{AspP}$ Asp[(im)perf] [$_{vP}$ [DP-nom] [$_{v'}$ v-1[act][$_{\sqrt{P}}$ $\sqrt{}$ [DP-acc] ...
      b. [$_{TP}$ T [$_{AspP}$ Asp[(im)perf] [$_{vP}$ v-1[pass] [$_{\sqrt{P}}$ $\sqrt{}$ [DP-nom] ...

Participles too show an active-passive voice distinction, though not a perfective-imperfective aspectual distinction. The voice distinction correlates with the same case properties for the internal argument. Active participles correlate with accusative case for the internal argument, while passive participles do not. Their internal argument appears in the nominative form, as with passive verbs. The element glossed as PRON in (12a and b) is a pronominal form that agrees in person, number, and gender with the subject and corresponds to INFL/T (Doron 1986; Eid 1983, 1991).

(12) a. al-walad-u   (huwwa)   kaatib-un   al-dars-a.
         the-boy-nom   PRON.3.m.s   write.act.part-ms.nom   the-lesson-acc
         'The boy writes the (class) lesson.'

      b. al-dars-u   (huwwa)   maktuub-un.
         the-lesson-nom   PRON.3.m.s   write.pass.part-m.s.nom
         'The (class) lesson is written.'

The absence of a morphological perfective-imperfective distinction in participles could simply be a function of the absence of the Asp[(im)perf] category in its structure. This essentially amounts to the claim that participles correspond to a structure that includes v-1 and a compatible root but no Asp[(im) perf] (13b). Otherwise, participles are similar to verbs that derive from the same root in that they include v-1.

(13)   a.   [$_{AspP}$ Asp[(im)perf] [$_{vP}$ *v-1*[act/pass] [$_{\sqrt{P}}$ $\sqrt{}$... (= Verb)
       b.   [$_{vP}$ *v-1*[act/pass] [$_{\sqrt{P}}$ $\sqrt{}$...   (= Participle)

Accordingly, sentences (12a&b) have the structures roughly shown in (14a and b), which do not show raising of DP-nom to Spec,T. PRON corresponds to T as observed above. Such sentences are described in the Semitic tradition as nominal or verbless, which in the current context reduces to the absence of Asp[(im)perf].

(14)   a.   [$_{TP}$ T (=PRON) [$_{vP}$ [DP-nom] [$_{v'}$ *v-1*[act] [$_{\sqrt{P}}$ $\sqrt{}$... [DP-acc]...
       b.   [$_{TP}$ T (= PRON) [$_{vP}$ *v-1*[pass] [$_{\sqrt{P}}$ $\sqrt{}$... [DP-nom]...

The conclusion that participles lack Asp[(im)perf] is consistent with the fact that they are compatible with D as is the case in attributive contexts such as (15). To the extent that such contexts do not involve a temporal structure of situations anchored in time by Tense, the fact that participles occur in them amounts to evidence that they lack Asp[(im)perf]. Because verbs include Asp[(im)perf], they are only compatible with T, and because participles do not include Asp[(im)perf], they are compatible with both T and D. Participles embedded under D have the representation roughly shown in (16), which abstracts away from structural derivational details affecting the argument/modified noun.

(15)   al-dars-u   al-maktuub-u
       the-lesson-m.s.nom   the-write.pass.part-m.s.nom
       'the written lesson'

(16)   [$_{DP}$ D [$_{vP}$ *v-1/2*[act/pass] [$_{\sqrt{P}}$ $\sqrt{}$...

Although the narrow structure corresponding to participles lacks Asp[(im) perf], it does not follow that all sentences with a participle necessarily lack Asp[(im)perf]. It is possible for a sentence with a participle to have Asp[(im) perf], as is the case in periphrastic sentences with the auxiliary BE in addition to a participle. The auxiliary can either be in the perfective or imperfective form and the participle can either be in the active or passive form. Example (17) includes the perfective form of the auxiliary and the passive form of the participle. Such sentences are classified in the tradition as being verbal compared to the ones with PRON.

(17)   kaan-a   al-dars-u   maktuub-an.
       be.perf-3.m.s   the-lesson-nom   write.pass.part-m.s.acc
       'The lesson was written.'

Periphrastic sentences such as (17) have the structure shown in (18), which is identical to that of sentences with a main verb alone (11a and b). The difference between the two types of sentences is derivational and has to do with head-raising discussed in more detail in section 7.3. To anticipate, in (11a and b) head-raising derives a single head-complex that includes $\sqrt{}$, *v-1*, Asp[(im) perf], and T and that corresponds to a verb. In (18), however, head-raising derives two head-complexes. One consists of $\sqrt{}$ and *v-1* and corresponds to a participle, and the other consists of Asp[(im)perf] and T and corresponds to BE.

(18)   [$_{TP}$ T [$_{AspP}$ Asp[perf] (=BE) [$_{vP}$ *v-1*[pass] [$_{\sqrt{}P}$ $\sqrt{}$ [DP-nom] ...

Next, consider the paradigm in (19a–c), which includes the stative root $\sqrt{KBR}$ 'to do with (become) big'. The paradigm includes an adjective form and verb forms, but no participle forms. Moreover, the verb forms show a perfective-imperfective aspect distinction, but not an active-passive voice distinction.

(19) $\sqrt{KBR}$ '(become) big'
     a. KaBiiR   'adjective'
     b. KaBuR   'perfective verb'
     c. aKBuR   'imperfective verb'

The properties of the paradigm in (19a–c) are reducible to the claim that stative roots are only compatible *with v-2*, which does not project an agent/causer. The absence of an active-passive distinction is a function of the fact that only verbs that have an agent/causer, that is, verbs that include *v-1*, can be passivized. In other words, the active-passive distinction is a property of *v-1*, but not *v-2*. The verbs in (19b and c) are neither active nor passive, although they resemble passive verbs in that they do not assign accusative case to their internal argument (the parallelism between passive and unaccusative verbs in Burzio's Generalization). The internal argument of stative verbs appears in the nominative form, as shown in (20). The latter has the syntactic representation shown in (21), which includes Asp[(im)perf].

(20)   kabur-a   al-wlad-u.
     become.big.perf-3ms   the-boy-nom
     'The boy has become big/has grown.'

(21)   [$_{TP}$ T [$_{AspP}$ Asp[perf] [$_{vP}$ *v-2* [$_{\sqrt{}P}$ $\sqrt{}$ [DP-nom] ...

Adjectives are to forms that include a stative root and therefore *v-2* what participles are to forms that include a non-stative root and therefore *v-1*. Participles were concluded above to correspond to a structure that includes a non-stative root and therefore *v-1*, but no Asp[(im)perf]. Likewise, adjectives correspond to a structure that includes a stative root and therefore *v-2*, but no Asp[(im)perf] along the lines shown in (22). This simultaneously accounts for the absence of participle forms derived from stative roots and the absence of a perfective-imperfective distinction with adjectives.[4]

(22)   [$_{vP}$ *v-2* [$_{\sqrt{P}}$ $\sqrt{}$ ... (=Adjective)

In predicative contexts such as (23), the adjective is embedded under T along the lines shown in (24). Like its counterpart with a participle above, (23) belongs to the group of nominal or verbless sentences, characterized by the lack of Asp[(im)perf].

(23)   al-bayt-u   (huwwa)   kabiir-un.
       the-house-m.s.nom   PRON:3.m.s   big-m.s.nom
       'The house is big.'

(24)   [$_{TP}$ T (= PRON) [$_{vP}$ *v-2* [$_{\sqrt{P}}$ $\sqrt{}$ (= Participle) [DP-nom] ...

In attributive contexts such as (25), the adjective is embedded under D along the lines shown in (26). As with participles, the absence of Asp[(im)perf] accounts for the ability of adjectives to be embedded under D. In other words, because adjectives lack Asp[(im)perf], they are compatible with both T and D.

(25)   al-bayt-u   al-kabiir-u
       the-house.m.s-nom   the-big.m.s-nom
       'the big house'

(26)   [$_{DP}$ D [$_{vP}$ *v-2* [$_{\sqrt{P}}$ $\sqrt{}$ ...

As with participles too, although the narrow structure that corresponds to adjectives lacks Asp[(im)perf], it does not follow that all sentences with a predicative adjective necessarily lack Asp[(im)perf]. Periphrastic sentences with an auxiliary BE and a predicative adjective such as (27) have a structure that includes Asp[(im)perf]. The structure, shown in (28), is identical to that of sentences with a stative verb. The difference between the two types of sentences is derivational and involves the scope of head-raising. In sentences with a stative verb, head-raising derives a single head-complex that includes $\sqrt{}$, *v-2*, Asp[(im)perf], and T, which corresponds to a stative verb. In their periphrastic counterparts, head-raising derives two head-complexes. One includes $\sqrt{}$ and *v-2* and corresponds to an adjective,

---

[4] According to this analysis, the distinction between 'verbal passives' and 'adjectival passives' reduces to the distinction between participles and adjectives. This is consistent with the view in Marantz (1997) that 'adjectival passives' are 'really, stative'.

and the other includes Asp[(im)perf] and T and corresponds to BE (see section 7.3 for more detail).[5]

(27) kaan-a   al-bayt-u   kabiir-an.
      be.perf-3.m.s the-house-nom   big-m.s.acc
      'The house was big.'

(28) [$_{TP}$ T [$_{AspP}$ Asp[perf] (= BE) [$_{vP}$ v-2 [$_{\sqrt{P}}$ $\sqrt{}$ (= Adjective) [DP-nom] ...

7.2.3 *Summary and Conclusions*

The classification of lexical categories in terms of v-Asp, understood as bundles of semantic-syntactic features, yields the distinction between verbs, participles, and adjectives. All three categories have v, but differ with respect to its features/values, which are reducible to related features of the roots it combines with. Verbs based on non-stative roots have v-1[act/pass], which shows an active-passive distinction. Verbs based on stative roots have v-2, which does show an active-passive distinction. Participles have v-1[act/pass], but adjectives have v-2. Participles are to non-stative verbs what adjectives are to stative verbs. Thus, all three categories are internally similar in that they include some form of v. Verbs include Asp[(im)perf] in addition, and therefore are compatible with T but not D. Participles and adjectives lack Asp[(im)perf] and therefore are compatible with both T and D. The next section shows how these semantic-syntactic properties correlate with agreement features to yield a different type of categorization at the syntax-PF interface level.[6]

7.3 Categorization and the Syntax-PF/Morphology Interface

This section includes brief outlines of the approaches to categorization based on morphosyntactic features outlined in Embick (2000) and Ouhalla (2005)

---

[5] There is a major difference between verbless sentences with PRON and a participle/adjective and periphrastic sentences with BE and a participle/adjective. In the former, the participle/adjective bears nominative case, traditionally thought of as an instance of concord with the subject. In the latter, however, the participle/adjective bears accusative case, traditionally thought to be governed by BE. This difference suggests an alternative structure for the periphrastic type whereby BE is a main verb of the raising type that takes the participle/adjective as its complement. I leave this issue open as it does not seem to have any significant implications for the issue of classification.

[6] As far as derived nouns are concerned, there is a widespread view in the literature on Semitic that they include a verb at least in contexts where they co-occur with an internal argument in the accusative form (Arad 1998, 2003; Fassi Fehri 1993; Hazout 1991, 1995; Ouhalla 1988, 1991; Siloni 1997). To the extent that the verb constituent corresponds to v, it is not clear if it is of type v-1 or type v-2 or a third type altogether in view of the fact that derived nouns do not exhibit an active-passive distinction. Presumably, the fact that derived nouns do not exhibit a perfective-imperfective aspectual distinction either implies that they lack Asp[(im)perf], which is consistent with the fact that they can co-occur with D on the account given here. Derived nouns raise other intriguing issues that are left for future research.

and a brief demonstration of their partly different consequences when applied
to Standard Arabic.

7.3.1 *Morphosyntactic Categorization*

Embick (2000) proposes an approach to parts-of-speech categorization that
treats lexical categories as 'morphological object[s]'. The approach is initially
based on capturing the distinction between verbs and participles in the Latin
Perfective (29), but is later generalized to other categories.

(29) *Perfect indicative active*   *Perfect indicative passive*
      1sg. am-ā-v-ī   1sg. am-ā-tus/-a/-um sum
      'I have loved'   'I was/have been loved'
      2sg. am-ā-v-istī   2sg. am-ā-t-us/-a/-im es
      'you have loved'   'you were/have been loved'

Embick argues that verbs and participles have the same constituent structure,
which consists of $\sqrt{}$, *v*, and Asp, and differ with respect to whether the
complex made up of these constituents raises to T or not. Raising to T results
in the derivation of verbs (30a) (Embick 2000: 213) and failure thereof results
in the derivation of participles (30b) (Embick 2000: 215). In the latter, failure
of raising to T is attributed to the presence in participles of the feature [pass]
claimed to be incompatible with T (Embick 2000: 205).[7] Instead, T is filled
with an auxiliary described as a 'sort of default instantiation of tense.'

(30) a. $[_{TP} [_T \sqrt{}-v\text{-Asp[perf]-T-Agr}] [_{AspP} t [_{vP} t [_{\sqrt{}P} t \ldots$
      b. $[_{TP} [_T \text{T-[be]-Agr}] [_{AspP} [_{Asp}\sqrt{}-v\textit{[pass]}\text{-Asp}] [_{vP} t [_{\sqrt{}P} t \ldots$

The analysis is extended to other lexical categories, including deverbal nouns
and adjectives. These resemble participles in that they fail to raise to T, although
for different reasons, including the absence of T in the case of deverbal nouns
(Embick 2000: 216–17). In the latter, the part of the structure corresponding to
the deverbal noun is included in a DP rather than a TP. Although this is not
stated in the article, the resulting classification is strictly binary in nature in that
it opposes verbs, which have T, to non-verbs (participles, deverbal nouns, and
adjectives), which lack T. The distinction does not allow for overlapping
membership and mixed categories of the type discussed above.

Ouhalla (2005) proposes an alternative approach that is also morphosyntactic in nature, but differs in that it bases the distinction on agreement
features, the archetypal morphosyntactic features that in the case of verbs,

---

[7] The incompatibility between T and [pass] is expressed in terms of the stipulation repeated in (i).
(i) [perf]Asp does not move to T when [pass] is present. (Embick 2000: 205)

participles, adjectives, and deverbal nouns have no relevance to meaning (are uninterpretable at LF). Verbs have person, in addition to gender and number, while non-verbs (participles, adjectives, and nouns) lack person and instead may have case, in addition to gender and number. This division can be seen in the Standard Arabic examples cited so far and others cited below. Verbs invariably bear person inflection, while participles, adjectives, and nouns do not (31a and b).

(31)   a. Person-set: Verbs
        b. Non-person-set: Participles, adjectives, and nouns

Like Embick's approach, this approach yields a binary distinction between lexical categories that opposes verbs, which have person, to non-verbs, which lack person. It differs in that it allows for categories with mixed feature-sets as is the case with at least first/second person pronouns on the view that they have person and case features. The two approaches are evaluated relative to relevant data from Standard Arabic in the remainder of this section.

7.3.2 *Tense*

As explained above, Embick (2000) defines verbs in terms of (raising to) T. Passive participles do not raise to T and therefore lack T. Both claims are inconsistent with Standard Arabic, where active imperfective verbs do not raise to T, and therefore lack T, and passive perfective verbs raise to T, and therefore have T.

There is straightforward evidence from Standard Arabic that perfective verbs, both active and passive, raise to T, while imperfective verbs, both active and passive, do not raise to T. The evidence is outlined and discussed in the literature (see Benmamoun 2000, Ouhalla 2002 and references cited therein) and is wide ranging in that it involves all contexts in which the two types of verbs may or may not occur. The presentation here is limited to negative sentences. Standard Arabic has two sentence negation markers. One is *maa*, which occupies a clause-peripheral position and does not bear tense. The other is *laa/lam/lan*, which occupies a clause-internal position and bears tense. Perfective verbs co-occur with the former (32a and b), while their imperfective counterparts co-occur with the latter (33a and b). This distribution cuts across the active-passive distinction.

(32)   a. maa   katab-a   al-wald-u   al-dars-a.
            neg   write.act.perf-3.m.s   the-boy-nom   the-lesson-acc
            'The boy did not write the lesson.'

b. maa   kutib-a   al-dars-u.
neg   write.pass.perf-3.m.s   the-lesson-acc
'The lesson was not written.'

(33) a. laa/lam/lan   yaktub   al-walad-u
         neg.pres/past/fut write.act.imperf.3.m.s   the-boy-nom
         al-dars-a.
         the lesson-acc
         'The boy is not writing/did/will not write the lesson.'

      b. laa/lam/lan   yuktab   al-dars-u.
         neg.pres/past/fut write.pass.imperf.3.m.s the-lesson-nom
         'The lesson is/was/will not (be) written.'

Negative sentences with a perfective verb have the structure and derivation shown in (34a and b), where the verb complex is located in T. Raising to T is unimpeded by Neg due to the latter's clause-peripheral position outside T.

(34) a. $[_{NegP}$ Neg ($=maa$) $[_{TP}$ T $[_{AspP}$ Asp[perf] $[_{vP}$ v[act/pass] $[_{\sqrt{P}}$ $\sqrt{}$...
      b. $[_{NegP}$ Neg ($=maa$)$[_{TP}$ $[[\sqrt{}]$-v[act/pass]-[Asp[perf]]]-T
      $[_{AspP}$...$[_{vP}$...$[_{\sqrt{P}}$...

Negative sentences with an imperfective verb have the structure and derivation shown in (35a and b), where the verb complex is located in Asp[imperf]. Raising of the verb complex T is blocked by Neg, which takes over the role of supporting tense via Neg-raising to T (Benmamoun 2000).

(35) a. $[_{TP}$ T $[_{NegP}$ Neg $[_{AspP}$ Asp[imperf] $[_{vP}$ v-1[act] $[_{\sqrt{P}}$ $\sqrt{}$...
      b. $[_{TP}$ [Neg]-T($=laa/lam/lan$)$[_{NegP}$...$[_{AspP}$ $[\sqrt{}]$-$[v$[act]]Asp
      [imperf] $[_{vP}$...$[_{\sqrt{P}}$...

Imperfective verbs pattern with participles and adjectives in this respect. These too co-occur with clause-internal negation in the form of what is often described in the literature as a negative auxiliary that inflects for subject agreement in addition to tense.

(36) a. la-ysa   al-walad-u   kaatib-an   al-dars-a.
         Neg-3ms the-boy-nom write.act.part.ms.acc the-lesson-acc
         'The boy is not writing the lesson.'

      b. la-ysa   al-dars-u   maktuub-an.
         neg-3.m.s the-lesson-nom write.pass.part-3.m.s.nom
         'The lesson is not written.'

(37)   la-ysa   al-bayt-u   kabiir-an.
        Neg.3.m.s the-house-nom big-m.s.acc
        'The house is not big.'

The sentences in (36a and b) and (37) have the structures and derivations shown in (38a and b) (participles) and (39a and b) (adjectives). Neg raises to T, deriving a head-complex that corresponds to the negative auxiliary. This pattern is essentially periphrastic in form and may involve an Asp category for the negative auxiliary, although this is not of major concern here.

(38)   a. [$_{TP}$ T [$_{NegP}$ Neg [vp v-1[act/pass] [$_{\sqrt{P}}$ $\sqrt{}$...
        b. [$_{TP}$ [Neg]-T (=$laysa$) [$_{NegP}$... [$_{vP}$ [$\sqrt{}$]-v-1[act/pass]]
           [$_{\sqrt{P}}$... (=Participle)

(39)   a. [$_{TP}$ T [$_{NegP}$ Neg [vp v-2 [$_{\sqrt{P}}$ $\sqrt{}$...
        b. [$_{TP}$ [Neg]-T (=$laysa$) [$_{NegP}$... [$_{vP}$ [$\sqrt{}$]-v-2 [$_{\sqrt{P}}$... (=Adjective)

It is clear that not all verbs necessarily raise to T and that the voice feature [pass] does not block raising to T and consequently is not responsible for the derivation of participles. The latter conclusion is trivially shown by the very existence of active participles in Standard Arabic, and arguably extends to morphological passives in general as opposed to periphrastic passives of the type found in Latin (Baker 1988; Ouhalla 1991).

7.3.3 *Agreement Features*

According to the analysis above, what verbs, both perfective and imperfective, have in common, which at the same time sets them apart from participles and adjectives, is Asp[(im)perf]. Verbs have Asp[(im)perf] while participles and adjectives lack this category. However, it is unclear if Asp[(im)perf] and *v* play a role in the classification of categories or for that matter in determining head-raising at PF. The reasoning extends to T on the assumption that tense features are semantic-syntactic in nature on a par with aspectual and voice features. More plausible candidates are the agreement features of verbs, participles, and adjectives, which are purely morphosyntactic in nature.

According to standard practice in Minimalism, functional heads are specified for bundles, sets of agreement features, which play a crucial role in syntactic derivation through the operation Agree. The claim here is that they also play a role in determining head-raising and consequently the derivation of head-complexes that correspond to various lexical categories. Association of functional heads with agreement features can take the form shown in (40a–c). The assignment of the person-set of agreement features to at least finite T is likely to be uniform across languages such that (40a) is arguably fixed for all languages. In comparison, the set of agreement features assigned to Asp[(im)perf] and v may vary across languages and even contexts within the same language. (40b and c) show the values/settings for Standard Arabic such that Asp[(im)perf] has the person-set while v can either have the person set or the non-person set.

(40)   a. T → T[agr:person]
       b. Asp[(im)perf] → Asp[agr:person]
       c. v → v[agr:person]/v[agr:case]

The agreement features assigned to functional heads, in particular Asp, can plausibly be view to determine head-raising to T.[8] The restriction in question can be stated as in (41), which is consistent with the independently established link between [person] and raising to T in connection to verbs (Rohbacher 1994; Vikner 1997) and indeed also clitic pronouns on the standard account that clitic movement targets T. As will be explained shortly, (41) has the desired effect of excluding participles and adjectives from raising to T on the grounds that their v has the wrong set of agreement features. Here again, the restriction may only apply to T in some languages. The formulation in (41) is tailored to Standard Arabic and similar languages.

(41)   Raising to T-Asp is restricted to categories or head-complexes with [person].

Prior to head-raising, sentences with a main verb alone such as (7a and b) and (8a and b) have the annotated representation shown in (42a), where v has the person-set of agreement features along with Asp. Raising of $\sqrt{}$ to v and of [$\sqrt{}$-v] to Asp apply in the derivation of both perfective and imperfective verbs. The difference lies in whether the head-complex [$\sqrt{}$-v-Asp] raises further to T or not. It does so in the derivation of perfective verbs (42b), but not in the derivation of imperfective verbs (42c). Both options are consistent with (41) along with raising of the head-complex [$\sqrt{}$-v] to Asp.

(42)   a. [$_{TP}$ T [$_{AspP}$ Asp[agr:pers] [$_{vP}$ v[agr:pers] [$_{\sqrt{P}}$ $\sqrt{}$...
       b. [$_{TP}$ [$\sqrt{}$-v-Asp[agr:pers]]+T [$_{AspP}$... [$_{vP}$... [$_{\sqrt{P}}$... (Perfective verbs)
       c. [$_{TP}$ T [$_{AspP}$ [$\sqrt{}$-v]+Asp[agr:pers]] [... [$_{vP}$... [$_{\sqrt{P}}$...
           (Imperfective verbs)

---

[8] In Ouhalla (1991), failure of participles and adjectives to raise to T is accounted for in terms of the assumption that these categories have the feature [N] in combination with the idea that T can attach to categories with the feature [V] (verbs) but not to categories with the feature [N] (participles and adjectives). The analysis here attempts to achieve the same outcome in terms of the independently needed agreement feature [person].

Verbless sentences with PRON and a participle or adjective such as (12a and b) and (23) have the annotated representation shown in (43a). It differs from the structure of sentences with a verb in that it lacks Asp, as concluded above. It also differs in that its v has the non-person set of agreement features. A person-set of features for v, which would permit raising to T, is arguably excluded on the morphological ground that the language lacks forms that correspond to the derived head-complex, that is, Aspectless verbs.

(43) a. $[_{TP}$ T $[vp$ $v[$agr:case$]$ $[_{\sqrt{P}}$ $\sqrt{}$...
    b. $[_{TP}$ T $(=$PRON$)$ $[vp$ $[\sqrt{}]+v$-$1[$agr:case$]$ $[_{\sqrt{P}}$...$($PRON$+$Participle$)$
    c. $[_{TP}$ T $(=$PRON$)$ $[vp$ $[\sqrt{}]+v$-$2[$agr:case$]$ $[_{\sqrt{P}}$...$($PRON$+$Adjective$)$

Periphrastic sentences with the auxiliary BE and a participle or an adjective such as (17) and (27) have the annotated structure shown in (44a). The structure is identical to that of sentences with a main verb alone in that it also includes Asp. It differs in that v is assigned a non-person set of agreement features, with implications for head-raising that result in a split between $[\sqrt{}$-$v]$ ($=$participle/adjective) and $[$Asp-T$]($=BE$)$. The choice between a simple pattern with the main verb alone and the periphrastic pattern with BE and a participle/adjective reduces as a function of the choice of the agreement features associated with v.[9]

(44) a. $[_{TP}$ T $[_{AspP}$ Asp$[$agr:pers$]$ $[vp$ $v[$agr:case$]$ $[_{\sqrt{P}}$ $\sqrt{}$...
    b. $[_{TP}$ $[$Asp$[$agr:pers$]]+$T$[_{AspP}$...$[vp$ $[\sqrt{}]+v$-$1[$agr:case$]$
       $[_{\sqrt{P}}$...$($BE$+$Participle$)$
    c. $[_{TP}$ $[$Asp$[$agr:pers$]]+$T$[_{AspP}$...$[vp$ $[\sqrt{}]+v$-$2[$agr:case$]$
       $[_{\sqrt{P}}$...$($BE$+$Adjective$)$

Finally, the proposed analysis is consistent with so-called complex tense sentences such as (45), which express the imperfective or progressive in the past. These sentences consist of the auxiliary BE in the perfective form and a main verb in the imperfective form. Their structure includes two Asp nodes, one has a [perf] value and is included in the auxiliary and the other has an

---

[9] A reviewer invoked the relevance of the concept of extended projection in the sense of Grimshaw (1991) and suggested an alternative formulation of the restriction on raising to T such that 'Only verbs can be part of an extended projection that includes T.' Indeed, it is conceivable that agreement features play a role in defining extended projections. Sentences with a main verb alone would be ones where v and Asp are both assigned a person-set of features along with T. Feature-matching then permits raising of v to Asp and v-Asp to T, resulting in the derivation of a tensed verb. Periphrastic sentences would in comparison be sentences where there is a split in agreement features such that v has the non-person set while Asp has the person-set along with T. Asp raises to T, resulting in an auxiliary. In contrast, v would be unable to raise to Asp, i.e. to be part of an extended projection that includes T-Asp, and consequently surfaces as a participle/adjective.

[imperf] value and is included in the imperfective verb. The auxiliary corresponds to the head-complex derived by raising of Asp[perf] to T, while the imperfective verb corresponds to a head-complex derived by raising of $[\sqrt{}+v]$ to Asp[imperf] along the lines shown in (46).

(45) kaana   al-walad-u   yaktubu   al-dars-a.
       be.perf.3.m.s   the-boy-nom   write.act.imperf.3.m.s   the-lesson-acc
       'The boy was writing the lesson.'

(46)   a. $[_{TP}$ T$[_{AspP}$ Asp[perf]/[agr:pers]$[_{AspP}$ Asp[imperf]/[agr:pers] $[_{vP}$
        v $[_{\sqrt{P}}$ $\sqrt{}$...
    b. $[_{TP}$ [Asp[perf]/[agr:pers]]+T $[_{AspP}$... (=BE)
       $[_{AspP}$ $[\sqrt{}$-$v]$+Asp[imperf]/[agr:pers] $[_{vP}$...$[_{\sqrt{P}}$...
       (= Imperfective verb)

7.3.4 *Summary and Conclusions*

There is a certain degree of overlap between the classification of categories in terms of semantic-syntactic features and their classification in terms of morphosyntactic features and head-raising. The structures of verbs include Asp and the head-complexes that correspond to verbs also include Asp. On the other hand, the structures of participles and adjectives do not include Asp and the head-complexes that correspond to participles and adjectives do not include Asp either. However, because head-raising is not sensitive to the semantic features of Asp and v, it does not make a distinction between verbs, participles, and adjectives. Instead, it makes a binary distinction between verbs on the one hand, and participles and adjectives on the other. This follows from the assumption here that head-raising is sensitive to the morphosyntactic features of agreement combined with the assumption that agreement features involve a binary opposition between person and case.

7.4 Conclusion

While the classification of lexical categories in terms of morphosyntactic features and head-raising may vary across languages, the classification in terms of semantic-syntactic features and constituent structure is expected to be uniform across languages. This is consistent with the view that variation is limited to PF. However, there is evidence of variation at both levels. This is the case with languages that lack adjectives (Bhat 1994; Dixon 1982; Hengeveld 1992; Schachter 1985). These languages include Berber, where the adjectival function is performed either by an attributive noun or a stative verb. Moreover, stative verbs show a perfective-imperfective aspectual distinction, though not an active-passive distinction, and bear the person-set of agreement features (Ouhalla 1988). In the present context, this would follow if Berber T were assumed to uniquely or obligatorily select Asp. Interestingly, the absence of adjectives in Berber appears to correlate with the absence of participles as well. There is one form in the language that is traditionally described as a participle on the grounds that it shows agreement in number and gender but not person. However, this form is restricted to subject extraction or anti-agreement contexts (Ouhalla 1993) and moreover shows both a passive-active voice distinction and a perfective-imperfective aspectual distinction. This form is essentially a verb that happens not to bear a non-person set of agreement features for reasons that have to do with subject extraction, at least on the analysis of anti-agreement outlined in Ouhalla (2005). The absence of participles from the language would also follow from the assumption that Berber T uniquely selects Asp given the parallelism drawn here between participles and adjectives. On a more general note, the existence of forms that show a mismatch between constituent structure and agreement features such as the so-called participle of Berber is not only consistent with the analysis proposed here, but arguably demonstrates the need to make a distinction between categorization in terms of semantic-syntactic features and constituent structure at the Syntax-LF interface and categorization in terms of morphosyntactic features and head-raising at the Syntax-PF interface.

8

Non-topical *wa*-phrases in Japanese*

REIKO VERMEULEN

8.1 Introduction

The information-structural status of an item, such as topic and focus, often influences its syntactic distribution. In this paper, I examine the syntactic distribution of topics in Japanese. The particle *wa* in this language is widely believed to be a marker for topic (Kuroda 1965; Kuno 1973). However, I will show that the syntactic distribution of a *wa*-marked item is at odds with the distribution of topics predicted by independent considerations at the interface between syntax and information structure: there are *wa*-marked items that show the predicted distribution of topics, but there are also *wa*-marked items that do not. I argue therefore that *wa*-marking is insufficient for identifying topics and *wa* should not be considered a topic marker. Rather, topics in Japanese should be identified solely on the basis of independently motivated discourse considerations. *Wa*-marked phrases identified as topics in this way display not only a distribution that is compatible with what is predicted by the interface considerations but also a set of syntactic properties that is not shared with those *wa*-phrases that are not identified as topics by the same considerations.

It is well known that at the level of information structure, a focus-background structure can be part of a comment, but a topic-comment structure cannot be embedded inside a background, an observation initially

* Earlier versions of this chapter were presented at Workshop on Information Structure/Syntax at Queen Mary, London 2007, LAGB 2007, Topicality Workshop at DGfS 2008, Information Structure session at CIL 18, 2008, and at UCLA 2008. I thank the organizers and participants at these events. I also thank Ad Neeleman, Vieri Samek-Lodovici, Kriszta Szendrői, Hans van de Koot, Hoji Hajime, and J.-R. Hayashishita for helpful discussion, an anonymous reviewer and my Japanese informants. This work is part of the output of an AHRC-funded project (Grant No. 119403) and a FWO-funded project (No. G091409).

noted by the Prague School (Hajičová *et al.* 1998).[1] This idea reflects the intuition that topic is an utterance-level notion, while focus is a propositional-level notion, and that utterances operate on propositions (Reinhart 1981; Krifka 2001, 2007; Tomioka 2009).

(1)   *Information structure*
  a.   topic [comment FOCUS [background ······]]
  b.   *FOCUS [background topic [comment ······]]

In relation to how such insights may be represented in the syntax, Rizzi (1997) and Neeleman and van de Koot (2008) have proposed that the sister constituent of a fronted topic is interpreted as its comment, while the sister constituent of a fronted focus is interpreted as its background, as illustrated below:

(2)   *Syntax—Information structure*

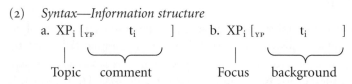

Neelemen and van de Koot argue that the two considerations in (1) and (2) together make predictions regarding the syntactic distribution of topic and focus, which are schematized in (3): a focus can follow a fronted topic, but a topic cannot follow a fronted focus. They show in detail that the predictions are borne out for Dutch. The cross-linguistic observation that topics generally precede foci also partially confirm these predictions (Hajičová *et al.* 1998).

(3)   a.   topic$_i$ [comment FOCUS [background t$_i$]]
  b.   *FOCUS$_i$ [background topic [comment t$_i$]]

In Japanese, however, a phrase marked with the putative topic marker *wa* can follow a fronted focus. Taking a constituent that answers the *wh*-part of a question to be focus, the object *John-o* 'John-acc' in the following exchange is a focus. As shown in (5b), the focus can be fronted to a position preceding the subject *wa*-phrase. Small capitals indicate an emphatic stress.

---

[1] For concreteness, I assume following Vallduví (1992) that information structure is a level of representation that mediates the mapping between surface syntax and a component that deals with pragmatic interpretation of sentences, just as LF mediates the mapping between syntax and semantic interpretation.

(4)   ano inu-wa dare-o   kande-simatta no?
      that dog-wa who-acc bite-ended.up Q
      'Who did the dog bite?'

(5)   a. ano inu-wa kinoo   kooen-de JOHN-O   kande-simatta
         that dog-wa yesterday   park-at John-acc bite-ended.up

      b. JOHN$_i$-o   ano inu-wa   kinoo   kooen-de t$_i$ kande-simatta
         John-acc   that dog-wa yesterday park-at   bite-ended.up
         'The dog bit John in the park yesterday.'

If the predictions in (3) are correct cross-linguistically, the post-focal *wa*-phrase in (5b) cannot be a topic. I argue that this is indeed the case. Concentrating mainly on *wa*-phrases that are not contrastive ('thematic' in Kuno's (1973) terminology), I provide arguments that it is not a topic, but is simply a discourse anaphoric item, in the sense that it has been previously mentioned (the notion 'topic' will be elaborated below). Specifically, I examine particular discourse contexts that require a topic and show that the word order in (5a), but not the one in (5b), is permitted in such contexts. The distribution of topics is in fact more restricted than what (3) suggests: they must occupy clause-initial position. I will demonstrate further syntactic differences between *wa*-phrases that must occupy clause-initial position and those that can appear in other positions.

In the next section, I will clarify the notion of 'topic' that this paper adopts. Section 8.3 illustrates that *wa*-phrases must occupy clause-initial position in discourse contexts requiring them to be topics. Section 8.4 provides evidence that *wa*-marking is available on items that are simply mentioned in the previous discourse. Such a *wa*-phrase need not, and sometimes cannot, appear clause-initially. Section 8.5 demonstrates that topic *wa*-phrases and discourse anaphoric *wa*-phrases are licensed in different syntactic configurations. Some implications of the findings for a theory of the syntax–information-structure interface are discussed in Section 8.6.

8.2 'Topic'

This paper is concerned with what is generally called 'sentence topic' rather than 'discourse topic'. Sentence topic is what the sentence is about and corresponds to a syntactic category, while discourse topic is what the whole discourse is about and can be more abstract (Reinhart 1981). I take the term 'sentence topic' to be further restricted, only referring to items that also affect the discourse topic, for example, by introducing one, reintroducing it, or shifting it from one item to another. This is roughly Givón's (1983) notion of 'chain-initial topic' and Vallduví's (1992) notion of 'link'.[2]

A sentence topic can be identified as the item *X* in the answer to the request *tell me about X*. Such a request is an explicit instruction to the hearer to introduce *X* as the discourse topic. Thus, *John* in (6B) is a sentence topic.

(6)   A: Tell me about John.
       B: John likes hiking.

That it is Speaker B who introduces *John* as the discourse topic, and not A, can be seen from the fact that B's utterance is still felicitous even if the request is less specific about what is to be the discourse topic, such as *tell me about someone in your class*.

Sentence topics must be distinguished from items that simply refer back to them (Vallduví 1992; Vallduví and Engdahl 1996; Neeleman *et al.* 2009). The point can be illustrated with the following discourse.

(7)   a. Maxine was introduced to the queen on her birthday.
       b. She was wearing a special dress for the occasion.

Uttered discourse-initially, *Maxine* in the example in (7a) is a sentence topic, introducing Maxine as the new discourse topic. The pronoun *her* in this utterance has the same referent as the discourse topic, but is not itself a sentence topic. It simply refers back to the discourse topic, indicating what other semantic role its referent plays in the event described by the sentence. By the same logic, I argue that the pronoun *she* in the subsequent utterance in (7b) only refers back to the discourse topic and is not a sentence topic itself. The utterance in (7b) can be described as an all-focus or all-comment structure where the discourse topic has been inherited from the previous utterance. Thus, the sentence in (7b) is understood as about the referent of the subject *she*, but this is so only because *she* happens to be anaphoric to the discourse topic.

The same considerations apply to the following type of exchange:

(8)   a. Who did Max see yesterday?
       b. He saw Rosa yesterday.

The pronoun *he* in (8b) is not a sentence topic. It refers back to the discourse topic Max, which is introduced as such in the preceding question in (8a). Thus, the information structure of the utterance in (8b) is that *Rosa* is the focus and the remaining items constitute the background. It is sometimes

---

[2] I refrain from using these terms however, as Givón also proposes several other types of topics and there are proposals that treat *wa*-phrases as links (e.g. Heycock 1993; Tomioka 2007). The data reported here are not compatible with either of these views.

assumed for this kind of context that the subject in the answer is a sentence topic (e.g., Reinhart 1981; Lambrecht 1994). However, there appears to be no reason why a pronominal that refers back to a discourse topic should also be a topic. An anaphoric item does not usually inherit the discourse-related properties of its antecedent. A pronoun that refers to a focus is not also therefore a focus, and a pronoun that refers to a contrastive topic is not therefore a contrastive topic.

In English, sentence topics are not necessarily marked overtly and can therefore be difficult to identify. However, the distinction mentioned above is formerly marked in some languages. For instance, in Catalan, the distinction reflects the direction of dislocation, i.e. left- or right-dislocation (Vallduví 1992). Frascarelli and Hinterhölzl (2007) also report similar syntactic and also prosodic effects of the distinction in Italian and German. I will show below that the distinction is crucial in explaining the syntactic distribution of *wa*-phrases in Japanese too. In sum, I will use the term 'topic' to refer to a sentence topic, i.e. a syntactic constituent that the sentence is about, that also affects the discourse topic.

8.3 The Syntactic Distribution of Topics

In Japanese, a topic must appear with *wa* and clause-initially. The point is illustrated below. The reply in (10b), in which the relevant *wa*-phrase is not in clause-initial position, is infelicitous. The sentence in (10b) is not ungrammatical, as it can be felicitously uttered in an exchange like (4)/(5b).

(9) ano   inu-nituite   osiete-kudasai.
     that   dog-about   tell-please
     'Tell me about that dog.'

(10) a. ano inu-wa   kinoo   kooen-de John-o   kande-simatta
         that dog-wa yesterday park-at   John-acc   bite-ended.up

     b. # John$_i$-o   ano inu-wa   kinoo   kooen-de t$_i$ kande-simatta
          John-acc   that dog-wa   yesterday park-at   bite-ended.up
          'The dog bit John in the park yesterday.'

Similarly, if the object in the reply is the topic, it must appear in clause-initial position (the nature of the empty category in (12a) will be discussed in section 8.5):

(11) ano boosi-nituite osiete-kudasai
     that hat-about   tell-please
     'Tell me about that hat.'

(12) a. ano boosi$_i$-wa   John-ga   kinoo e_i kaimasita
          that hat-wa   John-nom   yesterday   bought

      b. #John-ga   ano boosi-wa   kinoo   kaimasita[3]
          John-nom   that hat-wa   yesterday   bought
          'John bought that hat yesterday.'

Contrastive topics display the same pattern. Their typical functions include shifting the topic from one item to another. They are often compared to items that generally bear a B-accent in English or a rising pitch accent in German (Jackendoff 1972; Büring 1997, 2003, among others; for Japanese, see Hara 2006; Nakanishi 2007; Oshima 2008). Contrastive topics in Japanese are marked with *wa* and carry an emphatic stress. In the following discourse, information about John is requested in (13). Not knowing the relevant information regarding John, the speaker may provide the information about Bill, as in (14). In doing so, he has shifted the discourse topic from John to Bill, making *Bill-wa* a contrastive topic.[4] As the contrast between (14a) and (14b) demonstrates, *Bill-wa* must appear in clause-initial position.

(13) John-wa kinoo-no   party-de nani-o   tabeta no?
      John-wa yesterday-gen party-at what-acc ate   Q
      'What did John eat at the party yesterday?'

(14) Hmm, John-wa doo-ka   sira-nai   kedo,
      Hmm, John-wa how-whether know-not   but,
      'Well, I don't know about John, but...'

      a. BILL-WA 8-zi-goro   MAME-O   tabeteita   (yo)
          Bill-wa 8 o'clock-around   beans-acc was.eating particle

      b. #MAME$_i$-O BILL-WA 8-zi-goro t_i tabeteita (yo)
          beans-acc   Bill-wa 8 o'clock-around   was.eating particle
          'As for Bill, he was eating beans around 8 o'clock.'

Similarly, in (16), where the object in the answer, *mame-wa* 'beans-wa', is the contrastive topic, it must appear clause-initially.

---

[3] For reasons not entirely clear to me, an object *wa*-phrase does not surface easily adjacent to a verb. This may be due to the fact that an unstressed *wa*-phrase requires an intermediate phrase boundary following it (Nakanishi 2001 and references therein), while simplex verbs may not be preceded immediately by an intermediate phrase boundary (Nagahara 1994). Adverbials are inserted to avoid this effect. Following Neeleman and Reinhart (1998), I assume that a structure where the object precedes an adverbial can be base-generated, hence the absence of an empty position in (12b). This does not affect the discussion in the main text.

[4] The set-up of the context is due to Neeleman and van de Koot (2008).

(15) kinoo-no   party-de dare-ga   pasta-o   tabeta no?
      yesterday-gen party-at who-nom pasta-acc ate   Q
      'Who ate the pasta at the party yesterday?'

(16) Hmm, pasta-wa   doo-ka   sira-nai-kedo,
      Hmm, pasta-wa   how-whether know-not-but,
      'Well, I don't know about the pasta, but...'

    a. #BILL-GA MAME-WA 8-zi-goro   tabeteita   (yo)
        Bill-nom beans-wa 8 o'clock-around was.eating particle

    b. MAME$_i$-WA BILL-GA   8-zi-goro   t$_i$ tabeteita   (yo)
        beans-wa Bill-nom 8 o'clock-around   was.eating   particle
        'as for the beans, Bill was eating them around 8 o'clock.'

The examples in (13)–(16) demonstrate that the predictions in (3) are generally borne out in Japanese. (14b) and (16b) show, respectively, that a topic cannot follow a fronted focus, but a fronted topic can precede a focus. However, the distribution of topics is obviously more restricted. (16a) shows that a topic cannot follow an in-situ focus, and (10b) and (12b) illustrate that a topic cannot even follow a non-focus argument.

The standard characterization in the literature is that non-contrastive topics 'tend' to appear in a left-peripheral position, allowing for instances like the one in (5b), but contrastive topics need not (see Heycock 2008 for an overview). However, the examples in this section make it clear that both types of topics must appear in clause-initial position. I formulate this observation as in (17) and take it as a trigger for the displacement of *wa*-phrases. In terms of mapping between syntax and information structure, the constraint can be viewed as a reflection of the fact that Japanese transparently represents the topic-comment structure in its syntax, following the idea in (2).[5, 6]

(17) Topic is licensed in clause-initial position.

8.4 Discourse Anaphoric *wa*-phrases

According to the constraint in (17), *wa*-phrases in positions other than clause-initial position, such as the post-focal one in (5b), cannot be a topic. In this and the next sections, I provide arguments for their non-topical status.

---

[5] I will not discuss contrastive *wa*-phrases further here. See Vermeulen (2009a) for discussion on contrastive *wa*-phrases.

[6] Adverbials do not seem to count for the purpose of satisfying the clause-initialness of topics. In (16b), for instance, the adverbial *8-zi-goro* '8 o'clock-around' can precede *mame-wa* 'beans-wa'. I leave this issue for further research.

The main factor determining whether a *wa*-phrase must appear in clause-initial position, as in the exchange in (9)/(10), or not, as in the exchange in (4)/(5) is the context set up by the request. The request *tell me about X* in (9) instructs the *wa*-marked *X* in the reply to be a topic. By contrast, questions of the type in (4) introduce the *wa*-phrase as the discourse topic themselves and the *wa*-phrases in the answers are anaphoric items referring back to them. One argument for the topic status of the *wa*-phrase in the question is that it must appear in clause-initial position if the question is uttered discourse-initially. Thus, analogous to the English example in (8b), the sentences in (5) are understood as about the *wa*-phrases, not because they are themselves topics, but because their antecedent is the discourse topic.[7,8] I will call such non-topical *wa*-phrases 'discourse anaphoric *wa*-phrases'.

Some authors have argued that an item that refers back to a discourse topic is also a topic, but of a different kind to one that introduces the discourse topic (e.g Givón 1983; Chafe 1987; Lambrecht 1994). However, a discourse anaphoric *wa*-phrase need not refer back to a discourse topic. The example in (19), for instance, is a felicitous answer to the question in (18). Here, the object *ano hon* 'that book' is mentioned in the question, marked with the accusative marker *o*, indicating that it is not a topic, and yet it can be marked with *wa* in the answer. The standard description of an object *wa*-phrase in-situ is that it must bear an emphatic stress and be contrastively interpreted (Saito 1985; Fiengo and McClure 2002, Watanabe 2003; Tomioka 2009). However, in (19), no emphatic stress is required and no contrast is implicated.[9]

(18) Mary-wa ano hon-o   tosyokan-de karita   no?
      Mary-wa that book-acc library-at   borrowed Q
      'Did Mary borrow that book from the library?'

(19) Ie,   Mary-wa ano hon-wa   honya-de   kaimasita.
      No,   Mary-wa that book-wa book.shop-at bought
      'No, Mary bought the book in the end at the bookshop.'

---

[7] We cannot, however, rule out the possibility that the clause-initial *wa*-phrase in (5a) is a topic, reintroducing the discourse topic, though somewhat redundantly here. See Vallduví and Engdahl (1996: 474) for similar remarks for English. By contrast, we can be sure that the post-focal *wa*-phrase in (5b) is a discourse anaphoric *wa*-phrase due to (3b) and (17).

[8] One may wonder whether, being a pro-drop language, discourse anaphoric items are better expressed as empty pronominals and thus there might be awkwardness arising from the use of the full DP in (5). It is true that they are often not overtly expressed. However, there is evidence that an item must be mentioned twice before it can be pro-dropped (Clancy 1980). This is in contrast to English, where one mention licenses a subsequent use of a pronominal immediately, as in (8).

[9] Whether or not an object *wa*-phrase can appear in-situ seems to be influenced by whether the preceding subject bears *wa* or the nominative case marker *ga*. If the subject bears *ga*, an object *wa*-phrase in-situ indeed requires an emphatic stress and a contrastive interpretation. See Vermeulen (2009b) for discussion.

Further support for the non-topical status of the object *wa*-phrase in the above example comes from the fact that it cannot be fronted. The utterance in (20) is an infelicitous answer to (18). If it is not a topic, there is no trigger for its displacement. Examples such as (19) and (20) demonstrate clearly that previous mention of an item is sufficient for marking it with *wa*. Note that *Mary-wa* in (20) is referring back to the discourse topic introduced by (18), and therefore need not be in clause-initial position.

(20)   #Ie,   ano hon$_i$-wa   Mary-wa honya-de e_i kaimasita.
         No, that book-wa Mary-wa book.shop-at   bought

8.5 Topicalization and Island

There is a further syntactic difference between topic *wa*-phrases and discourse anaphoric *wa*-phrases. The standard view in the literature is that a non-contrastive *wa*-phrase is base-generated in a left-peripheral position and it can bind a *pro* in a thematic position internally to the clause, as illustrated below (Saito 1985).[10,11]

(21)   XP$_i$-wa   [$_{IP}$ pro$_i$]

This analysis explains the well-known observation that a *wa*-phrase can appear in a non-thematic, left-peripheral position and be construed as an argument inside a relative clause, without violating any island constraints. In the following example, *sono sinsi* 'that gentleman' is interpreted as the subject inside the following relative clause. Moreover, it is possible to overtly realize *pro* (Perlmutter 1972; Kuno 1973; Saito 1985).

(22)   sono sinsi$_i$-wa   [$_{TP}$[$_{NP}$ Ø$_j$ [$_{TP}$ pro$_i$/kare$_i$-ga e_j kitei-ta]
         that gentleman-TOP   he-nom   wearing-PAST
         yoohuku$_j$]-ga   yogoretei-ta.
         suit-GA   dirty-PAST
         'Speaking of that gentleman, the suit (he) was wearing was dirty.'

                                        (modified from Kuno 1973: 249)

---

[10] Clause-initial contrastive topics are usually assumed to have undergone movement, based on facts involving Weak Crossover, resumptive pronouns, and parasitic gaps (Hoji 1985).

[11] Kuroda (1988) and Sakai (1994) argue that topicalization always involves movement. However, the possibility of linking to a position inside a relative clause is still considered a characteristic of (a construction that can feed into) topicalization.

It seems reasonable to assume that generating a structure like (21), which involves displacement of XP from its thematic position, requires motivation. I propose that the motivation is the constraint in (17). It seems also reasonable to assume that a discourse anaphoric *wa*-phrase is base-generated in its thematic position in the absence of evidence to the contrary for discourse anaphoric items in general. We then predict a contrast between topic *wa*-phrases and discourse anaphoric *wa*-phrases: a structure such as (22) should be possible only if the *wa*-phrase is a topic and not if it is a discourse anaphoric *wa*-phrase.[12] The prediction is correct. In responding to the request in (23), *ano kodomo-wa* 'that child-wa', occupying clause-initial, non-thematic position in (24), can be construed as an argument inside the following relative clause.

(23)   ano kodomo-nituite osiete-kudasai.
        that child-about   tell-please
        'Tell me about that child.'

(24)   ano kodomo$_i$-wa kyoo kooen-de [$_{NP}$ [$_{TP}$ pro$_i$ e$_j$ kinoo
        that child-wa   today park-in   yesterday
        katta] inu$_j$]-ga John-o   kande-simatta.
        bought dog-nom John-acc bite-ended.up
        'As for that child, the dog that (he) bought yesterday bit John today in the park.'

To test the prediction for a discourse anaphoric *wa*-phrase is a little more complex and we need the following ingredients. First, the question must mention the phrase that is to be the discourse anaphoric *wa*-phrase in the

---

[12] Kishimoto (2006) claims that *wa*-marked phrases always move to the CP-zone, based on the observation that the focus particle *dake* 'only' attached to a tensed verb cannot associate with a *wa*-marked item. The point is illustrated below by the contrast in the available interpretations for a nominative subject and a *wa*-marked subject. He proposes that *dake* undergoes QR at LF, adjoins to TP and consequently associates with any item inside the TP. The fact that the *wa*-marked subject cannot be associated with *dake* shows that it is higher than TP.

(i) John-ga/wa   hon-o   yonda-dake (da)
    John-nom/wa book-acc read-only   (cop)
    a. 'Only [John] read the book.' (not available with *John-wa*)
    b. 'John read only [the book].'

Space limitation prevents a thorough discussion of Kishimoto's proposal here. However, crucially, he claims that a *wa*-phrase may move to SpecCP covertly. The data in section 8.3 show clearly that the constraint in (17) holds at the surface level. The prediction in the main text pertains to overt syntax: unless a *wa*-phrase is base-generated in a left-peripheral position, binding a *pro*, and hence is in a configuration like (21) at the surface level, it cannot take part in a structure like (22). My proposal here is that topic *wa*-phrases, but not discourse anaphoric *wa*-phrases, are licensed in this configuration in overt syntax, which is compatible with Kishimoto's proposal.

answer. Second, it must be possible for the focus in the answer to be fronted to a position preceding the *wa*-phrase to ensure that the latter is a discourse anaphoric item (see footnote 7). Thus, the question must be an object *wh*-question, as in the exchange in (4)/(5). In addition, object fronting is most natural if the thematic relations and word order among other material remained the same in the answer and the question. Consequently, the question must contain a *wa*-phrase that is already in a non-thematic position, binding a *pro* inside a relative clause, such as (25). The example in (26) shows that a discourse anaphoric *wa*-phrase cannot occupy a non-thematic position and be understood as an argument inside the following relative clause, as predicted.

(25)   ano kodomo-wa kooen-de [$_{NP}$ [$_{TP}$ e_j kinoo   katta] inu$_j$]-ga
        that child-wa   park-at   yesterday bought dog-nom
        dare-o   kanda no?
        who-acc bit   Q
        Lit.: 'Speaking of that child, who did the dog that he bought yesterday bite in the park?'

(26)   # JOHN$_k$-o ano kodomo$_i$-wa kooen-de [$_{NP}$[$_{TP}$ pro$_i$ e_j kinoo
        John-acc that child-wa   park-at   yesterday
        katta]   inu$_j$]-ga   t$_k$ kande-simatta.
        bought dog-nom   bite-ended.up
        'The dog that that child bought yesterday bit John in the park.'

If all *wa*-phrases were topics and licensed uniformly in the syntax as in (21), the contrast between (24) and (26) is unexpected.

8.6 How Much Information Structure is in Syntax?

In this section, I discuss the implications of the above findings for a theory of the interface between syntax and information structure. Neeleman and van de Koot (2008) view the schema in (2) as templates that constrain the mapping between syntax and information structure. These mapping rules are not associated with particular positions in the syntactic structure. An item that is interpreted as focus can undergo movement to an adjoined position internally to IP, for instance. Following Neeleman and van de Koot, I will call this the flexible approach.

   An alternative approach to the interface between syntax and information structure is the so-called cartographic approach, where functional projections associated with interpretations such as topic and focus are projected in a rigid order in the CP-domain of a clause (Rizzi 1997, 2004; Watanabe 2003 and

Endo 2007 for Japanese). Items that are to be interpreted as topic and focus bear syntactic topic and focus features, respectively, and move to the specifier positions of TopicP and FocusP, where the features are checked by the functional heads. Typically, Topic Phrase is projected recursively above as well as below Focus projection, as shown in (27).

(27)   ... TopP* FocP TopP* ...

On the cartographic approach, discourse anaphoric items are very often treated as topics. Thus, they also undergo movement to the specifier position of a TopP (Rizzi 1997, 2004; Belletti 2004; Grewendorf 2005, among others). Considering that I have argued that the Japanese particle *wa* can mark topics as well as discourse anaphoric items, data such as (5), which shows that a *wa*-phrase can precede or follow a fronted focus, may at first sight seem to give support for a clausal structure like (27). Watanabe (2003) and Endo (2007), for example, analyse a *wa*-marked phrase that follows a focus as a topic. However, as we saw in sections 8.3–8.5, discourse anaphoric *wa*-phrases have a distinct syntactic distribution from topic *wa*-phrases, suggesting that they are unlikely to bear the same syntactic topic feature and be licensed in the same manner in the syntax.

One may suggest that the post-focal Topic Phrases are perhaps functional projections associated with discourse anaphoricity instead, bearing the label Disc.Ana.P, for instance.[13] *Ano inu-wa* in the example in (5b) would occupy SpecDiscAnaP. In light of the fact that this *wa*-phrase in the same context can precede the focus, as in (5a), one might also postulate DiscAnaP above FocP, resulting in a structure like (28).

(28)   [$_{TopP}$ [$_{DiscAnaP}$ (ano inu-wa) [$_{FocP}$ JOHN-O
                        that dog-wa   John-acc
        [$_{DiscAnaP}$ (ano inu-wa) [......
                   that dog-wa

For sentences like (19), where both the subject and the object are discourse anaphoric *wa*-phrases, one might argue that the subject occupies the specifier position of the higher DiscAnaP, while the object is licensed in that of the lower DiscAnaP. On this account, however, it seems difficult to capture the

---

[13] Frascarelli and Hinterhölzl (2007) treat the kind of items that I call 'discourse anaphoric *wa*-phrases' as one of three types of topics ('familiar topic') and postulate a corresponding specific functional projection for this kind of item. However, the difficulty discussed above regarding DiscAnaP will extend to any analysis that postulates a differently labelled projection for items I have called discourse anaphoric *wa*-phrases.

observation that the object *wa*-phrase cannot appear in a position preceding the subject *wa*-phrase in the same context, which was demonstrated by the example in (20). Without further assumptions, it seems possible for the subject *wa*-phrase to be licensed in the lower DiscAnaP and the object *wa*-phrase in the higher DiscAnaP, as illustrated below:

(29)   [$_{TopP}$ [$_{DiscAnaP}$ ano hon$_j$-wa [$_{FocP}$ [$_{DiscAnaP}$ Mary$_i$-wa [$_{TP}$ e_i
                        that book-wa   Mary-wa
        honya-de e_j KAIMASITA]]]]]
        book.shop-at bought

By contrast, the idea that the particle *wa* marks topics as well as discourse anaphoric items is more easily accommodated on the flexible approach. Under this approach, nothing forces the particle to be directly associated with a topic interpretation. What *wa* marks is a separate issue from the syntactic representation of a sentence containing a topic. A displaced item is interpreted as a topic by virtue of its sister constituent being interpreted as the comment by the discourse.

One may wonder then why the particle *wa* appears on topics at all. Here, I speculate that there are functional reasons for this. In the case of objects, it would be difficult without the particle to distinguish topicalization from other kinds of structures. Unlike languages such as English and German, Japanese does not have prosodic means to distinguish topic from focus (Jackendoff 1972; Büring 1997; Hara 2006 and references therein for Japanese).[14] Consequently, a sentence containing an object topic has the same intonation as a sentence in which the object has undergone A-scrambling to above the subject (Ishihara 2001), as in (30). The subject *John-ga*, bears the main stress in both cases. Similarly, a sentence in which an object is a contrastive topic has the same intonation as a sentence with a fronted accusative object, which is interpreted as a contrastive focus, as demonstrated in (31). Here, the main stress falls on the object, with the rest of the sentence deaccented or showing downtrend (Ishihara 2007 and references therein).

(30)   ano hon-wa/o   John-ga   yonda.
        that book-wa/acc John-nom   read
         (i) with *wa*: 'Speaking of that book, John read it.'
         (ii) with *o*: 'John read that book.'

---

[14] Some researchers argue that Japanese has prosodic strategies indicating pragmatic effects similar to those associated with the B-accent in English (Oshima 2008; Hayashishita 2008). However, these strategies do not systematically distinguish topic in the sense discussed here from focus.

(31)   ANO HON-WA/O   John-ga   yonda.
        that book-wa/acc John-nom   read
        (i) with *wa*: 'John read that book(, but perhaps not another book).'
        (ii) with *o*: 'It is that book that John read.'

For subjects, it is widely reported in the literature that a nominative subject in the matrix clause is interpreted as either narrow focus or part of broad focus ('exhaustive' and 'neutral description' in Kuno's (1973) terminology; see also Heycock 1993; Kuroda 2005; Tomioka 2007). Thus, in order to receive a non-focal interpretation, which includes topic, a subject must be marked otherwise and I suggest that *wa* assumes this function. I leave further precise characterization of the function of *wa* for future research.

8.7 Concluding Remarks

I have argued in this chapter that the particle *wa* should not be considered a topic marker. It marks topics, but it can also mark discourse anaphoric items. It is therefore insufficient for identifying a topic. Rather, topics should be identified by means motivated by independent discourse considerations. *Wa*-phrases identified as topics in this way display syntactic properties that are not shared with discourse anaphoric *wa*-phrases. A topic *wa*-phrase must appear in clause-initial position, while a discourse anaphoric *wa*-phrase can appear in other positions including positions predicted not to be possible for topics by interface considerations. Secondly, in some instances, a discourse anaphoric *wa*-phrase cannot appear in clause-initial position. Finally, a topic *wa*-phrase can appear in a non-thematic, left-peripheral position and be construed as an argument inside a relative clause, but a discourse anaphoric *wa*-phrase cannot. The data observed here are difficult to explain on any account that treats the particle *wa* uniformly as a topic marker, or on the cartographic approach that proposes a rigid association between discourse-related interpretations and particular functional projections in the syntax.

Part II

The Morphological Properties of Words Interfacing with Syntax and Phonology

9

Word-internal Modification without the Syntax-Morphology Interface[*]

NAOKO TOMIOKA

9.1 Introduction

In the study of morphologically complex words, it is commonly stated that the morphemes that make up a word are initially represented separately. Pre-theoretically, this statement simply means that a word can be analysed into smaller meaningful units (morphemes). However, it is often claimed that the word is also a theoretically meaningful unit which has a special effect (hence-forth the *Word Effect*); due to this claim, hypotheses on word formation have played a central role in the debate on the architecture of grammar and the interfaces between its modules. Some argue that word formation and phrase formation take place in separate modules of grammar (i.e., morphology and syntax, respectively) and that the nature of the Word Effect reflects the interface conditions between these two modules (e.g., DiSciullo and Williams 1987). Others argue that word formation, as well as phrase formation, take place in syntax (McCawly 1971; Baker 1988; Halle and Marantz 1993).

The traditional debate on wordhood has focused on the question of whether or not the word is a theoretically sound and empirically definable unit of grammar (see e.g. DiSciullo and Williams 1987; Halle and Marantz 1993). This paper, however, takes a different approach to untangling the issue. The complexity of the traditional debate arises due to the difficulty in understanding the

[*] The research for this chapter was partially funded by CRSH412-2003-1003 and FQRSC103690 to Anna Maria Di Sciullo. The judgements reported here were collected via casual consultations with native speakers (English) and using questionnaires (Japanese), the latter was done as part of the experiment 'Processing of compounds in Japanese', project #R1-TOMN01. I would also like to thank the anonymous reviewer for his/her suggestions.

numerous phenomena which have been used to support the notion of the word as a theoretically useful unit. It is, however, possible to clarify certain empirical biases without having a clear definition of the word. I investigate a case that involves morphologically complex words and a syntactic operation (modification) and show that this phenomenon—which might be considered to reflect the Word Effect—in fact involves a purely structural restriction. It must be noted here that the proposed evidence for the Word Effect comes not just from modification, but also from binding and movement. I have, however, chosen to focus on modification so that a single phenomenon can receive full attention, which is necessary given the complexity of issues.

In order to fully comprehend the modification phenomena under consideration, we first need to understand the exact working of modifiers in Japanese. In Japanese, modifiers fail to pick out an element within a morphologically complex predicate. Consider (1).

(1)   Taro-wa bijutukan-de shasin-o   tori-wasure-ta.
       T.-TOP   museum-LOC   picture-ACC take-forget-PAST
       'Taro forgot to take a picture in the museum.'

The sentence in (1) involves a morphologically complex predicate *tori-wasure* 'take-forget', in which the first verb from the left, *tori*, can be taken as the embedded verb and the second verb, *wasure*, as the main verb. By selecting the right context (as given in section 9.4.1) we can see that the modifier *bijutukan-de* 'at the museum', can only be interpreted as modifying the matrix event of forgetting to take the picture and not the embedded event of taking the picture. This illustrates a case in which a locative modifier is unable to pick out the embedded event, expressed by an element which is realized as part of a morphologically complex word. The schema illustrates the kind of explanation this example would receive if one prematurely chose to use the Word-Effect hypothesis: an element X (the verb) appears as part of a word and the word boundary blocks the modification relation between the modifier Z and X.

(2)   [$_{word}$ X-Y]   Z
              ↑___* __|

The example in (1) however, does not show that the failure of modification is due to the Word Effect. As will be clear in section 9.4.1, the relevant restriction concerns the category of the embedded phrase. What this study shows is that the failure of modification, which at first seems to indicate the Word Effect, is in fact due to a completely different constraint on the modification relation. In the following sections, I give a detailed account of Japanese modifiers. They seem to consistently fail to pick out part of a complex predicate—a typical example that could support the Word Effect hypothesis. A closer investigation, however, reveals that this failure of modification should be associated with the structural restriction the modifiers are subject to, and not to wordhood. The present study thus demonstrates how a careful study of modification reveals that certain restrictions, which might be misunderstood as being due to the Word Effect, actually have their explanation in other sources. This case study should be taken as an example of how an apparent instance of the Word Effect in fact involves a subtler restriction of the grammar and that a better understanding of the phenomenon renders the Word Effect unnecessary. The finding of this study has greater consequences than the mere discovery of a language-specific constraint, as it represents an example of a case in which the Word Effect might be wrongly invoked. In order to situate this study, I thus start by describing the role the Word Effect plays in the theory of the architecture of the grammar and its interface conditions.

9.2 Theoretical Background

Theories about the architecture of the grammar differ from each other in whether or not they assume that word formation occurs separately from phrase formation. Some argue that morphologically complex words are formed in a module of grammar separate from syntax (i.e., morphology/lexicon) and that the internal structure of a word is invisible to syntax (e.g. DiSciullo and Williams 1987). Others argue that the atom of syntax is smaller than words and that syntactic operations, such as head movement, can create morphologically complex words (e.g. Baker 1988). Those who advocate this position in a stronger form argue that all structure-building, be it phrase or word, take place in syntax (Halle and Marantz 1993). Two central issues that have appeared in this debate are the notion of idiosyncracy and the accessibility of syntactic operations. The idea is that if word formation takes place in a module separate from syntax, we expect to observe two patterns: (i) the internal make-up of a word should be inaccessible to syntactic operations and (ii) this separate module is less systematic and provides room for more idiosyncratic meanings/forms to appear. The notion of idiosyncracy has made the division of structure formation more complex. Morphologically complex words have been classified into two types: 'lexical' and 'syntactic', where the former exhibits more irregularity in meaning and form than the latter. The classification based on the notion of idiosyncracy has the result that the division of 'lexical' and 'syntactic' differs from the traditional notion of 'word' and 'phrase'.

The difference between the lexical/syntactic and word/phrases classification, moreover, became even greater as researchers noted that phrases can exhibit irregularity in form-meaning pairings, as in the case of idioms. The idiosyncracy-based division thus provided the syntax-lexicon division at the sub-word level in one case, and at the phrasal level in another. This contradictory finding is taken as the evidence against treating word as a real grammatical element (Marantz 1997). Marantz's argument, combined with numerous pieces of evidence supporting Baker-type syntactic formation of morphologically complex words made the syntax-based word formation a generally accepted hypothesis for morphologically complex words. Such an approach must, however, explain the other empirical argument for the Word Effect, namely the apparent non-transparancy of words to syntactic operations; furthermore, it must do so without making recourse to words. An explanation of this type, however, has been neglected to this day, and the nature of Word Effect thus remains poorly understood.

Work on complex word formation often invoke the notion of Word Effect—i.e., that certain syntactic operations fail to access a constituent within a complex word because 'word' blocks such operations (see e.g. Lakoff and Ross 1979; DiSciullo and Williams 1987; Rapp and von Stechow 1999). This phenomenon of Word Effect, if it indeed is due to the nature of wordhood, would weaken theories which treat word formation and phrase-structure formation as syntactic operations, and may even require a re-thinking of the relation between the interfaces as conceptualized in the Minimalist framework.

To illustrate this theoretical problem, we shall consider a case of modification in the context of morphologically complex word formation. In studies that investigate the interaction between modification and morphologically complex predicates, researchers have often postulated that once two predicates combine to form a word, the constituent predicates are no longer accessible to word-external operations such as modification (see e.g. Rapp and Von Stechow 1999). This hypothesis has various unwanted consequences. First, head movement is no longer simply a case of movement; it affects the applicability of later operations. Second, this hypothesis entails that the PF realization of a structure has an effect on its semantic interpretation, which is not consistent with the assumptions of the Minimalist syntax. The Word Effect is postulated for a number of phenomena, including extraction and modification (Lakoff and Ross 1979; Di Sciullo and Williams 1987; Tada 1992), but its exact nature has remained elusive. Given the theoretical problem the Word Effect poses, there is a reason to reinvestigate the relevant facts in an attempt to eliminate the unwarranted use of this condition.

9.2.1 *The Essence of the Word Effect*

The exact definition of the Word Effect varies depending on the framework it is formulated in, but the motivation for the Word-Effect hypothesis follows the general pattern in (3):

(3)   (i)   there is a syntactic operation that targets a certain element
      (ii) this element may appear as part of a word
      (iii) the syntactic operation fails to pick out this element when it is part of a word.
      (iv) the failure is due to the Word Effect

The Word Effect, as stated in (3) appears in the Generative Semantics framework (Lakoff and Ross 1979), the Strong Lexicalist framework (DiSciullo and Williams 1987), and in the syntactic framework in which head movement creates morphologically complex words (Rapp and von Stechow 1999; Tada 1992). Various phenomena led to the postulation of the Word Effect (e.g., substitution in Lakoff and Ross 1979; movement in DiSciullo and Williams 1987; case assignment in Tada 1992), but for the current purpose, we focus on the Word Effect that is said to affect modification; a modifier fails to pick out a constituent of a morphologically complex word, and this failure is attributed to a blocking effect at the word boundary. As mentioned earlier, the traditional form of the Word Effect hypothesis attributes this effect to a property of the lexicon-syntax interface. In the Strong Lexicalist framework, the Word Effect arises because morphologically complex words are formed in the lexicon; when morphologically complex words enter syntax, their internal structure is inaccessible to syntactic operations. The critics of this approach point out that words do not define the basic building blocks of syntax and that the dissociation of word formation and phrase-structure formation is thus unwarranted (Lieber 1992; Ackema 1995; Halle and Marantz 1993). These works have already shown that words do not determine the minimal input at the lexicon-syntax interface, and that syntax can create morphologically complex words. However, the Word Effect still resurfaces in a new disguise, and raises the issue of the PF and LF interface interaction.

The issue of word-internal modification involves both the PF and LF interface because (i) a syntactic unit is classified as a word based on its PF realization and (ii) the property of modification is inferred from the LF interpretation of the relevant phrase structure. For example, Rapp and von Stechow (1999) claim that some modifiers (such as *fast* 'almost' in German) are sensitive to the phonological realization of the element they modify. Such modifiers can pick out an element if it is realized with a transparent form, but not if this element is realized as part of a word whose internal make-up is opaque. Such effects, however, are hard to formalize if words are not unit of syntax. Modification is an operation that must be read-off at the LF interface, since its effects are semantic. How, then, can the phonological realization of an element at PF influence the semantic effect at LF? These are the questions one must address in order to show words are not syntactically relevant entities. To put it more generally, an attempt to free a syntactic theory of wordhood must meet the challenge of accounting for the empirical data that has led to the postulation of Word Effect, without itself invoking the notion of wordhood. This paper is an attempt to solve this issue by providing a careful examination of some relevant data and by providing an account of that data without invoking the Word Effect.

9.3 Phrase-structure Based Account of Modification

The study of modifiers (mainly adverbs) suggest a close relation between the structural position of a modifier and its interpretation (e.g. Morgan 1969; Jackendoff 1972; von Stechow 1996; Cinque 1999; Morzycki 2005). For the sake of the discussion to follow, I take the strongest position concerning this correlation: the position of the modifier in the LF phrase structure is what determines speaker intuitions as to what the modifier modifies. In the Minimalist model of syntax (Chomsky 1995), syntax feeds into two interfaces, LF and PF; LF and PF, however, do not directly connect with each other. Given this assumption on the nature of modification, there is no longer a place for the Word Effect. A structure is realized as a word at the PF interface, subject to its PF properties. Crucially, the semantic interpretation of this structure at LF should not be sensitive to its PF realization. Word Effect, however, states precisely that this is the case: at LF, a modifier may not pick out a structure that is realized as part of a word at PF. Given this inconsistency, we have reason to examine how modification applies to morphologically complex predicates, and to provide an alternative account that does not rely on the PF-LF interaction.

Work on modifiers suggests that modifiers can be divided into two major classes. One type of modifier, which I call the event modifier, appears in functional domains outside of VP (Cinque 1999). The exact position of event modifiers varies from one individual modifier to another, and it is possible for the same modifier to appear in different positions and thus to receive different interpretations. Still, the distribution of event modifiers is limited to positions outside of the VP. The event-internal modifiers, in contrast, may appear inside VP, in addition to appearing in the functional domain. The best-known example of an event-internal modifier is *again* (and its counterpart in German), and this adverb has played a key role in the study of predicate structure (see e.g. McCawley 1968; Dowty 1978; von Stechow 1996; Beck and Johnson 2004). The crucial property of *again* is that it can attach to the small clause inside VP; in this position, the presupposition associated with *again* makes reference only to the content of the small clause. In the following discussion, I claim that the availability of the two attachment positions directly correlates with the availability of certain interpretations of a modifier. To make the point clear, the two positions are schematized in (4).

(4)   [[voiceP [VP [[small clause] {event internal modifier}]]]{event modifier}]

The voice head marks the attachment site of event modifiers; an event modifier picks out a voiceP and voiceP only. The position for the event-internal modifier can be identified in relation to the small clause. Some VPs contain a small-clause complement and event-internal modifiers pick out this constituent.

The structure-based account of the interpretation of modifiers makes predictions regarding when modification is possible and when it is not. In the following sections, the structure-based account of modification will be used to explain the failure of word-internal modification without recourse to the Word Effect. To put it simply, an adverbial modifier may inherently attach either to a voiceP or to a small clause.[1] The question is thus whether a given structure contains an embedded voiceP or a small clause. If the complex-predicate structure contains an embedded voiceP, an event-modifying adverbial can pick out this voiceP contained; if the complex predicate involves VP embedding (rather than embedding of voiceP) the adverb fails to modify the embedded structure. Similarly, if a complex predicate contains a small clause, adverbials may modify this small clause and provide an event-internal reading; if there is no small clause, the potential event-internal modifier does not yield an event-internal reading.

9.4 Complex Predicates in Japanese

Japanese exhibits numerous types of morphologically complex predicates, and a quick glance at traditional accounts of these predicates provides an

---

[1] I must warn the reader that this statement is oversimplified because there are adverbs that attach to higher functional projections than voiceP, as discussed in Cinque (1999). However, in the discussions involving complex predicates, the key criteria is whether an embedded clause contains a voiceP or a smaller constituent (Wurmbrand 2001; Tomioka 2006), and hence, given the scope of the current discussion, the simplified statement suffices.

example of cases where the Word Effect has been invoked. The Word Effect appears in the discussion of these predicates in two distinct forms. In one, researchers postulate that head movement has the effect of forming a complex predicate, whose constituent parts are no longer accessible to syntactic operations from without (e.g., Tada 1992). In the other, researchers invoke a weaker Word Effect in which the Word Effect affects only certain complex predicates, called lexical complex predicates (see e.g. Shibatani 1973; Kageyama 1989). In the following, I show that neither forms of the Word-Effect hypothesis are correct.

9.4.1 *Restructuring and Causatives: Event Modifiers and VoiceP*

The following is an example of a minimal pair, in which one sentence contains two separate predicates (5a) and the other contains the same predicates in a compound form (5b).

(5) a. Taro-wa Jiro-ni denwa-o   suru   no-o   wasure-ta.
        T.-TOP J.-DAT phone-ACC do-PRES NO-ACC forget-PAST
        'Taro forgot to call Jiro.'

     b. Taro-wa Jiro-ni denwa-o   si-wasure-ta.
        T.-TOP J.-DAT phone-ACC do-forget-PAST
        'Taro forgot to call Jiro.'

In their unmodified form, these two sentences seem to express the same proposition, as their translation suggests. However, the difference between the two becomes visible when a modifier is used. The sentence in (6a) is ambiguous; the modifier *mata* 'again' may pick out the main clause event or the embedded event. If it picks out the main clause event, the sentence has the presupposition that Taro had forgotten to call Jiro previously. The sentence thus means that it was the second time that Taro had forgotten to call Jiro. If it picks out the embedded event, the sentence has the presupposition that Taro had previously called Jiro. The sentence thus means that what Taro forgot to do was to make the second phone call to Jiro. The sentence in (6b), in contrast, is unambiguous. The only presupposition associated with this sentence is that Taro had previously forgotten to call Jiro. In other words, this sentence does not provide the reading associated with the modification of the embedded event.

(6) a. Taro-wa [Jiro-ni **mata** denwa-o   su-ru]   no-o   wasure-ta.
        T.-TOP   J-DAT again phone-ACC do-PRES NO-ACC forget-PAST
        'Taro forgot to call Jiro again.'

b. Taro-wa Jiro-ni mata denwa-o   si-wasure-ta
   T.-TOP   J-DAT again phone-ACC do-forget-PAST
   'Taro forgot to call Jiro again.'

These examples thus illustrate a phenomenon which on first glance seems to require the Word Effect for its explanation. (6a) and (6b) differ in the morphological realization of their predicates. In (6a), the two predicates appear separately; in (6b), they appear as a single word. Such an explanation, however, turns out to be an undesirable direction of analysis. Keeping this warning in mind, let us now consider sentences with a locative modifier, which exhibit the same pattern as (6a-b). In (7a), the two predicates again appear separately, and the sentence is ambiguous. In one reading, what Taro forgot to do was to take a picture in the museum. This is the reading one obtains when the locative modifies the embedded event. The second reading asserts that it was at the museum that Taro forgot to take a picture. This reading obtains when the locative modifies the main clause. As we saw earlier in (1), when the same locative is used with the complex predicate, shown here as (7b), it only yields the matrix-modification reading. The difference between the two sentences becomes apparent when the sentences are given in a context, where Taro did not go to the museum. With the first reading, Taro need not have gone to the museum at all, but with the second, Taro must have gone to the museum. Thus, given this background information, Japanese speakers judge (7a) to be true, but (7b) to be false.

(7) a. Taro-wa bijutukan-de shasin-o   toru-no-o   wasure-ta.
        T.-TOP   museum-LOC picture-ACC take-NO-ACC forget-PAST
        'Taro forgot to take a picture in the museum.'

     b. Taro-wa bijutukan-de shasin-o   tori-wasure-ta.
        T.-TOP   museum-LOC picture-ACC take-forget-PAST
        'Taro forgot to take a picture in the museum.'

Given this set of examples, it is tempting to postulate the Word Effect hypothesis, as other researchers have done upon observing a similar set of data (Shibatani 1973 for lexical causatives, Kageyama 1989 for lexical compounds, and Tada 1992 for restructuring and case-marking with verbal compounds); given the Word Effect hypothesis, the modifier fails to pick out the embedded event *because* the main predicate of the embedded clause appears in a compound form within the predicate of the main clause. In other words, the Word Effect hypothesis entails that head movement, which yields the head-adjoined structure realized as the compound, affects the LF interpretation by making the two clauses inseparable. This is an unconventional assumption of head movement. It is preferable if an analysis does not invoke such an unwarranted effect of a syntactic operation. We should instead consider the possibility that the two sentences differ in the type of embedded clause. In (6a) and (7a), the embedded clause is a full clause (IP or CP), as the embedded verb *su* appears with a tense-marker *ru* and the clause is followed by a complementizer *no*. All these morphemes are absent in (6b) and (7b). This could mean that these projections are absent and thus that the embedded clause is a VP. Wurmbrand (2001) argues that some verbs take a complement which lacks functional projections. Applying her idea to Japanese cases, I have previously argued that the complement of *wasure*, in a morphologically complex case (such as in (7b)) is a VP (or a CAUSEP) and thus lacks voiceP and higher projections (Tomioka 2007).

The following set of examples provide supporting evidence for my account because they are compatible with the structural account but not with the Word Effect hypothesis. These examples involve a construction called the 'syntactic causative'. In syntactic causatives, a causative suffix *(s)ase* attaches to a verbal stem, thus producing a morphologically complex predicate.[2] Contrary to what the Word Effect hypothesis would predict, modifiers *are* able to pick out the 'embedded' caused event in syntactic causatives, as shown below.

(8)   a.   Taro-wa Jiro-ni osiire no   naka-de   huku-o
            T.-TOP   J.-DAT closet-GEN inside-LOC clothes-ACC
            ki-ase-ta.
            wear-cause$_{synt}$-PAST
            'Taro made Jiro put on his clothes in the closet (Jiro was in the the closet).'

       b.   Taro-wa kodomo-ni hitoride huku-o   kis-ase-ta.
            T.-TOP   child-DAT   alone   clothes-ACC wear-cause$_{synt}$-PAST
            'Taro made the child put on her clothes by herself.'

                                                                        (Shibatani 1973)

In (8a), the locative can pick out the embedded event of Jiro's putting on his clothes. Similarly, the adverb *hitoride* can pick out the embedded event in (8b), i.e., the sentence could mean that no one helped the child put on the clothes. These examples indicate that two predicates may form a morphologically complex predicate and still allow for an event modifier to target the lower clause. Thus, the absence of the lower reading of (6b) and (7b) cannot

---

[2] Its meaning is transparent and its formation is productive, hence Shibatani (1973) classifies it as syntactic complex predicate, or syntactic causative. This classification does not save the Word Effect account since the restructuring compounds involving *wasure* are also syntactic compounds, as they are transparent and productive.

be attributed to head movement or morphologically complex formation. In other words, head movement may affect the morphological realization of a predicate at PF, but it does not block the interpretation of a modifier at LF, which singles out the embedded clause containing one of the predicates. As argued in Tomioka (2006), the absence of the lower reading in (6b) and (7b) should be attributed to a structural property of the sentences, namely the fact that the 'embedded' clause in these sentences is just a VP (lacking higher functional projections, including voice). As mentioned in section 9.3, the voice head is necessary for event modifiers, and its absence naturally accounts for the observation that the sentence lacks a reading associated with the modification of the embedded clause. Hence, the evidence from causative constructions like those in (8) supports a structural account of modification over the Word Effect-based account.

9.4.2 *Small-clause and Event-internal Modifiers*

The debate surrounding event-internal modifiers also includes cases where the Word Effect has been invoked. Event-internal modifiers are different from the event modifiers in being able to pick out constituents within VP, in addition to the regular positions associated with adverbial modification. The main focus of discussions on event-internal modification is the presence of a small clause in causative expressions, and how the event-internal modifier modifies it. The verbs discussed in this debate are often monomorphemic on the surface; despite their simple PF form, however, their interpretation involves the causative concept, a concept which is associated with a complex structural representation (see e.g. Hale and Keyser 1993). Event-internal modifiers, like *again*, are used in this discussion because they can single out the complement of CAUSE (as argued in numerous works cited above). The Word Effect has been invoked when an event-internal adverbial fails to pick out the presumed complement of CAUSE (Rapp and von Stechow 1999). Rapp and von Stechow (1999) propose that certain modifiers are sensitive to the phonological form of the predicate and that when the complement of CAUSE is phonologically opaque, the modifier fails to isolate it. This, again, is a problematic proposal in the current model of syntax, in which there is no mechanism which informs the LF of the PF realization. In this section, I show that event-internal modification is systematically absent in Japanese. I then provide an analysis of this phenomenon without invoking the Word Effect. My analysis relies on the structural difference between English and Japanese causative expressions. A detailed argument on this structural difference is provided in Tomioka (forthcoming). Here, I provide a summary of the arguments, and crucial evidence to illustrate the phenomenon.

The English example in (9) exemplifies event-internal modification. With the event-internal reading the durative phrase expresses how long the potatoes were in the oven. The event reading is also available, but for the purpose of our discussion, we focus on the event-internal reading only. The Japanese counterpart of this sentence, shown in (9b) differs from (9a) in not having the event-internal reading of the durative. Instead, the durative can only express the duration of the whole event, resulting in a pragmatically odd meaning.

(9)   a.   John put the potatoes in the oven **for 30 minutes.**
               VP internal reading: The potatoes were in the oven for 30 minutes.

      b.   #Kotaro-ga imo-o   oobun-ni **30-punkan** ire-ta.
            K.-NOM   potatoes-ACC oven-DAT 30-minutes put.in-PAST
            'Kotaro put the potatoes in the oven for 30 minutes [i.e., his putting
            took 30 minutes].'

Locative modifiers in Japanese are also limited to modifying the whole event, leading to a pragmatically odd interpretation, as shown in (10).

(10)   Kotaro-ga imo-o   oobun-no naka-de   yai-ta.
        K.-NOM   potato-ACC oven-GEN inside-LOC bake-PAST
        'Kotaro baked the potatoes in the oven [i.e., Kotaro was in the oven,
        baking the potatoes].'

The Japanese counterpart of *again, mata* also shows the same limitation, and provides an unambiguous reading, as shown in (11).

(11)   Kotaro-ga **mata** doa-o   ake-ta.
        K.-NOM   again door-ACC open-PAST
        'Kotaro opened the door again [and Kotaro had opened it before].'

These sentences show that there is something that is different between English and Japanese. Given that this phenomenon involves modifiers and semantically complex predicates, we have two logically possible accounts; either modifiers are different in English-type languages and Japanese-type languages, or semantically complex predicates come in different types. In Tomioka (forthcoming), I argue that the answer is the latter, attributing the unavailability of the event-internal modification to the structure of the CAUSEP in Japanese. Regardless of the choice between these two possible explanations, one thing is certain: the Word Effect cannot be the correct explanation. We have already seen that the Word Effect hypothesis is too strong: there are morphologically complex words in which modifiers may pick out constituent parts. In the following, I show that the Word Effect hypothesis is not sufficient to account for all the cases involving the failure of modification. That is, modifiers fail to provide the event-internal reading even when the presumed constituent appears as a separate phrase. The relevant case here involves resultative constructions in Japanese, as shown in (12).

(12) Taro-ga kami-o   kuroku some-ta.
      T.-NOM hair-ACC black dye-PAST
      'Taro dyed his hair black.'

The expression contains (i) the verb *some*, (ii) the adjectve *kuroku* which indicates the resulting state, and (iii) the nominal argument *kami* (the element that undergoes the dying action and becomes black). Before we examine the interaction of modifiers and resultatives in Japanese, let's first take a look at the English counterpart of this sentence. It is commonly assumed that in the English counterpart of this sentence, the nominal argument, and the result-expressing adjective form a constituent (small clause) that is the complement of CAUSE (Hoekstra 1988; Hoekstra and Mulder 1990; Hale and Keyser 1993). This constituent, moreover, can be singled out using an event-internal modifier, such as *again*, as (13) illustrates. The bracketing indicates the attachment site of the adverb.

(13) Taro dyed his hair again.
      Taro dyed [[his hair black] again]

The interpretation corresponding to this representation is that Taro's hair was black again as the result of his dying it. The presupposition derived by this structure makes reference to the content of the small clause (Taro's hair was black before), and not to the verb *dye*, and hence, the sentence is true even if it was the first time Taro dyed his hair. This English example thus illustrates how the inner reading of *again* works. Now let's return to the Japanese example, which differs from the English example in a crucial way.

(14) Taro-ga kami-o   mata kuroku some-ta.
      T.-NOM hair-ACC again black dye-PAST
      'Taro dyed his hair black again.'

The sentence in (14) unambiguously means that Taro had dyed his hair black previously and he did so again. This interpretation indicates that the adverb attaches in a higher position in Japanese than in English, as schematized below.

(15) Taro-ga [[hair black dye] again]

Since this is the only interpretation available in Japanese, this sentence is false if this is the first time Taro dyed his hair, regardless of whether his hair had been black before or not. This judgement clearly contrasts with judgements of the English counterpart in (13).

The Japanese example tells us that the morphological realization of a predicate does not affect the pattern of modification. In the Japanese resultative construction, the result expression is realized as a separate word (adjective), rather than as part of the causative predicate; still, the modifier fails to pick out only the caused event.

9.5 Conclusion

In this chapter, I investigated adverbial modification in the context of complex predicate formation. In previous studies, the Word Effect has often been invoked when a modifier fails to pick out a presumed constituent within a word. I examined two case studies in which the Word Effect has been invoked and have shown the empirical problems that arise with the Word Effect-based account. In both cases, the data first appeared to suggest that when two predicates formed a unit at PF (i.e., a morphologically complex predicate), they also formed an inseparable unit at LF, thereby blocking modifiers from singling out one constituent only. In both cases, however, a closer look revealed that it was a structural property of the complex predicate, rather than the Word Effect, which led to the failure of word-internal modification. The first case showed the apparent interaction between event modifiers and compounding, in which the modifier failed to pick out the embedded predicate. It was shown that this failure could not be due to the process of compounding, because another morphologically complex predicate—a causative predicate—does allow for word-internal modification. Hence, modification *is* possible in the context of morphologically complex predicates. The second case involved the interpretation of event-internal adverbials. Event-internal adverbs which pick out the small-clause constituents in English and Germanic languages fail to pick out the presumed equivalents in Japanese. I showed that event-internal modification fails in contexts where the presumed constituent is realized as a separate word, thereby dissociating availability of modification from the absence of the Word Effect. I argued that the failure of word-internal modification is instead due to a structural difference between Germanic VP and Japanese VP—namely, that Japanese causative expressions lack small clauses.

In light of both the empirical and the theoretical problems that the Word Effect faces, I conclude that the Word Effect cannot be the correct explanation of the observed phenomena. Instead, I argue that variation in the structural representation of predicates is what determines the interpretation of modifiers.

The current argument thus does not criticize any particular formulation of the Word Effect, but shows contexts in which an analysis other than the Word Effect is needed.

The alternative accounts I presented are meant to be a first step in re-evaluating and providing alternative accounts for cases involving the Word Effect hypothesis in general. The current account is more favourable than the Word Effect, given the current syntactic framework. Word Effect in the context of modification essentially involves the interaction between PF realization and LF interpretation. In the current model of syntax, syntax interfaces with PF and LF, but the two do not interface directly. Hence, the Word Effect is theoretically incompatible with the current model of syntax.

10

Affixation and the Mirror Principle

HEIDI HARLEY

10.1 Introduction

In a framework in which word formation, as well as phrase formation, is considered to be the output of the syntactic component, the Mirror Principle is expected to hold quite generally, cross-linguistically—in other words, morpheme order should respect the hierarchy of syntactic projections, as the default situation. In certain cases, however, this ideal situation does not seem to hold.

In this paper, I first outline three mechanisms that have been proposed to create the attested linear order of affixal morphological elements within a syntacticocentric architecture—head movement, morpheme-specific prefix/suffix specification, and Merger Under Adjacency. Each of these mechanisms is clearly motivated by data from relatively simple phenomena in individual languages. Given that each mechanism is independently well-motivated, we can ask what kind of patterns we might expect to see when they co-occur, and also in what ways we might expect these mechanisms to interact with each other. I show that two particularly flagrant cases of Mirror Principle violations, in Cupeño and Navajo, can be accommodated within the syntacticocentric framework using just these tools, without positing any additional special word-formation mechanisms, or any additional quasi-syntactic operations. The line of argumentation tracks closely that presented in Speas (1991).

10.2 Three Mechanisms for Syntactic Manipulation of Morpheme Order

Since Baker (1985), it has been recognized that something like the Mirror Principle is generally descriptively correct: morpheme order parallels the hierarchy of syntactic projections. In a syntacticocentric analysis of word formation, this descriptive generalization can be understood to fall out as a consequence of the basic operations which derive syntactic structures, given certain minimal assumptions concerning sub-word-level syntax. In particular, if bound morphemes occupy (or realize) syntactic terminal nodes just as free morphemes do, standard assumptions about the relationship between hierarchical structure and the linear order of terminals predict a very tightly constrained set of possible morpheme orders—too tightly constrained, as we will see, given the empirical situation in languages as familiar as English and as exotic as Cupeño.

Below, I first illustrate this typology with familiar data from French, showing a typical case of morpheme order predictions if complex words are formed by simple left-adjoining head-movement. Then I motivate enriching the head-movement mechanism to allow right-adjunction as well as left-adjunction with data from Cupeño (Hill 2005; Barragán 2003). Finally, I review the case from English proposed by Bobaljik (1994), among others, in favour of including a post-syntactic mechanism of Merger Under Adacency in the mix, as a supplementary word-formation strategy. With these two additional, simple, and independently motivated mechanisms supplementing basic head movement, I then go on to show that we have all the tools needed to syntactically produce the correct morpheme order in two particularly egregious cases of apparent Mirror Principle violations: the Cupeño complex predicate construction, and the Athapaskan verb.

10.2.1 *Head Movement*

First, consider the most constrained syntactic word-formation mechanism possible, namely, left-adjoining head movement, producing consistently right-headed complex $X°$ structures. In basic X-bar syntax, one key assumption is that word-sized phonological elements correspond to $X°$ terminal nodes. Morphologically complex phonological words, then, can be derived by head adjunction of one $X°$ to another, producing a larger $X°$ category with complex internal structure.[1] This is essentially Baker's (1986) theory of Incorporation, which, when applied generally, is one instantiation of a head-movement mechanism.

Left adjunction in head movement in a left-headed language will result in the type of right-headed word structures so familiar from English and French.

---

[1] Note that the complexity of the structure produced by head adjunction raises a serious theory-internal difficulty for the Bare Phrase Structure approach (Chomsky 1995). For discussion and some proposed solutions, see Matushansky (2006) and Harley (2004); in the analysis here, we will continue to assume that head adjunction which projects an $X°$ category is a theoretically straightforward and uncontentious operation.

A simplified derivation of a French past imperfect verb formed by head movement is illustrated in (1) below:

(1)   a. Structure before head movement

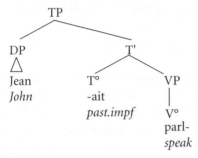

b. Structure after head movement with left adjunction

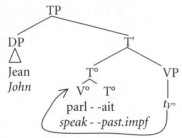

'John was speaking.'

If this were the only available mechanism for concatenating morphemes, the theory would be unable to generate any morpheme orders in which functional morphemes are prefixes to the lexical root in their extended projection.

10.2.2 *Prefixation of Functional Material: Affix-driven Adjunction*

Such orders do exist, however, and so the theory must be augmented with additional assumptions or mechanisms. Below, an example from Cupeño illustrates a case in which one functional affix is prefixed to the verb stem, and another is suffixed—an underivable order if left-adjoining head movement is the only option available.

Cupeño is a head-initial language described in-depth in Hill (2005), and whose verbal affixation patterns are analysed in Barragan (2003). See also Newell (2008) for a treatment of the prosodic phonology in these and related verbal constructions.

In Cupeño verbs, both Tense/Agr and Aspect are affixes to the verb stem, but the Tense/Agr affix is prefixal, and the Aspect affix is suffixal, illustrated below:

(2)   pe-ya-qál
       3sg.past-say-Imp.Sg
       'He was saying.'   (Hill 2005: ex. 2c)

Barragan (2003), following Halle and Marantz (1993), makes the simple assumption that morphemes can individually specify whether they are pre-fixal or suffixal—that is, whether they precede or follow their sister constitu-ent. Baker (1985) proposes that such prefix/suffix specification is possible on a language-wide basis; Barragan assumes it is possible for specific affixes within a language.[2]

Assuming that Tense/Agr is prefixal and Aspect suffixal in Cupeño, the derivation of the example in (2) will proceed as in (3) below. In this, for simplicity, I assume that TP dominates AspP, which in turn dominates VP (simplified here, as in the French tree above; really vP + VP). This Mirror Principle-predicted order is cross-linguistically attested as the most common one (Bybee 1985).[3]

(3)   a. Structure before head movement

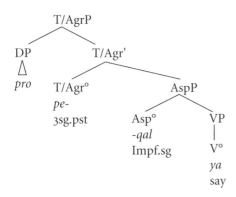

---

[2] Right-adjoining head movement is impossible in the antisymmetric theory of Kayne (1994); we do not assume antisymmetry here. See Koopman and Szabolci (2000) for an in-depth treatment of affixation in an antisymmetric approach. They treat affixation as the result of extensive remnant movement plus a species of Merger Under Adjacency (see section 10.2.3).

[3] Here, as noted, VP is shorthand for the usual vP+VP combination; the reader should assume that these verbs contain a null v° morpheme, picked up by the verb as it head-moves up the tree to Asp° and T°. For a full representation of the derivation of this form, see the fully specified tree in (10). This will be especially important as we consider the derivation of further Cupeño forms in section 10.3.

b. After the first step of head movement: *-qal* attaches to the right of its sister

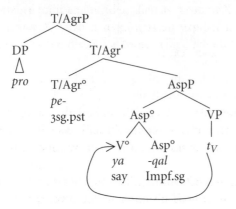

c. After the second step of head movement: *pe-* attaches to the left of its sister, the complex Asp° head

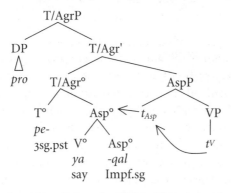

The choice of 'prefix' or 'suffix' is like a morpheme-driven variation on the Headedness Parameter. Just as the heads of phrasal syntactic projections may precede or follow their sisters, so too may the heads of X° constituents. With respect to the syntactic Headedness Parameter, intra-language consistency is the typological ideal (Japanese being consistently head-final, French consistently head-initial, for example), but nonetheless certain 'mixed' systems do appear (e.g. German head-final VP, head-initial CP). So too, we expect it to be the case that intra-language consistency is expected in word-level headedness, with e.g. English as a fairly solid example of a Right-Hand Head language at the word level,[4] but with Cupeño as an example of a

---

[4] Thanks to a reviewer for reminding me that even English shows some RHHR violations, e.g. *en-* is a verbalizer in words like *ennoble*.

mixed system, with certain $X°$ constituents being right-headed ($Asp°$) and others left-headed ($T°$).

Even the combination of optional, morpheme-driven headedness and head movement is inadequate to cover many important cases of word formation in familiar languages—like English. In the next subsection, I describe Bobaljik's (1994) approach to English *do*-support and the affixation of tense/aspect morphology, which adapts a mechanism first proposed by Marantz (1984): Morphological Merger, aka Merger Under Adjacency.

10.2.3 *Merger Under Adjacency: Word Formation without Head Movement*

Since Emonds (1976), the difference in the relative position of temporal adverbials and negation in English and French has been analysed as resulting from head movement of the verb out of the VP into the inflectional domain in the latter, but not the former (see, e.g. Carnie 2006 for an introduction). Head movement of the French verb to Tense accounts for the appearance of the tense/agreement morphology attached to the verb stem. The English verb, however, is also inflected for tense, except when negated or in questions, which presents a puzzle: How does English tense inflection come to be affixed to the $V°$ node, if the verb does not head-move out of the VP to Tense?

Bobaljik (1994) proposes a solution to this problem that exploits the post-syntactic operation detailed in Halle and Marantz (1993), Morphological Merger or Merger Under Adjacency (MUA).[5] MUA applies to adjacent terminal nodes, adjoining one to the other even across phrase boundaries, enabling the appearance of affixation of a structurally superior element to a structurally inferior one—essentially, an implementation of Chomsky's (1957) affix-hopping proposal within the context of modern generative grammar. Bobaljik shows that linear adjacency is a key restriction on the process; terminal nodes cannot undergo MUA if they are not linearly adjacent.[6] This restriction accounts for the need for *do*-support in negative contexts, when negation intervenes between Tense and V; in question contexts, when the subject intervenes between the T+C complex and V; and in emphatic contexts,

---

[5] I will use the acronym 'MUA' for this operation, rather than M-merger, since Matushansky (2006) uses 'm-merger' for a similar but slightly differently defined operation. Morphological Merger is of course not to be confused with Chomsky's (1995) phrase-structure-building operation Merge. For further discussion and development of the MUA operation, see Embick and Noyer (2001).

[6] Bobaljik excludes adverbs from intervention in the relevant sense, since Tense and V can combine despite the presumably intervening adverb in sentences like *I often walked to the store* (compare *I didn't often walk to the store*). He suggests that the failure of adverbs to intervene has a structural source in their status as adjuncts, rather than heads; apparently the MUA which applies in the English case cares only about linear adjacency relations between heads. See Embick and Noyer (2001) for further discussion and motivation for two distinct varieties of Merger Under Adjacency.

when a positive polarity item like *so* intervenes between T and V (*I did so file my paperwork!*).[7] The linear-order restriction also serves as an argument for locating the MUA operation post-syntactically. Bobaljik assumes that linearization is an operation that applies to a fully derived syntactic representation, in accordance with the Headedness Parameter. Since linearization occurs after the syntactic derivation is complete, and since MUA is restricted by linearity considerations, MUA must also apply after the syntactic derivation.[8] An MUA-like operation likely accounts for the dependent behaviour of a range of affixal items and clitics, especially 'leaner' clitics like English possessive *'s*.

Bobaljik's proposal for MUA of English past tense is illustrated in (4) below:

(4)   a. Before MUA of T to V   b. After MUA

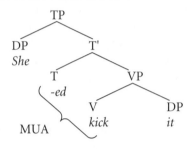
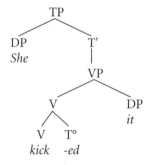

Note that MUA must right-adjoin T to V, rather than left-adjoin. This suggests that there could be morpheme-driven left or right adjunction resulting from MUA, just as there are left and right varieties of adjunction resulting from head movement and syntactic head adjunction. As for the head-movement case, it seems reasonable to treat this as a morphological specification—a property of the morphemes themselves, the phonological exponents that appear in each terminal node. It is a lexical property of *-ed* that it is suffixal, similarly of *-ais* in French; these specifications, I will assume, drive the left or right attachment

---

[7] Thanks to a reviewer for reminding me that positive polarity can also be indicated by prosodic emphasis; even this kind of non-segmental intervention can trigger *do*-support, and hence must be linearly present in the relevant sense: *I **did** finish my homework!* This is suggestive concerning the possible instantiations of vocabulary items, though orthodox DM proposals tend to only admit segmental VIs.

[8] It could well be that the process of vocabulary insertion and linearization occurs in several cycles, progressively deleting syntactic structure; consider Embick and Noyer's (2001) evidence that adverbs *do* intervene in the MUA computation in comparative formation. It cannot be that linearization of terminal nodes erases hierarchical structure from the morphological representation; vocabulary-item insertion often is sensitive to particular hierarchical structural contexts, not just linear ones, and VI insertion must follow (or be interleaved with) linearization phenomena.

of the affix to its host, provided they are sisters under an X° terminal node, regardless of whether that sisterhood relationship is derived via MUA or true syntactic head movement.

10.2.4 Summary: Three Tools

To summarize, we have outlined three mechanisms which can affect the formation of complex words in the syntax. These mechanisms are outlined in (5) below:

(5)   A. Head-movement (Combines morphemes under one mother node in the syntax)
       B. Affix-specific linearization requirement (Morpheme is a suffix/prefix with respect to its sister constituent)
       C. Merger under adjacency (Combines morphemes which are adjacent but not under one mother node at the end of the syntax)

It is perhaps worth observing that given the availability of both A and C as morphological concatenation mechanisms, the correct analysis of complex surface forms in certain cases will be underdetermined without further syntactic investigation, as famously is the case of English *He walked*—we can see there is concatenation of *-ed* and *walk*, but without further data we cannot be sure whether the V *walk* has raised to T, or whether T *-ed* has undergone postsyntactic MUA with V (Emonds 1976 provided that further data). The problem is especially acute in head-final languages, where all the ingredients in the extended verbal projection, even without head movement, are straightforwardly adjacent to each other and correctly ordered after the head-final headedness parameter is applied, as illustrated in (6).

(6)

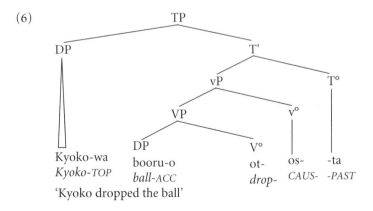

Kyoko-wa   booru-o   ot-   os-   -ta
Kyoko-TOP   ball-ACC   drop- CAUS- -PAST
'Kyoko dropped the ball'

Given the possibility of MUA, it requires quite sophisticated testing to determine whether head movement has occurred or not. See Koizumi (1995) for an example of an analysis which applies testing along these lines for Japanese.

We now turn to a consideration of how and whether these three independently motivated mechanisms can interact, proposing that it is precisely their interaction that leads to the derivation of certain apparent Mirror-Principle-violating morpheme orders in the polysynthetic languages Cupeño and Navajo. In particular, we will see that no special morphological or syntactic operations other than these are necessary to account for some extremely complex patterns.

10.3 Mirror Principle Violations I: Cupeño

As shown in Speas (1991), using just the first two of our three mechanisms, we can already derive several different morpheme orders, all of which respect the Mirror Principle—that is, morpheme orders in which the linear arrangement of morphemes will respect the hierarchy of syntactic embedding. Imagine a complex head produced by head movement of V up through three functional projections, v°, Asp°, and T°. If each of these projections can be specified as a prefix or a suffix, we predict the existence of eight Mirror-Principle-respecting possible morpheme orders. These orders are illustrated in (7) below:

(7) a. Everything suffixal

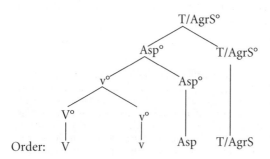

b. Everything prefixal

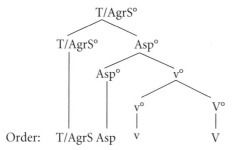

Order: T/AgrS Asp   V   V

c. Everything except T/AgrS suffixal, T/AgrS prefixal

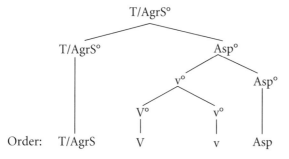

Order: T/AgrS   V   v   Asp

d. Everything except Asp suffixal, Asp prefixal

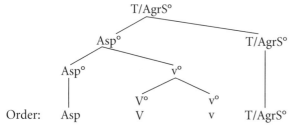

Order: Asp   V   v   T/AgrS

e. Everything except v° suffixal, v° prefixal

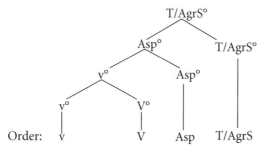

Order: v   V   Asp   T/AgrS

f. Both T/AgrS and Asp prefixal, v° suffixal

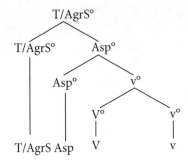

Order: T/AgrS Asp   V   v

g. Both Asp° and v° prefixal, T/AgrS suffixal

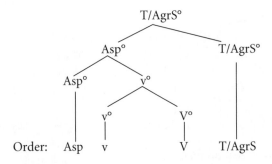

Order: Asp   v   V   T/AgrS

h. Both T/AgrS and v° prefixal, Asp suffixal

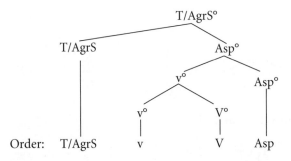

Order: T/AgrS   v   V   Asp

Despite the flexibility allowed by combining affix-specific linearization with head movement, certain morpheme orders are still predicted to be impossible—that is, the Mirror Principle is still a robust prediction, albeit somewhat lessened in force compared to a left-adjunction-only approach.[9]

---

[9] Speas (1991) doesn't appear to notice that certain orders remain impossible even assuming affix-specific ordering specifications; she states that in principle 'any order at all can be derived' (p. 183).

No morpheme order in which a higher morpheme like Asp° or T/Agr intervenes between v and V is possible, for example; similarly, no higher morpheme like T/Agr could intervene between v° and Asp°, between v° and V°, or between Asp° and V°.

However, this kind of intervention is exactly what is observed with two large subclasses of Cupeño verbs—that is, these Cupeño verbs represent true violations of the Mirror Principle. Below, I present the data and analysis first proposed in Barragan (2003). An example of a fully inflected Cupeño verb of the *in*-class is given in:

(8) Túku='ep   mi-**wíchax**-ne-**n**-qal   temá-t'a-yka
    yesterday=R 3PL.OB-**throw**-1sg.Pst-**v**$_{AGT}$-Imp.Pst.Sg ground-ACC-TO
    'Yesterday I was throwing them to the ground.'

Here we see a complex verb form in which the verb root is separated from a v° element by T/Agr° morphology—exactly the type of structure which head movement and affix-driven linearization, by themselves, cannot generate. However, if we allow affix-driven head movement and Merger Under Adacency to apply to different parts of the same structure, this order can be syntactically generated in a relatively straightforward manner.

First, we need a little more background on the Cupeño verb, to justify the analysis of the -*n*- in the structure as a realization of a v° terminal node. There are three major classes of Cupeño verbs described in Hill (2005). The first class are monomorphemic, like *ya*- 'say', which we saw exemplified in (2) above. The other two classes are bipartite, consisting of a root element, which occurs initially in the complex verb word, and a light-verb element which specifies the agentive status of the verb. *In*-class verbs have an Agent, while *yax*-class verbs do not. This is consistent with the analysis of these morphemes as realizations of v°, since the v° projection is associated with the appearance or absence of an external argument (e.g. Miyagawa 1994, 1998; Travis 2000).[10]

In any verb with a v° morpheme, the problematic pattern from (8) above appears, where the T/Agr morpheme intervenes between the V° morpheme and the v° morpheme. In the monomorphemic class, as illustrated in (2), the T/Agr morpheme simply appears as a prefix on the V°, an order which poses no Mirror Principle problems, as described above. Data illustrating the affixation patterns of the three classes of verbs are given below:

---

[10] As might be expected, inchoative/causative alternations in Cupeño often involve changing a -*yax*- for a -*in*-: *céne-in* is the basis for a sentence expressing 'x rolls y'; *céne-yax*, is the basis for 'y rolls'.

(9)   a.   pe-ya-qál   Ø-class verbs
           Pst.3sg-say-Imp.Sg   Monomorphemic
           'He was saying.'

       b.   mi=wíchax-ne-n-qal   *in*-class verbs
           3PL.OB=throw-Pst.1sg-vAGT-Imp.Sg   Bipartite: Agentive
           'I was throwing them.'

       c.   **nám-pem-yax-wen**   *yax*-class verbs
           cross-Pst.3pl-vNonAg-Imp.Pl   Bipartite: Non-agentive
           'They used to cross.'

Recall Barragan's derivation of the morpheme order of monomorphemic verbs like *pe-ya-qál*, in (2) and (9a). Above, we saw that head movement drove the affixation of (v+)V° to Asp° and then to T/AgrS°, and that affix-specific linearization requirements resulted in prefixal T/AgrS° and suffixal Asp°. The proposed structure for the final complex head in (3c) above is reproduced more fully, below, as a reminder. In this tree, the full structure of the VP is represented, with a null morpheme occupying the v° head and being carried along to Asp° and T° as the V° head raises. The null v° is represented as a suffix, though nothing hinges on this.[11] The subject is assumed to undergo A-movement from its base-generated position in spec-vP to spec-TP.

(10)

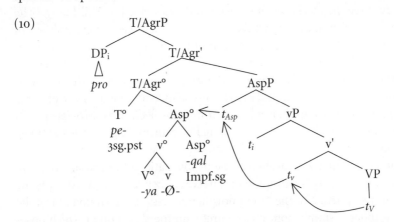

In order to derive the Mirror-Principle-violating morpheme order with bipartite verbs, Barragan carries this analysis over wholesale to the other classes of verbs, with one small adjustment: In the bipartite verbs, v°,

---

[11] The illustrated morpheme order is that in the hypothetical case illustrated in (7c) above; if the null v° were prefixal, then it would be like that in (7h).

rather than V°, head-moves to T°. In a sense, the pattern is exactly like that in a V2 language. There, a main verb will head-move to T except when there is an overt, intervening auxiliary verb, in which case the auxiliary moves to T, and the main verb remains *in situ* in the verb phrase. In the identical way, in Cupeño, V moves up to T iff there is no overt v° morpheme, i.e. when the verb is a member of the Ø-class. When there is an overt v° morpheme, as in the bipartite class, v° moves to T, stranding the main V.

Let us consider Barragan's proposal for the derivation of the form (9b) above. Cupeño is in fact head-final, like most Uto-Aztecan languages, so the derivations below are represented in head-final trees.[12]

We begin with a tree containing the subject pronoun (*pro*), an object clitic pronoun (*mi=*), and the verbal affixes in their base positions, V, v, Asp, and T/Agr°, illustrated in (11).

(11)

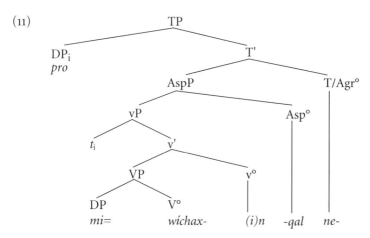

The v° morpheme is *-in-*, a non-null light verb which can behave like an auxiliary and support affixation, so the V° stays *in situ*. The v° raises by head movement up through Asp° and T°, which linearize according to the morpheme-specific prefix/suffix specifications that we observed above in the derivation of the zero-class form in (2). In particular, the Asp° morpheme *-qal* suffixes to the light v° *(i)n*, and the Tense° morpheme *ne-* prefixes to the complex Asp° head *(i)n-qal*. This results in the structure below:

---

[12] Nothing relevant would change about the initial discussion of (2) in a head-final structure; the structures in (2) are represented head-initally above just for ease of exposition and comparison with French and English.

(12)

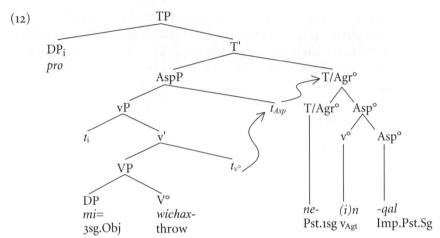

'Yesterday, I was throwing them to the ground.'

This structure is the output of the narrow syntax. Notice that the main verb, which has remained *in situ,* is adjacent to the T/Agr° complex to its right. Consequently we can then perform Merger Under Adjacency of the T/Agr° complex with V° to create the final complex V° form.[13] When v° is a zero-morpheme, all of the above operations still occur, but the V° itself must move, first through v° and then to Asp° and T/Agr°, as illustrated in (10).

In short, by exploiting the logical possibilities inherent in the three independently motivated word-formation techniques—head movement, affix-driven linearization, and Merger Under Adjacency—Barragan is able to derive the puzzling patterns of the inflected Cupeño verb in a principled manner. Note the diachronic plausibility of the account, as well: It seems likely that the v° affixes originally had their source as freestanding zero-class auxiliary-like verbs, patterning exactly like them and selecting perhaps some kind of nominalized or other non-verbal contentful complement. Over time, the complement itself was reanalysed as V or √, the auxiliaries lost their free-standing status, and the result was the peculiar hybrid pattern presented above.

Next, we turn to another, more famous, example of a Mirror Principle puzzle: the derivation of morpheme order in the Athapaskan verb.

---

[13] We can perform the same operation to add the base-generated object clitic to the entire complex verb form, or that clitic could be positioned by some other syntactic clitic-movement operation; I leave the question unresolved here.

10.4 Mirror Principle Violations II: Navajo

Some of the most famously intractable morphological systems are those of the Athapaskan languages, most often represented by Navajo (Speas 1990, 1991; Rice 2000; Hale 2004; Den Dikken 2003; Travis 2008, this volume, among others). Among their many other morphological complexities, these languages present a Mirror Principle problem similar to that of Cupeño, except even more elaborate in nature. Athapaskan verbal cores typically contain two or three 'lexicalized' parts which are separated by a host of inflectional material, occurring in a fixed order. I will argue that even these difficult systems are amenable to analysis with the same morphological tools we have introduced to date, and that no other novel word-building mechanisms need to be posited, despite many proposals to the contrary (see, e.g., Hale 2001, 2004; Travis 2008, this volume, as well as the family of templatic proposals argued against by Rice 2000).

In (13) below I present a sample Navajo verb, taken from Young and Morgan 1987: 283, as cited in Hale 2001:

(13) Ch'íshidiníɬdązh   Surface form
     ch'i-   sh-   d-   n-   ɬ-   **dązh**   Morphemic analysis
     out-   *1sgO* *limb-* *Perf-* *Trans-* *move*   given in Hale
     horizontally   *related* *(3sgO)*   *jerkily*
     'He jerked me.' (From a sentence translated *The policeman jerked me outdoors.*)

The bolded portion of the example above constitutes a single semantic unit, an example of the way in which the core Navajo verb is frequently morphologically bipartite, separated by considerable inflectional material, but semantically unified—here, the combination of *ch'i-* and *-dązh* are interpreted as 'jerk out'. The combination of the prefixal and root portions of the lexical verb can be perspicuously thought of as similar to Germanic verb-particle constructions (e.g. *look up* 'find entry in a reference work'), where the initial element corresponds to the particle and the root at the right of the complex verb word corresponds to the verb.

Following the initial particle is a range of more productive inflection-like markers, which occur in the following order: Object Agreement, Adverbial, Aspect, Subject Agreement, Transitivity. Following all of the above is the syllabic verb root.

I will begin by making the following assumptions concerning the general extended verbal projection in the Athapaskan verb, modelling the basic format on a version of that motivated for the Germanic verb word. The overall structure, indicating the assumed base-positions for the morphemes in (13) are illustrated below:[14]

(14)

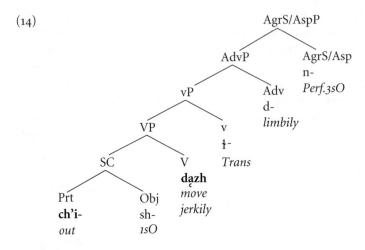

The key assumptions are the following:

(15)   a. Prt+Obj start out in a small-clause-like configuration (as for Germanic particles)
   b. Verb and v projected above that
   c. Aspectual, tense, and other inflectional-domain material projected above that as usual

Certain of these assumptions may be controversial in their specifics (for example, the assumption that a small clause contains both the particle and the object), but the overall architecture is quite familiar; perhaps the most unusual element is the inclusion of an AdvP containing the element denoting the instrumental manner in the extended verbal projection. However, this is in line with the proposal of Cinque (1999) that adverbial projections do form part of the inflectional spine. Here, the adverbial element is assumed to be realized in the head of the AdvP projection, consistent with

---

[14] I have omitted a *pro* DP in the specifier position of the AgrS/Asp projection for ease of exposition, though I assume it is present. I am assuming that the object morpheme is pronominal and clitic-like, occupying an argument position; adjusting that assumption to include an object *pro* and an object-agreement head position would not affect anything crucial about the analysis, as long as the AgrO projection occurred low enough in the structure, crucially below V°.

its status as an affixal element within a verb-word; in languages where adverbs are generally phrasal, like English, Cinque assumes that they occupy the specifier of AdvP. Positioning the adverbial affix *-d-* in the head position of AdvP should not affect the core ordering predictions of Cinque's proposal, however; presumably AdvPs, like other XPs, can exhibit spec-head agreement, such that specific adverbial features are present in both the head and the specifier. Whether a language chooses to realize the head Adv° position or the specifier of AdvP position or (perhaps) both could be a parametric property related to polysynthesis generally.[15] The overall picture is consistent with Rice's (2000) assertion that morpheme order in Athapaskan verbs respects semantic scope.

The three phrasal domains outlined in (15) correspond to the three general domains of the Athapaskan verb-word: the initial preverb domain, the central inflectional domain, and the root+transitivizer domain. Considered independently, none of these groups of morphemes violate any aspect of the Mirror Principle; it is only as a whole that the entire verb-word poses such significant problems. However, given the tools introduced above, we can easily assemble the entire complex verb—we need only assume two (syntactic) head-movement operations in combination with a pair of Merger Under Adjacency operations, conditioned by affixal preferences. The derivation, starting from the base-position illustrated in (14), is illustrated in (16)–(18) below.

First, V head-moves to v°, right-adjoining to it, as Navajo v° is specified as a prefixal element:

(16)   Step 1:
        V→v head movement

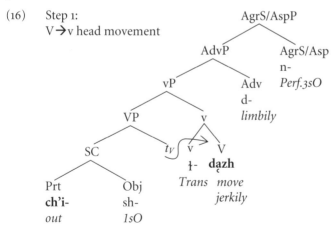

---

[15] Perhaps a language cannot choose to fill both the specifier and head positions of AdvP, if something like a generalized Doubly Filled Comp Filter is in effect for A-bar positions generally.

Next, Adv° head-moves to AgrS/Asp°, "this time left-adjoining to it", as Adv°
is specified as a prefixal element:

(17)   Step 2:
         Adv→AgrS head movement

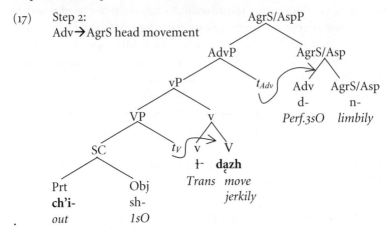

Note that these two movements, which I assume must take place in the
syntactic component, could occur in separate phases; nothing adverse
would result if the syntactic derivation proceeded stepwise, sending each
separate domain to spell-out as it is formed. However, it is crucial that all
three spelled-out domains are accessible in the morphological component
simultaneously, for the next steps.

   In the post-syntactic domain, the v+V complex and the AgrS/Asp complex
undergo Merger Under Adjacency—Affix-Hopping of complex X° constituents.
The former suffixes to the latter, as we assume that Agrs/Asp° is listed as prefixal:

(18)   Step 3:
         MUA of v° and AgrS°,
         inverting them

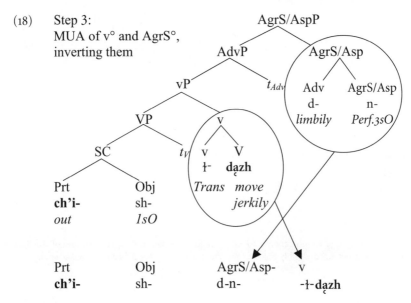

All the morphemes in (18) are now in the correct order. The particle and object can undergo MUA/cliticization with the remainder of the verb '*in situ*', as it were, and the complex morphophonological processes that derive the final surface form of the Navajo verb-word can be implemented.

10.5 Conclusions

In the above, following Speas (1991), I have simply drawn on extant, eminently reasonable proposals concerning affixation in various languages to spell out the notion that in addition to head movement, our arsenal of tools for coping with affixation must include both Merger Under Adjacency and a recognition that morphemes are inherently specified for their prefixal and suffixal selectional restriction (along with other specific selectional restrictions which it is clear that morphemes are subject to).

I have demonstrated that relaxing the assumptions surrounding affixation from strict left-adjoining head movement to allow for the occasional application of these other operations allows us to derive morpheme orders as complex as need be. Certain orders are predicted to be impossible in very complex contexts, given that syntactic head movement must precede Merger Under Adjacency, but for most purposes, pretty much any morpheme order could be generated with these quite simple mechanisms.

One could conclude, then, that in fact the Mirror Principle has been robbed of its predictive power entirely, and that it is never valid to draw conclusions about the order of syntactic projections from morpheme order. In fact, I would argue (following Rice 2000) that this is not so. Certain kinds of Mirror Principle violations have important implications for clausal syntax—in particular, situations in which morpheme orders clearly *respect* semantic scope, yet where the syntactic derivation seems to be at odds with that morpheme order in important ways. In other work (Harley 2007), I have argued that the interaction of Hiaki applicative and causative morphemes is such a case, where we are entitled to draw robust conclusions about the syntactic architecture because of scopally significant interactions depending on the order of these two morphemes.

It is only in cases like Cupeño, or Navajo, then, that appeal to these post-syntactic ordering mechanisms need be made. Indeed, in such cases the acquiring child could have positive evidence that such additional mechanisms have applied. Let us assume that the child's default assumption is that complex heads are derived by head movement, and that the hierarchical Mirror Principle applies. If the general order of the extended projection is provided by UG, interacting with conceptual structure, and assuming the child can identify morphemes in the input via a combination of morpho-phonological co-occurrence analysis and semantic deduction, mismatches between morpheme order and the extended projection can motivate the application of these limited additional mechanisms.[16] Economy constraints will dictate that as little use as possible should be made of such language-specific processes. The typological rarity of the Cupeño and Navajo patterns, then, is predicted; they require a complex combination of distinct affixation mechanisms to derive. Each mechanism by itself may well occur relatively frequently, and in familiar languages (Merger Under Adjacency in English verb tense specification, prefix/suffix specification in e.g. Swahili). Only in rare cases, however, will they interact with each other and with syntactic head movement simultaneously—hence the comparative markedness of the type of pattern analysed here.

---

[16] This type of consideration is key in any theory of these phenomena; for example, in Den Dikken's (2003) checking theory, involving a parameter for inside-out or outside-in mirroring, the choice between inside-out or outside-in for the acquiring child would also have to be driven by an observed mismatch of this type. However, the Cupeño pattern, where the mirror seems to apply in two different directions at once, seems potentially difficult for the restricted checking theory to account for.

11

Phases and Navajo Verbal Morphology*

LISA TRAVIS

11.1 Introduction

Navajo verbal morphology is a complex system that raises important questions about the interaction of various grammatical modules. In this paper, I seek to explain some of the more puzzling facts about Navajo verbal morphology by specifically addressing the interactions of the phonology, morphology, syntax, and semantics and the domains defined by them. By having some notion of how the components of the grammar pass on information at the interfaces one can provide better explanations of complex data.

11.2 Background

I start with some background on the facts that we will cover and the issues that these facts raise with respect to each of the grammatical components. At the outset, I acknowledge that there are two issues that I describe but leave unresolved with the hope that these two problems are not fatal to the account but rather point to interesting extensions of it.

11.2.1 *The Template*

Traditionally, the verbal system of Navajo has been described using a template (e.g. Young and Morgan 1987; Young 2000). Below I give an example of such a template with a brief description of the positions, adapted from Speas (1990: 205).[1]

* I am grateful for funding from SSHRC 410-2004-0966 and appreciate the feedback from the McGill PF Interface Reading Group (particularly Tobin Skinner and visitor Phil Branigan, who I probably should have listened more closely to), the OnLI audience (especially Heidi Harley, ditto), and an anonymous reviewer, who asked all the right questions. Some day I hope to be able to answer a few more.

[1] The problem of Navajo first came to my attention through Speas's work. For this reason, I often point to her book as a reference but there are, of course, many other sources for similar observations (e.g. Kari 1975; McDonough 2000, 2003; Young 2000; Young and Morgan 1987).

(1) Navajo Verbal Morpheme Order

DISJUNCT PREFIXES				CONJUNCT PREFIXES					
ADV	ITER	DIST-PL	#	D-OBJ	DEIC-SBJ	ADV	MODE	SBJ	VOICE/TRNS STEM
1	2	3	4	5	6	7	8	9√	

1 = ADVERBIAL: **manner, direction ... also indirect object pronoun**
2 = ITERATIVE: aspectual/adverbial prefix
3 = DISTRIBUTIVE PLURAL: plural and distributive, 'each one separately'
4 = DIRECT OBJECT: number and person of direct object
5 = DEICTIC SUBJECT: indefinite (someone) or fourth person (people in general)
6 = ADVERBIAL: **adverbial/aspectual notions**
7 = MODE: core of tense system
8 = SUBJECT: person and number of subject
9 = **voice/transitivity**

While it would be ideal to show the extent of this template through a series of examples, this, in fact, is quite difficult. However, below is one example taken from Speas (1990: 210) that gives a feel for the morphology.[2]

(2) Navajo Verbal Morpheme Order
Ná'ádidiists'in   'I hit myself once with a fist.'

Ná +	'ádi +	di	+ yi	+ sh	+ ts'in
up	REFL	*against*	SERIATIVE	1SGS	STEM
1	4	6	7	8	9

11.2.2 *The Issues*

Many generalizations about Navajo are embedded within this template—generalizations that span different modules of the grammar. I give a brief overview of some of these generalizations in order to set up subsequent sections of the paper, where these are addressed in more detail.

11.2.2.1 *The Morphology Issue*   We first can observe that the morphemes seem to be in the reverse order of what would be predicted by Baker's (1985) Mirror Principle along with Cinque's (1999) universal functional hierarchy. Given the Mirror Principle, we expect heads that are lower in the tree to be represented

---

[2] I have changed Speas's gloss from 2SGS to 1SGS. I assume that it is a typographical error. The original example is in Young and Morgan (1987: 71 Dictionary) without the morpheme breakdown or the translation. Abbreviations: REFL = reflexive; 1SGS = 1st person singular subject.

by morphemes closer to the stem. For example, in the Huichol example given in (3a) below (taken from Baker 1985: 389), object agreement appears closer to the root than subject agreement. In the Abkhaz example in (3b) below (taken from Cinque 1999: 155), iterative/frequentative marking appears closer to the stem than tense.[3]

(3)   a. Wan maria naa-ti   me-meci-miene   HUICHOL
         Juan Maria and-SUBJ 3PS-1SO-kill/SG
         'Juan and Maria are killing me.'

      b. ye-z-ba-ka-x'è-yt'   ABKHAZ
         it-I-see-FREQ-ANT-PRES
         'I have already seen it several times.'

These orders are expected since objects are lower in the syntactic structure than subjects and Aspect is lower in the syntactic structure than Tense (see Cinque 1999 for details on the hierarchies of different types of aspect).

In Navajo, however, we get the reverse order in both cases. First, the subject (agreement) position (#8) is closer to the stem than the object (agreement) position (#4). Second, the tense position (#7) is closer to the stem than the aspect position (#2). #7 is labelled Mode but according to Speas (1990: 206) this position 'marks the core of the tense system in Navajo'. #2 marks iterativity, i.e. a type of Aspect. These two pairs are shown schematically below.

(4)   ANTI-MIRROR PRINCIPLE
      Aspect Object Tense Subject Trans/Voice Stem
       2...   4...   7...   8   9√

In some sense, we want to attach the leftmost prefixes to the stem before we attach the rightmost prefixes given their syntactic position. An important task for the morphology, then, is to account for this reverse ordering of morphemes.

11.2.2.2 *The Phonology Issue*   Another generalization that is captured in this template involves a phonological distinction. Positions 1 to 3 are labelled disjunct prefixes and Positions 4 to 9 are conjunct prefixes. The difference in labelling encodes a difference in how these prefixes behave phonologically. Disjunct prefixes are 'loosely bound' while conjunct prefixes are 'tightly bound' based on 'functional, phonological, and positional criteria' (Young 2000: 27). The phonological information from the template now seems to be at

---

[3] Abbreviations: SUBJ = subject; 3PS = third person plural subject; 1SS = first person singular object; SG = singular; FREQ = frequentative; ANT = anterior; PRES = present.

odds with the morphological information. I suggested above that the leftmost morphemes are syntactically more closely related to the stem (i.e. need to be attached first). The phonology, however, suggests that the rightmost morphemes are attached first, accounting for why they are more tightly bound.

11.2.2.3 *The Semantics Issue*   There is also an interesting semantic issue embedded in the template. Note that positions 1 and 6 are both labelled Adverbial. These two positions house material that is often lexically and semantically idiosyncratic. Another way of looking at it is to say that lexical entries span positions 1, 6, and 9. We will see other examples later, but one is given in (5) below.

(5)   *kéé...ha...t'į* 'to reside'   1...6...stem

One might want to say that these three positions form a semantic unit and therefore should be merged into the structure together. We would now have three bits of contradictory information. The Mirror Principle suggests that the leftmost elements are attached to the stem first, phonology tells us that the rightmost elements are attached first and semantics tells us that Positions 1 and 6 are attached first.

11.2.2.4 *The Syntax Issue*   Syntax needs to create a structure that will produce the appropriate phonological and semantic representations at the interfaces. The main syntax issue is to find a structure that, when processed by the appropriate interface mechanisms, can account for the generalizations just discussed.

11.3 Introduction to the Phonology

Before delving into the structure that we will be using as a base for our account, it is helpful to know a bit about the phonology of Navajo. Disjunct and conjunct prefixes are phonologically distinguishable. Again we see below that the conjunct prefixes appear closer to the stem than do the disjunct prefixes.

(6)   DISJUNCT vs CONJUNCT prefixes

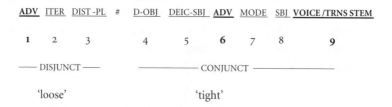

ADV	ITER	DIST	-PL	#	D-OBJ	DEIC-SBJ	ADV	MODE	SBJ	VOICE/TRNS	STEM
1	2	3		4	5	6	7	8	9		

—— DISJUNCT ——   ———————— CONJUNCT ————————

      'loose'   'tight'

In order to set up the distinction between the two types of prefixes, we must know (a) that all stems in Navajo are monosyllabic (Speas 1990: 208),[4] and (b) that the minimal word is two syllables (Speas 1990: 257). Conjunct prefixes differ from disjunct prefixes in often being analysed as just a C (less than stem size) while disjunct prefixes are always stem size (CV). We can see that the minimal word requirement of two syllables must be met at the edge of the conjunct prefix domain.

To make this clear, let us look at the progressive paradigm. The apparent form of this morpheme varies depending on the shape (C or CV) and type (conjunct or disjunct) of prefixes that combine with it. The assumption is that, underlyingly, the progressive prefix is null, and its two alternates (V and -*yi*) appear to meet the requirement of being a minimal word. In (7a), where the conjunct prefix *ni-* is attached in position 8, we see a case where the progressive morpheme does not appear phonetically. At the edge of the conjunct prefix domain, there is sufficient phonological material to meet the two syllable requirement. In (7b), however, the conjunct prefix *sh-* is added in position 8, not adding enough material for the two syllable require-ment, so an epenthetic syllable is added. In a more extreme case shown in (7c), both conjunct prefixes are null and again we have syllable epenthesis (from Speas 1990: 209).[5]

(7)   CONJUNCT prefixes
    a. nicha   'You are crying.'
        0+ni+cha
        PROG+2SGS+cry

    b. yishcha   'I am crying.'
        0+sh+cha
        PROG+1SGS+cry

    c. yicha   'S/he is crying.'
        0+0+cha
        PROG+3SGS+cry

Next, we can see in (8a) below that disjunct prefixes cannot help satisfy the minimal word requirement, i.e. the requirement must be met before the addition of the disjunct prefixes. The disjunct prefix *na-* in position 1 does not behave the same way as the prefix *ni-* that we saw in (7a) above. In this case the vowel is lengthened showing that there has been vowel insertion at

---

[4] Speas mentions that there are a few regular exceptions to this (Speas 1990: 257). These will be examined in future work.

[5] Abbreviations: PROG = progressive; SGS = singular subject.

the edge of the conjunct domain in order to satisfy the minimal word requirement (from Kari 1975: 338).[6] In (8b) we see this schematically where '[' marks the edge of the conjunct domain.

(8)   Disjunct prefix
    a. naashbé   'I am swimming around.'
        na+0+sh+bé
        ADV+PROG+1SSG+swim
    b. na + [V + sh + bé]

Following ideas from Newell and Piggott's (2006a, 2006b) analysis for Ojibwa, I assume that the distinct behaviour at this boundary indicates a phase edge, where a phase is a domain of the syntax that is passed to the phonology and transformed by the phonology into a single object.[7] The phonological component, upon receiving this material, will evaluate and repair the form according to the language-specific constraints. In the case we have just seen, the phonology will be ensuring that the material in this domain contains two syllables.

11.4 Syntax

Now we turn to syntax in order to fine-tune what we count as a domain or phase. We will be concerned with phrase structure and head movement. Anticipating a solution, we will first leave aside the problem of the disjunct prefixes (positions 1 to 3) and represent the conjunct prefixes as heads on a syntactic tree.

11.4.1 *The Structure*

In earlier work, I used the morpheme order within the verbal template of Navajo to support my proposal that there is an inflectional domain within the lexical domain of the *v*P (Travis 1992b). The structure below shows schematically how the conjunct prefixes line up with the domains I proposed.

---

[6] Vowel insertion is sufficient in this case unlike the examples in (7) where there is CV insertion.

[7] It is important to point out that I take a phase to be the material that is sent off to the interfaces, i.e. the extent of the phonological and semantic domain. In other words, the head of the phase does not send its complement to the interface but rather the projection of that head is what is transferred to the interface. *v*P is a phase and the whole *v*P is sent to the two interfaces. Given the space constraints on this paper, I cannot justify my underlying assumptions but refer the reader to Skinner (2009) and Dobler *et al.* (2009) for arguments.

(9)

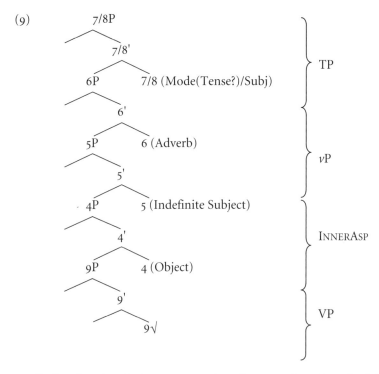

I will, for the time being, assume that the mapping given in (9) above is justifiable. First, it is not a stretch to assume that the morphemes encoding subject and tense features are housed within the TP domain. Further, I have argued elsewhere (e.g. Travis 1992a) that Inner Aspect is involved in the licensing of objects so it would be no surprise that object features are found within the Inner Aspect domain. Also, having the stem (9√) within VP is not unexpected. Three issues remain. One is the positioning of #6 in *v*P. I support this decision below in section 11.7. The remaining two have to do with the two questions mentioned at the outset of the paper. These are (i) the position of the indefinite subject features, and (ii) the clustering of morphemes (9+√) in V. I will discuss (i) in a bit more detail in section 11.7 below but immediately address (ii) to the extent that I can.

The clustering of morphemes as one head in (9) is problematic for two reasons. First, the actual content of Position #9 suggests it should be higher in the phrase structure.[8] We see in the template in (1) that the material of Position #9 encodes transitivity and voice. Given other analyses where this

---

[8] Heidi Harley pointed this out as a comment on my talk at OnLI.

sort of information in languages like Japanese is in v (e.g. Harley 2008), one might, in fact, hypothesize a very different mapping to phrase structure with Position #9 being housed in v. However, because of the interactions of the other grammatical modules, I have not been able to make this mapping explain as many of the generalizations. For this reason, I am assuming that this material is attached directly to the root.

The second problem is that, as we will see in the next section, I will need this cluster to act as an indivisible unit. There are phonological reasons to believe that there is also an edge of a phase between positions 8 and 9. Much has been written on what is called the d-effect in Navajo (see e.g. McDonough 2000). The boundary between 8 and 9 shows a special phonology. McDonough accounts for this special behaviour by positing a compound analysis of the Navajo verb form (inflection+V) where positions 1–8 are the first part of the compound and positions 9+√ are the second part of the compound. There are reasons to believe that the compound analysis cannot be the correct one (see Goad and Travis in preparation) but the direction of her proposal is right. I posit that 9+√ constitutes a phonological phase that has the maximal size of a syllable. This restriction on phonological size prevents vowel epenthesis from occurring.[9] Since the root itself will be a syllable, the additional material added in position 9 (e.g. the morpheme *d-*) will be forced to coalesce with the onset of the stem. Because of this different sort of phonology, I am assuming that there is a phase edge here, and that for further computation, the complex 9+√ acts as a unit.[10]

11.4.2 *Head Movement*

If we now add head movement to the picture outlined above, we get the right order of morphemes except for the positioning of the 9√ complex, which will appear at the left edge of the word instead of the right edge. The resulting bracketing after head movement is given in (10) below.

(10)   [[[[[[9√] 4] 5] 6] 7] 8]

I will assume that this is the appropriate bracketing to be derived from the syntax. We now turn to the tools available to us at the PF interface to see how the needed surface order can be derived.

---

[9] McDonough (2000) accounts for the lack of epenthesis by positing that the verbal part of the compound must align the right edge of the verbal domain with the right edge of the stem.

[10] One way of looking at this is that there is a prosodic phase (VP), and event-level phase (*v*P), and a proposition-level phase (CP). There are problems with this. I have never seen a case where there is an inner phase that has a maximality restriction (here one syllable) contained within a phase that has a minimality restriction (here two syllables). I leave further investigation of this for future research.

11.5 Morphology: Part I—Local Dislocation

There are a variety of ways that the order in (10) that has been produced by the syntactic component can be manipulated by the morphology at the PF interface to produce the correct order. I will choose from a group of analyses that all share a common mechanism that just varies in minor details. In Travis (1992b) I proposed that the morphemes were added sequentially to the lowest grouping of $9\sqrt{}$ but that each additional morpheme was prefixed to the left edge of that grouping. This has the effect that the last to attach (#8) ends up linearly adjacent to $9\sqrt{}$ while the first to attach ends up the furthest from this grouping. The detail question is what defines this grouping. Speas (1990) noted that every position in the template can be phonologically defined. Therefore, rather than resorting to a template, one could say that each affix had a phonologically identifiable attachment site. This creates a very powerful system that does not explain why the morphemes appear to be in the reverse order. One could, however, iteratively use her phonological condition for position #8 which is __ CV(C)#, in other words the final syllable. As each additional morpheme is added, it would attach to the final syllable pushing the previously attached morphemes to the left.

An alternative, which I use here, is iterative Local Dislocation (see Embick and Noyer 2001, and Embick 2007).[11] Local Dislocation is a process that attaches one element (either M-word or Subword) to another linearly adjacent element of the same type (either M-word or Subword). Local Dislocation occurs after Vocabulary Insertion and has the effect, in this case, of attaching one Subword to a phonologically adjacent Subword. It is important to note that here the Subword is attaching as a prefix.

In the bracketed structure in (10), every head is now a Subword. As such, Local Dislocation can apply to these heads. Local Dislocation would first apply to 4, which would dislocate with the adjacent Subword $9\sqrt{}$ (shown in (11b)). Next 5 would local dislocate with $9\sqrt{}$ creating (11c), and so on. At the end of the computation, we have the appropriate order of morphemes shown in (11f).[12]

---

[11] David Embick (p.c.) has suggested that Local Dislocation can only occur once as a repair mechanism, which is not what is happening here. If the process of Local Dislocation is not the appropriate mechanism, I would return to the previous solution of having all prefixation attach to the edge of the domain containing $9+\sqrt{}$. This latter solution would look like a head-movement version of tucking in as in Richards (1997, 2001). I owe much to Joey Sabbagh in helping me work this out. All mistakes and misunderstandings, however, are my own.

[12] Following convention, I use the symbol $\oplus$ to indicate two elements that have become attached via Local Dislocation.

(11)   a. [[[[[[9√] 4] 5] 6] 7] 8]

    b. [[[[[4⊕9√] 5] 6] 7] 8]

    c. [[[[4⊕5⊕9√] 6] 7] 8]

    d. [[[4⊕5⊕6⊕9√] 7] 8]

    e. [[4⊕5⊕6⊕7⊕9√] 8]

    f. [4⊕5⊕6⊕7⊕8⊕9√]

It is important to note the role of syntax in this account. First, the bracketing must be created by syntactic head movement. In other words, Local Dislocation is fed by the syntax, which has created a complex structure of Subwords allowing iterative Local Dislocation of this type. Further, as we have seen in section 11.3 above, the phonology of these forms suggests that all of the conjunct affixes are in the same phase—a surprising result given that the syntactic structure represents two phases (*v*P-internal and *v*P-external material). This is also explained through head movement as the *v*P-internal material will have moved, bleeding the spell-out of *v*P. All of the conjunct material will be spelled out in the CP phase.[13]

    Post-syntax and post-morphology, we now have the following structure.

(12)

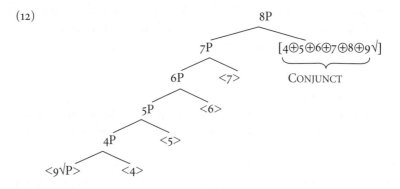

I am assuming (following Newell 2004) that syntactic structure is still available at this point for reasons that will become obvious in section 11.6 below. As we can see, all of the conjunct prefixes are part of a complex word.

---

[13] Given the conception of phases that I am using in this paper, we can have head movement both pre-spell-out and post-spell-out. Pre-spell-out movement will bleed spell-out and a phonological domain will be created that contains heads from two syntactic phases. See Dobler *et al.* (2009) for more discussion of these two types of head movement.

Now we turn to the issue of disjunct prefixes, starting with a phonological overview of the distinction. I then propose a morphological solution for the distinction.

11.6 Morphology: Part II—Late Adjunction

I start by looking at the disjunct morphemes themselves with the goal of aligning them to the relevant syntactic heads. As we saw earlier, the material in Position 1 presents a particular problem. As described in section 11.2.2.3, this position often houses material that acts as an idiosyncratic part of a lexical item. However, as a disjunct prefix, it is outside the phase that houses the conjunct prefixes. We start by looking at what the material in this position can encode (keeping in mind that the semantics is often not compositional). As we see in the lists below, the meaning is very similar to the meaning imparted by English particles (*throw **out**, toss **in**, take **away***) or German separable prefixes (*ab, an, auf, aus, ein*).

(13)   Position 1

    a. Bound postpositionals (Young 2000: 45)

      -kʼí-:   onto (e.g. pour onto)

      -í-:   against (e.g. lap against)

      -gha-:   away from (e.g. take away from)

      -ghá: through (e.g. penetrate through)

    b. Simple adverbials

      ʼa- ʼe- ʼi-: away, out of sight (e.g. the sun sets, moves away out of sight)

      ha-:   up, up out (e.g. climb up)

      ʼahá-: apart, in half (e.g. cut in two)

      ʼada-: downward from a height (e.g. descend)

      chʼi-: horizontally (e.g. carry outside)

      na¹-: around (e.g. walk around)

      na³-: downward (e.g. get down)

      ná¹-: around (e.g. extend around)

      ná⁴-: up from a surface (e.g. get up)

This parallel is interesting because English particles and German separable prefixes also have a semantically tight connection and phonologically loose connection to the stem, and, as such, present interesting problems for linguists. Newell (2005) outlines an analysis of separable prefixes in German that accounts for this dual behaviour. As we see in the German example below (shown in (14a)), the German verb moves to some higher functional category (in the structure here it is in C), leaving its prefix behind.[14] The structure in (14b) shows her account. Adapting ideas of Lebeaux (1991), Nissenbaum (2000), and Stepanov (2002), she posits late adjunction for these prefixes. After movement, the separable prefix is attached to the lowest copy of the verb.

(14) a. [$_{CP}$ Hans [fädelt [$_{TP}$ den   Faden [$_{VP}$ [$_{v}$ ein t]]]
            Hans   threads   the   needle   in
         'Hans threads the needle.'

    b.

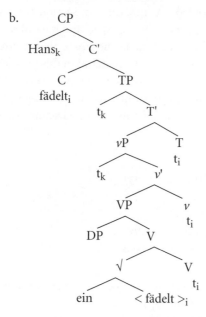

The prefix is loosely attached phonologically because it is adjoined late, after movement. It is closely attached semantically because in the semantic component, it is adjoined to the root. In later work (Newell 2008), she argues that the particle adjoins to Aspect, explaining why its presence interacts with the aspectual interpretation. I would rather that it adjoin to a lower projection that could encode the endpoint of an event that here I will call X (see Travis 2010 for more on this position). The tree in (15) below shows how the same ideas can be applied for the material in Position 1 and reapplied for Positions 2 and 3 (I return later to my justifications for the attachment sites for these latter two).

---

[14] I use a slightly different example from the one in Newell's work as German speakers found her sentence pragmatically odd.

(15)

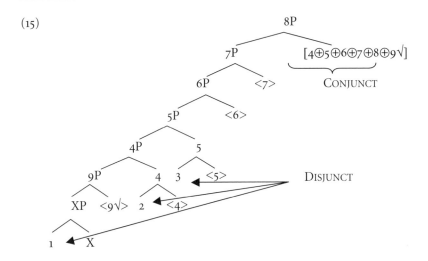

11.7 Syntax: Part II—More on Phrase Structure

Now let us look more closely at how more of the actual morphemes match up with syntactic heads. Here I look specifically at Positions 6, 2 and 4, and 3 and 5.

(16)

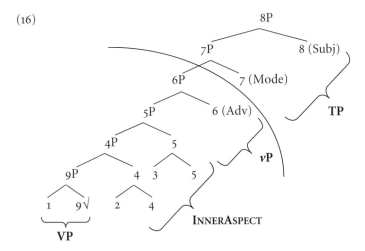

We begin by looking at the material that appears in Position 6, which I claim to be syntactically realized as *v*. This position is described as an adverbial element that is part of the lexical entry. I give some of the uses for this position (taken from Young 2000: 32).

(17)   Position 6
    (i)   thematic elements
        a. movement of arms/legs (e.g. reach with hand, step into)
        b. fire/light (e.g. to burn something, light shines through)
        c. stomach/food/oral noise (e.g. belch, say)
    (ii)   co-occurs with Position 1 downward prefix and acts as a unit meaning 'downward movement to a state of freedom'
    (iii)   inchoative (e.g. start to paint)
    (iv)   seriative (e.g. enter one after another)

This set of meanings is harder to characterize than that of Position 1 and at this point I can only make vague suggestions. These meanings clearly do not encode endpoints of events (which we earlier attached to V). The meanings we find here are either beginning points (inchoative) or manner/instrument (thematic elements). I claim that aligning these meanings with v is not unreasonable as they can be seen as 'manner tags' in the sense of Hale and Keyser (1993).

The two pairs of Positions 2 and 4 and Positions 3 and 5 I suggest are both part of an inflectional domain found within the vP (see Travis 2010). The first pair, Positions 2 and 4 are fairly straightforward. I have argued elsewhere (Travis 1991, 1992a) that direct objects are licensed by a functional category merged below the external argument (see also Koizumi 1993). In my work, this functional category is Inner Aspect. That this category would encode object agreement (Position 4) and be host for the late adjunction of the iterative morpheme (Position 2), then, is not surprising.[15]

We are left with the more difficult problem of Position 5 (deictic subject) and Position 3 (distributive plural), which has late adjoined to it. This is the second unresolved issue that I leave for further research. Here I just suggest a direction of a solution. Given the rest of my analysis, I am forced to say that these two are also part of the inner inflectional domain.[16] Now the question is: how defendable is this claim? At first it looks very surprising that a morpheme related to the subject would appear so low in the tree, below the position where the external argument is introduced. However, the use of this

[15] An anonymous reviewer points out that, following von Stechow's (1995) work, one would expect that a repetition morpheme attached so low would have a restitutive reading rather than an iterative reading. I would need more data to be able to address this.

[16] As pointed out by an anonymous reviewer, I have shoe-horned several morphemes (2,3,4,5) into one head (Inner Aspect), suggesting that I am using the label to designate a region of the tree rather than a head. Frankly, at this point, I'm not sure if one head can host several morphemes or if we have an articulated Inner Aspect, similar to Cinque's (1999) proposals. I leave this aside for now.

morpheme is to construct an impersonal passive (see Young 2000: 35)—a construction with an indefinite (someone) or fourth person (people in general) subject. This is less surprising, especially when thought of as a passive where external arguments are introduced differently. Perhaps this morpheme saturates the external argument before *v* is merged, giving the effect of something between an unaccusative (no external argument at all) and a passive (where an external argument can be realized with a *by*-phrase). The distributive plural (Position 3) late-adjoins to this position. Young (2000: 39–42) points out that the morpheme can be related to subjects or objects. Objects we know are licensed within this internal inflectional domain, and I have just proposed that external arguments may also be saturated here. However, much more work needs to be done to explain these relations satisfactorily.[17]

11.8 Semantics: Lexical Entries

The last issue that I address is the question of lexical entry. What does it mean to say that a lexical entry is spread over three positions? Young (2000: 27) makes a clear distinction between positions 1 and 6 on one hand and positions 2, 3, 4, 7, and 8 on the other hand calling the former derivational (thematic-adverbial) prefixes while the latter are called inflectional affixes. Speas gives the following examples of non-productive prefixes.

(18)   a. *yá...ti'*   'to talk'   1...   stem
       b. *di...lid*   'to burn something'   6 ...   stem
       c. *so...di...zin* 'to pray'   1... 6 ...   stem

She states 'None of these prefixes is derivationally productive, nor may these stems (a,b,c) occur without these prefixes' (Speas 1990: 208). I claim that these positions along with the stem account for the three lexical heads within the *v*P—*v*, V, and X. These are the three heads that we expect to contain idiosyncratic information.

We can see by looking at other languages that *v* can be idiosyncratic in morphological realization and in semantic composition. Starting with morphological shape, we can see in the table below that Japanese has a lexical causative that can be encoded by a variety of suffixes.

---

[17] In Travis (2010), I compare this morpheme to Spanish *se* which also has the effect of creating impersonal passives and unaccusatives and which has been argued by Bruhn-Garavito (2000) to appear below the theta position of the external argument.

(19)   Morphology for Japanese Lexical Causatives (from Harley 1996)

INTRANSITIVE

-ar-   (ag-ar-u *rise*)
-re-   (hazu-re-ru *come off*)
-ri-   (ta-ri-ru *suffice*)
-e-   (kog-e-ru *become scorched*)
-i-   (ok-i-ru *get up* (intr))
-Ø-   (nar-Ø-u *ring* (intr))
-Ø-   (ak-Ø-u *open* (intr))
-e-   (kir-e-ru *be cut*)
-ar-   (matag-ar-u *sit astride*)

TRANSITIVE

-e-   (ag-e-ru *raise*)
-s-   (hasu-s-u *take off*)
-s-   (ta-s-u *supplement*)
-as-   (kog-as-u *scorch*)
-os-   (ok-os-u *get up* (tr))
-as-   (nar-as-u *ring* (tr))
-e-   (ak-e-ru *open* (tr))
-Ø-   (kir-Ø-u *cut*)
-Ø-   (matag-Ø-u *straddle*)

We also know that the meaning of lexical causatives is not necessarily compositional. In English, transitive *redden* does not mean *cause to redden* as the sentence 'The make-up artist reddened the clown's cheeks' shows. Another example, this time from Tagalog, is given below.[18]

(20)   Tagalog
   a. Sumabog   sa Boston ang bomba[19]
       AT-PERF-*SABOG* in Boston NOM bomb
       'The bomb exploded in Boston.'

   b. # Nagsabog   ng   bomba sa Boston ang   terorista
       AT-PERF-*PAG*-*SABOG* ACC   bomb   in Boston NOM   terrorist
       cannot mean: 'The terrorist exploded the bomb in Boston.'
       get odd reading: 'The terrorist scattered the bomb in Boston.'

Just as *v* and V often do not have compositional meaning, V and X also combine unpredictably. This is easily seen in the examples below with English particles. For example, the meaning of *look up* 'to search for information' cannot be predicted from the meanings of *look* and *up*.

(21)   English particles
   a. look up
   b. throw up
   c. take in
   d. take up
   e. make out

---

[18] Abbreviations: AT = Actor Topic (i.e. the Actor is the subject); PERF = perfective; NOM = nominative; ACC = accusative.

[19] I use the Tagalog forms of *SABOG* and *PAG* here rather than glosses since the appropriate translation is part of the issue under discussion.

If *v*, V, and X can be shown in other languages to contribute in idiosyncratic ways—semantically and morphologically—to the predicate as indicated in (22) below, it should not be surprising that a language like Navajo would have idiosyncratic material in all three of these positions.

(22)

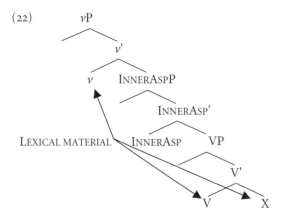

So far the three languages we have seen to support the claim that *v*, V, and X can be composed in idiosyncratic manners have all been agglutinating. This is not a necessary condition, however, as the same effects can be seen in extreme isolating languages, such as serial verb languages. Below we see that Yoruba predicates can be made up of two independent verbs. In (23) we see constructions where each verb has a meaning but together form a distinct lexical item. In (24) we see an extreme case where neither of the two verbal forms has a distinguishable meaning and they can only be used with another form to create a complex lexical item.

(23) Serial verb constructions: Yoruba (taken from Sebba 1987: 199)

	V1	V2	V1…V2 gloss
a.	*fa* 'pull'	*ya* 'tear'	'tear up'
b.	*là* 'cut open'	*yé* 'understand'	'explain'
c.	*pa* 'hit'	*de* 'cover up'	'close'
d.	*pa* 'hit'	*run* 'crush'	'destroy'
e.	*tàn* 'trick'	*je* 'consume'	'trick'
f.	*rí* 'see'	*gbà* 'take'	'receive'
g.	*gba* 'take, get'	*gbó* 'hear'	'believe'

(24) No identifiable meaning of the parts

omi   ti   bà á jé
water that ?   it ?
'Water has spoilt it.'

I propose that parts of lexical items can be inserted into lexical heads within the *v*P, i.e. spanning *v*, V, and X and that these elements must be interpreted in their merged positions.[20] Note that, just like larger idioms (see O'Grady 1998) these elements do not necessarily form a syntactic constituent. This is clearest in the case of serial verb constructions where the idiosyncratic elements are separate syntactic elements with intervening objects, but it is also true of Navajo where the idiosyncratic elements are found within the same word but do not form a Subword constituent.

11.9 Conclusions

While Navajo morphology is complex and presents apparent contradictions for any linguist, with a better understanding of the interfaces, we can begin to chip away at the problem. The contradictions lie in the fact that each module of the grammar appears to group the morphemes differently. Phonology sees positions 4–9 as one group and 1–3 as another (the conjunct/disjunct distinction). Syntax sees 1–6+9 as one grouping and 7 and 8 as another (*v*P-internal and *v*P-external). Semantics sees 1, 6, 9 as one grouping and 2–5, 7–8 as another (lexical entry vs inflectional material). Using PF interface processes such as Local Dislocation and late adjunction and LF interface processes such as lexical category (lexical item) interpretation, these contradictions can be given an explanation.

[20] In Travis (2000a, 2000b) I discussed the difference between lexical causatives (idiosyncratic) and productive causatives (non-idiosyncratic) as characterizing syntactic domains. Goldberg (2005) uses data from VP ellipsis to argue that Vs must be interpreted in their merged positions.

12

The Syntax and Prosody of Turkish 'Pre-stressing' Suffixes*

ARSALAN KAHNEMUYIPOUR AND
JAKLIN KORNFILT

12.1 Introduction

This paper is framed in the general context of the relation between phonology (in this case prosody) and (morpho)syntax. It has been observed that certain phonological rules are sensitive to syntactic structure in one way or another and many linguists have tried to account for such interactions (e.g. Selkirk 1980a, 1984, 1986; Nespor and Vogel 1982, 1986). These interactions have also been explored in the context of the syntax-prosody interface (e.g. Nespor and Vogel 1986; Hayes and Lahiri 1991; Nespor 1999; Hsiao 2002; Kahnemuyipour 2003, 2009; Wagner 2005; and Kratzer and Selkirk 2007). In particular, we discuss a set of suffixes in Turkish whose apparent effect is to put stress on the preceding syllable, thus the traditional term 'pre-stressing' suffixes. Regular stress in Turkish is word-final, and in this respect words involving these suffixes appear to have violated the regular pattern. Descriptively, some of these suffixes are verbal, some clausal,[1] some nominal, and a couple derive adjectives and adverbs. The focus of this paper is on the clausal and verbal suffixes in (1). (We provide a brief discussion of the non-verbal suffixes in the concluding section.)

* We thank Gabriela Alboiu, Marcel den Dikken, Elan Dresher, Robert Vago, and audiences at the 2006 CLA meeting, the CUNY Graduate Center, the ONLI conference at the University of Ulster, and SPINE 3 at Cornell University for their questions and comments on earlier versions of this chapter. Our special thanks go to two anonymous reviewers and the editors of this volume, Christiane Ulbrich and Raffaella Folli. The names of the authors are in alphabetical order.

[1] We take clausal morphemes to be those which take CP/TP as their complements.

(1)   (a) 'Pre-stressing' clausal suffixes:[2]
        ki: complementizer; *-(y)ken* 'when, while': temporal adverbial
        postposition

      (b) 'Pre-stressing' verbal suffixes:
        Agreement suffixes (reanalysed below as the inflected *y/Ø* copular
        clitic); *-mI*
        Yes/No question marker; *-mA* verbal negator[3]

There have been several attempts to account for the behaviour of 'pre-stressing' suffixes in Turkish (cf. Hameed 1985; Kaisse 1985, 1986; van der Hulst and van de Weijer 1991; Inkelas and Orgun 1995, 1998, 2003; Inkelas 1999; Kabak and Vogel 2001; Newell 2004b). While from a theory-internal perspective, these analyses may differ in terms of their degree of success in dealing with the Turkish facts, crucially, they all suffer from one major problem. In all these analyses, the 'pre-stressing' suffixes have been treated as a homogeneous group with a lexically pre-specified property that leads to their particular stress behaviour. According to such accounts, there is no principled reason why these (and not other) suffixes behave in this particular way.[4] In this paper we seek a principled explanation for the particular stress behaviour of these suffixes by tying their prosodic behaviour to their syntax. We argue that the 'pre-stressing' suffixes do not form a homogeneous class and that their similar stress pattern is an epiphenomenon. While some disparate suffixes will be unified, other apparently similar suffixes will be shown to need distinct syntactic analyses, while yielding similar stress effects.[5] The remainder of the paper is organized as follows. Section 12.2 deals with the clausal 'pre-stressing' suffixes. In section 12.3, we provide an account of the pre-stressing behaviour of the agreement suffixes building on Kornfilt (1996). Sections 12.4 and 12.5 are devoted to the question marker and the negation marker, respectively. Section 12.6 elaborates on the typology of 'pre-stressing' suffixes proposed in this paper. Section 12.7 concludes the paper.

---

[2] We do not take these to be genuine suffixes but rather enclitics. For the sake of convenience, we are extending the term 'suffix' to these elements as a merely descriptive term.

[3] We follow here general Turkological practice in indicating segments that undergo assimilation processes by using capital letters; in particular, capital letters for vowels indicate vowels that undergo Vowel Harmony for backness and rounding.

[4] Unfortunately, space limitations preclude a detailed discussion of these previous analyses in this paper.

[5] In the process of preparing this paper, we have been introduced to Kamali and Samuels (2008), a presentation at TIE3 in Lisbon, which addresses some of the same questions as ours and raises some criticisms of older versions of this paper. Time and space constraints do not allow us to give a full consideration and response to their paper.

12.2 Clausal 'Suffixes'

The clausal 'suffixes' (cf. footnote 1) in (1a) belong to separate syntactic (and as such independent stress) domains from the material on their left. To clarify, let us consider the examples in (2). (2a) shows the complementizer *ki*, a C head, which takes the TP on its right as its complement. Assuming that the syntactic boundary of a clause matches the phonological boundary of stress assignment, the fact that *ki* is not part of the preceding material follows straightforwardly. (2b) shows *(y)ken*, which we take to be a temporal P whose complement is the CP on its left. Therefore, *(y)ken* is outside the syntactic domain of the preceding material and by similar reasoning as in (2a) it is outside the stress domain of that preceding material.

(2)   a.   Duy -dú   -m   [$_{CP}$**ki** [Oya opera -ya   git -miş]]
            hear -PAST-1.SG   **that**   Oya opera -DAT go -RP
            'I heard that Oya went to the opera.'

        b.   Oya [$_{PP}$[$_{CP}$PRO kitap okú -r]   -**ken**]   uyu   -yakal -dı
            Oya   book read -AOR-**while** sleep -'fall' -PAST
            'Oya fell asleep while reading (a) book(s).'

It is worth noting that these clausal suffixes are the only ones among the 'pre-stressing' suffixes that do not undergo Vowel Harmony, as shown in (2), where the so-called 'pre-stressing' suffixes exhibit front vowels after a preceding back vowel, thus violating Vowel Harmony in Turkish (for general references on Turkish Vowel Harmony, see Lees 1961, Clements 1980, van der Hulst and van de Weijer 1991, 1995). This shows that they are not only outside the (smaller) domain of stress, but even outside the (typically larger) domain of Vowel Harmony.[6] This is precisely as expected given the clausal nature of these morphemes. Below, we turn to the verbal suffixes.

---

[6] Unlike stress, the domain of Vowel Harmony in Turkish does not completely correspond to syntactic structure and is determined more superficially, in that the backness (and rounding) of the final vowel in the root or any other element with lexically prespecified values for these two features extend to all the vowels in the following suffixes. This harmonizing process stops at the next vowel with prespecified backness (and rounding) features. Clausal morphemes (see note 1) have vowels prespecified for these features, while other morphemes that take smaller syntactic domains as their complements have underspecified vowels which therefore do get harmonized.

12.3 Agreement Suffixes

There are a large number of (apparently) verbal agreement suffixes (our Group A), traditionally characterized as 'pre-stressing', which attach to most *simple* tenses, as shown in (3). We have posited a null copula in these forms, an issue we will return to below.

(3)   Group A agreement suffixes: 'Pre-stressing' agreement markers with simple verbal tenses (limited to 1st and 2nd person)

	Future	Aorist	Reported Past
1.SG.	gid-ecéğ- Ø -im	gid-ér- Ø -im	git-míş- Ø -im
2.SG.	gid-ecék- Ø -sin	gid-ér- Ø -sin	git-míş- Ø -sin
1.PL.	gid-ecéğ- Ø -iz	gid-ér- Ø -iz	git-míş- Ø -iz
2.PL.	gid-ecék- Ø -siniz	gid-ér- Ø -siniz	git-míş- Ø -siniz
	go-FUT-COP-Agr.	go-AOR-COP-Agr.	go-RP-COP-Agr.

Another group of verbal agreement markers shown in (4) (our Group B) are regular with respect to stress, and attach to two forms: the definite past, and the simple conditional.

(4)   Group B agreement suffixes : 'Regular' agreement markers with simple verbal tenses (no copula):

	Definite Past	Conditional	(stem *gid* 'go')
1.SG.	git-tí-**m**	git-sé-**m**	
2.SG.	git-tí-**n**	git-sé-**n**	
1.PL.	git-tí-**k**	git-sé-**k**	
2.PL.	git-ti-**níz**	git-se-**níz**	
	go-PAST-Agr.	go-COND-Agr.	

To account for the apparently distinct stress behaviour of Group A and Group B suffixes in (3) and (4), we follow Kornfilt's (1996) claim that Group A suffixes are not 'pre-stressing' and in no way exceptional.[7] Rather, they are affixed to a (phonologically null) copula which introduces its own domain with respect to stress. Under this view, the contrast between (3) and (4) with respect to stress follows from the fact that the forms in (4) involve a single stress domain, while the ones in (3) involve two stress domains with main stress falling on the leftmost domain in line with regular phrasal stress in

---

[7] This claim follows Lees (1962), where the same essential claim was made, but with less detail, fewer relevant phenomena, and less argumentation, leading to a less spelled-out proposal.

Turkish (cf. Lees 1961; Kornfilt 1996).[8] Kornfilt's (1996) claim that Group A and B suffixes attach to distinct structural positions may also explain their distinct shape. More importantly, it paves the way for an account of a number of other syntactic and morphological phenomena. The most striking of these behaviours are illustrated below.

The examples in (5) illustrate what is known as suspended affixation. While the agreement suffix can be suspended in a conjoined structure involving most simple tenses exemplified by the future in (5a), it cannot be suspended in a similar construction involving the definite past or the simple conditional as shown in (5b).

(5) a. Suspended Affixation in simple tenses:
   [[oku-yacák] ve   [anla   -yacák]]   -Ø   -sın
   read-FUT and   understand-FUT   -COP-2.SG
   'You will read and understand.'

   b. Not possible without copula:
   *[[oku-du]   ve   [anla   -dı]]   -n
   read-PAST and   understand -PAST -2.SG
   Intended reading: 'You read and understood.'

To account for the facts in (5), we follow Kornfilt's (1996) claim about the affixation of Group A suffixes to a (phonologically null) copula. This copula introduces its own domain with respect to not only stress (as discussed above) but also suspended affixation illustrated in (5a). In fact, as shown in (6), the same type of phenomenon is found with straightforward copular constructions involving nominal and adjectival predicates. The parallel between (5a) and (6) provides further motivation for the analysis of the agreement suffixes as attached to a copula.

(6) a. [[yorgún]   ve   [hastá]]- Ø -sın
   tired   and   sick-COP-2.SG
   'You are tired and sick.'

   b. [[yorgún]   ve   [hastá]]-y   -dı   -n
   tired   and   sick   -COP-PAST -2.SG
   'You were tired and sick.'

---

[8] The claim that an apparently simple verbal form involves two syntactic and therefore also two stress domains is further motivated in Kornfilt (1996) by the parallel drawn with clearly complex verbs that consist of a root and two (rather than just one) tense/aspect forms with one agreement suffix. In these instances, the first tense/aspect form is a participle and receives the main stress, while the second tense/aspect form is a tensed auxiliary (or a tensed copula) which receives non-primary stress. In the apparently simple verbs which we deal with in the present paper, the second domain consists merely of a null copula and the agreement suffix, thus bringing the affix to the immediate proximity of the location of primary stress. This is why the agreement marker fails to realize the predicted non-primary stress in this domain, otherwise audible in the aforementioned complex verb forms.

Further support for the idea that the Group A forms in (3) (as opposed to the Group B forms in (4)) involve a complex structure with two separate domains comes from affixation by the Yes/No question marker. As shown in (7), while the question marker appears after Group B suffixes, it appears before Group A suffixes (in apparent violation of the word's integrity). Kornfilt's (1996) account of the Group A suffixes being affixed to a null copula provides an explanation for this phenomenon as well. Under this view, the form in (7a) is complex with the future morpheme demarcating a participle, a cliticization site for the Yes/No question marker. The form in (7b), on the other hand, is not complex, i.e. the definite past is verbal (as opposed to participial), the past morpheme does not introduce a cliticization site and as a result the cliticization of the question marker would violate the (simple) word's integrity.

(7)   a.   [[gid-ecék]-mi]- Ø -siniz]   *[[gid-ecék]- Ø -siniz]-mi]
            go-FUT-Q-COP-2.PL   vs   go-FUT-COP-2.PL-Q
            'Will you go?'

      b.   *git-tí-mi-niz   git-ti-níz-mi
            go-PAST-Q-2.PL   vs   go-PAST-2.PL-Q
                                                  'Did you go?'

The proposed account for the contrast in (7) finds support from parallel facts involving straightforward copular constructions with nominal and adjectival predicates. As shown in (8), the question marker has to appear before the copula. This parallel provides further motivation for the unified analysis of the Group A agreement suffixes as attached to the copula.

(8)   a.   hastá-mı- Ø -sınız   *hastá- Ø -sınız-mı
            sick-Q -COP-2.PL   vs   sick-COP-2.PL-Q
            'Are you sick?'

      b.   hastá-mı-y -dı -nız   *hastá -y -dı -nız -mı
            sick-Q -COP-PAST-2.PL   vs   sick-COP-PAST-2.PL-Q
            'Were you sick?'

To better understand our proposal, let us look at the relevant structures. The structures in (9) correspond to the examples in (7). In (9a) (corresponding to (7a)), we are positing a T/A/M head in the vP domain, which can be taken as the equivalent of an internal AspP (Travis 1991 and subsequent authors). The T/AgrP in the CP domain is equivalent of TP or IP. We are not taking a strong position on the exact nature of these heads or whether the structure of CP is more articulated (à la Rizzi 1997). Two points are crucial to our proposal. First, in (7b), we are dealing with one stress domain, while in (7a) there are two stress domains with the lower one receiving primary stress (see also Kahnemuyipour 2004, 2009 for a more elaborate analysis of stress domains and their correspondence with syntactic structure). Second, the question marker can be merged in the vP domain or the CP domain, in both cases immediately above the head which is the locus of Tense/Aspect in the corresponding domain (T/A/M in vP, T/Agr in CP).[9] This parallelism between the structure of vP and CP plays an important role in our proposed system and follows naturally, given the status of vP and CP as phases in the Minimalist framework (e.g. Chomsky 2001).

(9a) Corresponding to (7a)

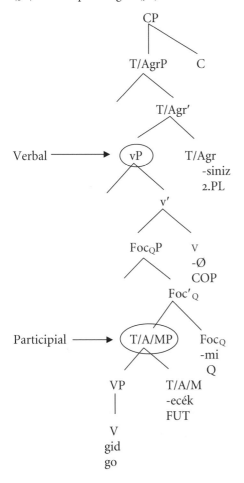

---

[9] An anonymous reviewer raises the question of why -*mI* cannot attach high (i.e. above T/AgrP) in (9a) or low (i.e. inside vP) in (9b). As for (9a), we take the obligatory low merger of -*mI* to be due to a requirement for merging as early (i.e. as low) as possible. In contrast, in (9b), the lower domain does not qualify for the merger of -*mI* as it lacks a fully realized functional projection of TAM. (This may

(9b)   Corresponding to (7b)

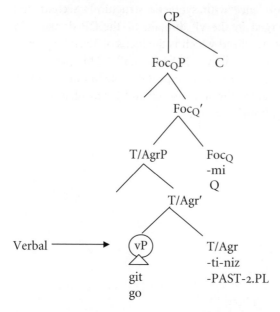

The Yes/No question marker illustrated in (7) to (9) is itself a 'pre-stressing' suffix. In the following section we sketch an analysis of its stress behaviour.

12.4 Question Marker

The question marker *-mI* is used either in the verbal domain as shown in (10) or attached to a focalized DP as shown in (11), with the vowel harmonizing with preceding vowels. In both cases in (10) and (11), stress falls on the element preceding this suffix, leading to its classification as a 'pre-stressing' suffix.

(10)   **Yes/No question marker as (high) focus marker in the verbal domain:**
mektub-u   oku -du   -núz-**mu**, yaz   -dı   -níz-**mı**[10]
letter -ACC read -PAST-2.PL-Q   write -PAST-2.PL-Q
'Did you **read** the letter, (or) did you **write** (it)?'

(11)   **Yes/No question marker as constituent focus marker:**
mektub-ú   -mu   oku   -du   -nuz, kitab   -í   -mı
letter -ACC Q   read -PAST-2.PL book   -ACC   -Q
'Did you read the **letter** or (did you read) the **book**?'

---

correspond to the notion of phases à la Chomsky 2000, 2001 and subsequent work.) Details of these proposals will be explored in future work.

 [10] For the sake of simplicity, we represent the Yes/No question marker as a suffix here, due to the fact that it undergoes Vowel Harmony with the preceding domain/syllable. As indicated in footnote 2, we actually analyse this suffix as an enclitic.

To account for the stress behaviour of the question marker, we propose that this marker is a focus marker both in the verbal domain shown in (10), in which we are primarily interested, and also when attached to focalized DPs as shown in (11). The focus marker attracts the focalized phrase in the case of DPs, and focalized small clauses in the case of the verbal domain to its specifier, accompanied by prosodic prominence. The relevant structure and corresponding movement for the example in (10) is given in (12). (For simplicity, we have shown in (12) only the structure for the first yes-no question in (10).)[11] (10)/(12) exemplifies the question particle merged in a high focus position above T/Agr. Recall from the previous section that the question particle can also be merged in a low vP-internal focus position (above T/A/M). The example and relevant structure are given in (7a) and (9a), respectively (see also note 9). A connection between wh-questions and focus in the domains of CP or vP has been made in the generative literature, for example by Horvath (1986), Rochemont (1986), Kiss (1995b), Bošković (1997, 2000), Ndayiragije (1999), Stjepanović (1999), Kahnemuyipour (2001), den Dikken (2003b), among others (see also section 12.5). This also follows naturally in the context of the parallel between vP and CP which we have drawn on in this paper.

(12)

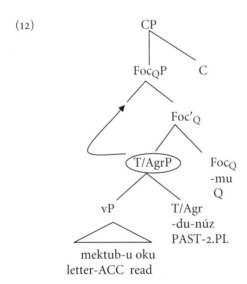

---

[11] This type of movement (complement-to-specifier), viewed as problematic by some, has been proposed in the context of roll-up movement by some linguists (e.g. Rackowski and Travis 2000, Kahnemuyipour and Massam 2006) but avoided by others (e.g. Cinque 2005) by positing an additional projection with a null head whose specifier is the target of such movement. We have sided with the former for the sake of simplicity.

12.5 Negation

The verbal negation marker -*mA* is another 'pre-stressing' suffix as shown in (13).

(13) **Verbal negation marker in lower focus position:**

köpeğ	-i	gez	-dír	-me	-di	-niz
dog	-ACC	walk	-CAUS	-NEG	-PAST	-2.PL

'You didn't walk the dog.' (i.e. 'You didn't let/make the dog walk.')

We propose that the negation marker is in a second focus head, a position lower than the question marker's focus position in the verbal domain (when focalizing small clauses). This low focus position explains the verbal negator's adjacency to 'voice' morphemes such as the causative marker in (13) as well as the passive marker not illustrated here. This negation/focus head attracts the negated predicate to its specifier, accompanied by prosodic prominence. This account captures both the *similarity* between the verbal negator and the question marker as ('pre-stressing') focus markers and their *different* positions. When both the negation marker and the question marker are present (in negative questions), the negation marker is closer to the verbal root, and the stress falls before the negation marker, as predicted by our analysis. (14a) shows an example and the structure of genuinely simple, verbal forms involving both negation and Yes/No question markers. (14b) shows the corresponding example and structure for what we have characterized as complex forms consisting of a participle and an inflected copula. In (14a) the question marker is in the CP domain, while in (14b) it is in the vP domain. In both examples, the negation is a low focus head right above the Voice phrase.[12]

---

[12] The proposed structures in (14) involve more than one focus (projection) within a clause, which may be problematic based on certain claims in the literature on the topic, e.g. Horvath (1995). In particular, in (14b), the two focus projections appear in a domain even smaller than a clause, namely vP. There are, on the other hand, certain facts which seem to defy this ban on the uniqeness of focus within a clause, e.g. responses to multiple wh-questions, or a combination of a wh-question and contrastive focus (if one takes wh-constituents to bear focus). Furthermore, to avoid the use of multiple focus projections, one might adhere to an approach such as Horvath (1995) which takes focus to be a feature hosted by certain heads. Under this view, we could reanalyse our Foc_{NEG} as a focus feature on a Neg head and our Foc_Q as a focus feature hosted by a C or v head. We leave these questions about possible constraints on the number of focus projections or focus features for future research.

(14a) köpeğ -i   gez   -dír   **-me** -di   -niz   **-mi**

       dog   -ACC walk -CAUS **-NEG**- PAST -2.PL. **-Q**

       'Didn't you walk the dog?' (i.e. 'Didn't you let/make the dog walk?')

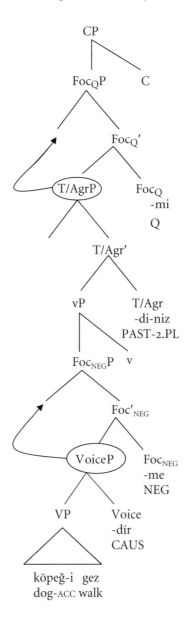

(14b) köpeğ   -i   gez   -dír   **-me** -yecek   **-mi** -siniz
       dog   -ACC   walk   -CAUS **-NEG** -FUT   **-Q**   -2.PL
       'Won't you walk the dog?' (i.e. 'Won't you let/make the dog walk?')

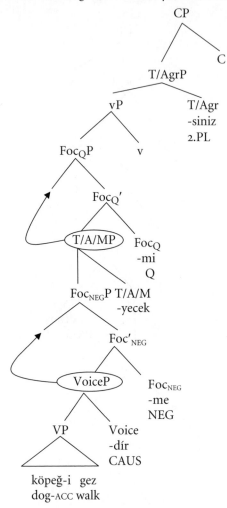

The syntax of negative sentences has often been connected to the syntax of interrogative sentences in the linguistic literature. Licensing of polarity items (see Progovac 1988, 1991; Laka 1990; Haegeman 1995, among others), subject-aux inversion (see, for example, Haegeman 1995), island effects (Rizzi 1990, Haegeman 1995, among others) are just a few phenomena which establish this parallelism. There are also many syntactic analyses in the literature which draw on this connection, e.g. Klima's (1964) treatment of Wh and Neg, Rizzi's (1990) analysis of island effects, the AFFECT-criterion (Haegeman 1992, 1995;

Kornfilt 1993; Rizzi 1996) and other instantiations of it such as the WH-criterion (May 1985, Rizzi 1996), the NEG-criterion (Haegeman and Zanuttini 1991) or the FOCUS-criterion (Brody 1990, Haegeman 1995).

In particular, Laka's (1990) analysis of the Basque negative particle 'ez' and Cheng *et al.*'s (1997) account of the Mandarin question particle 'ma' make a direct connection between negation and questions/focus. In her analysis of the negative particle 'ez' in Basque, Laka (1990) shows that this negative particle, the abstract affirmative morpheme and the emphatic particle 'ba' are in complementary distribution and all trigger auxiliary fronting. To account for this fact, she proposes a single functional projection whose instantiations are negation and emphatic affirmation.

Cheng *et al.* (1997) show that the Mandarin question particle 'ma' that marks Yes/No questions is in complementary distribution with a negative marker in sentence-final position, and it is concluded that the negative marker in Mandarin can fulfil the same function otherwise carried out by the Q particle, namely making a Yes/No question.[13,14] Our proposal finds a natural place in the context of this connection among negation, question, and focus.

We have argued above that what has been classified as 'pre-stressing' suffixes is not a homogeneous class, but rather two main groups. The behaviour of the first group essentially falls out from regular stress applied to a specific domain, as elaborated above (and in Kornfilt 1996). The second group, consisting of the negation and Yes/No question markers, represents focus stress. In the following section, we provide evidence to support the idea that the two groups should be distinguished.

12.6 Two Types of 'Pre-stressing' Suffixes

In this section, we provide support for the idea that 'pre-stressing' suffixes should be divided up in two groups as suggested above. We see below that

[13] A possibly similar phenomenon is observed in first language acquisition of Turkish negatives, where children, instead of producing the adult morpheme *-mA* and placing it within the verbal complex, produce different morphemes, placing them at the end of the clause, essentially in the same position where the yes/no question marker *-mI* would appear (cf. Ketrez 2005: 172, citing data from Aksu-Koç and Slobin 1985 and Köskinen 2000).

[14] In Niuean (an Oceanic language of the Tongic subgroup), there is a striking similarity in form between the question marker *nakai* (one of three question particles in the language) and the negative marker *na:kai*, where colon marks vowel length (see Massam 2003). Moreover, these elements are in complementary distribution. This striking similarity in form and the complementary distribution may find a natural place in a system like ours which takes negation and question to be two instances of the same phenomenon, namely focus. It should be noted that there is evidence in Massam (2003) showing clearly that the use of *nakai* in questions cannot be taken as an instance of the negation *na:kai* being used as a tag. We leave further exploration of these issues in Niuean for future research.

compound stress and phrasal stress exhibit behaviours that are different in the presence of the first group as opposed to the second group. We further argue that the behaviour observed with the second group lends itself to an analysis of the type we have presented above, where focus stress (for both negation and Yes/No question markers) is the result of the syntactic movement of a focused constituent to the specifier position of a Foc-head.

12.6.1 *Compound Stress*

In Turkish compounds, the first member receives primary stress, i.e. the first member gets the regular word-level stress as shown in (15):

(15) a. báş   -bakan
          head minister
          'prime minister'

      b. bak -á   # kal
          look -PRT   remain
          'remain looking; stare'

We focus here on verbal compounds exemplified in (15b). When the compound is used within a context involving a 'pre-stressing' suffix of the first kind, the main sentence stress remains on the compound, as shown in (16):

(16) bak   -á   # kal   -mış -Ø   -ız
      look -PRT   remain-RP -COP -1.PL
      'We reportedly were frozen in place, staring.'

A similar 'trapping' of regular compound stress takes place in front of 'non-pre-stressing' suffixes as well, as shown in (17):

(17) bak   -á   # kal   -dı   -k
      look -PRT   remain   -PAST   -1.PL
      'We stood in place, staring.'

Crucially, in the presence of the negation marker -*mA*, which, in this example, follows the modal verb *kal*, the compound stress moves over to immediately precede -*mA*, i.e. it falls on *kal*, as shown in (18):

(18) a. bak   -a   # kál   -ma   -mış   - ız
          look -PRT   remain-NEG -RP   -1.PL
          'We reportedly weren't frozen in place, staring.'

b. bak -a   # kál -ma -dı -k
   look -PRT   remain-NEG -PAST-1.PL
   'We didn't stand in place, staring.'

The contrast between (16) and (17) on the one hand, and (18) on the other, provides support for the separation between the two types of 'pre-stressing' suffixes. If we treat 'pre-stressing' -*mA* as a different phenomenon compared to other 'pre-stressing' suffixes, as proposed here, and say that -*mA* is a focus head, triggering movement to Spec, FocP of the constituent it negates, then these facts are not surprising in a system where focus stress is independent from and overrides regular stress (see also Kahnemuyipour 2004, 2009).[15] Similar supportive evidence is provided by the behaviour of phrasal stress in the context of the two types of 'pre-stressing' suffixes.

12.6.2 *Phrasal Stress*

A second observation can be conflated with our discussion of compound stress above, because phrasal stress works in similar ways as compound stress in Turkish; this is a general observation which has been made before (cf. Lees 1961). For example, in a sequence of object and verb, the object gets the primary stress in focus-neutral contexts exemplified in (19).

(19) Oya [kitab -í   oku -du]
      Oya book -ACC read -PAST
      'Oya read the book.'

This phrasal stress on the first element stays the same in the presence of a 'pre-stressing' suffix on the verb in a focus-neutral context as shown in (20).

(20) Oya [kitab -í   oku -muş   -Ø -tu]
      Oya book -ACC read -PastParticiple[16]-COP-PAST
      'Oya had read the book.'

Only when the verb is focused is it possible to 'move' the phrasal stress over to the verb, and then it will end up in the expected position to the left of the null copula:

---

[15] The Yes/No question marker on the verb exhibits behaviour very similar to the negation marker with respect to this 'untrapping' and attraction of compound stress (as well as of phrasal stress—see discussion in the next section). This is just as expected under our approach, where both Neg and the Yes/No question markers are treated as syntactic focus heads.

[16] We have analysed the suffix -*mIş* as a (past) participle throughout. In apparently 'simple' forms (which we have seen in previous examples) with the posited copula in the present tense this suffix has the additional evidential meaning of 'reported', reflected in our glosses.

(21)   Oya   kitab   -ı   oku   -múş   -Ø   -tu
      Oya   book   -ACC   read   -PastParticiple-COP-PAST
      'Oya had READ the book.'

In contrast, when the Neg marker is on the verb, the unmarked phrasal stress falls on the syllable to the left of Neg, which is expected if Neg is, as we claim, a Foc-head. This is shown in (22). Stress on the object would be possible here only if the object were focused.

(22)   Oya   kitab   -ı   okú   -ma   -mış   -Ø   -tı
      Oya   book   -ACC   read   NEG   -PastParticiple-COP-PAST
      'Oya had not read the book.'

We take the above evidence as a strong indication that the two types of 'pre-stressing' suffixes should be teased apart, with only one, namely focus stress interacting with regular compound or phrasal stress. We end this section with some speculations on the connection between negation and prosody across languages. We have argued above that the stress on the syllable preceding the negation marker in Turkish is the result of the movement of the negated constituent to the specifier of the negation head, accompanied by prosodic prominence on that moved constituent (on a par with focused constituents exhibiting a similar behaviour cross-linguistically). This proposal may take us a step closer to an understanding of the prosodic behavior of negation across languages. In Persian, for example, it is the negation itself that receives the main stress in the clause, as seen in (23).

(23)   ali   madrese   **ná**-raft
      Ali   school   NEG-went
      'Ali didn't go to school.'

It may be argued that the difference between Turkish and Persian with respect to stress is tied to the difference in the order of constituents, with overt movement of the negated constituent occurring only in Turkish. The claim is that in a language like Turkish with overt movement of the negated (or focused) constituent, stress falls on the negated constituent in the specifier of the negation (or focus) head; in Persian, where this movement does not occur overtly, stress falls on the negation (or focus) head itself (see also Kahnemuyipour 2005). Under this view, it is the edge of the focus phrase, i.e. its specifier, or its head if the specifier is null, which receives prosodic prominence.[17]

---

[17] We are not claiming that any language which lacks the overt movement of the negated constituent will necessarily exhibit primary stress on the negative marker. The negation may undergo further movement operations itself and consequently avoid sentential stress.

12.7 Conclusion

We have provided an account for the apparently pre-stressing behaviour of certain clausal and verbal suffixes in Turkish. We have shown that in the case of the clausal suffixes, their pre-stressing behaviour is the result of their syntactic position outside the clausal domain of the material preceding it. We have argued that one type of the so-called 'pre-stressing' agreement suffixes (our Group A) are really involved in a bi-clausal structure, thus motivating their stress behaviour. Finally we have proposed that another type of the so-called 'pre-stressing' suffixes, i.e. the negation and question markers, each head a focus projection, attracting the focused constituent to their specifier, accompanied by prosodic prominence. For the sake of completeness, it should be noted that there are several non-clausal/non-verbal 'pre-stressing' suffixes that have been left out of our discussion in this paper. These suffixes are listed in (24), adapted from Kabak and Vogel (2001).

(24) a. adverb/adjective-deriving suffixes (e.g. *-CA*, *-leyin* 'at' (as in *sabáh-leyin* 'at morning'; not productive), *-In* 'in/when' (as in *yáz-ın* 'in summer'; not productive)
   b. -DA   post-clitic coordinator
   c. -DIr   epistemic copula
   d. -(y)lA   comitative/instrumental (full form: *ile*)
   e. -gil   suffix that derives family names from nouns

While we leave a closer examination of these suffixes for future research, we believe most of the non-verbal suffixes in this list can be explained away as unproductive, and some are subject to analyses similar to those put forth in this paper, such as the epistemic copula -DIr in (24c) and the post-clitic coordinator -DA in (24b).

   To conclude, we hope to have provided a deeper understanding of the stress facts and the relation between syntax and prosody in Turkish. Further work is needed to explore the above proposals, in particular with respect to the syntactic and prosodic behaviour of negators in Turkish and across languages and the possibility of the extension of these proposals to non-verbal/non-clausal domains.

Part III
Sound Interfacing with Structure

13

Restrictions on Subject Extraction: A PF Interface Account

PETER ACKEMA

13.1 Introduction

In this chapter I will discuss a restriction on the possibilities of extracting subjects out of embedded clauses that is often referred to as the complementizer-trace effect. At first sight, this looks like a purely syntactic phenomenon, concerning the syntactic behaviour of subjects. Indeed, various accounts of it have been proposed in terms of syntactic principles alone. In this chapter, I will argue that an analysis that takes into account properties of the interface between syntax and the module of grammar that deals with the prosody of sentences, as proposed in Ackema and Neeleman (2004), gives a more straightforward handle on various empirical data connected to the complementizer-trace effect.

The chapter is structured as follows. I will first briefly describe what the relevant phenomenon is and introduce the account of it proposed by Ackema and Neeleman (2004), in section 13.2. Then in the subsequent sections I will show how this analysis makes correct predictions with regard to the following generalizations. (i) the complementizer-trace effect is suspended when a phrase intervenes between complementizer and trace (section 13.3); (ii) complementizer-trace effects can be observed when what is extracted is not the complete subject of the embedded clause but only a part of it (section 13.4); (iii) complementizer-trace effects do not occur when the subject extraction is 'covert' (section 13.5); (iv) there are no complementizer-trace effects in complementizer-final languages (section 13.6); (v) subject extraction is fine in the absence of a complementizer (section 13.7). Section 13.8 contains a brief general conclusion.

13.2 Subject Extraction

Chomsky and Lasnik (1977) introduce what they term a '*that*-trace filter'. This describes the phenomenon that, at least in English, it is less easy to extract a subject from an embedded clause than it is to extract other constituents, in particular when the embedded clause is introduced by a complementizer. This is illustrated by the contrast between (1a) and (1b,c).

(1)   a. *Who$_i$ do you think [that t$_i$ read that book yesterday]
      b. What$_i$ do you think [that Mary read t$_i$ yesterday]
      c. When$_i$ do you think [that Mary read that book t$_i$]

The same phenomenon can be observed with extraction out of clauses introduced by other complementizers than *that* as well, so a more general term for it, which I will use here, is the 'complementizer-trace effect'. This may seem to be a purely syntactic phenomenon, rather than being the consequence of the properties of some linguistic interface level. Indeed, quite a few purely syntactic accounts have been proposed for the phenomenon (e.g. Rizzi 1990, Lasnik and Saito 1992, and Rizzi 2006). However, some authors have argued that there are data that seem to indicate that the proper locus of dealing with it is in fact the interface level between syntax and phonology, PF (Ackema and Neeleman 2004; Kandybowicz 2006). I will argue that Ackema and Neeleman's (2004) PF interface account of this phenomenon makes a number of desirable empirical predictions about it that do not seem to follow directly from purely syntactic accounts.

Ackema and Neeleman (2004) propose that feature checking, the mechanism that ensures that a verb's uninterpretable agreement features are matched against the interpretable features of the agreeing noun phrase (cf. Chomsky 1995), can take place not only in local domains in syntax, but also within prosodic domains at PF. This can be expressed as in (2), where { } indicates prosodic phrase (φ) boundaries.

(2)   *PF feature checking*
      {[A (F1) (F2) (F3) ...] [B (F1) (F2) (F3) ...] } →
      {[A (F1$_i$) (F2$_j$) (F3$_k$) ...] [B (F1$_i$) (F2$_j$) (F3$_k$) ...] }

Prosodic phrasing in most of the languages under discussion below is determined by the following alignment principle (see Selkirk 1986; Tokizaki 1999). This says that right edges of syntactic phrases should be aligned with right edges of prosodic phrases:

(3)   Align (⟨right edge, XP⟩, ⟨right edge, φ⟩) (where φ is a prosodic phrase)

(3) has the effect that an XP ends up in the same prosodic phrase as a head when it is right-adjacent to this head, or when just another head intervenes, but not when another XP intervenes. An XP does not end up in the same prosodic phrase with a head to which it is left-adjacent, as the XP's right bracket induces φ-closure by (3).

The agreement between complementizers and subjects that is shown by some Germanic languages/dialects (cf. de Haan 1994; Zwart 1997) arguably involves such PF feature checking: it is subject to the type of right-adjacency effect predicted by this approach and it does not occur in embedded verb second clauses, which arguably constitute a prosodic domain separate from that of the complementizer under which they are 'embedded'. With this in mind, Ackema and Neeleman (2004) propose the condition in (4), which crucially holds at the PF interface rather than in syntax proper, as the origin of complementizer-trace effects:

(4)   Let α_i and α_{i+1} be links of the same chain such that α_i c-commands α_{i+1}. If agreement checking involves α_i and β, then α_{i+1} cannot be in a configuration that would allow agreement checking between it and β.

Extraction out of a clause in syntax proper is constrained by 'phase impenetrability' (Chomsky 2001). A strict version of this is the following:

(5)   *Phase impenetrability*
    a. Only the head of a phase is accessible to phase-external operations.
    b. A specifier of the phase can be made accessible by agreeing with the head.

Under the usual assumption that CP is a phase, it follows from (5) that extraction of an XP out of an embedded CP must involve movement to the left edge of this CP in syntax, where XP must establish a spec-head agreement relationship with C. (Evidence for such an agreement relation can be found in Irish, amongst other languages, where the form of C changes if a wh-phrase is extracted out of CP; see McCloskey 2001). But this means that at PF the condition in (4) will be violated if the extracted element originated in a position that allows PF feature checking against C's features. Subject extraction, but not extraction of elements that do not originate in a position right-adjacent to C, therefore usually violates (4) if there is a complementizer present:

(6)   syntax: $[\text{Wh}_i] \ldots [_{CP} [t_i]$ that $[_{IP} [t_i] \ldots$
       PF: $\{\text{Wh}_i\} \ldots \{t_i\} \{$ that $t_i\} \{ \ldots$

The intermediate trace is in an agreement relationship with C (or extraction could not have taken place in syntax given (5)), whereas at PF the lowest trace is in a potential checking configuration with C as well, as it ends up in the same prosodic phrase as C at this level (given (3)). Thus, (4) is violated.

13.3 The 'Adverb Effect'

The complementizer-trace effect disappears if there is an intervening phrase between C and the subject trace (the 'adverb effect', cf. Bresnan 1977, Culicover 1993):

(7) Who$_i$ do you think [t$_i$ that, according to the latest rumours, t$_i$ is quitting politics?]

This is predicted by the PF account: given (3), the intervening phrase prevents the lowest subject trace from ending up in the same prosodic phrase as C, so that (4) cannot be violated. In syntactic approaches, the intervening phrase must somehow affect the syntax of the construction in such a way that the embedded subject position is now allowed to contain a trace. No matter what assumptions are made in that respect, the problem with such an approach is that the intervening phrase need not be part of the syntactic structure that contains the complementizer and the trace. It can be a parenthetical. Parentheticals are arguably not syntactically present in their host structure—they are invisible to it (Haegeman 1988; Espinal 1991). Potts (2002) argues that *as*-clauses can be parentheticals. Indeed they seem to be absent from the syntactic structure of the host. For example, the usually required adjacency between verb and object in English is not disrupted by an apparently intervening *as*-clause:

(8) Harry likes, as we all know, silly books.

Similarly, the equivalent of an *as*-clause in Dutch can be invisible for the verb-second constraint operative in the syntax of this language:

(9) Marie, zoals we   allemaal weten,   gaat op zaterdag naar
     Mary   *as*   *we* *all*   *know*   *goes* *on*   *Saturday* *to*
     de   markt
     the   *market*
     'Mary, as we all know, goes to the market on Saturdays.'

Nevertheless, this type of clause has the same ameliorating effect on complementizer-trace configurations as other phrases in between C and the trace:

(10) Who$_i$ do you think [t$_i$ that, as the FBI discovered recently, t$_i$ was a spy?]

If parentheticals are not integrated in the syntactic structure of their host, this effect is unexpected for a syntactic approach. Parentheticals must be integrated somehow into the prosodic structure of the host, however, so the PF approach accounts for this in the same way as it does for the case in (7).

13.4 Subextraction

For reasons that we cannot go into here, the syntactic approach of Rizzi (2006) predicts that only extraction of a complete subject can give rise to a complementizer-trace violation; subextraction out of a subject should never produce such a violation. The PF account makes a different prediction: subextraction should be possible, but only as long as the trace of the subextracted phrase is not in the same prosodic phrase with C at PF. Given (3), this will be the case when this phrase is right-adjoined to the subject DP, but not when it is inside the subject DP, certainly not at its left edge (i.e. right-adjacent to C). When the trace of the subextracted phrase is in a potential checking configuration with C, problems with (4) may arise again at PF. It can be shown that elements within a subject can indeed establish an agreement relation with C, instead of the whole subject doing this. In some languages with overt complementizer agreement, complementizers can agree with the first conjunct of a coordinated subject only, as the Frisian example in (11) shows.

(11) Ik   tink   dat-st   do   en   Marie   dit   wykein
      I   *think*   *that*-2SG   *you*   *and*   *Mary*   *this*   *weekend*
      yn   Rome   west   ha   (van Koppen 2005)
      in   *Rome*   *been*   *have*
      'I think that you and Mary have been in Rome this weekend.'

The prediction that subextraction out of a subject can give rise to a *that*-trace effect just like extraction of the subject itself seems to be confirmed by Dutch examples like (12).

(12) a. Wat$_i$ denk   je   [t$_i$ dat   deze   week   [t$_i$ voor   boeken]
          what   *think*   *you*   *that*   *this*   *week*   *for*   *books*
          zijn   verschenen]?
          are   *appeared*
          'What kind of books do you think appeared this week?'

      b. ?*Wat$_i$ denk je [t$_i$ dat [t$_i$ voor boeken] zijn verschenen deze week]?

Right-alignment of syntactic and prosodic phrases results in the following partial initial PF structures, with the lowest trace and C in the same prosodic phrase in the PF of (12b) but not (12a). Thus, (4) is violated in (12b) but not (12a).

(13)   a. ...} {dat deze week} {t } {voor boeken} ...
       b. ...} {dat t} {voor boeken}{ ...

It might seem, however, that the difference between (12a) and (12b) is due to an independent factor, namely the subject island condition. Extraction out of subject DPs is prohibited, like extraction out of sentential subjects, if the DP is in a VP-external position (namely in spec-IP, the 'EPP' position), but not if the DP is VP-internal (see van de Koot and Mathieu 2003 and Adger 2003 on English, Bayer 2004 on German, Broekhuis 2006 on Dutch, Gallego and Uriagereka 2006 on Spanish). The order adverb-subject in (12a) might show that the subject is still in VP-internal position, whereas it would be in the VP-external EPP position in (12b). Moreover, the verb *verschijnen* 'appear' in (12) is unaccusative, so it may even be that subextraction in (12a) takes place when what is the subject on the surface is still in its underlying object position, before it is promoted to subject.[1] The idea that the contrast between (12a) and (12b) results from the subject island condition seems to be supported by the observation that a similar contrast can be found with *short* extraction out of subjects as well, although this contrast is markedly less sharp than the one in (12):

(14)   a. [Wat$_i$] zijn er   [t$_i$ voor boeken] verschenen deze week?
          what *are* *there* *for* *books* *appeared* *this* *week*
          'What kind of books have appeared this week?'

       b. ? [Wat$_i$] zijn [t$_i$ voor boeken] verschenen deze week?

I hypothesize that the contrast between (12a) and (12b) and that between (14a) and (14b) is not one between subextraction out of VP-external versus VP-internal position. All extraction takes place from inside VP and is unproblematic, except for the *that*-trace case in (12b). (14b) is somewhat degraded for a different reason. Bennis (1986) argues that the EPP may be violated in Dutch, so subjects need not move to a VP-external EPP position. He further argues that the apparent dummy *er* in sentences like (14a) does not occur to satisfy the EPP, but because certain presentational sentences, including those with a non-specific indefinite as subject, are degraded when not introduced with an adverbial element. If there is no other adverbial present that can fulfil this function (such as *deze week* in (12a)), adverbial *er* is used for this. I cannot discuss Bennis's arguments for these assumptions here, but will adopt them without discussion (see Ackema and Neeleman

---

[1] Such a derivation, appearing to involve A′-movement before A-movement, would seem to violate the 'extension' condition on derivations, but see Chomsky (2008).

1998 for more discussion on the violability of the EPP in Dutch). Given this, in all examples in (12) and (14) the subject may still be VP-internal, so we would not expect a problem with extracting anything out of it if the subject island condition does not hold of VP-internal subjects (as per the references given above). (14b) is relatively bad because a presentational sentence, with an indefinite subject, does not contain the proper adverbial element required to make this type of sentence felicitous. But (12b) is worse than (14b), indicating that, in addition to this, there is another problem with it.

The following two observations support the hypothesis that only in (12b) (the complementizer-trace case) is there a genuine problem with subextraction, whereas the contrast in (14) is not caused by a condition on movement such as the subject island condition, but exists for a different reason.

First, the contrast in (14) remains when there is no extraction out of the subject at all. For example, (15b) is degraded compared to (15a) just as (14b) is compared to (14a). Note that it is unlikely that this is because of a supposed EPP-violation (if the indefinite subject stays within VP), since (15b) is much better than an EPP-violation in languages that strictly adhere to this principle, such as English; compare the clear impossibility of a sentence like (16).

(15) a. Gisteren   zijn   er   een   paar   boeken   verschenen
          yesterday *are* *there* *a*   *couple* *books*   *appeared*
          'Yesterday a couple of books appeared.'

      b. ?Gisteren zijn een paar boeken verschenen

(16)   *Yesterday—appeared some books

The same contrast can even be detected in sentences that do not have a subject at all, namely impersonal passives, as in (17). Again, (17b) is somewhat worse than (17a), but is not impossible. Thus, the contrast in (14) is not caused by a problem with subextraction in (14b).

(17) a. Gisteren   werd   er   gefeest   in   de   stad
          yesterday *was* *there* *feasted* *in* *the* *city*
          'Yesterday people were partying in town'

      b. ?Gisteren werd gefeest in de stad

Second, although (14b) is marked compared to (14a), it is not nearly as bad as proper violations of the subject island condition seem to be. Extraction out of a subject that is VP-external in a language that adheres to the EPP, such as in English (18b), appears to lead to strong ungrammaticality, in contrast to (14b).

(18)   a.   Who is [$_{IP}$ there [$_{VP}$ [a description of t] in the book]]   (Adger 2003)
       b.   *Who is [$_{IP}$ [a description of t] [$_{VP}$ in the book]]

And crucially, however good or awkward (14b) is exactly, there is a contrast between this example and the example with long subextraction out of a complementizer-trace configuration in (12b), the latter being worse. This indicates that there really is a complementizer-trace effect in (12b).

The contrast can be made clearer in German, since here the expletive *es* (the counterpart of Dutch *er*) is not required to render a sentence with a non-specific indefinite subject felicitous, and in fact only appears in initial position in main clauses (to prevent a violation of the verb-second requirement). Thus, (19a) is perfectly well-formed in German, whereas (19a') is in fact impossible. Nevertheless, (19b) seems to be as bad as its Dutch counterpart (at least for those speakers who have the complementizer-trace restriction in the first place).[2]

(19)   a.   Was   sind   für   Leute   angekommen?
            what   are   for   people   arrived
            'What kind of people have arrived?'

---

[2] Many thanks to Patrick Brandt and Dirk Bury for discussion of German data. As noted, in Dutch (12) the verb in the clause out of which subextraction takes place is unaccusative, and the same in fact holds for the German examples in (19). It is standardly assumed that unergatives do not allow subextraction out of their subject, unless the subject is preceded by an adverbial (cf. den Besten 1985, Müller 2008):

(i)   a.   *Was   haben   für   Leute   telefoniert?
             what   have   for   people   telephoned

       b.   Was   haben   denn   für   Leute   telefoniert?
            what   have   then   for   people   telephoned
            'Well, what kind of people called?'

This has been taken, again, to reflect a distinction between a VP-external (ia) versus VP-internal (ib) extraction site (though it is difficult to see how insertion of the discourse particle *denn* in (ib) can influence the position the subject ends up in; interesting alternative accounts are given by Bayer 2004, Melchiors 2007, and Müller 2008). In fact, however, not all examples of short extraction out of an unergative's subject in the absence of a pre-subject adverbial are that bad; examples like the following are attested on the web and were readily accepted by my informants:

(ii)   a.   'Was   wohnen   für   Leute   in   Penang,   Sidhi?'   fragte   er   mich
            what   live   for   people   in   Penang,   Sidhi   asked   he   me
            ' "What kind of people live in Penang, Sidhi?" he asked me.'

       b.   Was   leben   für   Tiere   im   Ozean?
            what   live   for   animals   in-the   ocean
            'What kind of animal live in the ocean?'

Crucially, again there is a contrast with long subextraction out of a *that*-clause (for those speakers that have the complementizer-trace effect to begin with):

(iii) a.   ?*Was   glaubst   du   dass   für   Leute   in   Penang   wohnen?
       b.   ?*Was   glaubst   du   dass   für   Tiere   im   Ozean   leben?

a'. *Was sind es für Leute angekommen?

b. ?*Was glaubst du dass für Leute angekommen sind?

Another set of examples illustrating the same point comes from languages that allow left-branch extraction, such as Czech. Starke (2001) notes that this type of subextraction can take place from the subject of an embedded clause, but only if the subject is in inverted, post-VP, position, not when the subject is right-adjacent to C:

(20) a. Kolik$_i$ myslis [t$_i$ ze   [$_{VP}$ prislo] [t$_i$ dopisu]]?
          how-many *think*   *that*   *arrived*   *letters*
          'How many letters do you think arrived?'

      b. *Kolik$_i$ myslis [t$_i$ ze [t$_i$ dopisu] [$_{VP}$ prislo]]?

Right-peripheral subjects like the one in (20a) are presumably in a focus position, maybe in some designated Foc position, maybe adjoined to VP (cf. Godjevac 2004 on the equivalent construction in Serbo-Croatian). Thus, at the least a right VP-bracket triggers the insertion of a right prosodic phrase bracket between C and the trace inside the subject in this case (cf. (3)):

(21) ... {ze prislo} {t} {dopisu}

But in (20b) we have the standard comp-trace configuration, with the lower trace ending up in the same prosodic phrase as C:

(22) ...} {ze t} {dopisu} {prislo}

Again it turns out that it is irrelevant that it is not the subject itself that moves but only a sub-part—there still is a complementizer-trace violation, as expected given (4).

My own judgements for subextraction out of subjects of unergative verbs in Dutch are similar:

(iv) a. ?Wat wonen voor mensen in deze buurt?
          what *live* *for* *people* *in* *this* *neighbourhood*
          'What kind of people live in this neighbourhood?'

      b. ?*Wat denk je dat voor mensen wonen in deze buurt?
          what *think* *you* *that* *for* *people* *live* *in* *this* *neighbourhood*
          'What kind of people do you think live in this neighbourhood?'

      c. ?Wat denk je dat in deze buurt   voor mensen wonen?
          what *think* *you* *that* *in* *this* *neighbourhood* *for* *people* *live*

(iva) is somewhat marked because of the absence of *er*, but is acceptable; (ivb) is distinctly worse, showing there is a genuine complementizer-trace effect in this case of subextraction; (ivc) is on a par with (iva), rather than (ivb), because of the 'adverb effect' (see section 13.3).

13.5 Wh-in-situ

Wh-in-situ constructions are potentially relevant for the analysis of the complementizer-trace effect, but their exact relevance depends on whether or not the in-situ wh-phrase undergoes covert movement or not, which is a controversial issue. There appears to be evidence that wh-in-situ is not sensitive to Subjacency. This might seem to indicate absence of movement, but it has also been argued that there may be ways in which Subjacency violations can be circumvented by covert movement. Thus, Nishigauchi (1990) points out that Subjacency effects can be masked by the moving element pied-piping the complete island it is contained in, while Richards (1997) argues that some languages can circumvent Subjacency violations by allowing CP to have multiple specifiers (so there is an escape hatch present at the edge of the island); this is visible in some languages with multiple overt wh-movement, too (Bulgarian). (For discussion of other apparent differences between overt and covert movement see Nissenbaum 2000).

Crucially, Watanabe (1992) observes that Subjacency effects can in fact be detected in some cases of covert wh-movement with a single wh, but not if there is an additional wh-phrase present outside the island:

(23) a. ??John-wa [Mary-ga nani-o katta ka dooka] Tom-ni
          John   *Mary*   *what* *bought* *whether* *Tom*
          tazuneta no?
          asked   Q
          'John asked Tom whether Mary bought what'

     b. John-wa [Mary-ga nani-o katta ka dooka] dare-ni tazuneta no?
        John   *Mary* *what* *bought* *whether* *who*   *asked* Q
        'Who did John ask whether Mary bought what'

Suppose clauses must be 'clause-typed' at LF as being questions by having an appropriate Q element c-command the clause (cf. Cheng 1991). If there is only one wh-phrase, then this must move, and this movement may give rise to a Subjacency violation, as in (23a). In multiple questions, however, the lower wh-phrases can remain in situ, so that Subjacency effects are expected to be always absent (though see below).

Clearly, if an in-situ wh-subject does not move, it will not be sensitive to a complementizer-trace effect. If there is covert movement, however, a syntactic account would have to take extra measures (such as complementizer deletion at LF, as proposed in Lasnik and Saito 1992) to prevent this movement from being restricted by the complementizer-trace effect. The PF interface account, on the other hand, predicts that there should be no problem even if there is movement of in-situ wh-subjects at LF. This is because such movement occurs 'too late' to induce a violation of (4). At PF, the subject is in its base position. Hence, the PF approach predicts that wh-in-situ should under no circumstances give rise to a complementizer-trace effect. This generalization appears to be correct; as far as I can ascertain, there seems to be no language in which the equivalent of examples like in (24) is ruled out:[3]

(24)   a. Ni   renwei [shuo [shei hui
          you   *think*   *that*   *who*   *will*
          qu]]?   (Taiwan Mandarin, Cheng and Huang 2006)
          go
          'Who do you think will go?'

       b. Raam-ne   kyaa   socaa   [ki
          Raam-ERG SCOPE   *thought* *that*
          kOn aayaa   hE]   (Hindi, cf. Mahajan 2000)
          who come   *has*
          'Who does Raam think has come?'

A striking case is provided by Ancash Quechua. This language allows wh-movement to take place either overtly or covertly. Overtly moved subjects are restricted by the complementizer-trace effect, but covertly moved subjects are not (Cole and Hermon 1994) (note that 'who' in (25b) has matrix scope):

(25)   a. *Pi-taq Fuan   musyan [t tanta-ta   ruranqan-ta]?
          who-Q   *Fuan* *knows*   *bread*-ACC   *made*-ACC

       b. Fuan   musyan [pi   tanta-ta   ruranqan-ta]?
          Juan *knows*   *who* *bread*-ACC   *made*-ACC
          'Who does Juan know made bread?'

Note that the complementizer is null here, but, given the account defended here, it should not matter whether C ultimately receives a spell-out in phonology (after the PF interface)—on why this does seem to matter in English see section 13.7.

As for multiple wh-sentences, if the lower wh-phrases in situ do not move at LF (see above), any account predicts they should not be subject to the complementizer-trace effect. Dayal (2002) shows, however, there may be reasons

---

[3] Many wh-in-situ languages are head-final, and so may have final complementizers instead of initial ones, on which see the next section.

to believe that sometimes lower wh-phrases in a multiple wh-sentence do move. If the lower wh is not inside an island the answer to a multiple question may be either a single-pair answer or a multiple-pair answer (see (26)). But if the lower wh is inside an island (other than one that is induced by yet another wh), such as an adjunct island, only a single-pair answer is possible (see (27)).

(26)   Q: Which philosopher likes which linguist?
       A1: Professor Smith likes Professor Brown
       A2: Prof Smith likes Prof Brown and Prof King likes Prof Matthew

(27)   Q: Which linguist will be offended if we invite which philosopher?
       A1: Professor Smith will be offended if we invite Professor Brown
       A2: #Professor Smith will be offended if we invite Professor Brown and
           Professor King will be offended if we invite Professor Matthew

Dayal (1996, 2002) argues that this island sensitivity indicates that a multiple-pair answer is obtained by LF movement of the wh-in-situ to spec-CP at LF, where a semantic operation composes it with the other wh. In contrast, single-pair answers do not require movement of the lower wh; they are obtained by unselective binding of the lower wh by the higher one, or perhaps by existential closure involving a choice function interpretation for the lower wh (Reinhart 1998).

Most native speakers I asked allow a multiple-pair answer in (28b); no one noticed a difference between (28a) and (28b) in this respect.[4] (My own judgement for Dutch is the same). If so, this indicates the lower wh can covertly move in (28b) without this inducing a *that*-trace violation, as predicted.

(28)   a. Who said who left?
           A1: Sue said Bill left
           A2: Sue said Bill left and Carl said Pauline left
       b. Who said that who left?
           A1: Sue said that Bill left
           A2: Sue said that Bill left and Carl said that Pauline left

13.6 Extraction Out of Complementizer-final Clauses

In a purely syntactic account, it is not immediately expected that the linear position of C should have an influence on the extractability of the subject, but it does matter in the PF interface account. If the language adheres to

---

[4] All my informants found (28b) grammatical, *pace* Aoun *et al.* (1987), but in line with Lasnik and Saito (1992).

right-alignment between syntactic and prosodic phrases as in (3), the subject will never end up in a prosodic phrase with a sentence-final C, and so should be freely extractable. Head-final languages seem to be subject, however, to the mirror image of (3), i.e. left-alignment between syntactic and prosodic phrases (see Selkirk 1986; Tokizaki 1999):

(29)   Align (⟨left edge, XP⟩, ⟨left edge, φ⟩)

This would mean that any XP that is left-adjacent to C in syntax ends up in the same prosodic phrase with C initially at PF, which could give rise to problems with (4) if the XP is extracted out of an embedded clause. If so, subjects should usually be extractable in C-final languages, as any intervening XP between them and the sentence-final C has the result that subject and C are not in the same prosodic phrase. But if the subject is the sole XP in the VP, then, it seems, there may be trouble. Moreover, we would now expect that objects are more difficult to extract than subjects, since in a strict SOVC language objects would not have other XPs between them and C. If the language adheres to (29) this would result in the following syntax-PF correspondence, with YP ending up in the same φ with C at PF.

(30)   syntax: XP [$_{VP}$ YP V] C
          PF   {XP} {YP V C}

However, a typological property of OV languages seems to be that they allow leftward clause-internal scrambling of objects quite freely (see for instance Haider 2005 on this correlation between headedness and possible word orders in the VP of a language). This means that, if a phrase is extracted out of a clause, we cannot be certain that extraction from that clause took place out of the phrase's base position, or whether the phrase scrambled clause-internally first and then got extracted. If scrambling is adjunction to VP (or any higher phrase), a phrase in scrambled position does not end up in the same prosodic phrase as C at PF under (29), since at least a left VP-bracket triggers a φ-boundary between the phrase and the complementizer:

(31)   syntax XP [$_{VP}$ YP [$_{VP}$ ... V]] C
          PF   {XP} {YP} {V C}

Thus, YP in (31) should be extractable without problems.

   The prediction under the PF account, then, is that the linear position of C does have an effect: right-peripheral complementizers should not give rise to the mirror image of complementizer-trace effects, that is, to trace-complementizer effects (except in those C-final languages that do not allow for scrambling, if such exist). It has been hypothesized that this is indeed the case:

(32) '(Conjecture) *That*-trace effects are found only with initial comple-
      mentizers'

(Kayne 1994: 53)

It is difficult to test this, however, as a lot of head-final languages are also wh-
in-situ languages (on which, see the previous section). As for other types of
movement than wh-movement, it can be observed that there is nothing wrong
with long-distance scrambling out of complementizer-final clauses in a language like Japanese. This can affect elements that have only the verb (so not an
XP) between their base position and C:

(33) Hon-o$_i$ John-ga   [Mary-ga   t$_i$ yonda
      book-ACC   *John*-NOM   *Mary*-NOM   *read*
      to]   omotte-iru.   (Kawamura 2004)
      COMP   *think*
      'John thinks that Mary read a book.'

It can also affect subjects, as long as they do not carry the nominative particle
ga (*ga*-marked NPs do not seem to scramble at all, not even clause-internally,
cf. Saito 1985; see Whitman 2001, from which (34) comes, for one possible
explanation of this):

(34) [Sono   hon   mo / dake]$_i$ Taroo ga   [t$_i$ ii   to]   omotte
      that *book* *even/only*   *Taroo*-NOM   *good* COMP   *thinking*
      iru   (koto)
      is   *fact*
      'Even/Only that book, Taroo thinks (that) is good.'

Ishii (2004) argues that if comparative 'deletion' involves empty operator
movement, then this too shows there is no complementizer-trace (or rather
trace-complementizer) effect in Japanese:

(35) John-ga   Mary-ni   hanasi kaketa   to   omotteiru yorimo
      John-NOM   *Mary*-DAT   *talked to*   COMP   *think*   *than*
      harukani   ookumo   hito-ga   Susy-ni   hanasi   tagatte   ita
      far   *more*   *people*-NOM   *Susy*-DAT *wanted*   *to*   *talk*
      'Far more people wanted to talk with Susy than John thinks talked
      to Mary.'

      [OP$_i$ [John-ga [t$_i$ Mary-ni hanasi kaketa to] omotteiru] yorimo] harukani
      ookuno hito-ga Susy-to hanasi tagatte ita

'In [(35)], the empty operator OP, which originates in the embedded subject
position, undergoes movement to the matrix Spec of C crossing over the

embedded overt complementizer *to* "that." The result is acceptable. This shows that Japanese lacks the that-t effect.' (Ishii 2004: 212).

Similar observations can be made for other complementizer-final languages. Bayer (1999) notes that both Indo-Aryan and Dravidian languages can be shown to permit overt as well as covert movement from complementizer-final clauses. This holds, again, both for elements whose base position is left-adjacent to the V-C sequence...

(36) [tomar beral-ke]ᵢ amra SObai [paS-er baRi-r
your cat-ACC *we all side*-GEN *house*-GEN
kukur ti tᵢ kamRe-che bole] Sune-chilam (Bengali, Bayer 1999)
dog bite-PTS3 COMP *hear* −PTS1
'Your cat, we have all heard that the dog from next door has bitten'

...and for subjects (note that in (37) we are dealing with a wh-in-situ subject though, so it also falls under the generalization discussed in the previous section). In (37), *ke* 'who' can have either narrow scope ('They have heard who will come'), or wide scope ('Who have they heard will come?'). In the latter case, *ke* moves to the matrix clause at LF (note there is no second, higher, wh in (37), cf. section 13.5), across the complementizer.

(37) ora [[ke aS-be] bole] Sune-che (Bengali, Bayer 1999)
they who come-FUT3 COMP *hear*–PTS3

13.7 Extraction Out of Complementizer-less Clauses

Ancash Quechua (25a) showed that complementizer-trace effects can be induced by complementizers that do not receive a phonological realization. Indeed, the PF account presented here predicts it should not matter whether C is spelled out or not in phonology (though this is also true of a number of purely syntactic accounts). So why *does* it seem to matter in English? After all, in contrast to (1a), a sentence like (38) is perfectly fine.

(38) Whoᵢ do you think [tᵢ read that book yesterday]?

One possible approach involves truncation (cf. Rizzi 2006). Perhaps the higher part of the clausal functional structure, including C, is absent altogether if we do not see *that* appearing. In that case, (4) cannot be violated. This may be the proper way to deal with a type of subject extraction that is generally unproblematic, namely raising (A-movement).

Infinitives arguably have a smaller clausal structure than tensed clauses (see Wurmbrand 2000 for detailed discussion and references). Compare the situation in Dutch: some infinitival clauses can optionally be introduced by a complementizer, and so be CPs, but in that case subject raising out of them is impossible. In other words, only control infinitives can be introduced by a complementizer; raising is only possible out of complementizer-less infinitives:

(39) a. Jan   probeert [(om) PRO het boek te lezen]   (control)
          John   tries   for   the   book   to   read
          'John tries to read the book.'

      b. Jan$_i$ schijnt [(*om) t$_i$ een moeilijk boek te lezen]   (raising)
          John   seems   for   a   difficult book   to   read
          'John seems to read a difficult book.'

For tensed clauses, assuming there is truncation if there is no visible complementizer is not a very attractive solution, however. The diagnostics that show some infinitival clauses can have a reduced clausal structure (e.g. the infinitive undergoing verb raising in German and Dutch, scope-taking elements in the infinitival clause taking matrix scope, 'long passive' in German) are absent in the case of tensed clauses.

The PF approach allows for another possible analysis, however. PF is the interface level between syntax and phonology:

(40) syntax ↔ PF ↔ phonology

If something does not show up in phonology, this can mean one of three things. (i) It is not there. This would be the case for C under truncation. (ii) It is present in syntax and initially in the derivation of PF, but it gets deleted at PF (and so is not present in phonology). I assume this is the case for 'null' elements, including traces and the null complementizer in Quechua (25a). (iii) It is present initially in the derivation in syntax, but it gets deleted in syntax; thus, it is not present at PF (nor in phonology). I assume this is the case for elements that undergo an ellipsis process (e.g. gapping, VP-deletion, conjunction reduction).

If the 'null C' in English (38) is a deleted C (one that is present in syntax but not at PF), rather than a non-spelled-out C (one that is present at PF but not in phonology), then (4) cannot be violated (the lowest subject trace does not find itself in a potential checking configuration with C at PF, as C is not present there). Independent evidence for this deletion approach may come from the observation, made by Merchant (2001), that other processes of ellipsis that target not just C but a complete clause containing a complementizer-trace configuration also void the effect:

(41)   a.   *John said that someone would write a new textbook but I can't
            remember who$_i$ John said that t$_i$ would write a new textbook

       b.   John said that someone would write a new textbook but I can't
            remember who$_i$ ~~John said that t$_i$ would write a new textbook~~

                                                                    (sluicing)

13.8 Conclusion

The main point of this chapter is that, although the complementizer-trace effect looks like a purely syntactic phenomenon at first sight, it turns out that the data pertaining to it fall out from an account that takes into account the interplay between syntax and PF. A general methodological conclusion that can be drawn form this is that, although most likely purely syntactic principles must be assumed to account for various phenomena, it can be fruitful to consider the interplay of multiple modules to account for a phenomenon that seemingly pertains to only one of them.

Acknowledgements

For helpful comments on earlier versions of this chapter I am indebted to audiences at UCL, University of Ulster at Jordanstown (OnLI workshop) and Catholic University Brussels (BCGL 2), as well as two anonymous reviewers.

14

An Experimental Approach to the Interpretation of wh-phrases: Processing and Syntax-Prosody Interface

SUWON YOON

14.1 Introduction

This chapter argues against previous uniform approaches for wh-phrases, showing that there exists an argument/adjunct asymmetry with respect to the interpretation of wh-phrases: argument wh-phrases trigger Intervention Effects, but adjunct wh-phrases do not. Though there have been discussions on the idiosyncratic lack of IEs for reason *why* (Cole and Hermon 1998; Kuwabara 1998; Miyagawa 2001; Ko 2005), the systematic asymmetry of argument wh-phrases '*what/who/where*' versus adjunct wh-phrases '*how/when/why*' has never been noticed in the literature (section 14.2). The current chapter sheds light on this novel division of wh-phrases by rigorously investigating empirical facts in this domain from Korean, Japanese, and Turkish, calling into question previous approaches.

The empirical facts on argument/adjunct asymmetry are established by a series of experiments in different perspectives: First, since the judgements about IEs are often considered to be extremely subtle (Lee and Tomioka 2001), they require a verification process by a valid method. A total of 156 score responses from a Magnitude Estimation Task (Bard, Robertson, and Sorace 1996) manifests a sharp contrast in acceptability judgements in the course of processing between argument and adjunct intervention stimuli. Furthermore, the insignificant difference between two subject groups (linguist vs non-linguist) in the experiment is shown by a three way ANOVA (section 14.3). Second, substantial prosodic adjustment taken only for argument intervention stimuli (but not for adjunct intervention stimuli) indicates ungrammaticality, which has been elucidated by the comparison of recordings by Praat (section 14.4).

Furthermore, the new dichotomy between '*what/who/where*' and '*how/ when/why*' is supported by their inherently distinct morphological and syntactic properties. First, an ambiguity between interrogative and existential indefinite interpretation only holds for the argument wh-phrases in these languages. Second, a syntactic division is evidenced by structural case-attachment tests and formation of complex wh-expressions, which are available only for the arguments (section 14.5).

After showing that this dichotomy is empirically robust, I suggest different syntacticosemantic locations for wh-arguments (inside *v*P) and wh-adjuncts (outside *v*P) in order to account for the relevant asymmetry (section 14.6). The conclusion follows (section 14.7).

14.2 Intervention Effects

14.2.1 *Uniform Analyses*

Korean, Japanese, and Turkish lack the obligatory overt wh-movement of English-type languages. Instead, wh-phrases can be scrambled over to the initial position of the wh-question sentence in these wh-in-situ languages. As Beck and Kim (1997) note, scrambling is an optional operation in general, since it triggers neither grammaticality differences nor notable meaning contrasts between the sentences in (1a) and (1b). Thus, both sentences are perfectly grammatical wh-questions with the identical meaning of 'what did Suna buy?' in Korean.

(1)   a. Suna-ka   *mwues-ul*   sa-ss-ni?
          Suna-nom   what-acc   buy-Past-Q
      b. *Mwues-ul* Suna-ka   sa-ss-ni?
          what-acc   Suna-nom   buy-Past-Q
          'What did Suna buy?'   [Korean]

However, Beck and Kim (1997) argue that the scrambling of wh-phrases is obligatory in cases where the element preceding the wh-phrase is a scope-bearing element such as a negative polarity item (NPI; e.g., *anyone* 'amwuto' in Korean, 'taremo' in Japanese). Therefore, the in-situ counterparts of wh-phrases as seen in (2b) and (3b) result in ungrammaticality, despite the fact that they are remaining in their canonical positions.

(2)   a.   *Nwukwu-lul* amwuto   manna-ci anh-ass-ni?
            who-acc   anyone   meet-CI not. do-Past-Q
      b. *Amwuto   *nwukwu-lul* manna-ci anh-ass-ni?
            anyone   who-acc   meet-CI not. do-Past-Q
      'Who did no one meet?'

(3)   a.   *Mwues-ul* amwuto   sa-ci   anh-ass-ni?
            what-acc   anyone   buy-CI   not. do-Past-Q
      b. *Amwuto   *mwues-ul* sa-ci   anh-ass-ni?
            anyone   what-acc   buy-CI   not. do-Past-Q
      'What did no one buy?'   [Korean]

The surprising fact that wh-phrases cannot follow an NPI has been accounted for as an Intervention Effect (IE), as in (4).

(4)   Intervention Effects (IEs)
      In LF, a wh-phrase may not move across certain Scope-Bearing
      Interveners.   (e.g. NPI, not, only, even)

                    (Beck and Kim 1997; cf. Hagstrom 1998, Pesetsky 2000)

In order to capture the empirical facts, Beck (1996; Beck and Kim 1997) proposes the following: (i) the notion of Negation Induced Barrier (NIB) defines an intervener; (ii) the Minimal Negative Structure Constraint (MNSC) accounts for the IE data by restricting the binding relation of LF traces.

(5)   Negation Induced Barrier (NIB):
      The first node that dominates a negative quantifier, its restric-
      tion, and its nuclear scope is a Negation Induced Barrier
      (NIB).

(6)   Minimal Negative Structure Constraint (MNSC):
      If an LF trace β is dominated by a NIB α, then the binder of β
      must also be dominated by α.

In the course of the interpretational computation, a wh-phrase needs to covertly move up to the higher position (spec CP) across the subject in order to receive an interpretation at Logical Form (LF). According to the definition of IEs, however, semantically negative scope-bearing elements act as a harmful intervener for this movement of wh-phrases. Therefore, the wh-phrase ends up being uninterpretable, hence ungrammatical. The scrambling of the wh-phrase to the initial position in (2a) and (3a), however, seems to ameliorate the situation. The newly adopted linear order at the surface structure—the wh-phrase preceding the intervener—reflects a different LF structure in which the NIB (the VP-dominating Neg) is located below the LF trace of the wh-phrase and hence the LF does not violate the MNSC. In this vein, they argue that scrambling is not a semantically vacuous operation since the scrambling of a wh-phrase has the effect of altering the structural hierarchy at LF. Thus it provides evidence against Hale's (1980) claim that free word order in Japanese is due to non-configurational, flat phrase structure, or the abovementioned claim that scrambling is a strictly optional movement.

14.2.2 *Asymmetry Analysis*

Although previous analyses of IEs seem to correctly predict the interactions between interpretation components in questions with wh-arguments, the theory requires a revision because I am suspicious of the sensitivity of adjunct wh-phrases (*when, how, why*) to IEs.

Starting here, additional data on IEs in other wh-phrases are going to be examined to show that the important asymmetry between argument and adjunct wh-phrases went unnoticed by previous analyses. To illustrate, wh-arguments such as *what, who,* and *where* as in Beck and Kim's examples in the previous section reveal a strong constraint on triggering their scrambling over the intervening NPI. However, empirical discoveries show that the IEs do not strictly hold for adjunct wh-phrases in Korean and Japanese. As seen below, the constraint becomes far weaker or does not exist at all with adjunct wh-phrases such as *when, how,* and *why*. In the following data (7) and (8), the scrambling of adjunct wh-phrases across NPIs seems to be optional even in the presence of interveners, in contrast with the wh-arguments discussed in the preceding sections.

(7)   *Way/encey/ettehkey(hayse)* amwuto swukcey-lul   ceychwulha-ci
       why/when/how(manner)   anyone   homework-acc submit-CI
       anh-ass-ni?
       not.do-Past-Q

(8)   (?)Amwuto *way/encey/ettehkey(hayse)* swukcey -lul
           anyone   why/when/how(manner)   homework-acc
           ceychwulha-ci anh-ass-ni?
           submit-CI   not.do-Past-Q
           'Why/when/how(manner) did nobody submit their homework?'
                                                                [Korean]

An analogous conclusion is drawn from the evidence that Beck and Kim's own ungrammatical sentence in (9) becomes perfectly grammatical if the argument wh-phrase *what* is replaced by an adjunct wh-phrase such as *how*, *why*, or *when* in (10).

(9)   *Suna-ka   amwu-ekey-to *mwues-ul* poyeochwu-ci anh-ass-ni?
       Suna-Nom anyone-Dat   what-Acc   show-CI   not.do-Past-Q
       'What didn't Suna show to anyone?'   [Korean] (Beck and Kim 1997)

(10)   Suna-ka   amwu-ekey-to *way/encey/ettehkey(hayse)* kukes-ul
        Suna-Nom   anyone-Dat   why/when/how(manner)   it-acc
        poyeochwu-ci anh-ass-ni?
        show-CI   not.do-Past-Q
        'Why/when/how(manner) didn't Suna show it to anyone?'   [Korean]

More importantly, the plausibility of an asymmetry analysis is further supported by the fact that such phenomena are observed in another wh-*in-situ* language. The Japanese data given below also show a parallel pattern between obligatorily scrambled argument wh-phrases in (11) and (12), and optionally scrambled adjunct wh-phrases in (13).

(11)   a.   *Dare-o*   dare-mo   mi-na-katta–no.
              who-acc anyone-even see-not-Past-Q

        b.   *Dare-mo   *dare-o*   mi-na-katta-no.
              anyone-even who-acc see-not-Past-Q
              'Who did no one see?'

(12)   a.   *Nani-o*   dare-mo   kawa-na-katta–no.
              what-acc anyone-even buy-not-Past-Q

        b.   *Dare-mo   *nani-o*   kawa-na-katta-no.
              anyone-even what-acc buy-not-Past-do-Q
              'What did no one buy?'

(13)   a.   *Naze/itu/doo(nikasite)*   dare-mo   shukudai-o
              when/why/how(manner) anyone-even homework-acc
              tasa-na-katta-no.
              submit-not-Past-Q

        b.   (?)Dare-mo   *naze/itu/doo(nikasite)*   shukudai-o
              anyone-even why/when/how(manner)   homework-acc
              tasa-na-katta-no.
              submit-not-Past-Q
              'Why/when/how(manner) did no one submit their homework?'
                                                                    [Japanese]

Finally, a similar asymmetry is also observed in Turkish where only NPs create IEs but PPs with non-structural cases do not. In (14), an accusative object induces IEs according to Cagri (2005). She (p.c.) also mentions that this NP versus PP asymmetry corresponds to the proposed new dichotomy (i.e., *what/who/where* vs *how/when/why*) in Turkish wh-phrases.

(14)   *[Ø ı çocuk-lar-ı   arı sok-an]   ormanı
       Ø children-ACC bee sting-SUBJECT-RELATIVIZATION woods
       'the woods where a bee/bees sting(s) children'   [Turkish]

Thus far I have shown that there is a clear discrepancy between argument wh-phrases such as *what/who/where* and adjunct wh-phrases such as *how/when/why* with respect to IEs at least in the abovementioned languages. Before turning to the question of why the asymmetry exists, I provide a confirming process for the asymmetric data in the following sections (section 14.3, 14.4).

14.3 The Experiment Part I: Processing of wh-questions

14.3.1 *Magnitude Estimation Task*

In this section, the results of an experiment conducted with Korean native speakers are presented.[1] The purpose of the experiment is to lay a solid empirical basis for my claims regarding the argument-adjunct asymmetry. This additional substantiation is advisable since judgements for IEs are claimed to be extremely subtle (Lee and Tomioka 2001). For the analytic method, I adopt the 'Magnitude Estimation Task (MET)' of linguistic acceptability developed by Bard, Robertson, and Sorace (1996). The test is designed to reveal the gradience in relative acceptability perceived by the subjects assuming that the acceptability is a reflection of the grammatical effects. Thus the test is used to manifest the asymmetry of the intervention data in terms of relative acceptability and hence grammaticality. In the experiment kit, the stimuli consist of the following twelve wh-questions.

14.3.1.1 *Stimuli*

Non-IE stimuli: (a) sentences
IE stimuli: (b) sentences

---

[1] As for the Japanese IE data, the judgements were also tested by Japanese linguists at the University of Chicago. Although informally surveyed, the obvious argument-adjunct asymmetry was commented on by all the informants while judging the Japanese data.

(15) a. *Nwukwu-lul* amwuto   manna-ci anh-ass-ni?
          who-acc   anyone   meet-CI   not.do-Past-Q
      b. Amwuto   *nwukwu-lul* manna-ci anh-ass-ni?
          anyone   who-acc   meet-CI   not.do-Past-Q
      'Who did no one see?'

(16) a. *Mwues-ul* amwuto   sa-ci   anh-ass-ni?
          what-acc   anyone   buy-CI   not.do-Past-Q
      b. Amwuto   *mwues-ul* sa-ci   anh-ass-ni?
          anyone   what-acc   buy-CI   not.do-Past-Q
      'What did no one buy?'

(17) a. *Eti-lul*   amwuto   ka-ci   anh-ass-ni?
          where-acc   anyone   go-CI not.do-Past-Q
      b. Amwuto   *eti-lul*   ka-ci   anh-ass-ni?
          anyone   where-acc go-CI not.do-Past-Q
      'Where did no one go?'

(18) a. *Encey*   amwuto swukcey-lul   ceychwulha-ci anh-ass-ni?
          when   anyone homework-acc submit-CI   not.do-Past-Q
      b. Amwuto *encey*   swukcey-lul   ceychwulha-ci anh-ass-ni?
          anyone when   homework-acc submit-CI   not.do-Past-Q
      'When did nobody submit their homework?'

(19) a. *Ettehkey* amwuto say-pepan-ey panungha-ci anh-ass-ni?
          how   anyone new-bill-to   respond-CI   not.do-Past-Q
      b. Amwuto *ettehkey* say-pepan-ey panungha-ci anh-ass-ni?
          anyone how   new-bill-to   respond-CI   not.do-Past-Q
      'How did nobody respond to the new bill?'

(20) a. *Way*   amwuto swukcey-lul   ceychwulha-ci anh-ass-ni?
          why   anyone homework-acc submit-CI   not.do-Past-Q
      b. Amwuto *way*   swukcey-lul   ceychwulha-ci anh-ass-ni?
          anyone why   homework-acc submit-CI   not.do-Past-Q
      'Why did nobody submit their homework?'

14.3.1.2 *Subjects* The experiment was conducted with two subgroups of subjects, a group of eight non-linguist graduate students and a group of five linguists. After each subject scored twelve wh-question sentences (the a/b sentences given above), a total of 156 score responses was acquired.

14.3.1.3 *Results* The arithmetic means of the judgements are represented in the following Figure 1. As can be clearly seen in the contrast between

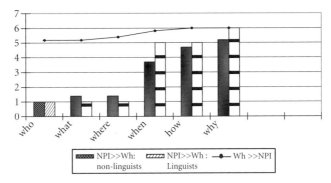

Figure 1. Strength of preference for acceptability with Intervention data in Korean wh-questions (The first dotted bars in each pair represent the mean number by the non-linguist group, and the following line shaded bars by the linguist group.)

wh-phrases, the preference of wh-adjuncts over wh-arguments in intervention environments is borne out.

The subjects scored the acceptability of each sentence from 0 (terribly ungrammatical) to 6 (perfectly grammatical) given in the experiment kit. First, the judgements for the (a) sentences are given as diamonds connected by a line in Figure 1 (Wh>>NPI case: Wh-phrase preceding NPI). As can be inferred from the uniformly high scores assigned to these items, these are grammatical sentences (with scrambled wh-words, hence not giving rise to IEs) provided only for comparison purposes.

Rather, let us focus on the double bars that give the mean scores for the (b) sentences in (13-18), where the interveners precede the wh-phases (NPI>>Wh). Drastic contrasts between wh-argument (who/what/where) vs wh-adjunct (when/how/why) are revealed here, which shows that the intuition about the asymmetry is robust.

14.3.2 *Variation in Responses*

In the bar graph (Figure 1) above, the double bar of each wh-phrase designates two subgroups of subjects, the former being the non-linguist group and the latter the linguist group. As the more distinctive scores in Figure 1 allude, linguists seem to have more decisive views on the asymmetry than non-linguists. The difference between the two subject groups (linguist vs non-linguist) turns out to be statistically insignificant in this experiment (see p-value of 'major' in (1) and (2) of Figure 2).

Three-way ANOVA (Analysis of Variance) in Figure 2 below provides empirical evidence that both the sentence types (a/b) and the wh-phrases have a significant effect on collected sentence-evaluation scores while the type

(1) Six types of Wh-phrase.

Source of Variation	d.f.	Sum sq.	Mean Sq.	F statistic	p-value	Remark
Major (Ling/non-Ling)	1	0.85	0.85	0.76	38.6 %	Insignificant
Sentence (a/b)	1	280.01	280.01	248.34	<10−14%	Significant
Wh-phrase (6)	5	191.26	38.25	33.93	<10−14%	Significant
Residuals	148	166.87	1.13			

(2) Only two group of Wh-phrase (argument / adjunct).

Source of Variation	d.f.	Sum sq.	Mean Sq.	F statistic	p-value	Remark
Major (Ling/non-Ling)	1	0.85	0.85	0.74	39.1 %	Insignificant
Sentence (a/b)	1	280.01	280.01	243.14	<10−14%	Significant
Wh-phrase (arg./adj.)	1	183.08	183.08	158.98	<10−14%	Significant
Residuals	152	175.05	1.15			

FIGURE 2. Three-way ANOVA(Analysis of Variance) Table: (1) Six types of Wh-phrase (2) Only two group of Wh-phrase (argument/adjunct).

of respondent (linguist vs non-linguist group) does not. This result turns out robust regardless of how six wh-phrases are grouped.

Given the statistical significance, both groups can be concluded to show reliable judgements within and across the groups. In fact, these variations are unsurprising considering that linguists are more sensitive to acceptability judgements, intentionally disregarding the extra intonational factors since prosodic effects may play an active role in ameliorating the ungrammatical sentences, especially with IEs. The role of prosody in improving the degenerated sentences will be discussed in the next section, and it will provide further evidence for the asymmetry between wh-questions.

14.4 The Experiment Part II: Prosody-Syntax Interface

In this section, an analysis of wh-questions is presented based on prosody experiments assuming the intersecting nature of prosody and syntax.

14.4.1 *Theoretical Background*

The theoretical background of this experiment can be found in the 'cue-based interpretation theory' developed by Pickering and Barry (1991) who argue that if one cue is low in validity, it can be compensated for by the other cue. In the ungrammatical IE sentences in (21) below, for instance, the interpretation of the wh-argument 'who' is difficult to acquire due to the coexistence of two focusing elements, *amwuto* 'anyone' and *nwukwu-lul* 'who-acc' at LF. Hence, a speaker's strategy to express an intervention sentence with a correct interpretation can be either to adjust the 'syntactic cue' by wh-phrase scrambling (and hence reordering the LF structure), or to strengthen the 'phonetic cue' by producing an extra prosodic effect on the wh-phrase. Observing that scope inversion is signalled by a pause or prosodic focus to license an NPI in special prosodic environments in Korean and Japanese, Sohn (1999) assumes this kind of prosodic remedy to be 'string vacuous scrambling'. Furthermore, the interaction between syntax and prosody has been extensively discussed in recent literature based on the common assumption that the interpretation of wh-questions is significantly affected by prosody (Lee and Tomioka 2001; Deguchi and Kitagawa 2002; Ishihara 2003; Hirotani 2003; Kitagawa and Fodor 2003; Kitagawa and Tomioka 2003). It is unsurprising that research in similar aspects are also discovered in Korean literature: the interactions between focus and phonological prominence and between pitch accent and length in Korean are discussed by Choi (1985), Lee and Chung (1999), and Jun and Oh (1996). More importantly, Choi, and Jun and Oh show how the prosodic effects work with wh-phrases in Korean.

In this vein, the present experiment is conducted based on the assumption that syntactically caused IEs can be fixed to some extent by rearranging the prosodic structure, following Bruce (1998) and others. As will be shown shortly in the phonetic descriptions, if extra-prosodic effects are given on wh-phrases, it seems to strengthen its focus at higher prosodic phrasing and therefore remedy the violation (IEs) incurred at lower syntactic levels as already noted by Pickering and Barry (1991), Sohn (1999), and Pesetsky (p.c. in Ko (2005)).

14.4.2 *Prediction*

Based on the theoretical background, the crucial assumption is that there will be two possible prosodic strategies to be employed by a speaker to improve the syntactic ungrammaticality: higher pitch and long pause. Hence, if there is any hint of extra-prosodic effects in a given sentence, it can be analysed as having been adopted by the speaker in order to ameliorate the degenerated sentence. Thus the anticipated result of the experiment is that the degree of prosodic effects will differ between (ungrammatical) wh-arguments and (grammatical) wh-adjuncts in the IE data corresponding to their asymmetry in acceptability.

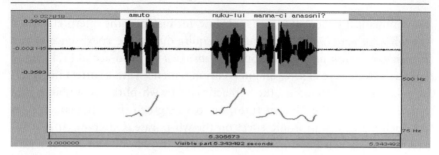

FIGURE 3. The IE wh-argument question remedied by prosodic aid.

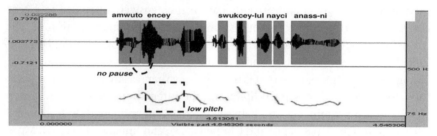

FIGURE 4. The IE wh-adjunct question remedied by prosodic aid.

14.4.3 *Results*

This prediction is borne out as shown in the prosodic descriptions, analysed by Praat, in Figure 3 and Figure 4 above.

(21)   Amwuto *(##)* *nwukwu-lul* manna-ci anh-ass-ni?
        anyone   who-acc   meet-CI   not.do-Past-Q
        'Who did no one meet?'

(22)   (?) Amwuto *encey* swucey-lul   nay-ci   anh-ass-ni?
            anyone   when homework-ACC submit-CI NEG-PST-Q
            'When did nobody submit their homework?'

First of all, compare the 'pause length' difference in Figure 3 and Figure 4. Since a pause can cancel the IEs (Sohn 1995; Ko 2005), the 'long pause' between *amwuto* (anyone) and *nwukwu* (who) indicates that there is supposed to be a high degree of grammaticality violation before it was remedied by this prosodic cue in Figure 3. In contrast, no noticeable pause is observed between *amwuto* (anyone) and *encey* (when) in Figure 4 due to the lack of IEs to be cured to begin with.

The second difference is the 'pitch' level, indicated by F0, between *nwukwu* (who) and *encey* (when). As shown in the lower part of each figure above, a strong extra-prosodic effect on the wh-argument (*nwukwu* 'who') is expressed as higher pitch, resulting in a circumvention of the IEs. On the other hand, the equivalent pitch height of the wh-adjunct (*encey* 'when') and the intervener (*amwuto* 'anyone') shows that this sentence is already grammatical before any prosodic aid is taken. Once again the asymmetry is supported by the 'no violation, no remedy' rule.

Thus far the asymmetric pattern in IE wh-questions has been established by presenting previously unnoticed crucial data and by examining them with acceptability and prosody experiments. In order to understand the origin of the asymmetrical behaviours between wh-arguments and wh-adjuncts with respect to IEs, inherently different properties between the wh-phrases in Korean and Japanese will be discussed in section 14.5.

14.5 Further Evidence for the New Dichotomy

14.5.1 *Interrogative vs Existential Indefinite*

In order to correctly capture the source of the wh-phrase dichotomy, their semantic ambiguity needs to be considered. As in many other languages, wh-phrases in Korean and Japanese have both interrogative and existential indefinite meaning. To illustrate, 'nwukwu' in Korean can either mean 'who' or 'someone/anyone' depending upon the context.[2] One notable argument/adjunct asymmetry arises in this NPI formation from wh-phrases. As illustrated in (23) below, argument wh-phrase '*what/who/where*' plus particle '*to/mo*' (even) tend to acquire a strong NPI status whereas wh-adjunct '*when/how/ why*' are very reluctant to combine with the NPI-inducing particle.

(23)   wh-phrases + NPI particle (even) ((a)Korean and (b)Japanese)

(a)Korean wh-phrases	wh+'to' (wh+*even*):NPI	(b)Japanese wh-phrases	wh+'mo' (wh+*even*):NPI	meaning
who: nwukwu	nwukwu-to	who: dare	dare-mo	anyone (NPI)
what: mwues	mwues-to	what: nani	nani-mo	anything (NPI)
when: encey	??encey-to	when: itu	*itu-mo (→'always')	anytime (NPI)
where: etise	etise-to	where: doko	doko-mo	anywhere(NPI)
how: ettehkey	??ettehkey-to	how: doo	*doo-mo	anyhow (NPI)
why: way	*way-to	why: naze	*naze-mo	for any reason(NPI)

---

[2] This formation of strong NPI from wh-phrase is universally observed if the wh-phrases have indefinite use in the language. (e.g., Mandarin Chinese)

14.5.2 *Structural Case Attachment*

Given the semantic polarity difference, let us move on to the syntactic properties of wh-phrases. Another piece of evidence that '*what/who/where*' are nominals and '*when/how/why*' are adverbials is given by structural case attachability tests (NOM/ACC particle) in (24) and (25).

(24)   NOM/ACC-marker attachability test: Korean wh-phrases
       mwues-i/lul   'what-nom/acc'   *ettehkey-ka/lul '*how-nom/acc'
       nwukwu-ka/lul 'who-nom/acc'   *encey-ka/lul   '*when-nom/acc'
       eti-ka/lul   'where-nom/acc' *way-ka/lul   '*why-nom/acc'

(25)   NOM/ACC-marker attachability test: Japanese wh-phrases
       nani-ka/o   'what-acc'   *doo-ka/o   '*how-acc'
       dare-ka/o   'who-acc'   *itu-ka/o   '*when-acc'
       doko-ka/o³ 'where-acc'(limited use) *naze-ka/o '*why-acc'

Furthermore, the relevant distinction between wh-arguments and wh-adjuncts can be found in complex wh-phrase formation in Korean, noted by Chung (2000). As seen in (26), Korean wh-arguments are able to form a wh-phrase cluster attached to another wh-phrase *enu* (roughly translated as *which*⁴). Along with the case facts, the asymmetry in complex wh-phrase formation also supports the nominal property of wh-arguments and adverbial property of wh-adjuncts because *enu* can only modify nouns.

(26)   Formation of complex wh-expressions:

       enu {nwukwu/mwues/*eti⁵/*encey/*ettehkey/*elma/*way}
       which who/what/where/   when/how/how much/why

---

³ The usage of Japanese *doko-o* (where-acc) is limited to nominal sense 'which place' in (i), whereas *eti-lul* (where-acc) in Korean is more widely used as 'where' in (ii).

(i) Nihon-de doko-o   mita-ka?
    Japan-in   where-acc see-Q   (Which place did you see in Japan?)

(ii) Eti-lul   ka-ni?
     where-acc go-Q? (Where do you go?)

⁴ These complex wh-phrases convey either D-linking or rhetorical usage on *who* or *what* in Korean, so 'enu nwukwu (which who)' means something similar to 'who the hell/who in the world'.

⁵ As for the argument vs adjunct property of 'where' in Korean and Japanese, I assume that it might be ambivalent. Or, one can also claim that there are two different lexical items, i.e. argument *where* and adjunct *where*, in these languages.

14.6 Proposal: The Locus of wh-phrases

Based on the observations so far, I suggest the syntacticosemantic location of each wh-phrase (27) in these languages. Note that the wh-adjuncts *why/how/when* are located higher than *v*P (and hence higher than NegP), while the core wh-arguments *who/what/where* and other ACC-attachable wh-expressions such as *how many N* and *which N* are located under *v*P either at subject or object position where structural case is assigned. The (in)sensitivity to IEs is now predictable from the original position of each wh-phrase at LF.

(27)   The locus of wh-phrases in Korean/Japanese/Turkish-type languages (simplified version)

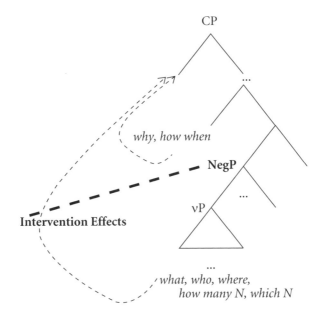

14.7 Conclusion

In this chapter I have argued for a new dichotomy between argument and adjunct wh-phrases in Korean, Japanese, and Turkish-type languages. The proposal is significant in two respects: First, although there has been a long-standing debate between syntactic (Beck and Kim 1997; Hagstrom 1998) and semantic approaches (Honcoop 1998; Kim 2002; Beck 2006) to Intervention Effects, the empirical finding of the asymmetrical pattern in IEs suggests that the blocking effects must be analysed as syntactic LF constraints, rather than a purely semantic focus clash. Second, given that the *who/what/where* vs *why/how/when* dichotomy exists in these languages while no such asymmetry is observed in languages like German, it reveals a significant cross-linguistic variation in syntacticosemantic characteristics of wh-phrases.

15

Acoustic, Articulatory, and Phonological Perspectives on Allophonic Variation of /r/ in Dutch[*]

JAMES M. SCOBBIE AND KOEN SEBREGTS

15.1 Introduction

One of many difficult areas for the phonology-phonetics interface is the phenomenon of allophony. When some lower unit of structure (typically something equivalent to a segment) appears in two distinct positions in higher structure then the potential arises for phonological allophony. By 'phonological', here, we mean that the representation of the segment in the surface phonological level of representation occurs in two variants, predictably conditioned by categorically distinct phonological contexts. 'Phonetic' allophony refers to the far greater number of cases of predictable contextual differences which exist but which are not thought to be represented by changing the internal phonological content of segments—even though these are still conditioned by categorically distinct contexts. (We do not include phonetic changes due to non-phonological variations, e.g. in speech rate, or style or affect, in our definition of allophony.)

For a textbook example, in some varieties, English /t/ is often said to be [tʰ] in the onset and [ʔ] in the coda and [t] in initial /s/ clusters, etc. It is important to note that the prosodic structures and linear order of segments in the surface level of representation already provide all the information required for the necessary translation into the various allophonic variants, whether the relations are phonetic or phonological. What is contentious is, of

[*] This is a reduced version of Scobbie, Sebregts, and Stuart-Smith (2009), narrowed to focus on Dutch /r/. The authors would like to thank Jane Stuart-Smith and Alan Wrench for extensive and continued input and discussion and to acknowledge the support of SRIF funding for ultrasound infrastructure.

course, the amount of detail represented in surface structure by virtue of encoding fewer or more allophones: the more allophones are phonological, the more phonetic detail surface structure contains. For recent reviews of different approaches to the content of surface structure and the relationship with different conceptions of the interface, see Pierrehumbert, Beckman, and Ladd (2000), Cohn (2006), and Scobbie (2007).

We have previously made the criticism of phonology (Scobbie 2007) that there is no scientific, or analytically consistent or agreed means for determining which fineness of phonetic transcription constitutes the raw data for phonological analysis. It seems sometimes that transcription data is claimed, by a category error, to **be** a level of representation. Furthermore, given the preference for phonological data to derive from broad transcription, this means that surface structure consists mainly of those forms which are easy to transcribe and often which have been conventionally analysed in a previous cycle of theoretical analysis (cf. also Simpson 1999; Port and Leary 2005). Stating /t/ allophony in terms of transcribed segments begs the question: it is no wonder so many phenomena can appear segmental and categorical, and hence phonological, if the data is prepared at the appropriate level of granularity. Using fine-grained phonetic data might change our conception of the phenomenon, revealing it to be more subtle, variable, and less phonological (Docherty 1992; Browman and Goldstein 1989, 1992; Pierrehumbert 2002), but it might also reinforce its phonological status from a firmer empirical base. Instrumental analysis provides far more raw information than transcription about the phonetic exponents of phonological systems, but *neither* type of data is a level of representation. From the analytic perspective, phonetic data of any type is a resource which enables a proper consideration of relationships and structures, and is always an abstraction from the real world. Arguments against a naïve phonological interpretation of transcribed phonetic substance can equally be applied to complex phonetic observation. In the end, however much descriptive detail we have, the analyses of phonological allophony and contrast are fundamentally abstract processes. Allophones may be radically different at a phonetic level yet still be argued to belong to the same phonological structure, where general processes of phonetic implementation account for the allophony, or similar phonetically yet differing in phonological specification.

In this paper we will look at one element in Dutch, namely /r/, following in the wake of previous work which has uncovered wide variation in Dutch /r/ realizations while considering the implications for phonology (e.g. Van der Velde and Van Hout 2001; Plug and Ogden 2003; Sebregts and Scobbie 2005). The detail of such variation lets us consider the tension between an apparently simple phonological abstraction with its theoretical phonological label and feature content (here we use a neutral /r/ symbol) and the rich and complex phonetic phenomena associated with it.

The question of whether a phoneme has one phonological allophone which varies phonetically in onset vs coda, or whether it has two (or more) phonological allophonic categories exercises the mind of every phonologist. We explore this issue via a qualitative instrumental articulatory analysis supplemented with acoustic analysis, to explore the nature of this rhotic consonant from speaker-oriented and listener-oriented points of view. Specially, we have used an ultra-sound scanner to capture time-varying images of the tongue (Stone 1997).

One of the main issues of interest for Dutch /r/ allophony suitable for ultrasound investigation is the relationship between a uvular trill as an onset allophone in combination with a post-alveolar approximant coda allophone, a pattern increasingly found in modern Standard Dutch (Van Bezooijen 2005). The radically different allophones [R] and [ɹ] appear easy to distinguish, and it is a priori tempting therefore to describe /r/ as requiring two different categories which differ in both manner and place. But is this phonologization? Let us consider more carefully. The basic analytic decision is whether to use feature theory or a language-specific phonetic specification. How are the very different places and manners encoded and distributed phonologically, if indeed they are at all? How powerful is phonetic imple-mentation, if mere phonetics can turn one of these categories into the other?

In the rest of this paper we will describe our articulatory and acoustic studies, highlighting the differences between speakers and the allophonic patterns that exist within speakers. We conclude with a discussion about the implications of such data for phonology.

15.2 Method

15.2.1 *Participants*

We present data from five native Dutch speakers staying in Edinburgh, Scot-land, with an aim of exploring /r/ systems in which the onset was a uvular trill and the coda a post-alveolar approximant. Please see Scobbie, Sebregts, and Stuart-Smith (2009) for more technical details of this study. All were bilingual in English, and the sample is not representative of anything more than a random set of younger Dutch overseas students or émigrés. Impressionistic-ally, their Dutch sounded native without traces of second language interfer-ence and we have no reason to think that their systems show attrition towards English (de Leeuw 2009), but this has to be acknowledged as a possibility. All speakers spoke Standard Dutch with few traces of regional accents.

The types of systems that were found can be grouped into three types, with subject pseudo-initials given accordingly. As will be shown later, these initials are mnemonics for the speakers' articulations. The ordering of the two initials indicates onset, then coda articulations, and U = uvular trill, B = bunched post-alveolar approximant, and R = retroflex alveolar approximant. Numbering is used to distinguish the two speakers who both have a UB system.

- Onset and coda both uvular trill ($n = 1$, with 4 rejected) **UU**
- Onset uvular trill, coda post-alveolar approximant ($n = 3$) **UB1, UB2, UR**
- Onset and coda both post-alveolar approximants ($n = 1$) **RR**
- These five speakers were all from the western or central Netherlands. All three onset/coda patterns are well known from previous descriptions of Standard Dutch /r/ (Van Reenen 1994; Voortman 1994; Van de Velde 1996).

15.2.2 *Data Collection Procedure*

All subjects were recorded in a sound-treated room at QMU using the equipment and methodology reported by Vazquez Alvarez and Hewlett (2007), which comprises ultrasound scans digitized at 25Hz with an associated acoustic signal synchronized with a temporal alignment error of at worst ±30ms. A headset was used to provide stability, holding the ultrasound probe in a fairly fixed location. Clearly, analysis of acoustic/articulatory timing relations is the most problematic analysis type from this body of data, compared to pure formant analysis or pure ultrasound analysis, due to the variable error in alignment. Thus we will approach articulatory and acoustic correspondences cautiously, and qualitatively. The relatively slow-moving gestures required to bring the tongue into target position for both uvular trills and post-alveolar gestures are, however, clearly visible and easy to extract.

The ultrasound probe was held by the headset under the speaker's chin and touching the submental surface, to provide a steady mid-sagittal image, with the tongue blade and tip to the right of the image (Figure 1) and the root to the left (Stone 1997). As a prompt, speakers were presented with a picture on screen. The list of materials was collected in three blocks, each in random order. At least three tokens of each word were collected, and the final three produced were analysed.

15.2.3 *Materials*

A short set of materials was used, comprising pictures representing common single-word items in Dutch. To control for C-to-C co-articulation as much as possible, an /r/ was placed as a singleton either in word-initial onset or word-final coda position in a monosyllabic word, with /i/, /u/, or /a/ as the

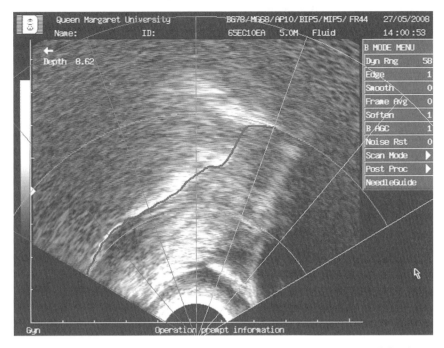

FIGURE 1. Ultrasound Tongue Imaging, with tip and blade to right, root to left. This is a token of a post-alveolar approximant. An analysis curve has been superimposed onto the raw data, at the base of the bright white areas created by reflections from the tongue surface.

adjacent vowel. The particular focus was /r/ in a pre-pausal coda context, with just one onset type for comparison. The contexts /ir/ and /ri/ are thus the closest onset-coda comparison possible with these materials. In addition, two cluster contexts were examined, /rt/ and /rs/, in which the presence of /r/ created a minimal pair with comparable /t/-final and /s/-final words. These /r/ can be expected to be different from singleton /r/ phonetically, due to co-articulation. There were about a dozen semantic distracters, including some words with /r/ in a different position (e.g. *draad* 'thread') which are not analysed here.

Onset:	/ri/	*riem*	'belt'
Bare coda:	/ir/	*mier*	'ant'
	/ar/	*schaar*	'scissors'
	/ur/	*boer*	'farmer'
Coda cluster:	/ɔt/ - /ɔrt/	*bot* vs *bord*	'bone' vs 'plate'
	/as/ - /ars/	*kaas* vs *kaars*	'cheese' vs 'candle'

15.2.4 *Measurement*

15.2.4.1 *Acoustics*   Acoustic measurements were made on the basis of the acoustic data alone, and we undertook two types of acoustic analysis of the four subjects with approximant codas. These measures are indicative and suitable for qualitative analysis, and are not intended for quantitative statistical analysis. First, we measured the duration of quasi-segmental components of the rimes /ir/ /ur/ /ar/. The word was segmented into a steady-state vowel portion (if any), a transitional formant movement, and finally a steady-state rhotic (if any). We noticed that there was frequently a voiceless offglide from the end of the word, a transition into post-speech silence which could have a rhotic quality, so this was also annotated if present. It was a weak fricative which could be uvular, post-alveolar, or like a voiceless vowel in character. Duration measures are presented not normalized in order to present more direct and qualitative characterization of timing and duration. No durational analyses of the minimal pairs were undertaken.

Second, we made manual formant measurements of F_1, F_2, and F_3 (in the AAA software) at a single point in each of the three voiced events, to see how closely approximated F_2 and F_3 are, which is a typical correlate of a post-alveolar rhotic (e.g. Guenther *et al.* 1999). For /ur/, /ir/, and /ar/, the measure was taken at the time when the formants were most closely approximated, which was late in the rime. For the minimal pairs *bot* vs *bord* and *kaas* vs *kaars*, a point approximately midway in each of the three events (vowel, transition, and rhotic) was chosen. If there was no steady-state rhotic, then the end of the voiced transition portion was chosen because it would be the most rhoticized part of the voiced part of the rime, immediately before the final consonant. The final consonant could well be co-articulated and thus reflect the presence of /r/, but we have not measured it here (though such variation would illustrate our theoretical questions about what level of phonetic detail is encoded in surface structure.)

15.2.4.2 *Articulation*   As mentioned above, a line is fitted by hand using AAA software onto any ultrasound frame which is to be used for further analysis. Here we have chosen frames judged to be the one containing the most extreme, clearest articulation of /r/. By and large, this frame was at the end of phonation in the transition to silence.

The curve drawn onto the raw ultrasound image (Figure 1) was exported in Cartesian coordinates to a spreadsheet, using AAA software (Articulate Instruments, 2008), as the basis of an impressionistic analysis. Tongue shapes can be qualitatively assigned, based on the types of /r/ constriction proposed by Delattre and Freeman (1968).

15.3 Results

15.3.1 *Impressionistic Results*

Speaker RR sounds highly derhoticized in the coda (Vieregge and Broeders 1993; van den Heuvel and Cucchiarini 2001; Plug and Ogden 2003), especially after /a/, with residual weak anterior rhoticity of some kind in some tokens. Unlike the other speakers, she clearly has a post-alveolar approximant in the onset rather than a uvular trill. Other speakers sound more rhotic in codas but vary greatly in the apparent dynamics and vowel duration. Speakers UR, UB1, and UB2 sound particularly rhotic. Finally, UU has uvular trills mostly, but a few tokens sound more like voiced fricatives, which is expected from descriptions of Dutch (Collins and Mees 1996: 200) as well as cross-linguistically (Lindau 1985). We are not confident that we can correctly label the approximants as being bunched or retroflex on an impressionistic basis.

15.3.2 *Acoustic Results*

We will present the durational characteristics of the speakers first, then the formant measurement results.

15.3.2.1 *Durational Analysis*   Figure 2 reflects our impression that speaker RR differs from the other subjects in being derhoticized, because she has long steady-state vowels, with an audible offglide but without the period of qualitatively stable phonetic rhoticity that the other subjects have. UR, on the other hand, sounds appreciably rhotic, even though her steady-state

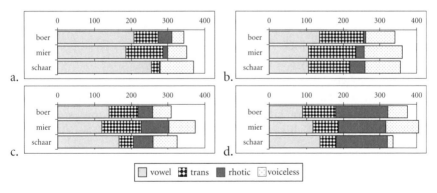

FIGURE 2. Durations (ms) of acoustic events in syllable rime of /r/-final words; speakers a. RR b. UR c. UB1 d. UB2.

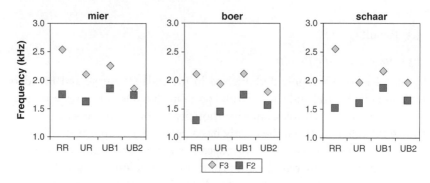

FIGURE 3. Second and third formants during their closest approximation in a rime ending with phonological /r/.

rhoticity is also short, and the V-/r/ transition is long, showing that the auditory percept of rhoticity is not necessarily conveyed by a stable rhotic post-alveolar approximant, and that quality (unsurprisingly) is also important. But, the differences between the speakers in their rhotic portion is remarkable. UB2 has very long steady-state rhoticity and much shorter vowels. Overall, all speakers have comparable rime durations, at around 250 ms to 300 ms, with on average a bit more than 50ms of weak voiceless friction, typically from a glottal source, which can have a faint rhotic quality.

15.3.2.2 *Spectral Analysis*   First, we present the results for the simple rimes. Figure 3 shows that three speakers approximate F2 and F3 much more closely than the fourth, RR, reflecting the impressionistic derhoticization of this speaker. Recall from Figure 2 that RR has long steady-state vowel with short offglide transitions and little rhotic steady state, if any (so that /ar/ was nearly monophthongal), while UR had long transitions towards a relatively short rhotic steady state, which perhaps accounts for her F2-F3 approximation appearing to be slightly less tight than UB1 or UB2.

Across speakers, there is some consistent co-articulation with the preceding vowel, such that F2 and F3 are both lowered following /u/. The consistently higher formant values for UB1 likely reflect a smaller vocal tract size. Table 1 shows the mean F3-F2 value calculated from the nine pooled tokens per speaker.

TABLE 1. F3-F2 (Hz) in the approximant singleton coda /r/.

	RR	UR	UB1	UB2
mean	884	443	222	359
s.d.	*180*	*70*	*110*	*81*

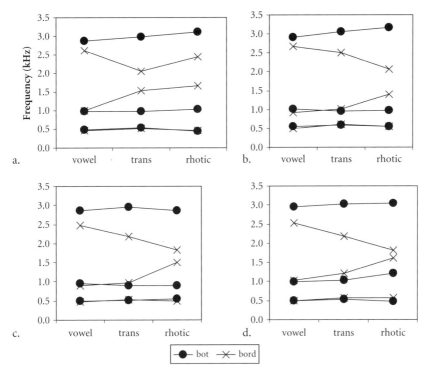

FIGURE 4. The first three formants in a rhotic (crosses: bord) vs rhotic-less (circles: bot) stop-final minimal pair, normalized time; speakers a. RR b. UR c. UB1 d. UB2.

We turn now to the minimal pairs. In Figure 4 and particularly in Figure 5 RR (a) again has far weaker acoustic contrast in terms of the formant frequency in F2 and F3, especially for the low vowel context (about an 800Hz difference in *kaars* vs about 1,200Hz in *kaas*). The other speakers' rhotic formant values (with the crosses) show clear approximation of F2 and F3 in the rhotic phase (R) (about 200Hz vs about 1,200Hz). In addition to these spectral differences, the rhotic rimes tend to be longer in duration and there are some co-articulatory effects attributable to /r/ in the final stop and fricative. But even in these tokens, as in those shown in Figure 2, RR has a long vowel with shorter transition and an almost absent rhotic steady state. On the other hand, the F1 values show that there is no transfer of contrast to a vowel-quality difference. We are not claiming that there is neutralization here in RR's speech, but rather we have shown that the impression of derhoticization in RR's speech (stronger in some tokens than others) is supported by acoustic analysis. Even within the category of 'post-alveolar approximant' for coda /r/, there may be a wide range of variation in the acoustics, from a strong to an almost absent rhotic quality on

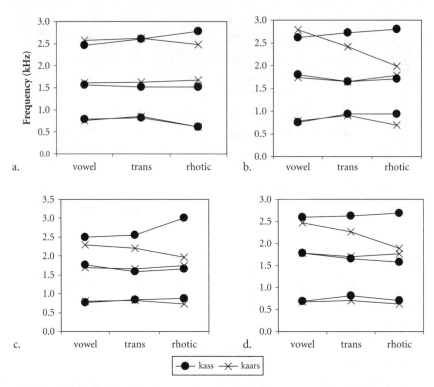

FIGURE 5. The first three formants in a rhotic (crosses: kaars) vs. rhotic-less (circles: kaas) fricative-final minimal pair, normalised time; speakers a. RR, b. UR, c. UB1, d. UB2.

average, with individual tokens completely lacking any impressionistic quality of rhoticity at all in the case of the rime /ar/.

15.3.3 *Articulatory Analysis*

Three speakers appear to have a strong categorical distinction between onset and coda allophones, given that onsets are uvular trills and codas are post-alveolar approximants. In the articulatory analysis we look at singleton /r/, contrasting the tongue shapes of onsets and codas within speaker. For the non-dynamic analyses presented below, a single representative tongue curve representing the vowel and another representing the /r/ were taken from the dynamic sequence, typical cases of which are shown in Figure 6. In Figure 7 (Speaker UR) and Figure 8 (Speakers UB1 and UB2) are the three tokens each from onset /r/, from /ri/, with three tokens from coda /ir/, overlaid in articulatory space. (Not shown is the tongue shape for /i/, which is, in both *mier* and *riem*, a palatal constriction with advanced tongue root very different from the shapes for /r/.)

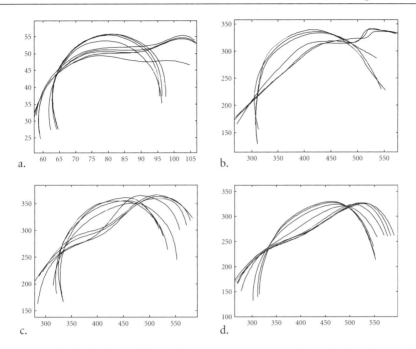

FIGURE 6. Individual tokens of boer with tongue curves at 40ms intervals (varying spatial scales); speakers a. RR, b. UR, c. UB1, d. UB2.

Both speaker UB1 in Figure 8a and UB2 in Figure 8b show a large onset-coda allophonic difference. They have a post-alveolar approximant coda /r/ which is bunched (tip down), unlike UR (Figure 7) or RR (Figure 10 below) who have a tip-up or retroflex articulation (finally providing the evidence for the five speakers' code names as mentioned in section 15.2.1). Note, however, that in Figure 8a in Speaker UB1, the anterior part of the tongue in the onset uvular trill appears to be approximated to the post-alveolar region as a secondary articulation, just as closely as it is for the coda, where this is said to be the primary articulation, a pattern which UB2 may have too.

For speaker RR, who has an approximant onset, Figure 10 shows that articulatory rhoticity in the coda is clear and comparable in strength to the onset, despite both impressionistic and acoustic coda derhoticization. Although the acoustic point at which this occurs cannot be identified with high temporal accuracy, it appears that this constriction target occurs roughly at the termination of phonation or even <u>after</u> its offset, which would explain why the degree of raising that is present does not appear to generate such a strong impression of rhoticity as it does in the onset. Of particular interest is the clearly visible but acoustically covert tip raising in *schaar* (Figure 10), the rime of which is nearly monophthongal (Figure 3).

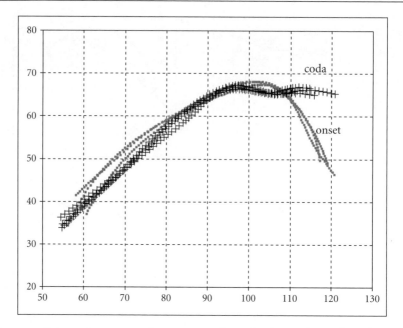

FIGURE 7. Extracted tongue surface contours from the three tokens of speaker UR's onset /ri/ (crosses) and coda /ir/ (small squares), showing broadly comparable pharyngeal contours (on the left of the image) but with clear anterior tip raising (on the right) in the coda but not in the onset. Horizontal and vertical measures are in mm from an arbitrary origin. Subsequent figures follow these same conventions.

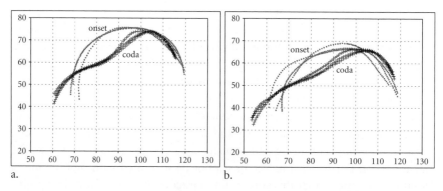

a.   b.

FIGURE 8. Extracted tongue surface contours from a. UB1 and b. UB2. Both show a near semi-circular shape for the uvular trill in onset /r/ vs. a clear double articulation for the post-alveolar approximant coda /r/. The latter has a retracted tongue root, a tip-down post-alveolar constriction, and a saddle in between.

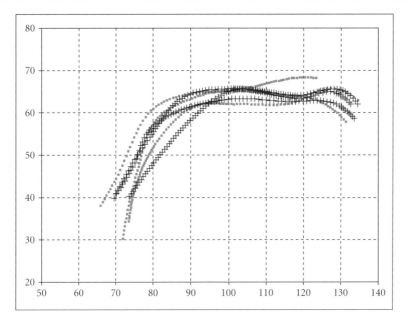

FIGURE 9. Extracted tongue surface contours from the three tokens of speaker RR's onset /ri/ (crosses) and coda /ir/ (small squares), showing comparable retroflexion in both, with greater token-to-token variation than other speakers.

Examination of static and dynamic ultrasound data and further tongue curves for this speaker show that RR has a post-alveolar tip up approximant articulation after all three vowels /i/, /u/, and /a/, where it is very clear that the tongue tip is raising away from the configuration required for the preceding vowel nucleus. The label 'covert' is most appropriate in the context of /a/, since /i/ and /u/ have centring and slightly rhoticized offglides, but RR generally has a disparity between the more strongly rhotic articulation and the more weakly rhotic acoustics in all rimes. In addition to the articulatory comparisons between onset and coda /r/ in the /i/ context (Figure 9), we looked at the /r/-ful

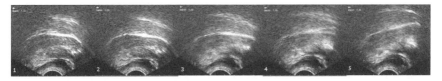

FIGURE 10. Time series of ultrasound images (speaker RR, *schaar*), showing tongue raising in the four frames (120ms) leading to a tip-up constriction in the fifth. Offset of voicing occurs roughly around frame 4.

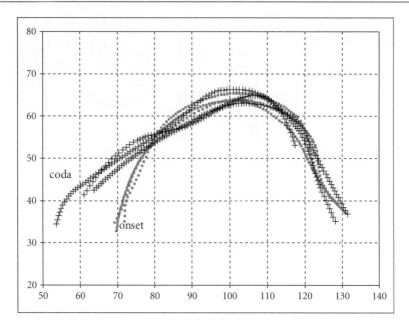

FIGURE 11. Coda uvular trill /r/ from UU with a pharyngeal retraction not present in the onset.

words (*mier, boer, schaar*) vs /r/-less rimes (*riem, koe,* and *sla*). All the articulatory evidence points to there being rhotic post-alveolar and pharyngeal approximant targets conditioned by /r/ in onset and coda alike, whereas the acoustic evidence points to a lack of acoustic rhoticity in the coda.

RR does, however, appear to show more co-articulation between her /r/ and the preceding vowel than any of the other speakers, and more token-to-token variability, suggesting the gestural target location is more likely to be undershot and co-articulated. Though onset and coda /r/ appear comparable in constriction strength and place, perhaps better data would reveal that gradient contextual weakening of the critical articulatory gesture contributes to the acoustic derhoticization, but it seems clear at least that the late timing of the tip raising to a post-alveolar or alveolar location gives rise to a. long vowels, b. late transitions, and c. weak acoustic rhoticity.

Finally, consider speaker UU (Figure 11), who has uvular trills in the coda as well as the onset. Like speakers UB1 and UB2, her coda has an extra, strong, pharyngeal constriction. Thus overall, all speakers have a pharyngeal constriction for coda /r/. Examination of dynamic changes in articulation show that UU's tongue root is advanced for /i/ and /u/ vowels in *mier* and *boer* and then clearly retracts for /r/. She has a pharyngeal constriction already during the /a/

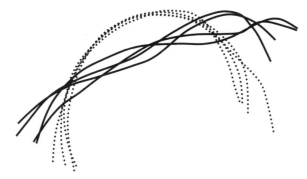

FIGURE 12. Overlaid tongue curves from 'boer', showing consistency in /u/ (dotted lines) and variation in /r/ (solid lines) with two bunched tip-down (UB1, UB2) and two tip-up slightly retroflex (RR, UR) post-alveolar approximants.

vowel in *schaar*. The same is true for UB1. UB2 shows much more co-articulation throughout the vowel before the /r/, so that /i/, /u/, and /a/ before /r/ all have a more similar constriction to each other, as well as similar to /r/, than /i/, /u/, and /a/ from /r/-less rimes (*koe, sla,* and *riem*).

The clear division into tip up (UR, RR) and bunched (UB1, UB2) approximants can be emphasized by informally overlaying all the speakers (Figure 12). Taking a token from *boer*, we extracted a curve for /u/ and another for /r/. We rotated and translated each speaker's pair of curves (i.e. without transforming the size or shape of the curves at all) so the /u/ curves were aligned as far as possible: the two types of /r/ appear quite distinct and comparable to the patterns presented by Delattre and Freeman (1968).

15.4 Discussion and Phonological Interpretation

Our study adds further phonetic detail to previous work which shows that different speakers of Dutch have different systems of onset-coda allophony for phoneme /r/. Since allophony can include both abstract categorical relationships **and** subtle phonetic contextual variation, the Dutch situation is just one instance of a common interface problem for phonetics and phonology: it is necessary for generative phonology to say which allophonic relationships are abstract and phonological, requiring different specifications of place and manner in surface structure. Otherwise the allophony would be phonetic, where a single segmental specification is realized differently by phonetic implementation on the basis of the difference in higher structure.

The phonetic data presented here are tantalizing, rather than conclusive, and serve both to remind us how inadequate a source of data a broad impressionistic transcription is, how indeterminate and complex a small sample of phonetic data can be, and, most importantly, that it is necessary to provide direct evidence of claimed articulatory factors. Phonological theory relies rather heavily on articulatory labels for its categories, both in terms of manner and place, so there is a clear advantage for the theorist in seeing some of the articulatory details of the phenomena they discuss.

Our acoustic and impressionistic data superficially support previous impressions that Dutch /r/ allophony is abstract, categorical, and phonological, with different place and manner features required for onset and coda allophones. There are, in addition, some differences in the timing of the vowel-approximant rime, where these appear subtle and are probably specified phonetically through differences in gestural strength and timing. Most significant in that regard is speaker RR, whose approximant /r/ in the coda can be heavily derhoticized (cf. similar cases in Plug and Ogden 2003), apparently even deleting /r/ in some tokens. Her deletions are probably variants due to gestural weakening (in the sense of Browman and Goldstein 1992). However, the articulatory data reveals that in every case things are more complex and subtle, and that the drawing of the interface as stated above would be inadequate.

First, consider the simplest case, speaker UU, who lacks overt allophony because she has a uvular trill for /r/ in both onset and coda (Figure 11). Ultrasound reveals that she has an extra secondary pharyngeal constriction in the coda. Whether this specification is gestural or feature-based, such a pattern, if general, would be a challenge for most theoretical approaches (e.g. the otherwise very different Goldsmith 1990 and Browman and Goldstein 1992), which argue for the coda being a location for phonological and phonetic weakening, rather than augmentation by a gesture or feature.

Speakers UB1, UB2, RR, and UR have a post-alveolar approximant coda, but in two cases it is bunched (UB1, UB2), and in two, retroflex (RR, UR). Is this configuration of the active articulator encoded in phonological structure? If not, this is presumably because the distinction is assumed to have no phonological relevance beyond cueing the phonotactic context (Mielke *et al.* forthcoming), but this is something that must be investigated further. All four approximants have some degree of pharyngealization, but the bunched approximants might be phonetically more retracted, which is another avenue for future work. Finally, the fact that approximant /r/s are doubly articulated (in the coda and, in the case of RR, in the onset) means that the traditional label of 'post-alveolar' is oversimplistic.

The speakers with trill/approximant allophony appear to be superficially the most abstract and phonological, changing manner and place, but the articulatory data suggest a phonetic gestural approach may be more appropriate than it seems at first. First, consider our new finding that speakers UB1 and UB2 have an additional pharyngeal constriction in the coda, like UU. This suggests they have a general coda pharyngealisation, since it appears in variants of /r/ which impressionistically have quite different places and manners. The second new finding which we have made relates to the onsets of UB1 (and of UB2 to a lesser extent). These speakers' uvular trills involve a post-alveolar secondary articulation.

There may be functional reasons for both these secondary articulations. If a uvular trilled /r/ contains a post-alveolar constriction, rhotic correlates due to F3/F2 approximation will still occur even if there is no trill. It appears from a major cross-linguistic survey (Jones 2009) that lack of actual trilling (what Jones called 'trill failure') is typical of trilled /r/, due to undershoot, increased lingual tension, or other causes. It seems reasonable that since weakening processes particularly affect codas, an approximant production instead of a uvular trill may become the established target for coda /r/. What would appear arbitrary—that the approximant resulting from uvular undershoot is post-alveolar—appears to be less surprising now that we have seen the UTI data showing double articulation.

Moreover, it appears that perhaps we can understand that there may be articulatory commonalities behind the impressionistic variety that exists in Lindau's (1985) family of rhotics, though we still need to explain the ultimate origin of these secondary articulations. We cannot tell whether a post-alveolar constriction is present for perceptual reasons (to ensure alternative rhotic cues are present for the listener's benefit on cue failure), or as an articulatory side-effect (generating a rhotic approximant by accident, as it were), or both. All we can do here is note that it appears that a combination of phonetic factors such as trill failure, the presence of an appropriate secondary articulation, and a tendency for phonetic coda weakening together could be the origin of the apparently abstract onset/coda allophonic pattern of uvular trill vs post-alveolar approximant. Distinct phonological representations would not be needed as part of an **explanation** of the origin of the allophony, though they could be a diachronically later development. The post-alveolar constriction could be covertly present in onset and coda in speakers with uvular trills (though whether this is in some or all remains to be seen), 'waiting for its chance to emerge' on trill failure. We could thus conclude that a phonetic account of the origin of the allophony seems more likely.

Turning now to the pharyngeal articulation which appears to be added in the coda, this is not predicted by either a phonological or a phonetic account of coda weakening. Thus we need to take into account both individual systems and the existence of variation in the community. Perhaps speakers like UB1 and UB2 are at a more advanced stage than UU of re-phonologization. They may be part of a group of uvular-trill-in-onset speakers for whom the pharyngeal constriction in the coda has enabled the loss of trilling in the coda and the establishment of a more abstract allophonic relationship between the forms of /r/, as suggested above. Perhaps, however, the causality runs the other way, and a pharyngeal constriction is present for speakers like UU during their coda uvular trills precisely because some Dutch speakers have approximant coda /r/ already.

The strongly rhotic post-alveolar approximant found here with speakers UB1 and UB2 is also found with speakers of Standard Dutch who have apical alveolar trill or tap onset allophones (Sebregts *et al.* 2003). For a postalveolar approximant to arise diachronically from a more constricted apical alveolar /r/ is considerably less surprising phonetically than the possible link between such an approximant and uvular /r/. Given the sociolinguistic status of the post-alveolar coda approximant in the Netherlands (a rapidly spreading prestige variant, associated with younger speakers, middle-class and female), the wholesale borrowing of this variant by speakers that do not have an articulatorily relatable onset /r/ cannot be excluded as a possibility. It is of course impossible to tell if borrowing has indeed taken place for the speakers in our sample, or whether they have simply acquired this now well-established allophony due to it being present in their ambient environment. In any case, the presence of a post-alveolar constriction during the articulation of the uvular trill for speaker UB1, as well as the presence of a pharyngeal constriction throughout the articulation of both the uvular and post-alveolar allophones for UB1 and UB2 suggests that these speakers have some sort of concrete and systematic link between their onset and coda allophones that is not obvious from impressionistic analysis.

Finally, let us consider the derhoticization of RR. It appears impressionistically that RR deletes /r/ in some tokens, and weakens it in others, and on average, she generates very small F_3/F_2 cues to rhoticity. In fact, the articulatory evidence reveals that in pre-pausal position, she has a strong and consistent post-alveolar retroflex articulation, one which seems to generate very little overt acoustic rhoticity. Our view is that this covert rhoticity highlights the complex relationship between articulation and acoustics even more keenly than the secondary articulations that accompany the very salient acoustic effects of trilling discussed above. Before silence, word-final /r/ seems to involve some kind of gestural delay rather than gestural weakening, but not any categorical phonological deletion. Such covert rhotic articulations have been further evidenced in recent work on Scottish English (Lawson, Stuart-Smith, and Scobbie 2008; Scobbie, Stuart-Smith, and Lawson 2008; Scobbie, Sebregts, and Stuart-Smith 2009), and Scobbie *et al.* (2008) explore the implications of such data: /r/ derhoticization is socially-distributed in Scottish English (Romaine 1979; Stuart-Smith 2007). Our hypothesis is that the anterior constriction for /r/ is made by RR, but close to and often after the offset of phonation. At most, she generates a very weak voiceless excitation of the rhotic constriction.

In connected speech and word-internally, further variants appears to occur. When /r/ is immediately followed by an anterior lingual consonant within the same word, the anterior constriction appears to be very weak or even absent as an independent consonant. The following consonant can be, however, slightly rhoticized. In pairs like *kaas* vs *kaars*, the contrast seems very weak indeed, so perceptual analysis of the output of such speakers is clearly a priority for future research. Our acoustic and articulatory data appear to support the observation by Plug and Ogden (2003) that a variety of phonetic correlates other than formants cue the presence of /r/, such as, in -/rs/ and -/rt/ clusters, the place of articulation of the following obstruent.

As for word-final /r/ phrase medially, a small follow-up study with RR reveals strong variation, which if recorded in broad transcription would likely be treated as a categorical external sandhi (van den Heuvel and Cucchiarini 2001).[1] Word-final /r/ before some consonants (*ik zie vier mieren* and *een paar vazen*) has scarcely any post-alveolar gesture—it is reduced rather than delayed and is barely still visible articulatorily. However, RR's word-final /r/ is realized as a post-alveolar tap or an impressionistically strongly rhotic approximant before a following word-initial vowel (e.g. in *een paar azen*, *ga er maar aanstaan*, and *de boer oefent*). The preceding vowel sounds long and monophthongal. Rhoticity is present even if word-boundary glottalization intervenes, arguing against phonological resyllabification (Scobbie and Pouplier 2010).[2] If the follow-ing word begins with a voiceless /p/ (*de boer poetst*), the acoustic

---

[1] In this work, an automatic speech-recognition device decides on the presence of /r/, where only categorical absence or presence is allowed. In other works, such as Vieregge and Broeders (1993) and Van de Velde (1996), some /r/s are transcribed as 'zero' on the basis of purely acoustic data.

[2] Even so, gestural delay might give some insight into the diachronic origin of floating phonological features and external sandhi 'resyllabification'.

and impressionistic story is still that RR is derhoticized. However, unlike the other phrase-medial cases above involving gestural reduction, there can be, just like in the pre-pausal case, a strong rhotic gesture, masked by the silence of /p/.

Our hypothesis (which cannot be tested without further data) is that the variation presented here in the coda forms of RR is gradient in character, suggesting that the choice between spatial undershoot vs temporal delay implementations of weakening may be structurally conditioned by prosodic categories but not be categorical or deterministic, making them less likely to be encoded categorically in phonology as alternatives. Additionally, we think that the acoustic consequences of the undershoot (e.g. derhoticization) count as a target and therefore as a representation of phonological structure at least as much as the articulation does. So, the phonological representation of /r/ ought to be abstract, and not too wedded to phonetic substance, since the substance has articulatory and acoustic characteristics trading off each other in a complex pattern which reflects phonological and prosodic context, patterns which may have to be understood via far more phonetically detailed models than those offered in traditional phonological formalisms, more along the lines of Browman and Goldstein (1992), Docherty (1992), Boersma (1998), Pierrehumbert (2002), or others.

It should be clear that neither the acoustic nor the articulatory patterns found need to be the **automatic** consequence of some strategy. Functional explanations, such as preservation of contrast, or ease of articulation, are not deterministic, though they surely have a role to play. This lack of determinism means that formal models of such patterns are descriptive but not explanatory (Scobbie and Stuart-Smith 2008). It is not to be denied that formal descriptions are preferable to informal ones, but explanation is too strong a claim.

To conclude, 'the' phonetics-phonology interface is multifaceted. The data presented here suggest a complex interplay between observable and measurable phenomena and the abstract systems which underlie them, whether those systems be formalized in theoretical frameworks which stress categorical algebraic relationships (typically phonology) or are heavily quantificational (typically phonetic). This is typical of detailed phonetic data (whether from articulatory, acoustic, or perceptual research), which is why studies in laboratory phonology (Pierrehumbert *et al.* 2000) may suggest different and more complex conceptual relationships between phonetics and phonology than are normally entertained when the only source of 'information about phonetics comes from pre-categorized, segmental transcriptions.

Are uvular trill and coronal approximant allophones of Dutch /r/ discretely different? If so, how do they emerge as allophones of the same phoneme? The first answer is yes **and** no. For the second, we think a phonetic explanation is more likely to be successful. However, it is not clear from our small study whether it makes sense to allocate the more discrete aspects of allophony exclusively to phonetics or phonology. The structural conditioning factors we have examined are discrete, so even phonetic allophony can appear to involve categorical distinctions. What is just as important as the clear differences between trills and approximants are the hidden details of secondary articulations. Our initial data appear to challenge both phonetic and phonological explanations of coda weakening while providing some rationale for a phonetic continuity between uvular trill and post-alveolar approximant, thus providing insight into what appears initially to be a case of straightforward phonological allophony. We conclude that some fundamental phonological questions need to be addressed through large-scale studies which provide detailed data about phonetics, including speech production, as part of a renewed commitment to the empirical underpinnings of our field.

16

Second Occurrence Focus and the Acoustics of Prominence*

JONATHAN HOWELL

16.1 Introduction

The interpretation of a variety of different linguistic expressions shows sensitivity to phonological prominence, among them quantificational adverbs, determiner quantifiers, counterfactuals, generics, modals, comparatives, superlatives, and negation. Jackendoff (1972) called this phenomenon 'association with focus'. The constituent which receives prominence and associates with a focus-sensitive expression is known as the focus associate, focus argument, or simply the focus. Often, the choice of focus associate yields truth-conditional effects, as illustrated by the minimal pair in (1) with the focus-sensitive adverb *only*. We can imagine a scenario on which (1a) is true and (1b) false, and vice versa. Prominence on the focus associate is marked with capital letters.

(1)   a. Mary only offered CAKE to Sue.
      b. Mary only offered cake to SUE.

Second occurrence focus (SOF) is the label given to the repeated occurrence of a particular association with focus. One of the first examples in the formal semantics literature comes from Partee (1991).[1]

* I was fortunate to present different versions of this chapter at several venues. I wish to thank audiences at the Cornell Linguistics department, 4th Joint ASA/ASJ Meeting, 2007 LSA Annual Meeting, MOT2007, WCCFL26, SPINE2007 and OnLI2007. Thanks also to the participants of the experiments for their patience and to the following individuals for discussion: Johanna Brugman, Abby Cohn, Adam Cooper, Effi Georgala, Carlos Gussenhoven, Hyun Kyung Hwang, Florian Jaeger, Dan Kaufman, Bob Ladd, Amanda Miller, Mats Rooth, and Michael Wagner. And last but not least, thanks to two anonymous reviewers.

[1] She notes that similar examples are found in Gussenhoven (1983), Roberts (1990), and Krifka (1991).

(2)   A: Eva only gave xerox copies to the GRADUATE STUDENTS.

       B: No, PETR only gave xerox copies to the <u>graduate students</u>.

Rooth (1996, 2004) also includes in the category of SOF those cases in which an association with focus has not previously been uttered, but may be implicated. We assume in his example (3) that Susan and Harold are among the set of younger candidates.

(3)   A: The provost and the dean aren't taking any candidates other than Susan and Harold seriously.

       B: Even the CHAIRMAN is only considering <u>younger</u> candidates.

The empirical question addressed in this chapter is whether a potential associate (e.g. *graduate students* in 2B or *younger* in 3B) has phonological prominence. The answer has important consequences for our understanding of focus and the modules of language that conspire to produce it. First, syntactic and semantic theories of association with focus predict that the underlined constituents in (2) and (3) should have prominence; pragmatic theories of association with focus predict that they do not. Second, we also want to understand whether focus phenomena can be modelled in terms of a single notional category focus or givenness, or whether it is necessary to posit two distinct mechanisms. SOF plays an important role in arguments for both views. In the rest of this section, we'll briefly review the role of SOF in these debates and the growing but not yet conclusive experimental research on SOF, which has found small but controversial phonetic differences between SOF associates and their unfocused counterparts.

   In section 16.2, I report on a new production study of the acoustics of SOF. The results do not support the view that the associate of a focus-sensitive expression in general, or of *only* in particular, must always have phonological prominence. Indeed, a conflicting prominence pattern is observed, which in section 16.3 I attribute to rhythm based on the results of a second, follow-up production experiment. In section 16.4, I present a perception experiment using a subset of the production data. The perception results do not support the view that listeners use prominence to determine an SOF associate.

16.1.1 *Second Occurrence Focus and Semantic Theory*

According to a grammaticized theory of association with focus (cf. Jackendoff 1972; Rooth 1985; von Stechow 1991) the focus sensitivity of an expression is achieved by a lexical rule that makes direct reference to syntactic annotation, usually known as F(ocus)-marking, or to focus-determined semantic objects, such as Rooth's (1985, 1992) focus semantic value (FSV). By way of illustration, consider the following simplified definition for *only*.[2]

(3) $[[$only $[\Phi]]]$ is true iff Φ, and for all $p \in FSV(\Phi)$, if p is true then $p = \Phi$

Roughly, (3) states that the constituent of *only* and its semantic argument Φ[3] is true if and only if Φ is true and there is no other true alternative in its FSV. The FSV is determined by making substitutions for an F-marked constituent. In (4a), the FSV of *John eats [dinner]$_F$* is the set in (4b).

(4)   a. John only eats [dinner]$_F$.
       b. FSV = {'John eats breakfast', 'John eats lunch', 'John eats dinner',...}

These theories are considered 'weak' (Rooth 1992) because it must be stipulated for each focus-sensitive expression how it operates on its focus.

A pragmatic account holds that a more general extra-grammatical principle is responsible, indirectly, for association with focus.[4] In particular, the 'domain selection' type of pragmatic account (cf. Rooth 1992; von Fintel 1994; Kadmon 2001; Martí 2003; Krifka 2004) seeks to analyse association with focus by capitalizing on extant theories of other context-sensitive expressions. Consider the domain of the universal quantifier *everyone* in (5).

(5)   Mary had a party. Everyone danced.

Since in context *everyone* does not to refer to every individual in the world, some pragmatic mechanism is responsible for specifying its domain (e.g. to the set of attendees at Mary's party). Similarly, a focus-sensitive expression such as *only* also has a domain. Following Rooth (1992), let's assign that domain a variable C and suppose that the definition of *only* refers to C (rather than to the FSV as above).

(3') $[[$only $[\Phi]]]$ is true iff Φ, and for all $p \in C$, if p is true then $p = \Phi$

The role of focus is to constrain the domain C to a subset of the FSV.[5] Suppose that C is fixed to (6a) in one context and to (6b) in another. C_1 is an appropriate domain for *only* in (4a) since C_1 is a subset of the FSV (4b); C_2 is not an appropriate domain, since it is not a subset of the FSV.

---

[2] See Kadmon (2001: 299) for a more formally explicit definition of *only* within a rule-based theory of focus association.

[3] For presentational purposes, I assume that *only* takes a propositional argument (e.g. *John eats dinner*).

[4] Examples of such 'strong' theories appear in Vallduví (1990), Jacobs (1991), Rooth (1992), von Fintel (1994), Dryer (1994), Roberts (1996), Schwarzschild (1997), Partee (1991,1999), Kadmon (2001), Martí (2003), Geurts and van der Sandt (2004).

[5] We must also stipulate that the subset includes Φ and at least one other alternative.

(6)   a. C_1 = {'John eats breakfast', 'John eats lunch', 'John eats dinner'}
      b. C_2 = {'John eats dinner', 'John hates dinner', 'Tom eats dinner'}

On this type of analysis, the meaning of a focus-sensitive operator like *only* does not refer directly to focus-dependent objects like F-marked syntactic constituents or FSVs. Consequently, the pragmatic account allows for occurrences of focus-sensitive expressions without an associating focus (and therefore without prominence on a potential associate). Grammaticized accounts, on the other hand, require an associating focus, and thus predict that an associate must always have prominence.

Beaver and Clark (2008) propose an intermediate or hybrid account (see also Rooth 1992) according to which the semantics of some but not all focus-sensitive expressions refer directly to focus, among them *only* and *even*. On this intermediate account, prominence is only predicted for the associates of these particular focus-sensitive expressions.

A second, related debate concerns the mapping between the semantic representation of focus and the phonological representation of prominence. On the semantics side, it is often debated whether focus phenomena should be modelled in terms of a single notional category 'focus' (e.g. Rooth 1992), a single notional category 'givenness' (e.g. Schwarzschild 1999), or two distinct notional categories 'contrastive focus' and 'givenness' (e.g. Selkirk 2008). On the phonology side, there is general agreement that prominence is hierarchical, with relative prominence existing in English at the word level (e.g. Chomsky and Halle 1968), at the sentence level, and at various other levels of stress in between (e.g. Selkirk 1980; Nespor and Vogel 1986; Beckman and Pierrehumbert 1986). We also know, since Liberman (1979) and Pierrehumbert (1980) that intonational events (i.e. tones or pitch accents) belong to a semi-autonomous, highest level of prominence.

The existence of different levels of phonological prominence means there need not be a single phonological correlate of semantic focus, such as pitch accent. Indeed, most formulations of the mapping between the scope of a focus-sensitive expression and phonology allow for this, referring to relative stress or prominence, rather than one particular level of stress or prominence (e.g. Truckenbrodt 1995; Rooth 2008).[6]

(7)   Stress F (Rooth 2009)
      Let β be an F-marked phrase with scope ϕ. Then the strongest stress in the phonological realization of ϕ falls within the realization of β.

(8)   Destress Given (Féry and Samek-Lodovici 2006)
      A given phrase is prosodically non-prominent.

---

[6] See also Chomsky (1971), Jackendoff (1972), Zubizarreta (1998), Büring (2008).

Selkirk (2008) (see also Féry and Ishihara 2009) advances SOF as one piece of evidence for the coexistence of two distinct categories of contrastive focus and discourse-givenness in the grammar, the former mapped to phonology according to a principle like (7) and the latter according to a rule Destress Given (cf. 8). Since in SOF examples both the focus-sensitive expression and everything in its scope are already given (or may be taken to be so, cf. (3)), they must be phonologically less prominent relative to the rest of the sentence. For example, in (2B), *only gave xerox copies to the graduate students* is given, and is therefore predicted to have less prominence (e.g. reduced or no pitch accenting) than *Petr*. However, the focus associate within *gave xerox copies to the graduate students*, namely *graduate students*, will still have greatest relative prominence (e.g. stress) within that constituent. Selkirk's theory is therefore motivated in part by putative prominence in SOF.

Rooth (2006, 2009) and Büring (2008), who are inclined towards a single-notion theory of focus, offer proposals relating the phonological realization of focus to the relative scope of different focus-sensitive operators. As schematized in (9), a focus-sensitive operator semantically embedded under another focus will have a focus associate that is realized with SOF phonology (e.g. lacking a pitch accent), while the associate of the widest-scope focus operator will have regular focus phonology (e.g. with a pitch accent). In (3b), for example, *only* is embedded under *even* and therefore the associate of *only* will have second occurrence focus.

(9)   Configurational SOF (adapted from Rooth 1996)
       $[\dots F \dots [[\dots SOF \dots] \, Op_2] \dots] \, Op_1$

These analyses allow for the phonological realization of SOF to differ from regular focus, but the semantic notion of relative scope itself is independently motivated and does not by itself necessitate that the focus associate in an SOF utterance have prominence.

16.1.2 *Previous Investigations of Prominence*

Several experimental investigations followed Partee's (1991) first observations, beginning with Rooth (1996). Investigating the acoustics of his own speech, Rooth compared three different acoustic measures. The first, *fo* movement, is the change in fundamental frequency, the physical correlate of pitch; the second is syllable duration; and the third, root mean squared (RMS) amplitude, is calculated from the sound wave and measures acoustic intensity. Rooth found in his data, uncontroversially, that that regular focus (henceforth 'first occurrence focus' FOF) showed large *fo* maxima, while SOF lacked any significant *fo* movement. However, in comparing an expected SOF associate and an adjacent unfocused (unF) word, Rooth found that the SOF associate had a measurably longer syllable duration and greater RMS amplitude. This is illustrated in (10), with the direction of comparison illustrated with a horizontal arrow: in (10aB), *named* had a greater syllable duration and amplitude than *Manny* in Rooth's data, and vice versa in (10bB). Perceptually, he judged it possible to identify the correct association with focus listening only to an SOF utterance (i.e. 10aB or 10bB), in the absence of the context-supplying FOF sentence (i.e. 10aA or 10bB).

(10)   a. A: Paul only NAMED Manny today.
          B: So what. Even EVA only <u>**named**</u> **Manny** today.

       b. A: Paul only named MANNY today.
          B: So what. Even EVA only **named** <u>**Manny**</u> today.

Bartels (2004) later determined in a production experiment with six native English speakers that the acoustics of FOF and SOF were statistically different. She measured relative *fo* maxima, RMS amplitude, and word duration, calculated as ratios of a focus associate and its preceding words or syllables. The results support the intuition that FOF and SOF have different realizations—overall, the SOF associates had reduced relative *fo* maxima, RMS amplitude, and word duration compared to FOF associates. Unlike Rooth (1996), Bartels's experiment did not test whether an SOF constituent had greater prominence compared to an unF constituent.

Beaver *et al.* (2007) and Jaeger (2005) conducted a large production study with twenty native English speakers. In addition to *fo* maxima, RMS amplitude, and word duration, the authors also measured *fo* minima, *fo* mean, *fo* range, and acoustic energy, a function of amplitude and duration, within a target utterance. The direction of comparison was both within a given utterance ('syntagmatic' comparison), as in Rooth (1996), and across utterances ('paradigmatic' comparison). Two minimal discourse pairs from the study are given in 11–12). The (b) sentence contains an FOF and the (c) sentence an SOF. In (11c), *Pete* is the potential associate; in (12c), *a pill* is the potential associate. The syntagmatic comparison (cf. horizontal arrow) contrasts *Pete* with *a pill* in the same utterance. The paradigmatic comparison (cf. vertical arrow) contrasts *Pete* in (11c) with *Pete* in (12c), and *a pill* in (11c) with *a pill* in (12c). Note that the inclusion of both syntagmatic and paradigmatic comparisons is important, since it remains an open question whether speakers and listeners produce and perceive focus prominence syntagmatically or paradigmatically.

In confirmation of previous studies, Beaver *et al.* and Jaeger found that *fo* was not a significant predictor of SOF. However, the authors report a statistically significant difference in duration between SOF and unF, both syntagmatically[7] (10.1ms and 8.1ms) and paradigmatically (6ms). Intensity and energy were also significant or approaching significance, both syntagmatically (.8519/.6354 dB and 0.0049/0.0027) and paradigmatically (0.13 dB and 0.0011).

(11)   a. Context sentence
           Both Pete and Edward are suffering from the flu.
        b. FOF sentence
           But the nurse only gave PETE a pill today.
        c. SOF sentence
           Even THE DOCTOR only gave <u>**Pete a pill**</u> today.

(12)   a. Context sentence
           Pete really needed an injection to ease the pain.
        b. FOF sentence
           But the nurse only gave Pete A PILL today.
        c. SOF sentence
           Even THE DOCTOR only gave **Pete <u>a pill</u>** today.

While statistically significant, these acoustic values fall short of some published just noticeable differences (JNDs) (i.e. smallest perceivable differences) for speech sounds: 10–40ms (Lehiste 1980) and ~25ms (Klatt 1976) for duration; 1–4dB (Stevens 1998) for amplitude. The authors, therefore, conducted a perception experiment.

Beaver *et al.* presented native English-speaking listeners with minimal SOF pairs (e.g. (11c) and (12c)) from a subset of their production data and asked them to identify in which of the two renditions the second target (e.g. *a pill*) was more prominent. Subjects performed above chance in this discrimination task, but averaged only 63 per cent accuracy. The authors speculate that the less than perfect performance may be due to reader disfluencies in the laboratory-elicited production stimuli. Further, as the authors admit, it is impossible to conclude from these results alone whether listeners actually

---

[7] The two syntagmatic differences reported correspond to different linear orderings: SOF-unF and unF-SOF, respectively.

exploit this discrimination in interpretation, or even whether the discrimination reflects purely linguistic competence.

Féry and Ishihara (2009) investigated SOF in German. In a 29-subject production experiment, they compared mean fo and word duration paradigmatically (cf. (13a–c)), although unlike Beaver *et al.* (2007) they measured unF targets in an unrelated discourse (cf. (13c)). A major concern[8] in this study is the phonological notion of nuclear accent (see Newman 1946: 176; Chomsky and Halle 1968: 90), namely that the last pitch accent in an utterance is perceived as most prominent and any following material in the utterance is reduced in pitch. This reduction phenomenon in English and German is known as post-nuclear deaccenting. Since an FOF associate is typically a nuclear accent, Féry and Ishihara investigated both SOF associates which *preceded* an FOF (cf. (13b)), as well as SOF associates which followed the nuclear accent (cf. all previous studies).

(13)   Context sentence:
        Die meisten unserer Kollegen waren beim Beriebsausflug lässig angezogen.
        'Most of our colleagues were dressed casually at the staff outing.'

   a. FOF sentence
      Nur PETER hat eine Krawatte getragen.
      'Only Peter wore a tie.'

   b. SOF sentence
      Nur Peter hat sogar einen ANZUG getragen.
      Only Peter has even a   suit   worn
      'Only Peter even wore a suit.'

   c. unF sentence
      Wen hat Peter geküsst?
      'Who did Peter kiss?'
      Peter hat MARIA geküsst.
      'Peter kissed Maria.'

The authors found a significant paradigmatic difference in fo and word duration between SOF and unF in both pre-nuclear and post-nuclear positions, although they report that the difference in fo is 'radically reduced' in the post-nuclear position.

---

[8] The authors also investigated sentence position and found that SOF has a higher mean pitch and a longer word duration sentence-initially than sentence-medially. They attribute this to the phonological phenomena of intonational downstepping and phrase-final lengthening.

Finally, Bishop (forthcoming) tests pre-nuclear SOF and unF in English in a five-speaker production experiment, using the methodology of Rooth (1996) and Beaver *et al.* In a paradigmatic comparison, Bishop found, contra Féry and Ishihara (2009) for German, that the pre-nuclear SOF associates did not have significantly greater *f*o maxima than the related unF targets. It is not clear whether this contrast is due to differences in methodology or due to differences between English and German. Bishop did confirm, however, that the duration of SOF and unF differed significantly, although as in Beaver *et al.* the durational differences were small and hovered around the JNDs mentioned above.

In summary, previous investigations confirmed that potential SOF associates are less prominent than FOF associates. Small, but statistically significant acoustic differences were observed between SOF associates and their unF counterparts, both syntagmatically and paradigmatically, and both pre-nuclearly and post-nuclearly. Presented with a minimal pair of SOF sentences, listeners identified prominence poorly, but above chance.

16.2 First Production Experiment

16.2.1 *Method*

16.2.1.1 *Subjects* I ran a small production study with three male speakers, including myself. Sophisticated, non-naïve speakers were chosen in order to complement the results of Beaver *et al.* (2007)/Jaeger (2005) who used naïve speakers, and in answer to the speculation that speakers' naïveté and reading disfluencies weakened their results.[9] Recall that Rooth (1996) reported clear results in his own speech.

16.2.1.2 *Recording* Subjects were recorded in a sound-attenuated room, using a Plantronics DSP-500 headset to control for head movement. Recording and analysis were both conducted with Praat 4.2.29 (Boersma and Weenink 2008). Subjects repeated each discourse five times for a total of sixty tokens per speaker. The subjects were asked to read the stimuli as naturally as possible, and without exaggeration. One token produced with a pitch accent on a SOF word was deemed unnatural by one speaker, who asked to rerecord the token without prompting.

16.2.1.3 *Stimuli* Following the methodology of Rooth (1996) and Beaver *et al.* (2007), the elicited discourses consisted of a context sentence with FOF and a target sentence with SOF, allowing paradigmatic and syntagmatic comparison.

---

[9] Another methodological approach would try to elicit stimuli in a communicative task. See the conclusion for some comments on why this approach may not be useful.

The target words were noun/verb homophones (*peddles/pedals, patches, labels*), used in order to avoid *post-hoc* normalization and in order to control for vowel quality. Similar to Féry and Ishihara (2009) and Bishop (forthcoming), I included SOF and unF targets which preceded FOF as well as those which followed FOF. Finally, with the intent of controlling for possible isochronic effects (disruptions to regular rhythm, cf. Lehiste 1980), I limited my target words to bisyllabic trochees (two-syllable words with first-syllable word stress). Some examples follow; (14) contains a post-nuclear SOF and (15) a pre-nuclear SOF.

(14) Post-nuclear
  a. A: Johnson only **PATCHES patches** for Microsoft. (He doesn't create them.)
      B: That's right. Even THOMPSON only <u>patches</u> **patches** for Microsoft.
  b. A: Johnson only **patches PATCHES** for Microsoft. (He doesn't patch the programs themselves.)
      B: That's right. Even THOMPSON only **patches** <u>patches</u> for Microsoft.

(15) Pre-nuclear
  a. A: Johnson only **PATCHES patches** for Microsoft. (He doesn't create them.)
      B: That's right. Johnson only <u>patches</u> **patches** even for APPLE.
  b. A: Johnson only **patches PATCHES** for Microsoft. (He doesn't patch the programs themselves.)
      B: That's right. Johnson only **patches** <u>patches</u> even for APPLE.

16.2.1.4 *Measurements*   The target words were manually annotated in Praat for stop closure, aspiration, first vowel duration, and second syllable duration. The following values were then automatically extracted using Praat scripts:[10] maximum *fo*, minimum *fo*, mean *fo*, stressed syllable duration, mean RMS intensity, energy, power, and spectral balance. Spectral balance (aka spectral tilt), not used in previous investigations of SOF, measures relative amplitude at different harmonic frequencies, rather than over the entire spectrum and has been claimed to be an acoustic correlate of stress in English and Dutch (Campbell and Beckman 1997; Sluijter and van Heuven 1996). The following spectral-balance values were calculated from differentials of harmonic frequencies (H) and amplitudes (A) using a 10ms window centred at the time of the first formant maximum: H1-H2, H1-H3, H1-A1, and H1-A2.

---

[10] Thanks to Amanda Miller for assistance, and to Marc Brunelle and Mietta Liennes for related scripts.

16.2.1.5 *Statistical Analysis*   For the syntagmatic comparison, a paired t-test was conducted to compare the means of adjacent verb and noun targets in the FOF sentences, and then in the SOF sentences. For the paradigmatic comparison, a t-test was also conducted to compare the means of the focused targets (FOF or SOF) to those of the unfocused targets among verbs, and the means of focused targets to those of the unfocused targets among nouns. The differences are summarized in Tables 1 and 2; significance is indicated by (*).

Finally, a 2x2 analysis of variance (ANOVA) was conducted for focus value (focused vs unfocused) and word position (verb vs noun, or equivalently first position vs second position), both for the FOF condition, as a kind of baseline, and for the SOF condition of interest. The ANOVA tests the hypothesis that focus value and word position are significant predictors ('main effects') of the observed differences of an acoustic measure.

Statistical tests were also performed by speaker, by nuclear position (prenuclear or post-nuclear) and by word type, but did not pattern differently from the complete dataset and so are omitted here for space. Transformations of the data were performed for non-linear measurements, including the natural log of duration, the square of energy, and root mean square of

TABLE 1. Summary of mean syntagmatic differences between focused and unfocused by focus type (verb focus vs noun focus) for FOF and SOF. Significance of $\alpha < 0.05$ on a paired t-test indicated by (*).

| | | FOF | | SOF | |
| | | Verb Focus | Noun Focus | Verb Focus | Noun Focus |
	N	$[verb]_{FOF}$ - $[noun]_{unF}$	$[noun]_{FOF}$ - $[verb]_{unF}$	$[verb]_{SOF}$ - $[noun]_{unF}$	$[noun]_{SOF}$ - $[verb]_{unF}$
Duration (ms)	90	31.0*	61.4*	21.0*	−1.7
Mean f_0 (Hz)	83	50.3*	29.3*	0.75	0.81
Max f_0 (Hz)	83	57.4*	38.0*	−2.8	2.3
Min f_0 (Hz)	83	39.6*	19.1*	2.1*	−0.4
RMS Intensity (dB)	90	7.66*	4.70*	1.14*	−0.05
Energy	90	0.00386*	0.00369*	0.000005	0.00029
Power	90	0.038*	0.029*	0.001*	0.0009
H1-H2 (Hz)	90	−0.867*	−0.998*	−0.482	0.137
H1-H3 (Hz)	90	−1.227*	−1.68*	−0.672	0.337
H1-A1 (Hz)	90	−7.747*	−5.655*	−0.728	−0.284
H1-A2 (Hz)	90	−7.542*	−5.737*	−1.146	0.83

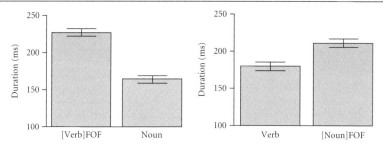

FIGURES 1A AND 1B. Mean stressed syllable durations for verb FOF and adjacent unfocused noun, and noun FOF and adjacent unfocused verb, respectively (with 95% confidence interval).

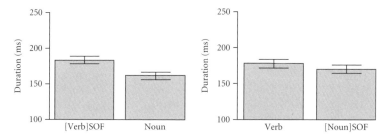

FIGURE 2A AND 2B. Mean stressed syllable durations for verb SOF and adjacent unfocused noun, and noun SOF and adjacent unfocused verb, respectively (with 95% confidence interval).

energy. All tests were performed in the statistical computing environment R (R Development Core Team 2008).

16.2.2 *Results*

16.2.2.1 *Syntagmatic Comparison*   Unsurprisingly, results of the syntagmatic comparison revealed that an FOF target was more prominent than its adjacent unfocused target. All measures in the FOF condition were significant, as summarized in Table 1. A few of the measures were statistically significant for the SOF condition—duration, minimum fo, intensity and power—were significant, but only in the verb focus comparison.

Looking specifically at duration, we can see that an FOF verb had significantly greater duration than the adjacent unF noun (Figure 1A), and an FOF noun had significantly greater duration than the adjacent unF verb (Figure 1B). It is also worth mentioning that, intuitively, the magnitude of difference is much greater for the verb-focused condition than for the noun-focused condition. This will be relevant for the discussion of rhythm in section 16.3.

TABLE 2. Summary of mean paradigmatic differences between focused and unfocused by word position (verb position vs noun position) for FOF and SOF. Significance of $\alpha < 0.05$ on a paired t-test indicated by (*).

| | | FOF | | SOF | |
| | | Verbs | Nouns | Verbs | Nouns |
	N	[verb]$_{FOF}$ - [verb]$_{unF}$	[noun]$_{FOF}$ - [noun]$_{unF}$	[verb]$_{SOF}$ - [verb]$_{unF}$	[noun]$_{SOF}$ - [noun]$_{unF}$
Duration (ms)	180	48.4*	45.1*	10.4*	8.9*
Mean fo (Hz)	173/4	35.5*	44.1*	2.47	−0.91
Max fo (Hz)	173/4	48.6*	50.8*	2.58	−3.11
Min fo (Hz)	173/4	24.5*	34.2*	2.74	−1.08
RMS Intensity (dB)	180	5.78*	6.57*	0.57	0.53
Energy	180	0.00353*	0.00402*	0.00015	0.00018
Power	180	0.033*	0.034*	0.002	0.001
H1-H2 (Hz)	180	−0.7900+	−1.0742*	−0.0269	−0.0762
H1-H3 (Hz)	180	−1.0500	−1.8599*	−0.395	0.0604
H1-A1 (Hz)	180	−5.4910*	−7.9117*	−2.089	1.078
H1-A2 (Hz)	180	−5.1442*	−8.1350*	0.002	−0.3189

A SOF verb did have significantly different duration from the adjacent noun (Figure 2B); however, an SOF noun was not significantly longer than the adjacent verb (Figure 2A). In fact, the direction of difference, like most of the other measures, favoured the verb.

Previous investigations of SOF, in particular Jaeger (2005), would lead us to expect parallel behaviour between the FOF condition and the SOF condition, i.e. that a focused target will have greater prominence than the adjacent unfocused target, regardless of whether the focus is FOF or SOF, at least for some measures. Instead, we observe some significant differences among verb-focused SOF cases, and no significant differences among noun-focused SOF cases.

16.2.2.2 *Paradigmatic Comparison*   As seen in Table 2, paradigmatic difference between FOF and unfocused verb targets and between FOF and unfocused noun targets were statistically significant for almost all measures. Those same differences between SOF and unF targets lacked statistical significance for nearly all measures, with the notable exception of duration.

The mean durations of FOF, SOF, and unfocused targets (adjacent to FOF and adjacent to SOF given separately) are illustrated in Figures 3A, B. The contrast between the FOF targets and the other targets is clear; as in the syntagmatic comparison above, the contrast between the SOF targets and the unfocused targets, while statistically significant, is much less striking.

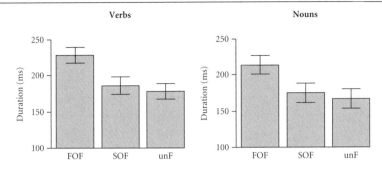

FIGURES 3A AND 3B. Mean stressed syllable durations of FOF, SOF, and unF verbs and nouns, respectively (with standard deviations).

16.2.2.3 *Analysis of Variance* In the FOF condition, there was a main effect of focus value (focused vs unfocused) for all measures. There was also a main effect of word position (verb vs noun, or 1st vs 2nd position) for all but the energy and spectral balance measures. No interaction effects were observed.

In the SOF condition, there was a main effect of focus value and of position on duration only, mirroring the pattern observed in the paradigmatic comparison. From Beaver *et al.* (2007), we would predict main effects of both focus value and position on several of the measures.

16.2.3 *Discussion*

The results of the first production experiment partly confirm previous experimental results. Paradigmatically, there is indeed a small but significant difference in duration between SOF and unF. The ANOVA also revealed a main effect of focus on duration.

Surprisingly, however, none of the other measures showed a main effect. Furthermore, there was also a main effect of position. Syntagmatically, the results strongly suggest a tendency towards greater relative prominence on the verb, independent of which target was the intended focus associate. In the next section, I explore this tendency towards prominence on the verb with a second production experiment and hypothesize that it is due to rhythm. Whether or not this hypothesis is correct, the results of the main production experiment reported in this section caution against absolute syntagmatic comparison as a reliable correlate of focus in SOF.

Section 16.4 explores whether listeners can perceive SOF in these data, either given the admittedly weak paradigmatic information or in spite of the seemingly misleading syntagmatic information.

TABLE 3A. Analysis of Variance (ANOVA) by focus value (focus vs unfocus) and word position (verb vs noun) for FOF. Significance of $\alpha < 0.05$ on a paired t-test indicated by (*).

	N	FOF Focus Value	Word Position
Duration	360	$F = 337.49$, $p < 0.001^*$	$F = 34.60$, $p < 0.001^*$
Intensity	360	$F = 189.88$, $p < 0.001^*$	$F = 11.74$, $p < 0.001^*$
Energy	360	$F = 115.58$, $p < 0.001^*$	$F = 1.03$, $p = 0.31$
Mean fo	353	$F = 277.65$, $p < 0.001^*$	$F = 19.29$, $p < 0.001^*$
Max fo	353	$F = 341.66$, $p < 0.001^*$	$F = 14.06$, $p < 0.001^*$
Min fo	353	$F = 138.27$, $p < 0.001^*$	$F = 17.07$, $p < 0.001^*$
Power	360	$F = 318.41$, $p < 0.001^*$	$F = 4.60$, $p < 0.01^*$
H1-H2	360	$F = 9.81$, $p < 0.01^{**}$	$F = 0.05$, $p = 0.83$
H1-H3	360	$F = 7.94$, $p < 0.01^{**}$	$F = 0.19$, $p = 0.66$
H1-A1	360	$F = 28.57$, $p < 0.001^*$	$F = 0.70$, $p = 0.40$
H1-A2	360	$F = 25.79$, $p < 0.001^*$	$F = 0.48$, $p = 0.49$

TABLE 3B. Analysis of Variance (ANOVA) by focus value (focus vs unfocus) and word position (verb vs noun) for SOF. Significance of $\alpha < 0.05$ indicated by (*).

	N	SOF Focus	Position
Duration	360	$F = 13.05$, $p < 0.001^*$	$F = 20.78$, $p < 0.001^*$
Intensity	360	$F = 1.19$, $p = 0.28$	$F = 1.75$, $p = 0.19$
Energy	360	$F = 1.14$, $p = 0.29$	$F = 1.46$, $p = 0.29$
Mean fo	353	$F = 0.22$, $p = 0.64$	$F < 0.01$, $p = 0.99$
Max fo	353	$F = 0.02$, $p = 0.90$	$F = 1.30$, $p = 0.25$
Min fo	353	$F = 0.28$, $p = 0.59$	$F = 0.63$, $p = 0.43$
Power	360	$F = 2.91$, $p = 0.09$	$F = 0.37$, $p = 0.54$
H1-H2	360	$F = 0.37$, $p = 0.55$	$F = 1.18$, $p = 0.28$
H1-H3	360	$F = 0.11$, $p = 0.74$	$F = 1.01$, $p = 0.32$
H1-A1	360	$F = 0.15$, $p = 0.70$	$F = 0.03$, $p = 0.87$
H1-A2	360	$F = 0.01$, $p = 0.90$	$F = 0.57$, $p = 0.45$
H1-A3	360	$F = 0.01$, $p = 0.90$	$F = 0.57$, $p = 0.45$

16.3 Second Production Experiment

16.3.1 *Methods*

Two of the speakers from the first production experiment were recorded under the same conditions. The stimuli were constructed to closely resemble the SOF sentences in the first production experiment, but without the

TABLE 4. Analysis of Variance for Adverb Condition (adverb vs no adverb) and word position (verb vs noun or 1st vs 2nd).

	N	Adverb (yes/no)	Word Position (verb vs noun)
Duration	120	$F = 15.52$, $p < 0.001^*$	$F = 0.10$, $p = 0.75$ n.s.
Intensity	120	$F = 0.45$, $p = 0.50$ n.s.	$F = 1.16$, $p = 0.28$ n.s.
Energy	120	$F = 0.09$, $p = 0.76$ n.s.	$F = 1.53$, $p = 0.22$ n.s.
Mean fo	101	$F = 2.09$, $p = 0.15$ n.s.	$F = 2.28$, $p = 0.13$ n.s.
Max fo	101	$F = 0.25$, $p = 0.62$ n.s.	$F = 0.63$, $p = 0.43$ n.s.
Min fo	101	$F = 1.43$, $p = 0.23$ n.s.	$F = 4.06$, $p < 0.05^*$
Power	120	$F = 1.12$, $p = 0.29$ n.s.	$F = 2.02$, $p = 0.16$ n.s.
H1-H2	120	$F = 1.09$, $p = 0.30$ n.s.	$F = 0.19$, $p = 0.66$ n.s.
H1-H3	120	$F = 1.77$, $p = 0.19$ n.s.	$F = 0.36$, $p = 0.55$ n.s.
H1-A1	120	$F = 6.69$, $p < 0.01^*$	$F = 0.13$, $p = 0.71$ n.s.
H1-A2	120	$F = 6.10$, $p < 0.05^*$	$F = 0.40$, $p = 0.53$ n.s.

focus-sensitive adverb *only*. Half of the stimuli contained instead no adverb at all (e.g. (16B)); the other half contained a non-focus-sensitive adverb (e.g. (17B)). The target sentence was the answer to a wh-question, which meant that the subject, *Johnson*, was always an FOF, and the target words (e.g. *patches* and *patches*) were always unfocused. Any prominence found on the target words would not, therefore, be attributable to SOF. Each discourse was repeated five times in each condition, for a total of sixty discourse tokens. Recordings were manually annotated, as before.

(16)   A: Who patches patches for Microsoft?
        B: JOHNSON patches patches for Microsoft.

(17)   A: Who **poorly** patches patches for Microsoft?
        B: JOHNSON **poorly** patches patches for Microsoft.

16.3.2 *Results*

To test whether adverb condition (presence vs absence of the adverb) or word position (being the verb or the noun) was a predictor of any of the acoustic measures, I carried out a two-way ANOVA. A main effect of adverb condition emerged for duration, as well as two of the spectral measures. There were no main effects of word position for any measure except minimum *fo*: the nouns were a significant 2.08 Hz lower than verbs (paired t-test: $t(45) = 2.59$, $p < 0.05$). A possible hypothesis for the main effect of position on minimum *fo* is the phenomenon of declination, the tendency for *fo* to decrease over the course of an utterance, all else being equal.

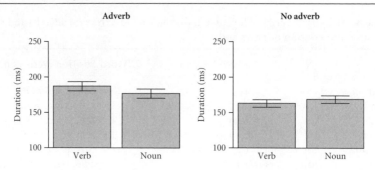

FIGURE 4A AND 4B. Mean stressed syllable durations for verbs and nouns in the adverb and no adverb conditions, respectively (with 95% confidence interval).

Among the utterances with the adverb, verbs had significantly longer stressed syllable duration than the nouns (mean difference 9.8 ms, paired t-test: t(29) = 2.87, p < 0.01) (Figure 4A). Among the utterances without an adverb, verbs had significantly shorter stressed syllable duration than the nouns (mean difference 5.7 ms) (Figure 4B).

16.3.3 *Discussion*

Perhaps surprisingly, the presence of the adverb had a clear effect on acoustic prominence in the rest of the utterance. The utterances with the adverb are relevant because they closely resemble the stimuli in the first production experiment, with the difference that the adverb in this experiment is not a focus-sensitive expression. In the first production experiment, we also noted a tendency towards a more prominent verb, both paradigmatically and syntagmatically. The tendency is not categorical, i.e. present in every production, but it is overall statistically significant.

The important point for our discussion of SOF and acoustic prominence is that we have observed a statistically significant difference that is not attributable to semantic focus. Notably, the difference for duration is on the same order of magnitude as that attributed to SOF in previous investigations.

I also want to speculate that the particular source of the observed prominence is eurhythmy, or regular rhythm. I will discuss two studies. First, according to the Phonetic Spacing Hypothesis of Hayes (1984), speakers attempt to produce phonetic prominence at regular intervals, either with respect to actual physical time or to abstract phonological timing units. Hayes proposes the hypothesis as an alternative to purely phonological analyses of a stress-shift phenomenon known as the 'rhythm rule'. For example, many speakers who would consistently utter *fourtéen* in isolation demonstrate a preference for *foúrteen wómen* over *fourtéen wómen*, the latter of which involves a 'clash' of stress on two adjacent syllables (stress indicated by accent marks). However, Hayes notes (see also Liberman and Prince 1977) that another strategy employed is to lengthen a syllable to create greater phonetic distance between adjacent stresses (i.e. lengthening of the *-téen* in *fourtéen*).

Second, while little study has been undertaken on the phonetics of prominence in the postnuclear domain, an experiment by Huss (1978) is of particular note. Huss compared the production and perception of stress-sensitive noun-verb pairs like *íncrease* and *incréase* following a nuclear accent, or what we could call an FOF (e.g. (18) vs (19)). He found that the stressed syllable of the *noun* had longer relative duration and intensity than the unstressed syllable, but the two syllables of the verb were largely even. Further, when listeners listened to the target sentence without the preceding context, they were most likely to identify nouns.

(18) Noun rendition
      (Whereas formerly the workers' increase used to benefit from inflation)
      now the EMPLÓYERS' íncrease benefits.

(19) Verb rendition
      (Whereas formerly government used to increase benefits)
      now the EMPLÓYERS incréase benefits.

Huss attributed this behaviour to the tendency towards regular rhythmic intervals: speakers' productions tended towards first-syllable prominence on *increase* in (18)–(19) in order to achieve even spacing between the stress on *increase* the preceding stress on *employers*.

In a second experiment, Huss recorded the same target words in sentences with a rhythmic context favouring second-syllable prominence; cf. (20)–(21). The opposite effect was observed: the second syllable had greater duration and intensity in the verb rendition, and even the noun rendition.

(20) Noun rendition
      (Whereas formerly the French increase was worse)
      now the DÚTCH íncrease is worse

(21) Verb rendition
      (Whereas formerly the French increased their stock)
      now the DÚTCH incréase their stock.

The targets *pátches pátches* in the present experiment have word stress at equal levels. If, however, we imagine the phonetic spacing hypothesis also holds at a higher level between phonological words (bisyllabic trochees in our data), the observed tendency parallels the results of Huss at the syllable level. In (22)–(23), the adverb leaves exactly one word or trochee between the FOF and the verb. By hypothesis, the verb therefore receives greater prominence in order to maintain eurhythmy. I leave more rigorous investigation of this phenomenon to future study.

(22)   [JÓHNSON poorly] [pátches patches] for Microsoft.

(23)   Even [THÓMPSON only] [pátches patches] for Microsoft.

16.4 Perception Experiment

16.4.1 *Methods*

Six linguistically trained listeners participated in a forced-choice and acceptability listening experiment. Stimuli were presented in the form of a context retrieval task (cf. Gussenhoven 1983). Subjects chose between two discourses: the SOF sentence was the same in both discourses; in one of the two discourses the context sentence matched in intended focus association; in the other discourse the context sentence did not match (cf. (24)). Stimuli were taken from the '*pedals*' recordings of all three speakers in the first production experiment, and the pairs of discourses were presented twice each in random order (n = 60). In a forced-choice judgement, listeners were asked to choose one of the two discourses as more felicitous. Then in a rating task, listeners would also choose one of the following three categories: (i) only the selected discourse is acceptable; (ii) both are acceptable, or; (iii) neither is acceptable.

(24)   *Matching discourse*
        FOF_v: Johnson only PEDDLES pedals lately.
        SOF_v: Even THOMPSON only <u>peddles</u> pedals lately.
        Non-matching discourse
        FOF_n: Johnson only peddles PEDALS lately.
        SOF_v: Even THOMPSON only <u>peddles</u> pedals lately.

16.4.2 *Results*

Table 5 gives the percentage of stimuli correctly identified (i.e. the appropriately matching discourse was selected as 'better') and the percentage of stimuli judged as 'both acceptable' for each listener. The average success rate was 57.5 per cent, and listeners judged the stimuli as both acceptable at 69.8 per cent, with three of the listeners judging all or nearly all discourses as

TABLE 5. Rates of correct identification, and rates of acceptability of both discourses ($n = 60$)

	L1	L2	L3	L4	L5	L6	Total
%correct	55	50	68	65	47	60	57.5
%both acceptable	61	100	93	28	37	100	69.8

acceptable.[11] Not surprisingly, duration had a significant effect on overall correct identification ($p = .0054$). Finally, listeners' successes were normally distributed over the different stimuli: listeners did not perform consistently better for any particular stimuli.

16.4.3 *Discussion*

While the context retrieval task is somewhat more complex than the discrimination task in Beaver *et al.* (2007)/Jaeger (2005),[12] it more closely approaches listeners' intuitions about the semantic/pragmatic felicity of prominence, and the use of sophisticated listeners was intended to mitigate the complexity. Additionally, by including both FOF and SOF sentences, listeners have access to explicit paradigmatic comparison, in addition to syntagmatic comparison.

If the statistically significant paradigmatic differences observed in the production data are indeed perceptually significant, listeners ought to be able to exploit this for correct identification. This prediction was not borne out.

If the statistically significant syntagmatic trend for greater prominence on the verb in the production data were perceptually significant, we might expect listeners to hear SOF on the verb more often than the noun. Alternatively, we might imagine listeners are able to 'filter out' the non-semantic prominence in order to identify the intended focus associate. These predictions were also not borne out.

Overall, the sophisticated listeners were not particularly successful at identifying the matching discourse. I believe it is telling that two of the listeners (L2 and L6) were willing to accept all discourse pairs as prosodically felicitous, and that even for the best performing listener (L3), an association with focus in the SOF sentence could be essentially 'coerced' by the FOF context sentence.

---

[11] L2, a trained phonetician, reported guessing for each stimulus and judged all discourses acceptable. L3, a trained musician as well as linguist performed best (65% correct), although this listener judged nearly all discourses acceptable.

[12] Regarding the complexity of the task, a simple matching task was also run (omitted here for space) where a matching/not matching judgement was elicited for a single discourse only. Results were largely the same: low success and reports of 'guessing'.

16.5 Deciding Among Semantic Theories

How do these results inform our choice between a grammatically mediated or purely pragmatic account of association with focus? Let us consider the possibilities.

First, suppose that a SOF associate is always syntactically F-marked. The results of the first production experiment suggest, however, that the focus associate is not always realized as most prosodically prominent. Listeners could in principle disambiguate a SOF sentence, as they do in Rooth's bridging examples (cf. (3)). This possibility, criticized by Partee (1999) as 'phonologically invisible focus', certainly undermines the interface principle Stress-F, either on its own or in conspiracy with Destress-Given. Either a revision of the principle or an account of its neutralization under certain conditions would be required.

Second, consider an account on which SOF is never grammatically marked. On this scenario, what remains to be explained is the documented phonetic differences that sometimes arise. For example, Krifka (2004) suggests that SOF amounts to an anaphor (cf. *he, her, it*) without internal compositional semantics. The weak but observable production effects are due to phonetic copying, motor planning, or some other 'low-level' phenomenon. This provides a way of maintaining a grammaticized theory of focus, and one which observes Stress-F.

Third, consider an account according to which SOF is only sometimes marked. SOF is not marked when contextually recoverable; it is marked otherwise. Since all experimental investigations elicited SOF productions by using contexts in which the phonetically identical associate is identified, we would again require an explanation for any production effects, such as phonetic copying. A way of testing this account against the others would be to investigate the production of SOF in bridging examples. If prominence is required to license bridging inferences (e.g. that Harold and Susan are among the younger candidates in (3)), that may suggest that SOF is indeed sometimes marked. Selective or contextually dependent marking of SOF would potentially be consistent with Stress-F. As a theory in which SOF is sometimes realized with relative prominence, it is also consistent with a multi-notional theory of focus (cf. Selkirk 2008).

Despite the impressive and promising results of Beaver *et al.* and others, it appears that the debate over SOF is still open. There is indeed an observable and repeatable effect of focus in the acoustic signal. From this study, however, it seems unlikely that English speakers and listeners consistently exploit these acoustic contrasts in the perception of second occurrence focus in all contexts.

17

Loan Adaptation of Laryngeal Features[*]

SANG-CHEOL AHN AND JUHEE LEE

17.1 Introduction

Numerous previous works on loanword phonology have centred on the issue of whether the input is phonetic (Silverman 1992; Yip 1993; Dupoux *et al.* 1999; Peperkamp and Dupoux 2003) or phonological in the borrowing language (Paradis and LaCharité 1997, LaCharité and Paradis 2005, etc.). First of all, Silverman (1992) proposed a concrete model of loanword phonology with a perceptual level added to the loanword input. With this view, he distinguishes between a perceptual level at which segmental adaptations take place and which is phonetic and automatic in nature and an operative level, which is phonological in nature. Silverman's model is reflected in the later works by Dupoux *et al.* (1999) and Peperkamp and Dupoux (2003), which have been discussed in psycholinguistic experimental work in the loanword context. On the other hand, LaCharité and Paradis (2005) argue that the tradition of 'Category Preservation and Proximity' in loanword adaptation is, by and large, based on the perception by the bilingual speaker's contrastive categories in the source language. More recently, many researchers take into account the intermediate position (Shinohara 1997, 2006; Steriade 2001; Kenstowicz and Suchato 2006), in which the adaptation process can account for a variety of factors to achieve the best match to the source word. In this paper, however, we propose another model of 'typological adaptation,' in which we examine the loanword adaptation patterns for laryngeal features. To attest our proposal, we examine the role of phonetic factors such as closure duration, voice onset time (VOT), and F_0 in loanword adaptation. We then argue that the representational, i.e., laryngeal, contrast and the phonetic factors play crucial roles in loan adaptation as the loan adaptation of laryngeal features heavily depends on

[*] We are very grateful to the two reviewers for their detailed comments and suggestions.

the language typology. In this way, the phonology of loanwords provides a window that enables us to understand the native phonology more deeply.

17.2 Typological Characterization of Laryngeal Contrasts

The conventional description of the two-way laryngeal contrast categorizes all languages with respect to the phonological voicing distinction even when their phonetic properties are substantially different (Ahn and Iverson 2004). However, the voice onset time (VOT) values of Romance and Slavic languages, on the one hand, and most Germanic languages, on the other, are quite different (Lisker and Abramson 1964). For example, the voiced stops of French or Russian are thoroughly voiced, with early VOT, but the 'voiced' stops of English or German are often not voiced at all at the beginning of the word and in other voicing-unfriendly environments, with comparatively late VOT. Similarly, the voiceless stops of French or Russian are produced with relatively early VOT (at or just after their release), whereas the VOT of the English voiceless stop series is considerably delayed, well into a following vowel or sonorant consonant. Therefore, French or Russian voiceless stops are regularly 'unaspirated' whereas those of English are rather heavily 'aspirated' (Iverson and Salmons 1995; Flemming 1995; Ewen and van der Hulst 2001, etc.).

All known laryngeal systems can now be represented via combinations of the three privative features [voice], [spread], and [constricted] (Avery and Idsardi 2001). For a system with no laryngeal feature specifications (one series is always marked), there are no laryngeal feature specifications, whereas languages with a two-way contrast require specification of just one of the three (Ahn and Iverson 2004). In English, for example, the distinction is expressed in terms of the feature [spread] standing in opposition to laryngeally unmarked ([ ]) segments, whereas for the other two-way systems, the marked features is [voice]. The feature [spread] and [voice] are also involved in many three-way contrastive systems, distinguishing, for example, the voiceless, voiced, and aspirated phonemes of Thai.

(1)

	/p ∼b̥/	/b/	/pʰ/	Other
Japanese, French	[ ]	[voice]		
English, German	[ ]		[spread]	
Korean	[ ]		[spread]	CC (tense C)
Thai	[ ]	[voice]	[spread]	

We observe that Thai belongs to the [voice] group just like Romance or Slavic languages as the [voice] feature plays a distinctive role, while English and Korean belong to the [spread] type, lacking the voicing distinction. Despite the typological difference, moreover, both Korean and Thai show the three-way laryngeal contrasts in stops. Unlike Thai, however, Korean shows a tense (i.e., geminate) stop, while lacking a voiced stop employed in Thai (Ahn and Lee 2008). Note that there is no velar voiced stop in Thai.

(2)   Korean

[ ]		[spread]		CC (=[C'])	
pul	'fire'	pʰul	'grass'	ppul	'horn'
tal	'moon'	tʰal	'mask'	ttal	'daughter'
kɨn	'weight unit'	kʰɨn	'large'	kkɨn	'rope'

(3)   Thai

[ ]		[voice]		[spread]	
pâː	'aunt'	bâː	'crazy'	pʰâ̄a:	'cloth'
tāː	'eye'	dàː	'curse'	tʰầ:	'landing place'
kāː	'teapot'	–		kʰā̄:	'(die) immediately'

As the [spread] property plays a major role in the distribution of stops, English and Korean belong to the same 'laryngeal typology,' lacking the [voice] property. The laryngeal distinction of a word-initial English stop thus employs the [spread] property, rather than the [voice] distinction. Thai also employs the [spread] property for phonemic distinction but the function of the [voice] distinction is crucial as well since Thai has phonetically long VOT just like other [voice] languages. The interrelationship among the three languages can be schematized as follows.

(4)

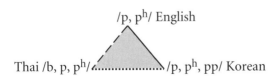

The solid line indicates that both English and Korean belong to the aspiration group. The long broken line is marked for their different laryngeal typologies, as the feature [± voice] is distinctive only for Thai. Moreover, the dotted line indicates that both Korean and Thai have the three-way laryngeal contrasts.

17.3 Typological Factor in Substitution[1]

17.3.1 *Adaptation of English Loanwords in Korean and Thai*

Korean and Thai have adapted numerous English loanwords as shown in the following table.

(5)

Korean	English	Thai
pʰe.ni	p[pʰ]enny	pʰēnnīi
tʰim	t[tʰ]eam	tʰīim
kʰyu.pʰi.tɨ	c[kʰ]upid	kʰīwpît
pa.i.pɨl	b[b̥]ible	bāibân
tal.la	d[d̥]ollar	dɔ̄nlâa

The substitution pattern in Korean is more like a phoneme-based pattern, whereas the pattern in Thai is more phonetically motivated. This observation therefore contradicts both Paradis and LaCharité (1997) and LaCharité and Paradis (2005), claiming that loanword adaptations are phonological/categorical since phonetic approximation does not have much influence in loanword adaptation. Moreover, the opposite view, based on phonetic details, cannot account for the current observation either since their claims (Silverman 1992; Peperkamp and Dupoux 2003, etc.) are based on language-particular processes. We thus need an alternative view employing the 'typological characteristics' between the target and the recipient languages.

We first observe the mapping process between English and Korean since they belong to the same laryngeal typology.

(6)

Eng /C/ [C]	Kor /C/	Eng /Cʰ/ [Cʰ]	Kor /Cʰ/	Eng /C/ [C]	Kor /Cʰ/
bin [b̥](=[p])	pin	pin [pʰ]	pʰin	spin [p]	sipʰin
desk [d̥]	tesɨkʰɨ	test [tʰ]	tʰesɨtʰɨ	strike [t]	sitʰɨlaikʰɨ
google [g̥]	kukɨl	can [kʰ]	kʰɛn	ski [k]	sikʰi

[1] A part of this section is included in Ahn and Lee (2008).

Here the phonetic details are not reflected in the laryngeal mapping in that the allophonic variation does not affect the phoneme-to-phoneme transfer process as claimed in Paradis and LaCharité (1997) and LaCharité and Paradis (2005). For example, English words beginning with *sC* are realized as unaspirated [p, t, k] phonetically, but they are adopted for the phoneme-to-phoneme mapping as /p^h, t^h, k^h/ in Korean. That is, as schematized below, Korean speakers prefer a phoneme-to-phoneme mapping, reflecting that both languages belong to the aspiration group (<> stands for the orthography).

(7)   English → Korean mapping (phoneme-based)

English	[spread]/p^h/<p>		[ ] /p/ <b>		phonemic rep.
	[p^h]	[p]/[b̥]	[p]/[b̥]	[b]	allophonic rep.
Korean	[spread]		[ ]		
	/p^h/		/p/		

On the other hand, the phonological view of loanword adaptation faces a different problem in the adaptation of English loanwords in Thai (Kenstowicz and Suchato 2006).

(8)

English	Thai	English	Thai	English	Thai
penny [p^h]	phēnnī	sponsor [p]	sᵊpɔɔnsɔ̂ə	bible [b̥]	bāibân
team [t^h]	thīim	sticker [t]	sᵊtíkkôə	dollar[d̥]	dɔ̄nlâa
cone [k^h]	khōon	screen [k]	sᵊkrīin	-	-

The loanword mapping processes between English and Thai are fundamentally phonetically based in that the allophonic details in English stops are reflected in Thai. In particular, the 'unaspirated' phonetic information in the English *sC* cluster is reflected in Thai.

(9)   English → Thai mapping

English	[spread] /p^h/ <p>		[ ] /p/ <b>		phonemic rep.
	[p^h]	[p]/[b̥]		[b]	allophonic rep.
Thai	[spread]	[ ]		[voice]	
	/p^h/	/p/		/b/	

At a glance, the mapping process looks very simple since there is a one-to-one allophone-phoneme correspondence between the two languages: i.e., three allophones ([pʰ], [p], [b]) in English → three phonemes (/pʰ/, /p/, /b/) in Thai. We note, however, that the adaptation process is not as straightforward as is the case with Korean. Although the English initial /pʰ/ is uniformly adapted as the corresponding aspirated stop /pʰ/ in Thai, a non-initial English /pʰ/ (following an /s/) is adapted as a plain stop /p/, reflecting the allophonic pronunciation in English [p].

This phonetically motivated adaptation process, however, shows further complication in the adaptation of English voiced stops since an English devoiced initial stop as in *bible* is mapped into the Thai voiced stop /b/, rather than the plain stop /p/. Note that the VOT values of the English stops are much longer than those in Thai (Lisker and Abramson 1964) and presuming a phonetically based adaptation process may cause the wrong /b/ → /p/ mapping in this case. Thus, neither a phonetic nor a phonological adaptation process seems to function in a straightforward way.

(10)   VOT for stops (Lisker and Abramson 1964)

	English	Thai
/p, t, k/	> 58 ms	6~25 ms
/b, d, g/	0~21 ms	−97~ −78 ms²

Numerous studies (House and Fairbanks 1953; Lehiste and Peterson 1961) show that English word-initial voiced stops lack closure voicing but still lower the pitch (i.e., F_0) of the following vowel.[3] According to Abramson and Lisker (1985), the F_0 differences can be used as cues to stop identification by English subjects. In a perceptual experimental study with Thai, Abramson and Erickson (1992) also show that the two-way interaction between the VOT category of the stop and the tone (F_0) on the following vowel is an important factor as the identification of /b/ increases systematically as the F_0 value decreases.[4] Similarly, higher F_0 facilitates /p/ identification.[5] It can therefore be argued

---

[2] As Thai lacks the velar stop /g/, this negative VOT value is only for the /b, d/.

[3] According to Cho and Ladefoged (1999), the language variation is largely predictable as languages choose one of the three possibilities for the degree of aspiration of voiceless stops. In a similar way, the VOT values may vary, depending on the given context, as shown in Scobbie (2005) for Shetlandic and Docherty (1992) for British English.

[4] English F_0 contours are interpreted only in stop identification in loan adaptation, not in the tonal representation of a vowel (Kenstowicz and Suchato 2006).

[5] There is no comparable F_0 effect on the /pʰ/ identification.

that Thai speakers use the low F_0 value for the adaptation of the devoiced initial stops in English and match them with the Thai voiced stops. That is, the F_0 effect on the following vowel overrides the VOT identification of the stop.

(11)   English   allophone   Thai

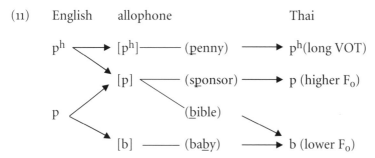

Here we may consider the P-map hypothesis (Steriade 2001), which states that when the pair of sounds (a-b) is perceptually more similar than the pair (y-z), substitution between /a/ and /b/ is favoured, because the change is less perceptible and hence less noticeable. In the case of Thai, however, the F_0 of a neighbouring vowel is an additional factor as we judge the perceptual similarity in the substitution between two consonantal segments.[6]

(12)   English $\rightarrow$ Thai mapping (allophone-based)

English	[spread] /p^h/<p>		[ ] /p/ <b>		phonemic rep.
	[p^h]	[p]/[b̥]	[p]/[b̥]	[b]	allophonic rep.
Thai	[spread]	high F_0 (V)	low F_0 (V)	[voice]	factors
	/p^h/	/p/	/b/		consequences

17.3.2 *Loan Adaptation of Thai Words in Korean*

The phonetic mapping method, however, does not work in Thai loanword adaptation in Korean even though both languages have three-way laryngeal contrasts in stops.[7]

---

[6] Silva (2006) also observes that the VOT overlap in lax and aspirated stops of the young speakers indicates that VOT by itself is no longer sufficient for the distinction of three types of stops in Chinese Korean (Yenben dialect).

[7] Our generalization is based on the consonantal chart in H.-W. Lee (2002: 8).

(13)

Thai		Korean	
/pʰ/⁸	ผ พ ภ	/pʰ/	ㅍ
/p/	ป	/pp/	ㅃ
/b/	บ	/p/	ㅂ

The aspirated stop in Thai is mapped to the corresponding aspirated one in Korean, while a plain stop is adapted as a tense stop, rather than as a plain stop, in Korean. Moreover, the Thai voiced stop is realized as the plain stop in Korean lacking the voicing distinction phonemically. Recall that being a [voice] language, Thai shows a negative VOT value for voiced stops and Korean speakers take the closest VOT match for the Thai voiced stop in Korean, which turns out to be a plain stop. Moreover, having three types of laryngeal contrast, Thai shows a shorter VOT for a plain stop than for a Korean plain stop. Then, the unmarked Thai plain stop is mapped onto the tense stop in Korean. Consider the VOT values between Korean and Thai in order to understand the adaptation process (Lisker and Abramson 1964; Kim 1965).

(14) Mapping by VOT (word-initial)

	Thai	Korean
/b, d, –/	−53~ −35 ms	–
/p, t, k/	8~15 ms	7~20 ms
/p', t', k'/	–	22~48 ms
/pʰ, tʰ, kʰ/	37~69 ms	89~125 ms

Based on the VOT values, we can describe the following mapping result in these two typologically different languages.

⁸ There are multiple letters for certain consonants in Thai. Those letters represented separate sounds in the past, but over the years the distinction between those sounds was lost and the letters show the tonal difference in Modern Thai.

(15)   Thai → Korean mapping

Thai	[spread] /pʰ/	[ ] /p/	[voice] /b/	phonemic
	[pʰ]	[p]	[b]	phonetic
	①salient VOT	②closer VOT	③default	mapping procedure
Korean	[spread]	tense/CC/	[ ]	mapping
	/pʰ/	/pp/	/p/	consequences

First of all, the aspiration value is regarded as the most salient in Thai and thus matches to the corresponding aspirated one in Korean. Secondly, the plain stop /p/ is adapted as a geminate tense consonant, due to the closet VOT value. Finally, the voiced /b/ in Thai is mapped to the unmarked sound /p/ in Korean by default. We summarize the substitution pattern in the following manner.[9]

(16)   1st stage: /pʰ/ in Thai → /pʰ/ in Korean
        (e.g.) Phuket [pʰ] → [pʰu.kʰet] 'place name'
        2nd stage: /p/ in Thai → /pp/ (=p') in Korean, i.e., gemination [pp] (= [p'])
        (e.g.) Paknam [p] → [p'ak.nam] 'place name'
        3rd stage: /b/ in Thai → no match in Korean (i.e., default)
        (e.g.) Baht [b] → [patʰɨ] 'monetary unit',
            Bankok [b] → [paŋ.kʰok] 'Bankok'

17.4 Further Developments

17.4.1 *Closure Duration and F₀*

Japanese has both two-way voicing distinction and length distinction for voiceless stops, unlike Korean, having the three-way contrasts. Given the typological difference, therefore, there is no direct corresponding relationship between these two languages, as (18) shows the 'voiced stop → plain stop' adaptation pattern (Ito *et al.* 2006).

---

[9] This adaptation process is supported by the experimental study by Wayland (2000) arguing that VOT is also the main perceptual cue for the discrimination of Korean stops (/p/, /pp/, /pʰ/) for the speakers of Thai. She further argues that laryngealization seems to play only a minor role in the perception of Korean stop consonants.

(17)

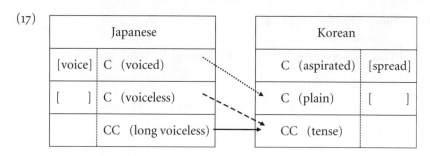

(18)   Japanese Korean
  beNtoo pent'o (t'=tt) 'lunch box'
  dai tai   'table'
  gara kara   'fake'

As Korean lacks phonemic voiced stops, we could consider possible VOT mapping. But the average negative VOT value of the Japanese 'voiceless' stops is closer to that of the Korean 'tense' stops, rather than the plain ones. Having the shortest VOT, moreover, the 'plain' stops are chosen as the correspondents for the Japanese 'voiced' stops. Therefore, VOT may not be a deciding factor in perceptually distinguishing tense and plain stops.

(19)   Average VOT values (ms) (word-initial)

	Korean Lisker and Abramson (1964)		Japanese (Honma 1981)	
	Word-initial	Word-medial	Word-initial	Word-medial
/b, d, g/	–	–	−27~0 ms	No data in Honma
/p, t, k/	7~20 ms	5~21 ms	27~53 ms	7~24 ms
/p', t', k'/	22~48 ms	13~44 ms	11~28 ms (intervocalic geminate)	
/pʰ, tʰ, kʰ/	89~125 ms	75~93 ms	–	

We may therefore consider the closure duration of the Korean plain stops, which is close to that of the Japanese voiced stop.

(20)   Relativized closure duration of Korean and Japanese stops (Ito *et al.* 2006: 95)

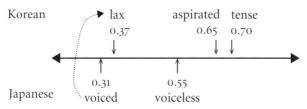

On the other hand, the earlier studies (Han 1996; Ahn 1999; Ahn and Iverson 2004; etc.) show that the closure duration of tense stops is much longer than those of the lax and aspirated ones (by about 1/3, according to medial measurements reported by Ahn (1999: 30) [207 ms, 145 and 146 ms]). The tense series also differs from the others by not undergoing medial lenition, while the plain and aspirated series experience substantial reduction in VOT lag in the same (i.e., intervoiced) environments.

Consideration of duration gets further support from the adaptation of Japanese geminates.[10] Japanese has the single vs geminate distinction for word-medial stops as the phonemic voiceless stops are used as geminates, adding an extra mora to the preceding syllable, i.e., *Nippon* 'Japan', *ippai* 'fully', *tekkiri* 'certainly', etc. Moreover, the distinction is realized in two different mapping patterns as Japanese voiceless singleton stops are adapted as tense stops in Korean only word-medially (and as plain stops word-initially), whereas the geminates are always adapted as tense stops in Korean.

(21)   Japanese Korean (p'=pp, t'=tt, k'=kk)

Japanese	Korean	
tama	tama	'ball'
kao	kao	'face'
itai	it'ai	'painful'
Kyoto	kyot'o	'place name'
sake	sak'e	'Japanese liquor'
kaNpai	kanp'ai	'cheers'
ippai	ip'ai	'fully'
tekkiri	tek'iri	'certainly'

---

[10] Ito *et al.* (2006), however, employ another criterion replacing the VOT consideration, i.e., vocalic cues for tense and aspirated consonants: i.e., higher F_0 values in vowels following tense/aspirated stops.

Note that Japanese voiceless stops have a longer duration than voiced stops and voiceless geminates, which are close to three times longer than voiceless singletons.

(22)   Average closure duration of intervocalic stops (ms) (Honma 1981)

/b/	55	/p/	77	/pp/	183
/d/	35	/t/	62	/tt/	170
/g/	41	/k/	61	/kk/	175

Regarding the closure durations, geminates are adapted as Korean tense stops whose closure duration is much longer than that of the aspirated stops.

17.4.2 *Sequential Mapping*

As we move on to the adaptation of the Japanese voiceless stops, however, both closure duration or F_0 accounts do not work since the voiceless stops are realized as tense, rather than aspirated. The closure duration account incorrectly predicts the mapping of aspirated stops since their duration is the closest to that of Japanese voiceless stops. On the other hand, the F_0 account would face an indeterminacy problem in that both tense and aspirated stops elevate the F_0 values of the following vowels. Citing Kawahara (2005), Ito *et al.* (2006) claim that F_0 overrides closure duration and VOT as a cue to distinguishing tense and lax stops when in conflict. But such a solution does not provide any mechanism to determine between tense and aspirated stops.

Following the transcription guideline of *The National Institute of the Korean Language*, however, numerous studies (Nozawa *et al.* 2000; H. Kim 2006) claim that Japanese voiceless stops are adapted as aspirated stops in Korean. The guideline requires that all of the Japanese voiceless sounds be transcribed as aspirated ones. For example, place names such as *Tokyo* and *Osaka* are to be written as <tok^{h}yo> and <osak^{h}a> in Korean, but these transcriptions merely reflect the orthographic guideline, rather than the actual pronunciation like [tok'yo] and [osak'a] with tensing. Therefore, the practical motivation for the unrealistic transcription is merely the tendency to avoid tensed consonants in writing.[11] This tendency is observed not only in Japanese loanwords, but also in the transcription of the loanwords of other

---

[11] For example, the Chinese loanword <cajangmyeon> (*<c'ajangmyeon>) 'Chinese noodle with blackish sauce' is actually pronounced as [c'ajaŋmyɔn] by most Korean speakers. According to a report from *The National Institute of the Korean Language*, 72% of Korean speakers would pronounce it as tense.

languages. For example, English /s/ (unless in a consonant cluster) is adapted as a tense [s'] (i.e., /ss/) in Korean, but it is written as a single /s/.

(23)   <seil>   [s'eil]   *[seil]   'sale'
       <saunti>   [s'aundi]   *[saundi]   'sound'
       <soŋ>   [s'oŋ]   *[soŋ]   'song'

Moreover, those loanwords from non-aspiration languages, such as *Paris* and *Espagna,* are transcribed with aspiration, i.e., <pʰali> and <esipʰanya>, not representing the more natural pronunciations, [p'ari] and [esip'anya].

As mentioned above, Korean aspirated stops should be a match for Japanese voiceless ones in terms of closure duration. But this incorrect mapping, based on closure duration, causes artificial or unrealistic pronunciation. Therefore, none of the earlier accounts (i.e., VOT, closure duration, and F_0) would work for the realization of tense stops for the Japanese voiceless stops. Considering the typological difference, we therefore employ a mapping procedure to be applied in a sequential way due to the typological difference. The adaptation process is rather phonetically based, but we need further refinement (The shaded area will be filled in later[12]).

(24)

Japanese	[voice] /g/	[ ] /k/			phonemic
	[g]	Initial	elsewhere	[kk]	allophonic
Korean	/k/		/kk/		*/kʰ/

The first step of the adaptation process is the substitution of the more salient /g/ as /k/ in Korean, showing that Korean speakers adapt the Japanese voiced stops as voiceless ones in Korean, based on phonetic information, i.e., closure duration. Moreover, the same procedure applies to the adaptation of the geminate consonants. The closure duration account, however, does not hold for the adaptation of /k/ as the tensed /kk/ (*/kʰ/). Thus, we go back to the VOT measurements for this case, as the VOT of the Japanese voiceless stop is close to that of the Korean tensed consonant, which is far shorter than that of the Korean aspirated stop. Consequently, we need to employ both criteria for these two processes.

---

[12] In Japanese phonology, there is a constraint against single [p]. Yamato (native) and Sino-Japanese forms tolerate /p/ only in a geminated or at least partially geminated form (*kappa* 'river imp', *nippoN* 'Japan', and *kampai* 'cheers', but never *kapa or *nipoN). The *P-constraint, however, governs neither mimetics (cf. *pika-pika* 'glittering') nor foreign items (cf. *peepaa* 'paper').

17.4.3 *On Word-initial Neutralization*

Here a question arises as to why Korean speakers prefer a plain stop to an aspirated one in word-initial positions. We argue that this preference, however, is manipulated by the transcription guideline requiring that Japanese voiceless stops be adapted as aspirated ones in Korean. Perceiving the short VOT of Japanese voiceless stops, however, most Korean speakers do not follow the guideline in actual pronunciation and voiceless stops are realized as plain stops word-initially just like voiced stops, while non-initial voiceless stops are adapted as tensed/geminates.

This initial laryngeal neutralization is quite peculiar in that, unlike those of Japanese, initial stops in English and French loanwords can be realized as aspirated or tensed stops, depending on the laryngeal type of the target language as shown in (25).

(25)

English	Korean	French	Korean	Japanese	Korean
pet	pʰetʰɨ	Paris	p'ali	teNpura 'fry'	temp'ula
tank	tʰɛŋkʰɨ	Toulouse	t'ulluci	teriyaki 'grilled beef'	teliyak'i
kit	kʰitʰɨ	Claude (Monet)	k'illotɨ	kawasaki 'name'	kawasak'i

The asymmetric adaptations of the English and French initial stops can be attributed to the difference in the laryngeal typology, as English belongs to the aspiration type, while French to the voice type. As for the difference between French and Japanese loanwords, we first consider the suggestion in Ito *et al.* (2006), citing Honma (1981) and Shimizu (1999), for measuring the F_0 values for Japanese vowels following voiceless stops, while also noting O'Shaughnessy's account (1981) for French. According to these works, French voiceless stops are slightly lower for the F_0 values than those of corresponding Japanese stops. Ito *et al.* (2006) thus argue that the different adaptation patterns of initial stops of French and Japanese words (i.e., French /t/ → Korean /t'/, Japanese /t/→Korean /t/) are due to the different roles of F_0 in these languages.

This account, however, cannot explain why the initial voiced and voiceless stops of Japanese loanwords undergo neutralization. For this problem, we argue that the neutralization is a result of the effort required to avoid initial tense stops. Having been introduced after the Middle Korean period, tensed consonants are the new members of the Korean phonemic system and seem to be avoided in the adaptation of loanwords, especially in word-initial positions. And this tendency ends up with the guideline for loanword transcription. The word-initial realization [p, t, k] for both /p, t, k/ and /b, d, g/ is thus a result of laryngeal neutralization reflecting the *psychological tendency* (orthography and sociolinguistic context) to avoid tenseness which risks possible semantic ambiguity.

(26) [kin]:   <u>kin</u> medaru, 'gold medal'   vs <u>gin</u> medaru 'silver medal'
              <u>kin</u> kakuji 'Golden pavillion' vs <u>gin</u> kakuji 'Silver pavillion'
     [tok'yo]: <u>Tokyo</u> University   <u>Dokkyo</u> University

Given that a voiceless stop lowers the F_0 of the following vowel, it is difficult to account for the initial neutralization with the F_0 account. We need to incorporate the tendency to avoid initial tensing/aspiration for Japanese loanwords.

(27)

Japanese (initial)		Korean	Japanese (medial)		Korean
<u>t</u>ama	'ball'	<u>t</u>ama	kanpai	'cheers'	kanp'ai
<u>T</u>okyo		tok'yo	Sapporo	'place name'	sap'oro
<u>k</u>ao	'face'	<u>k</u>ao	beNtoo	'lunch box'	pent'o
			nattoo	'fermented bean'	nat'o
			sake	'Japanese liquor'	sak'e
			tekkiri	'certainly'	tek'iri

In sum, unlike the claim in Ito *et al.* (2006),[13] the F_0 factor does not play much of a role in the adaptation of Japanese loanwords, although typologically different Japanese and Korean loanwords do undergo phonetically based adaptation patterns.[14]

(28)

Japanese	[voice] /g/		[ ] /k/		phonemic rep.
	[k]	W-initial	elsewhere	[kk]	allophonic rep.
Korean	/k/		/kk/		*/kʰ/

In (28), we first search for the optimal Korean correspondent for the more salient /b/ in Japanese, as Korean speakers adapt Japanese voiced stops as

---

[13] Ito *et al.* (2006) propose the hierarchy, 'F_0 > VOT > Vowel quality', for Japanese loanword adaptation.

[14] The typological adaptation pattern can be verified in other languages. For example, Shinohara (1997) shows that the adaptation pattern of French loanwords in Japanese follows the voicing correspondence between these two [voice] languages: e.g., *pâté* → *pate*, *bagatelle* → *baga'teru*.

voiceless ones in Korean, based on closure duration. Then, the same procedure applies for the adaptation of geminate consonants, mapping a Japanese geminate /CC/ to a tense stop in Korean. Next, the least marked voiceless stops are mapped to the tense stops /CC/, rather than the aspirated ones. As the closure duration account does not work, we re-employ the VOT account as the VOT value of Japanese voiceless stop is as short as the Korean tensed consonant, that is, far shorter than that of the Korean aspirated stop. Thus, both closure duration and VOT accounts are required for different steps of adaptation, i.e., closure duration for more marked stops but VOT for unmarked ones. Therefore, the initial neutralization of Japanese /k, g/ cannot be accounted for by the F_0 account in Ito *et al.* (2006). Rather, it is explained in terms of the tendency to avoid initial laryngeal marking. Thus, we propose the following sequential mapping procedure for the adaptation of Japanese stops in Korean.

(29)   Mapping procedure
    1) Voice (i.e. marked) in Japanese
      → Plain in Korean (closure duration)
    2) Voiceless (i.e. unmarked) in Japanese
      → Geminate (*aspirate) in Korean (VOT (?), *Closure duration/*F_0)
    3) Geminate in Japanese
      → Geminate in Korean (closure duration, VOT)
    4) Word-initial voice/voiceless
      → Plain in Korean (neutralization)

17.5 Concluding Remarks

We have so far examined loanword adaptation patterns for laryngeal features in several languages, e.g., English, Korean, Thai, and Japanese, etc. To investigate laryngeal features in these languages, we first observed the loan adaptation patterns of English loanwords in Thai and Korean, and moved on to the adaptation pattern of Thai words in Korean and vice versa. In order to analyse loan adaptation patterns, we proposed 'typological adaptation' as the model of loanword phonology. Within this model, we argued that typological categorization, either phonemic or phonetic mapping, plays an important role in determining the strategy for loan adaptation. In this line of analysis, we proposed to refine the P-map hypothesis (Steriade 2001) in loan adaptation, as the loan adaptation of laryngeal features depends heavily on the language typology as well as orthographic identity. More specifically, we argued that the phonemic vs phonetic mapping patterns can be decided based on the laryngeal typology of the target and the recipient languages, e.g., mapping from English-Thai-Korean. Then, we discussed how phonetic factors such as closure duration and VOT function play major roles in the adaptation of Japanese loanwords in Korean.

Before concluding this chapter, however, we need to note that there are many cases where a [voice] language speaker may not employ the phonetic-based adaptation process for English loanwords. For example, if a [voice] language such as Spanish adapts voiced English stops, the result is realized as a corresponding voiced stop, rather than a voiceless one, even though the VOT values of English voiced stops phonetically correspond to those of Spanish voiceless stops.

(30)   VOT contrasts in English and Spanish (LaCharité and Paradis 2005)

	English	Spanish
/p, t, k/	+VOT (> 50 ms)	+VOT (0~30 ms)
/b, d, g/	+VOT (0~30 ms)	−VOT (−40~0 ms)

(31)   Loan adaptation in Spanish (data from LaCharité and Paradis 2005)

		English	Spanish	
/b/	bar	[bɑɹ]	→ [baɾ]	*[paɾ]
/d/	dip	[dɪp]	→ [dip]	*[tip]
/g/	golf	[gɑlf]	→ [gɔlf]	*[kɔlf]

Being Indo-European, both languages have the same orthographic system using Roman alphabets, so the orthographic information here seems to override the phonetic factor, forcing Spanish speakers to follow the voiced stops. Note that there is only one laryngeal distinction in English and Spanish and there exists an orthographic similarity between those stops in the two languages. Therefore, Spanish speakers match English /p, t, k/ with Spanish /p, t, k/ even though the VOT values of English stops are much longer than those in the [voice] language Spanish.[15] This result shows that if the target language has the same number of laryngeal contrasts, the recipient language chooses the phonemic match, following the orthographic similarity reflecting the etymological connection. Therefore, for two typologically different languages, the orthographic information of the two languages should be incorporated for the adaptation strategies if they share the same type of orthographic representation (e.g., Indo-European languages using similar orthographic [i.e., alphabet] systems).

15 Also, refer to Ladefoged (2001: 120–1) for a relevant observation.

Part IV
Experimental Work on Interface Issues

18

Scope Ambiguity in Child Language: Old and New Problems*

ANDREA GUALMINI

18.1 Introduction

This chapter is concerned with the resolution of scope ambiguities in child language, a domain which arguably involves different levels of linguistic knowledge. An issue which has attracted much recent attention is how the syntactic and semantic properties of scope-bearing elements, in particular negation and quantifiers, interact with children's performance mechanisms. Our focus will be on the role of pragmatic factors. Despite the efforts of recent research, pragmatics continues to be one of the least understood submodules of children's developing knowledge. Recent advances in the theoretical literature call for a change, however. In this paper, we will illustrate how we can bring theoretically motivated notions to bear on the debate, by showing how explicitly formalized pragmatic notions can explain facts that were previously attributed to syntactic factors. More generally, this is used to illustrate how the interactions between different aspects of children's linguistic competence are likely to conspire in determining their behaviour, as well as making an explanation for their behaviour harder to come by. Then, drawing upon recent work with Bernhard Schwarz, we will show how the child could in principle exploit pragmatic information in the process of language development itself.

* I am indebted to Bernhard Schwarz for discussion and advice on all the issues discussed here. I also thank Michelle St-Amour and the audience at OnLI for comments on previous versions of this paper. This work was partially supported by a McGill VP-Internal research grant, a grant from McGill's Arts Undergraduate Society, and by a Standard Research Grant from the Social Sciences & Humanities Research Council of Canada (SSHRC). The author is currently supported by a VIDI fellowship from the Netherlands Organization for Scientific Research (NWO) and Utrecht University.

18.2 Teasing Apart the Relevant Contribution of Different Linguistic Levels

In recent years, much research has focused on children's interpretation of scopally ambiguous sentences. An influential line of research draws upon the work of Musolino (1998), who investigated children's interpretation of sentences containing negation and a quantifier. An experimental result that has attracted considerable attention pertains to children's interpretation of the sentences below.

(1)   Every horse didn't jump over the fence.

(2)   The detective didn't find some guys.

(3)   The smurf didn't catch two birds.

The experiments conducted by Musolino (1998) focused on the inverse scope interpretation of the sentences above. In particular, Musolino (1998) wanted to determine whether children have access to such interpretations to the same extent as adults. To find out, Musolino put children in what seemed to be the most favourable circumstances for the inverse scope interpretations of (1) through (3), namely contexts that made the inverse scope interpretations true and the surface scope interpretations false. For instance, children were presented with (1) as a description of a story in which some horses had jumped over the fence, but one horse hadn't. The reasoning followed by Musolino (1998) was that if children's grammar could generate the inverse scope interpretation of the relevant sentence (i.e., *It is not the case that every horse jumped over the fence*), then children would access that interpretation. This assumption rests on the hypothesis that children, like adults, assume that speakers follow the Principle of Cooperation, and in particular the Maxim of Quality (see Grice 1975). Musolino's finding was that children's responses were predominantly dictated by surface scope interpretation of (1) (i.e., *None of the horses jumped over the fence*). More generally, despite being placed in the most favourable circumstances, children, unlike adults, resorted to the surface scope interpretation of the sentences in (1) through (3). In particular, across all those sentences children resorted to the surface scope interpretation, at the cost of rejecting the target sentence. Since surface scope seemed to be a common denominator to children's responses, Musolino (1998) proposed to capture the facts through the Observation of Isomorphism, the claim that semantic scope coincides with syntactic scope in children (see also Musolino, Crain, and Thornton (2000)).

For present purposes, let us take the Observation of Isomorphism as a generalization. In other words, let us simply take the Observation of Isomorphism as the claim that, when it comes to potentially ambiguous sentences involving scope-bearing elements, if children differ from adults, the difference takes one particular form: children select surface scope interpretations to a larger extent than adults. The next question is what explains this difference. Given that scope resolution involves a great deal of distinct factors, children's non-adult behaviour could in principle depend on children's failure with any one of those factors. For instance, since scope-bearing elements often show lexical restrictions in their interaction with other elements, children might differ from adults in that they allow a given element to be interpreted in a different range of environments than adults. Alternatively, on the assumption that children and adults have access to the same ambiguity (i.e., the same range of interpretations), they might differ in how they resolve that ambiguity. Since ambiguity resolution can be affected by a great variety of factors, it is not surprising that over the years different proposals have been put forward, each one focusing on a different component of children's developing system. Let us introduce some of the accounts that have been put forward, by considering what knowledge is required by the adult interpretation of the sentences above.

The first piece of knowledge that is required by the adult interpretation of sentences (1) through (3) is the availability of the inverse scope reading. A child who for some reason has not acquired the existence of such a reading has no option but to interpret the relevant sentence on its surface scope interpretation. According to Musolino (1998), this is exactly what children do (see also Musolino, Crain, and Thornton 2000): the data ultimately result from children entertaining a grammar that is different from the one of the local community. Interestingly, Musolino's original outlook on the findings seemed to comport well with an independently proposed principle of the Language Acquisition Device, namely the Semantic Subset Principle proposed by Crain, Conway, and Ni (1994). These authors studied the acquisition of so-called privative ambiguities, namely ambiguities in which one reading entails the other. According to Crain, Conway, and Ni (1994), if children hypothesized the existence of the weak reading (i.e., the reading that is entailed by the other) right off the bat, they could never find truth-conditional evidence for the existence of the strong reading (i.e., the reading that entails the other). Thus, children must start off from the assumption that only the strong reading is available, i.e., the interpretation that is true in the narrowest set of circumstances. This is the Semantic Subset Principle (see Crain *et al.* 1994). As it turns out, the strong reading of

(1) is their surface scope interpretation.[1] On this view, children in the relevant stage still have not encountered the input that is necessary for them to learn the existence of the weak reading.

A second study attempting to relate children's behaviour to more general aspects of the language acquisition process is due to Gennari and MacDonald (2005/2006) who focus on sentences like (1) and (3). The contribution of Gennari and MacDonald (2005/2006) is twofold. First, they show experimentally that in contexts like the ones tested by Musolino (1998), adult speakers of English refrain from using sentences like (1) or (3), and in particular adults make use of sentences that do not include negation. Second, Gennari and MacDonald (2005/2006) show that sentences such as (1) and (3) are virtually non-existent in child-directed speech. On their account, children's behaviour with sentences like (1) and (3) must be explained along the same lines as adults' reluctance to use those kind of sentences. Furthermore, Gennari and MacDonald (2005/2006) argue that children's experience, mostly consisting of sentences that need to be interpreted on their surface scope interpretation, leads them to interpret sentences on surface scope interpretations.

Having illustrated two accounts of Musolino's original generalization, we can turn to further data, data that contributed to a significant refinement of Musolino's original generalization. The first piece of evidence against the view of Isomorphism proposed by Musolino (1998) and Musolino *et al.* (2000) comes from Gualmini (2003) and was later refined by Gualmini (2004a, b). These studies demonstrate that when it comes to sentences equivalent to (2) (i.e., *The detective didn't find some guys*) children are indeed capable of accessing either scope assignment. Gualmini drew upon the observation that negative sentences ordinarily are used to point out a discrepancy between an expected outcome and the actual outcome (see Glenberg, Robertson, Jansen, and Johnson-Glenberg 1999; Horn 1989; Wason 1965, 1972). In order to evaluate whether expectations can mitigate children's difficulty with sentences like (2), Gualmini presented children with stories in which a character had a task to carry out. In one of the trials, children were told a story about a troll, who is supposed to deliver four pizzas to Grover. Unfortunately, on the way to Grover's house

---

[1] In the case of weak quantifiers such as the ones occurring in (2) and (3), the explanation proposed by Musolino (1998) was slightly different in that it focused on the grammatical operations that are needed to generate the inverse scope reading, as opposed to the entailment relations between the two readings. For present purposes, we can ignore this issue, and focus on the what is common to the differences between children and adults, namely the fact that they are ultimately due to a difference in the grammar that they entertain.

two pizzas fall off the delivery truck and the troll only manages to deliver two pizzas. Children were then asked to evaluate either (4) or (5).

(4)   The troll didn't deliver some pizzas.

(5)   The troll didn't lose some pizzas.

Notice that both (4) and (5) are true in the context under consideration on the inverse scope interpretation. (4) is true because there are some pizzas that the troll didn't deliver, namely the ones he lost on the way; (5) is true because there are some pizzas that the troll didn't lose, namely the ones he managed to deliver. The two sentences differ in appropriateness, however. Whereas (4) pertinently points out that the troll failed in carrying out his task, upon hearing (5) the hearer has the impression that the speaker is not addressing what's at stake. Gualmini (2003) argued that this difference has an effect on children's responses. Thirty 4- and 5-year-olds participated in the experiment. Children accepted sentences like (4) in fifty-four out of sixty trials (90 per cent) but they accepted sentences like (5) in only thirty out of sixty trials (50 per cent). Similarly, Gualmini (2004a) demonstrated that children are perfectly capable of assigning wide scope to the indefinite *some* with sentences such as (6).

(6)   Every farmer didn't clean some animal.

More recently, Gualmini, Hulsey, Hacquard, and Fox (2005) have shown that the same contextual manoeuvre discovered by Gualmini (2004a, b) leads children to select the inverse scope interpretation of sentences equivalent to (1) (e.g., *Every pizza wasn't delivered*) and (3) (e.g., *The troll didn't deliver two pizzas*) to a higher extent than observed in previous literature.

A second piece of evidence against the view of Isomorphism proposed by Musolino (1998) and Musolino *et al.* (2000) comes from Musolino and Lidz (2006). They also demonstrated that when it comes to sentences like (1), children are capable of accessing either scope assignment. This conclusion was supported by the finding that children selected the inverse scope interpretation of (7) to a larger extent than they did for (1).

(7)   Every horse jumped over the log, but every horse didn't jump over the fence.

The finding that children's behaviour changes systematically across contexts poses a challenge for the original view of Isomorphism, especially since the studies we mentioned focused on the exact same sentence types which, according to Musolino, were predicted to be interpretable exclusively on their surface scope interpretation, due to parameter mis-setting.

Not surprisingly, the challenge was recognized by most researchers, and the original view was abandoned (see Gualmini 2004a, Lidz and Musolino 2005/ 2006, Musolino 2006, and Musolino and Lidz 2002, 2003). Despite the failure of the original view, however, some later developments attempted to account for the data preserving the spirit of Isomorphism. In particular, some accounts attributed children's non-adult behaviour to a preference for surface scope interpretations, which could be mitigated by the context, rather than to a strict constraint against inverse scope interpretations. In turn, recent studies have attempted to derive this preference from different features of children's processing system.

A more recent incarnation of Isomorphism attempts to link children's interpretation of scopally ambiguous sentences to children's failure to compute scalar implicatures. This novel view of Isomorphism was proposed by Musolino and Lidz (2002) and further developed by Musolino and Lidz (2006). First, these authors argue that adults' preference for inverse scope interpretations results from a pragmatic reasoning (see Grice 1975; Horn 1989). This is what Musolino and Lidz (2006: 842) write:

That is, adult speakers of English prefer to produce/interpret sentences like *Every/all N neg VP* on a 'not all' interpretation because of the availability of sentences of the form *Nobody/no-none VP* to express the alternative interpretation, i.e. the 'none' reading.

Furthermore, Musolino and Lidz (2006) argue that, given children's well-documented reluctance to compute scalar implicatures (see Guasti *et al.* (2005) for a recent review), their behaviour with inverse scope interpretations is hardly surprising.

Yet another component of children's fragile linguistic system was singled out by Musolino and Lidz (2003, 2006). The proposal offered by Musolino and Lidz (2003, 2006) attempts to analyse the data as resulting from two factors: a default preference for surface scope interpretations and a preference for true interpretations. In particular, the former factor is supposed to take precedence over the latter, in order to explain the fact that children often select false, surface scope interpretations over true, inverse scope interpretations. Here is a representative quote:

one approach, inspired by recent models of sentence processing (Trueswell et al. 1999), would be to view relative processing difficulty and satisfaction of the principle of charity as probabilistic constraints exerting antagonistic forces: The greater the processing difficulty associated with a particular reading, the more likely it is that this difficulty will override the application of the principle of charity. Musolino and Lidz (2003: 288).

On this view, the cases in which children indeed manage to access true inverse scope interpretations represent the exception and the cases in which children select surface scope interpretations represent the rule. In turn, the difference in behaviour between children and adults derives from a quantitative difference in how heavily children and adults rely on syntax in parsing.

It is time to take stock. We reviewed Musolino's data, which led to the Observation of Isomorphism, a precise hypothesis about what form children's non-adult behaviour should take. We then reviewed several explanations that have been proposed to account for those data. These explanations may seem very different in nature, as the focus shifts from UG-based parameter setting to frequency effects in the input, or from pragmatically based inferences to parsing mechanisms. Yet, all these studies seem to share one assumption, namely the assumption that differences between children and adults always surface as a preference on children's part for surface scope interpretations. To account for the fact that in some contexts no difference seems to surface, these proposals would have to make room for the role of contextual factors in helping children in overcoming their default tendency.

A good illustration of this working strategy comes from Musolino and Lidz (2006). These authors interpret the data presented by Gualmini (2003) as well as the data that they produced as showing that children's preference can be over-ridden if (a) the inverse scope interpretation makes the target sentence true and (b) that interpretation is supported by the context. Nevertheless, Musolino and Lidz (2006) do not provide an explicit model of what it would mean for the inverse scope interpretation to be supported by the context. This represents a weakness of their account. Once it is recognized— as Musolino and Lidz (2006) do—that the context plays a role in the resolution of scopally ambiguous sentences, it is important to explain *how* this happens. In particular, in absence of any proposal on this matter, we need to consider the possibility that once the role of context is formalized, we might have a mechanism that makes other factors unnecessary— including the putative preference for surface scope. This is exactly what emerges from a study by Hulsey, Hacquard, Fox, and Gualmini (2004) (see also Gualmini *et al.* 2008).

The paper by Hulsey *et al.* (2004) proposed a new model of scope resolution that makes reference to independently motivated principles of communication. According to this model, which Hulsey *et al.* (2004) call the Question-Answer requirement, children select the scope assignment which allows them to address the Question under Discussion. Focusing on 'yes/no' questions, the case which is most relevant for our purposes, an interpretation addresses a question, if that interpretation entails the proposition that is being questioned or the negation of that proposition. According to this model, what is relevant in the pizza story used by Gualmini (2003) is the troll's task. At the end of the story, one wants to know whether the troll has carried out his task or not. This amounts to asking the 'yes/no' question *Did the troll deliver all the pizzas?* Notice that either scope assignment of (4), repeated below as (8), entails an answer to that question. Thus, either scope assignment is viable as far as the Question-Answer requirement is concerned. Since the Question-Answer requirement is satisfied by either interpretation of the target sentence, children can make use of the Principle of Charity and select the interpretation that makes the target sentence true, namely the inverse scope interpretation (i.e., *There are some pizzas that the troll didn't deliver*).

(8)   The troll didn't deliver some pizzas.

By contrast, consider (5) repeated below as (9). In this case, only the surface scope interpretation addresses the contextually relevant question, as shown below.

(9)   The troll didn't lose some pizzas.

(10)   Question: Did the troll deliver all the pizzas?
        Felicitous Answer: He didn't lose any.
        Infelicitous Answers: There are some pizzas he didn't lose.

Given that only one interpretation satisfies the Question-Answer requirement, the only relevant interpretation is selected and the Principle of Charity is violated. The inverse scope interpretation is not selected—even though it would make the target sentence true—because it does not entail an answer to the Question under Discussion.

A prediction of the QAR model is that, for any given context and for any given predicate, children should prefer the same interpretation, regardless of whether it amounts to surface scope or inverse scope. Hulsey *et al.* corroborated this prediction in an experiment testing children's interpretation of the following sentences, in the same contexts investigated by Gualmini (2004a, b).

(11)   Some pizzas were not delivered.

(12)   Some pizzas were not lost.

The results show that all English-speaking children accepted (11), but half of them rejected (12). In particular, half of the subjects interviewed by

Hulsey *et al.* (2004) rejected (12) on the grounds that some pizzas were indeed lost, thereby accessing the inverse scope interpretation of (12) (i.e., *it is not the case that some pizzas were lost*). As predicted by the QAR model, the rate of rejection for (12) closely mirrors the rate of rejection for (5) documented by Gualmini (2004a, b). From the point of view of Isomorphism, by contrast, the results are unexpected. In particular, if we consider that adult controls accepted both (11) and (12), we see that the difference in behaviour between children and adults does not take the shape that Isomorphism expected. In particular, the results show that children can differ from adults, in that children select inverse scope in a context in which adults select surface scope.

Aside from the significance of the results for the debate on scope resolution, we would like end by stressing the methodological lesson that can be drawn from the development of the debate on scope resolution in child language. The study of any system involving the interaction between different levels of linguistic knowledge requires a hypothesis about all of those levels. That hypothesis might be wrong, but we cannot proceed in a vacuum. Furthermore, privileging the role of one module of the performance system might be very tempting, yet it can have a great deal of negative consequences. In the case at hand, the most influential line of research has focused on the role of syntactic factors in parsing and has assumed that contextual factors would only play a secondary role. In particular, it has been assumed that context may help subjects in overcoming the difficulties they would otherwise encounter, without considering the possibility that contextual factors might actually be *responsible* for those difficulties. As appealing as this approach may seem, the very first attempt to formalize the role of context has lead to experimental findings that falsify the view of contextual factors as secondary and reparatory factors.

Although the rejection of any theory is a welcome result, one might wonder how this particular theory came about. In our view, it arose as a result of a methodological mistake. The emphasis was placed on a subset of the data that were available. This is most evident if we consider that data from languages other than English that falsify even the weakest version of Isomorphism were available since the publication of Krämer (2000), since that study shows that Dutch-speaking children initially differ from Dutch-speaking adults in that they overwhelmingly select inverse scope interpretations (see also Unsworth 2005 and Unsworth, Gualmini, and Helder 2008). Once again, this reminds us of the importance of being able to consider and draw upon data coming from a wide array of sources.

18.3 Exploiting Different Linguistic Levels

The previous section focused on the interaction of different levels of linguistic representation for the resolution of scope ambiguities. We concluded by highlighting how the interaction between different systems might make it difficult for the researcher to tease apart their relative contribution. In this section, we would like to shift our focus and consider what benefits might arise from the interaction between different levels of linguistic representation. In particular, we will review a recent proposal developed in joint work with Bernhard Schwarz that illustrates how children might make use of pragmatic information to learn semantic properties.

Let us focus on children's interpretation of scopally ambiguous sentences containing negation and the positive polarity item *some*. As we saw above, previous research has shown that English-speaking children may assign to *some* both wide and narrow scope with respect to clausemate negation (see O'Leary and Crain 1994; Gualmini 2004a; Hulsey *et al.* 2004). The way children resolve that ambiguity has stirred much debate. A different issue has been largely overlooked, though, namely the fact that children have access to an ambiguity whereas, under current assumptions, adults don't. In particular, under the assumption that adults can't interpret *some* in the scope of negation (see Ladusaw 1979), children may be facing a learnability problem. Mechanisms of scope resolution aside, children's development must include the expunction of one reading. This is the problem addressed by Gualmini and Schwarz (2009).

It should be noted that a solution to this problem was already offered by Musolino *et al.* (2000). According to this account, children first need to notice the similarities between *some* and *any*. Then, guided by the assumption that no two lexical items can be exactly identical in meaning, children are forced to posit a difference between the two items. Here is an obvious shortcoming of this proposal: if children always interpret *any* in the scope of negation whereas they can interpret *some* both within and outside the scope of negation (as shown by the data reviewed above), then the polarity properties of the two items are already different.[2]

A different proposal was advanced by Gualmini and Schwarz (2009). To illustrate, consider the dialogue below.

(13) Speaker A: Some pizzas were not lost.
       Speaker B: Well, no pizza was lost!

---

[2] This observation emerged in conversations with Bernhard Schwarz during the preparation of Gualmini and Schwarz (2009).

As far as Speaker B knows, no pizza was lost. Furthermore, Speaker B's utterance signals that Speaker A's utterance does not count as a cooperative contribution to the conversation. If *some* receives wide scope over negation in Speaker A's utterance, then we know why his utterance is uncooperative: the proposition that some pizzas were not lost triggers the implicature that some pizzas were indeed lost, but this implicature is not met in the context, since no pizza was lost. If *some* could receive narrow scope below negation, however, Speaker A's utterance would be true and cooperative, as it would express the same proposition expressed by Speaker B, namely that no pizza was lost. The question for anybody witnessing the dialogue above then would be: why can't Speaker B be charitable to Speaker A and interpret Speaker A's utterance on the meaning that would make the sentence true and felicitous in the context? A plausible answer would be the following: because Speaker B cannot generate that meaning. In other words, Speaker B's contribution signals that Speaker B has no choice but to access the interpretation that gives rise to such an implicature, i.e., the surface scope interpretation of Speaker A's utterance.

Scalar implicatures play a crucial role for the acquisition scenario envisioned by Gualmini and Schwarz (2009). Any witness to the dialogue above who cannot compute scalar implicatures would not be able to make sense of Speaker's B reply, because Speaker B's contribution is in fact consistent with the surface scope interpretation of Speaker A's utterance. Given that young children have often been reported not to compute scalar implicatures, the consequences for the learner are straightforward: even though the relevant information might be there, at the initial stages of language development, children might not be able to make use of it. Only after the mechanism for computation of scalar implicatures is in place can children draw useful inferences from dialogues like (13). In turn, this might explain why children as old as 5 may be able to interpret *some* in the scope of negation to a larger extent than adults.

Gualmini and Schwarz's reasoning summarized above has far-reaching consequences. The idea that children might be able to bootstrap from syntax to semantics (see Gleitman 1990) or from semantics to syntax (see Pinker 1984) has generated a great body of research. As our theoretical understanding of pragmatics deepens, new potential sources of evidence for the young learner also need to be considered. An interesting issue for further research is whether anything like pragmatic bootstrapping should be available to children.

18.4 Conclusions

In this chapter, we discussed two issues that arise whenever a linguistic phenomenon depends on different interacting modules. As the case of scope ambiguity shows, the interaction between several different modules makes the researcher's task harder, but it may also present a welcome consequence for the learner, as the learner might in fact draw upon multiple sources of information.

19

Interaction of Syntax and Discourse Pragmatics in Closely Related Languages: How Native Swedes, Native Germans, and Swedish-speaking Learners of German Start their Sentences

UTE BOHNACKER AND CHRISTINA ROSÉN

19.1 Introduction

Non-native performance in second language (L2) acquisition can have many causes, transfer from the native language (L1) being one of them. It has recently been suggested that L2 learners have particular problems in integrating different kinds of grammatical knowledge, for example morphology with phonology, morphology with syntax, syntax with the lexicon, or syntax with discourse/pragmatics. These are areas where different components of the linguistic computational system interact (or 'interface') with each other or with language-external cognitive systems, such as the articulatory-perceptual and conceptual-intentional systems.

There is a growing body of evidence that L2 learners master pure syntax long before they are able to put that syntax to appropriate discursive use (White 2009).[1] In this paper, we investigate the interaction of syntax and

---

[1] For instance, Italian and Spanish exhibit Subject-Verb (SV) and Verb-Subject (VS) word orders depending on verb type (unaccusative/unergative), but for presentationally focused subjects, native speakers prefer VS irrespective of verb type. As shown by e.g. Hertel (2003), Belletti and Leonini (2004), and Lozano (2006), L2ers of Italian and Spanish acquire VS word order relatively easily but have protracted problems with VS in focused contexts: unlike native speakers, L2ers fail to produce VS in focused contexts or accept both VS and SV in equal proportions. Word-order alterations that interface with discourse pragmatics thus seem hard to acquire.

discourse-pragmatic requirements in two closely related languages, Swedish and German, and in the L2 German of native Swedish speakers, concerning the clause-initial position of declaratives. Swedish is typologically, grammatically and lexically very close to German, and syntactically both languages adhere to the V2 constraint that requires the finite verb in declaratives to be the second constituent. In non-subject-initial main clauses, inversion of the subject and the verb is required, and V3 is generally ungrammatical.[2] The position to the left of the finite verb is called the 'pre-field' (e.g. Reis 1980). Even though this position in principle can be occupied by almost any type of constituent, irrespective of syntactic category, complexity, and semantic function, we present empirical corpus data from German and Swedish speakers that indicate language-specific patterns: the frequencies of pre-field constituent types differ substantially, with a higher proportion of subjects and fewer objects and adjuncts in this position in Swedish than in German. Moreover, Swedish speakers postpone new information and instead fill the pre-field with given elements and elements of no or low informational value (e.g. expletives) to a far greater extent than German speakers do (Bohnacker and Rosén 2007, 2008). One might thus say that an identical V2 syntax interfaces differently with discourse pragmatics in the two languages. We compare native speakers to beginning, intermediate, and advanced Swedish learners of German. Our findings indicate that the learners master the syntactic properties of V2 but start their sentences in ways that diverge from the native German corpus data, and—as shown by an additional study where German informants were asked to assess and rewrite advanced L2 productions—native Germans consider many of the learners' sentence openings unidiomatic. We argue that this is because the learners overapply the Swedish information-structural principle of 'rheme later' in their L2 German, and fill the pre-field largely with elements of low informational content. In our view, this indicates L1 transfer at the interface of syntax and discourse pragmatics.

The chapter is structured as follows. Section 19.2 summarizes the learners' acquisition of V2 syntax in oral and written productions. In section 19.3, we discuss discourse-pragmatic and interface issues concerning the pre-field (19.3.1), compare the pre-field of V2 declaratives in native Swedish and German on the basis of corpus data (19.3.2), and introduce our L1 corpora (19.3.3).

---

[2] (i)   In Schweden lernen alle Englisch in der Schule.   (V2, XVS)
          in Sweden   learn   all   English   in the school
          'In Schweden everybody learns English at school.'

  (ii) *In Schweden alle lernen Englisch in der Schule.   (V3, XSV)

Section 19.4 provides some background to our L2 corpora and presents learner results. Quantitative (19.4.2) as well as qualitative differences (19.4.3) between native and L2 data are discussed, and supporting evidence from a judgement and rewriting task by native informants is reported on. Section 19.5 contains concluding remarks.

19.2 Acquisition of Verb Second in L2 German

There are many empirical studies of the acquisition of verb placement in L2 German, and there is by now good evidence that learners transfer their L1 syntax, producing and processing L2 utterances largely through the L1 grammar at first (Schwartz and Sprouse 1996). In Bohnacker (2005, 2006) we showed that this also is the case for the acquisition of V2 by Swedish learners of German, and the results are briefly summarized here.[3] Swedish beginning learners of German productively use non-subject-initial V2 declaratives in oral narratives after only four months of exposure to a few hours of German per week, unlike what has been found for L2ers whose L1 is non-V2 (Italian, Spanish, Turkish, Korean, English), who acquire V2 late (e.g. Clahsen and Muysken 1986; Schwartz and Sprouse 1996). Bohnacker also found an interesting difference between Swedes who started to learn German as their first foreign language as adults and perfectly adhered to V2 right away (Figure 1, left), and Swedes who had learnt English before and in adult age took up German as their second foreign language. Those who knew English did not fully adhere to V2, but produced both non-targetlike V3 and targetlike non-subject-initial V2 (Figure 1, right). This suggests that they partially transfer V2 syntax from their L1 Swedish, but that prior knowledge of a non-V2 language (English) interferes.[4] The V3 influence of English on the learners' German diminishes over time, as illustrated in Figure 2: intermediate learners produce a majority of subject-initial (SVX) and non-subject-initial V2 (XVS), but only 2 per cent non-targetlike V3 after three years of German. For individual results, raw figures and detailed discussion, see Bohnacker (2005: 56–66, 2006: 19–38).

---

[3] Generative grammars typically model V2 as a syntactic double-movement transformation: leftward movement of the finite verb to a functional head position on the left sentence periphery, plus movement of a constituent into the specifier position of that projection, often identified as CP. Alternatively, the pre-field constituent is not moved but generated in that position. Here we concentrate on the linear order of constituents (SVX, V1 (= VSX), V2 (= XVS), V3 (= XSV, SXV)), since our findings do not hinge on any specific structural account.

[4] The influence of L2 English on the acquisition of word order in L3 German is also discussed in e.g. Dentler (2000).

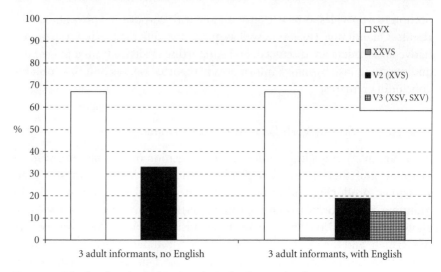

FIGURE 1. Word orders in declaratives in L2 beginners (oral).

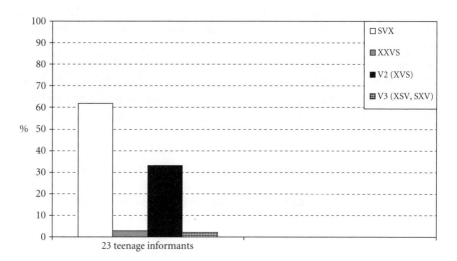

FIGURE 2. Word orders in declaratives in L2 intermediates (oral).

Written data from Swedish beginning and intermediate learners of German are very similar (Bohnacker 2005: 56–8, Bohnacker and Rosén 2007), but for reasons of space we only show the results for a group of beginners we studied (for learner background, see section 19.4). They produce a majority of subject-initial (SVX) and non-subject-initial V2 (XVS), and only 3 per cent non-targetlike V3 (Figure 3).

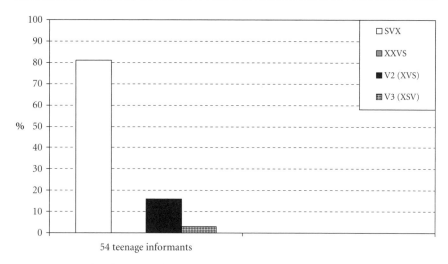

FIGURE 3. Word orders in declaratives, L2 beginners (written).

Closer investigation of these L2 productions indicates however that they are not necessarily adequate in the context they occur in, i.e. they do not always comply with native German discourse-pragmatic requirements. Rosén (2006) found that the very same learners who produce correct V2 clauses appear to be organizing and structuring information in a way that disturbs German readers, which will be discussed in more detail in sections 19.4.2 and 19.4.3. When native Germans were asked to assess advanced L2 productions, they described them as non-nativelike, choppy, and textually incoherent, and when asked to make the L2 texts 'sound more German', native speakers homed in on the beginning of sentences and consistently changed these in certain ways. Why would changing the beginnings of sentences make texts less choppy and more German? This is discussed in section 19.3, where we compare information-structural patterns in Swedish and German.

19.3 The Pre-field in Swedish and German

19.3.1 *Some Comments on Discourse Pragmatics, Syntax, Interfaces, and the Pre-field*

The syntax of a language is commonly described as a set of rules, parameters, or constraints on which orderings are possible *irrespective of context*. In a particular context, certain word orders may be more likely or more felicitous than others but this variation is typically not ascribed to pure syntax, but to semantic and discourse-pragmatic factors. Discourse pragmatics covers many phenomena including politeness marking and language choice in multilingual contexts, but for our purposes another area of discourse pragmatics is relevant, namely the way in which speakers/writers of a particular language organize and present information. Such information management can be studied at a global or text level (e.g. Halliday and Hasan 1976; von Stutterheim 1997) or at a local (i.e. utterance or clause) level. It is this latter, local level that interests us here—information-structural influence on constituent ordering and language-specific differences related to this. Discourse-pragmatic aspects of information structure do not affect the factual information or truth value of the sentence, whilst certain semantic aspects of information structure may do so (e.g. Krifka 2007).[5]

The pre-field is especially important for communication as it anchors the clause in discourse. At the inter-sentential level, the pre-field contributes to textual coherence by linking up with preceding discourse; at the intra-sentential level, it often establishes the topic identified by the speaker, about which s/he then provides information, the comment (e.g. Reinhart 1982; Lambrecht 1994; Krifka 2007). Moreover, the pre-field typically contains an element of low informational value, *given* information, i.e. the 'theme' in the terminology of Ammann (1928) and the Prague School. New information, the so-called 'rheme', is usually provided later, after the finite verb in V2 clauses, giving rise to 'theme-rheme' order (cf. Daneš 1970; Beneš 1971). The term *theme* here stands for what the speaker/writer assumes the listener/reader to know; it is given information in the sense that it has previously been explicitly mentioned or is inferable with recourse to the linguistic discourse or the discourse situation. *Rheme* stands for what the speaker assumes to be new information for the hearer.[6] Alternatively, the pre-field can also be used to focus or contrast members of some evoked set of alternatives (cf. e.g. Zifonun *et al.* 1997; Prince 1998; Schmid 1999; Teleman *et al.* 1999).

How to view and formalize the relation between syntactic form and discourse function is much debated, and as far as we understand, three major lines of approach can be distinguished. One is the (in essence) functionalist view that the grammatical form directly follows from the communicative function of a sentence (cf. Kuno 1987). Another is the 'traditional' generative view that syntax is autonomous and discourse function is external

---

[5] For example, consider the semantic uses of focus as expressed via focus-sensitive particles such as *only* and *even* in connection with sentence accent.

[6] Dividing the clause into theme and rheme (given and new) is not always straightforward, as clauses may contain several thematic elements, and some contain none but are informationally all-new. Thematicity/givenness may also be viewed as a graded property, where recency of mention and other factors influence just how accessible a thematic/given element is.

to syntax (e.g. Chomsky 1965; Prince 1981, 1998; Fanselow 2007; Féry 2007). Prince (1998: 281) puts it as follows: 'the relation between syntactic form and discourse function is no less arbitrary than, say, the relation between phonological form and lexical meaning'. Structural possibilities are provided by the grammar *independently* of discourse pragmatics, and discourse-pragmatic notions do *not* play a role in the identification of syntactic slots or categories, nor in the triggering of syntactic operations. A multitude of grammatical devices (phonological, morphological, and lexical markers, syntactic structures, and surface positions) may be employed to support different discourse functions, but there is great cross-linguistic variation and particular discourse functions do not invariably correlate with any grammatical reflex, according to the autonomous-syntax view (e.g. Prince 1998; Féry 2007). Any mapping between language-specific form and pragmatic function can thus only be indirect and takes place not in syntax but in separate cognitive components (e.g. Lambrecht 1994).[7]

This view contrasts with a third approach, where discourse-pragmatic notions such as topic, focus, givenness are incorporated into formal theories of syntax via an articulated hierarchy of functional projections and corresponding 'syntactic' features. Whilst such a 'cartographic' approach (e.g. Rizzi 1997, 2004) is gaining popularity, proponents do not agree on the details of this proliferated phrase structure. As Benincà and Poletto (2004: 52) put it, 'there is no limit, in our view, as to how many of these projections there will ultimately be'. This may raise questions about learnability and concerns that formal theories of syntax try to account for phenomena that would better be handled in semantic, pragmatic, or processing terms (Polinsky and Kluender 2007: 277).

There is thus little agreement on whether and how much discourse pragmatics should be represented in the syntax, and we won't be taking a stand on this matter here. However, depending on which line of approach is chosen, the locus or type of the interface in one's model of language knowledge may change. In the generative tradition, linguistic competence is mentally represented by means of an abstract linguistic system, the grammar. In this grammar, different components or modules interface with each other (White's 2009 'grammar-internal interfaces'), and they also interface with other, grammar-external, domains such as the conceptual-intentional system. A 'discourse-free' syntax approach thus necessarily involves an external

---

[7] Due to effects of pressure on planning and language production in real time, there may also be processing explanations for correlating linguistic-form/discourse-function tendencies (Arnold *et al.* 2000).

interface with an interpretive module. A 'discourse-laden' syntax à la Rizzi strives to treat discourse-pragmatic notions essentially as syntactic and as part of the computational system of the grammar. But if they are part of the computational system this suggests a grammar-*internal* interface (notwithstanding the existence of a grammar-external interface with an interpretive module). As mentioned in section 19.1, recent L2 research points fairly consistently to learner problems associated with interface phenomena that involve a relationship between syntax and discourse pragmatics. But it seems to us that there is no theory-neutral answer to the question whether L2ers have greater problems at grammar-external interfaces than at grammar-internal interfaces, and to whether the problems are pragmatic or grammatical in nature, since the answer very much depends on the formal theory of syntax chosen.

19.3.2 *Language-specific Differences in the Pre-field*

Let us now turn again to the pre-field. In principle, this clause-initial, pre-verbal position in V2 declaratives can contain virtually any constituent in German and Swedish, some modal particles excluded (e.g. Zifonun *et al.* 1997; Teleman *et al.* 1999). On the view that a description of syntax of a language should aim for specifying the possible strings, regardless of the likelihood that such strings will sound felicitous in a particular discourse context (e.g. Prince 1998), we can say that the syntactic constraints on the pre-field and on how to start a V2 declarative clause in the two languages are the same. Not surprisingly, Swedish and German as well as other Germanic V2 languages are often assumed to behave alike concerning the function and frequency of pre-field constituents. A distribution of 70 per cent or 60 per cent subject-initial vs 30 per cent or 40 per cent non-subject-initial is assumed—implicitly or explicitly– for all V2 languages (e.g. Håkansson 1997: 50), though such figures are not based on corpora counts.

However, our own work suggests that V2 languages may differ substantially in the way they make use of the pre-field, both quantitatively and qualitatively. We will start with some quantitative differences. Subject-initial clauses are consistently more frequent in Swedish than in German corpora, especially so if genre is kept constant, whereas object-initial clauses are much less frequent than in German: For German newspapers for instance, Fabricius-Hansen and Solfjeld (1994) report 54 per cent subject-initial and 7 per cent object-initial main clauses. For Swedish by contrast, Westman (1974: 155–9) finds 66 per cent subject-initial and only 2 per cent object-initial main clauses in a corpus of newspaper articles and other non-fiction texts from textbooks

TABLE 1. Overt constituents in the pre-field, written L1 data (informal letters).[8]

	Subjects & expletives	Objects	Temporal & locational adverbials	Other adverbials	Other constituents
Adult L1 Swedish (30)	73% 388/535	3% 14/535	14% 77/535	6% 30/535	2% 10/535
Adult L1 German (35)	50% 587/1173	7% 87/1173	17% 199/1173	18% 215/1173	1% 13/1173

and brochures issued by the authorities. Other corpora show very similar distributions, as reported on in Bohnacker and Rosén (2007).

19.3.3 Language-specific Differences in Our Own Corpus Data

In order to verify and further investigate these language-specific tendencies, we collected informal written data from native speakers matched for age. These Swedish and German corpora consist of 150 compositions (informal letters and essays, 46 000 words) from 15-to-16-year-old pupils and 20–25-year-old university students. Informants were chosen to match the ages and backgrounds of our L2 learners (to be reported on later).

Clear differences emerge concerning the frequencies of constituent types in the pre-field (Table 1, from Bohnacker and Rosén 2008). Swedish has a stronger subject-initial preference (73 per cent) than German (50 per cent); objects are fronted more often in German (7 per cent) than in Swedish (3 per cent), and adverbials other than temporal and locational are fronted more frequently in German (18 per cent) than in Swedish (6 per cent). These differences are statistically significant for subjects and expletives ($\chi^2 = 75.797$, $p < 0.001$), objects ($\chi^2 = 15.216$, $p < 0.001$) and other adverbials ($\chi^2 = 58.951$, $p < 0.001$), but not for temporal and locational adverbials. Here we compare only informal letters in order to avoid any potential confounding effects that different text types might cause. Table 1 shows the results for our 20-to-25-year-old informants; the data from 15-to-16-year-olds look very similar (Rosén 2006: 78–82).

19.3.3.1 *Subjects and Expletives in the Pre-field* Concerning subjects, it is particularly interesting to see that expletive *det* 'it' in the pre-field is much more frequent in Swedish than expletive *es* 'it' in German. In Rosén's (2006) corpora of informal letters, 22 per cent of all subject-initial sentences

[8] The figures in Table 1 do not add up to 100%. The remaining percent are made up of 16 subordinate clauses for Swedish and 72 for German (see Rosén 2006).

TABLE 2. Expletive subjects in the pre-field, written data (informal letters).

	Expletives out of all overt pre-field constituents	Expletives out of all subjects
Adult L1 Swedish (30)	16% 85/535	22% 85/388
Adult L1 German (35)	6% 66/1173	11% 66/587

beginning with an expletive in Swedish, but only 11 per cent do so in German, as shown in Table 2.[9]

Percentages may be different for corpora of other text types, but our point here is that when keeping genre constant, there is a clear asymmetry between German and Swedish, and as we will presently argue, this is likely to be due to different tendencies concerning information structure and thematic progression.

Swedish declaratives that contain an informationally new ('rhematic') subject typically have a clause-initial expletive subject, *det* 'it', as in (1). The proper subject (*många utbytesstudenter* 'many exchange students', *mycket* 'much') occurs post-verbally. Alternatively, one could front an element encoding new information, like the rhematic subject *många utbytesstudenter* or the locational adverbial *i stan*, as in (1'). But such sentences are dispreferred in Swedish and rarely occur in our native-speaker corpus. By contrast, native Germans hardly ever use a clause-initial expletive subject here, but start the clause with a phonologically heavier rhematic element, as in (2).

(1) a. **Det** studerar många utbytesstudenter   här.
        it   study   many exchange-students here
        'Lots of exchange students study here.'

     b. **Det** händer   mycket i   stan.
        it   happens much   in town
        'There's a lot going on in town.'

(1') a. <u>Många utbytesstudenter</u>   studerar här.   (dispreferred)
         many exchange-students study   here

      b. <u>I   stan</u> händer   mycket.   (dispreferred)
         in town happens much

<hr>

[9] A similar asymmetry emerges for informal speech: in two corpora of spoken Swedish, 16% (99/623) and 19% (578/3068) of all subject-initial declaratives start with an expletive, but in a comparable corpus of spoken German only 3% (39/1190) do so (Bohnacker 2010).

(2)   a. <u>Viele AustauschstudentInnen</u> studieren hier.
      many exchange-students   study   here
      'Lots of exchange students study here.'

    b. <u>In der Stadt</u> ist   viel   los.
      in the town   is   much   on
      'There's a lot going on in town.'

(2′) a. **Es** studieren viele AustauschstudentInnen hier. (dispreferred)
      it study   many exchange-students   here

    b. **Es** ist viel   los in der Stadt.   (dispreferred)
      it is much on in the town

The following authentic, representative examples illustrate that German speakers easily start a sentence with a rhematic constituent (underlined, (3/4a)), whilst Swedish speakers preferably do so with a thematic subject or an expletive (boldface, (3/4b)).

(3)   Context: A student comments on the mentality of other students at her university

    a. Ger. Ich habe den Eindruck,   daß   alle sehr offen sind.
             I   get   the impression that   all very open are
             <u>Viele Freunde meines festen</u>   <u>privaten Freundeskreises</u> habe
             many friends my   regular personal friend's-circle have
             ich allerdings   schon   während meiner Schulzeit [...]
             I   though   already   during my   school-days
             kennengelernt.
             got-to-know (L1 German student)

    b. Swe. **Jag** har   lärt känna flera   av mina nära vänner redan
             I   have got know several of my   close friends already
             tidigare.
             earlier
             'I got to know many of my close friends already back at school though.'

(4)   a. Ger. <u>Mit</u>   <u>den Übersetzungsklausuren</u> lief   es nicht so gut.
             with   the translation-exams   went it not   so well

    b. Swe. **Det** gick inte så bra   med översättningstentorna.
             it   went not so well with translation-exams-the
             'Things didn't go so well with the translation exams.'

The difference between the two languages is not categorical; it would be grammatical to rephrase (3a) to begin with an informationally old element such as pronominal *ich* 'I' instead of the informationally new *viele Freunde meines festen privaten Freundeskreises*, and it would also be grammatical to begin (4a) with an expletive *es* 'it' instead of informationally new *Mit den Übersetzungsklausuren*. Likewise, it is possible to rephrase the Swedish sentences in (3b/4b) and start with an element of new information instead of an informationally old subject or expletive. But this is not what native speakers tend to do.

Our corpus data suggest that Swedish has a stronger preference for 'rheme later', where rhematic/new information is realized further to the right in the clause. This discourse-pragmatic difference, we believe, lies at the heart of why corpus data exhibit quantitative differences as in Tables 1–2 and why native Germans change the beginnings of sentences in L2 texts to make them 'sound more German' (see 19.4.2–19.4.3).

19.3.3.2 *Other Elements in the Pre-field*   There is a range of constructions with an element of low informational content in the pre-field (e.g. *så*-constructions, clefts), but for reasons of space we cannot go into all of them here. In Bohnacker and Rosén (2007, 2008) we show that these are used more frequently in Swedish than in German.

A similar tendency manifests itself in the case of fronted objects. Recall that object-initial declaratives, though generally uncommon, are more frequent in German (7 per cent) than in Swedish (3 per cent, Table 1). In our corpora, Swedish native speakers typically front objects that are given information, mostly in the form of the definite inanimate pronoun *det* ('it/that'), as in (5).

(5)   Jag tänker lära   mig segla i   sommar, men **det** har jag   inte
       I   intend learn me sail in summer but it   have I   not
       bestämt ännu.
       decided yet
       'I'm thinking of learning how to sail this summer, but I haven't decided yet.'

Such thematic *det* is much more frequent than equivalent *das/es* in our German data: *det* makes up 82 per cent of all fronted object pronouns, but *das* only 24 per cent (Rosén 2006: 99–102). This distribution appears to be common in informal written Swedish texts by young people and colloquial speech (cf. Jörgensen 1976: 110–13, Bohnacker and Rosén 2008).

Native Germans front a wider range of objects, both lexical and pronominal (e.g. *mir* 'me', *ihn* 'him'). And they make use of 'pronominal adverbs' (*Pronominaladverbien*). These are thematic elements that are compounded of a locational adverb (typically, *da* 'there') and a preposition. Some examples are *dazu* 'there-to/with that', *darauf* 'there-on/on that', *daran* 'there-on/on that'. Their morphological complexity makes pronominal adverbs informationally more specific than simple thematic *das/det* 'it/that' or *da/där* 'there'. Some pronominal adverbs also exist in Swedish but are restricted to archaic expressions and formal registers and do not occur in our corpus. Pronominal adverbs maintain a referent in spatial, temporal and other terms, and are thus a means to establish textual coherence in German. In (6) for instance, the rhematic information of the first clause, *segeln zu lernen* 'learning how to sail', is turned via *damit* 'with that' into the theme of the next. This corresponds in Swedish to a sentence without a pronominal adverb; cf. (5) above.

(6) Außerdem habe ich vor segeln zu lernen, aber **damit**   werde
     moreover have I   PRT sailing to learn   but there-with will
     ich wohl   bis zum   Sommer warten.
     I   probably till till-the summer wait
     'I'd also like to learn how to sail, but I'll probably wait with that till the summer.'

In sum, German and Swedish employ slightly different means to establish textual coherence. German has a stronger preference for new/rhematic information in clause-initial position compared to Swedish, where rhematic information is realized further to the right in the clause ('rheme later').[10] To achieve this, Swedish speakers start their sentences with elements of no or low informational value, such as expletives, thematic subjects, and object pronouns.

19.4 The Pre-field in L2 German

19.4.1 *Informants*

Our L2 learners are those whose V2 acquisition we reported in section 19.2. The oral L2 production data (30 000 words) come from six Swedish L1 adults, taking evening classes in German as a foreign language for beginners, and from twenty-three Swedish L1 teenagers learning German as a foreign language at secondary school in Sweden. Data were elicited from all learners with the same narrative task, the telling of a monologue on a given topic (see Bohnacker 2005: 56, 2006: 15–18). The teenagers were tested once, at the end of

---

[10] Swedish also seems to have a stronger tendency to start the sentence with a phonologically light element than German does. Light weight and thematicity/givenness go hand in hand (cf. Arnold *et al.* 2000).

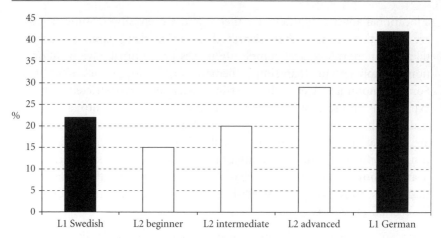

FIGURE 4 Percentages of non-subject-initial declaratives in L2ers and L1ers (letters).

their third year of German (age 16). They are referred to as intermediates. The adults (age 60–70) were tested twice, after four months or forty-five hours of classroom German, and again after nine months or ninety hours of German, and are referred to as beginners. Three adults did not know any language other than Swedish before taking up German, whilst the other three, and the teenagers, had learnt English earlier at school.

Our written L2 data consist of texts produced by teenage and adult Swedish learners of German at secondary schools and universities in Sweden. The informants had all learnt English at school before taking up German. 245 German compositions, comprising informal letters, essays, and summaries, totalling 100 000 words, were collected between 1999 and 2005 (Rosén 2006: 73–5). There were fifty-five 14-year-old beginners (with 200 hours of classroom German), fifty-five 17-year-old intermediates (with 830 hours of classroom German), and 135 L2 advanced productions by 20–25-year-old university students who had taken German classes for six years.

For a follow-up assessment and rewriting task, we recruited fifty-eight native German speakers. These were divided into three groups (students, teachers, and 'others') and judged and commented on two advanced learner texts each. Twenty native German university students were also asked to rewrite one advanced learner text each, to 'make it sound more German'.

19.4.2 *Quantitative Results*

The frequencies of constituents in the pre-field in our L2 German data differ from those of L1 German but resemble those of L1 Swedish. Figure 4 illustrates

TABLE 3. Non-subject constituents in the pre-field, L2 learners.

	Objects	Temporal & locational adverbials	Other adverbials	Other constituents
L2 beginner (oral)	10% 37/381 all: *das*	83% 317/381 incl. 146 *dann*	7% 27/381	0% 0/381
L2 intermediate (oral)	10% 37/386 incl. 22 *das*	81% 314/386	9% 33/386	1% 2/386
L2 beginner (letters)	3% 3/87	81% 70/87	16% 14/87	0% 0/87
L2 intermediate (letters)	11% 33/295 incl. 16 *das*	70% 207/295	18% 53/295	1% 2/295

this for the text type of informal letters. Black bars show the percentage of non-subject-initial clauses out of all declaratives for L1 Swedish (22 per cent) and for L1 German (42 per cent). Compare this with the L2 productions (white bars): For the L2 beginners, the pre-field contains a constituent other than the subject only 15 per cent of the time (85/569), for the intermediates, 20 per cent (281/1413), and for the advanced learners, 29 per cent (343/1175). Thus, non-subject-initial clauses become more common with increasing proficiency level, but even the most advanced learner group has not reached nativelike levels after six years of German.

The non-subject-initial clauses of the learners can be broken down further by constituent type (Table 3). Here, the figures for the L2 oral and written letter data are strikingly similar.[11] Fronted objects are rare (10–12 per cent) and largely take the form of object pronominal *das* 'it/that'. Most non-subject-initial clauses start with a temporal or locational adverbial (70–83 per cent). Fronted temporals are particularly frequent in the oral narratives, with a preponderance of *dann* 'then'. Other adverbials (e.g. modal, speaker attitude, and connective adverbs) are much less frequent in the pre-field (7–18 per cent). Fronted pronominal adverbs are not found at all.

Results from a rewriting experiment bolster the differences we found concerning constituents in the pre-field (Rosén 2006: 96–7, 102–38). When twenty German informants were asked to rewrite twenty advanced L2 texts produced by learners their own age to 'make them sound more German',

[11] Note that despite the difference in modality, the two genres are related: informal oral mono-logical narratives on a given topic and informal monological letters on a given topic.

TABLE 4. Constituents in the pre-field in twenty L2-German texts and L1-German rewritings.

	Subjects & expletives	Objects	Temporal & locational adverbials	Other adverbials
Advanced L2 German	68% 366/538	3% 17/538	16% 88/538	8% 42/538
Rewritten by natives	55% 363/658	7% 43/658	18% 120/658	14% 95/658

rewriting resulted in a reduction of clause-initial subjects and expletives from 68 per cent to 55 per cent, and in a doubling of the figures for objects and adverbials other than temporal and locational (Table 4). These differences are statistically significant for subjects and expletives ($\chi^2 = 19.295$, $p = 0.000$), objects ($\chi^2 = 6.932$, p. $= 0.001$), and other adverbials ($\chi^2 = 8.998$, $p = 0.003$), but not for temporal and locational adverbials ($\chi^2 = 0.639$, $p = 0.424$).[12]

Thus, the distribution of constituent types in the rewritten texts became very similar to the distribution independently found in the L1 German corpus (Table 1). This strongly suggests that the differences between the groups cannot be dismissed as stylistic variation in the sense of idiosyncratic preferences of individuals, but that they are in fact consistent, language-specific differences.

19.4.3 *Qualitative Results*

In contrast to the native Germans, our L2 learners rarely start their sentences with an element of new information, but tend to produce expletive-initial clauses where rhematic information is postponed, e.g. (7). These are dispreferred in German, but correspond to the expletive-initial constructions preferred in Swedish.

(7)   Autobahn! **Es** ist nicht mehr eine gleich aggressive Stimmung
       motorway   it is not   more a   same aggressive mood
       auf Autobahn...
       on motorway
       'Motorways. There isn't this aggressive mood on the motorways in
       Germany any more'

(advanced L2 summary)

---

[12] The figures in Table 4 do not add up to 100%. The remaining percent comprise 25 subordinate clauses in the advanced L2 German and 37 in the native German rewritings.

Supporting evidence also comes from a judgement, or rating, task (Rosén 2006) where 58 native speakers commented upon the L2 texts, pointing out "zu viel *es* am Satzanfang" [too many *es* in clause-initial position], un-German *es*-constructions, and "zu viel *es gibt*" [too many *es gibt* 'it is/exists']. Native Germans prefer to use alternative ways of connecting sentences, for instance by fronting an adverbial, as in (8'), which is the rewritten version of the L2 version in (8), or by adding a connective adverb.

(8)   Es ist in dem königlichen Zimmern, wo   den Besuchern die
      it is in the   royal   rooms   where the visitors   the
      Motive aus   Mittelalterem   Märchen begegnen [. . .]
      scenes from mediaeval   sagas   meet   (advanced L2)
      'In the royal rooms visitors will see scenes from mediaeval sagas.'

(8') In den königlichen Zimmern begegnen den Besuchern
      in the royal   rooms   meet   the visitors
      Motive aus   mittelalterlichen Märchen.
      scenes from mediaeval   sagas
                                        (rewritten by native speaker)

As for objects, our L2ers only rarely produce an object in the pre-field, but when they do, they predominantly front pronominal *das* (80 per cent), and such *das* is always thematic, as in (9). The native judges of our L2 texts comment on such *das*: 'zu viele Sätze fangen mit *das* an' [too many sentences start with *das*].

(9)   Ab   und zu   machen wir auch Sachen zusammen, **das**
      now and then make   we too   things together   that
      muss man.
      must you
      'Now and then we do things together, you have to.'
                                        (advanced L2 essay)

Fronted object *das* as produced by our L2 learners is not ungrammatical in German, it is simply less common. The native Germans front *das* as well but also a wider range of objects, and they front pronominal adverbs (11 per cent). None of our L2ers do so at beginner and intermediate level (0 per cent), and even at advanced level, pronominal adverbs in the pre-field remain rare (4 per cent).

There are many other adverbials that can be used in the pre-field to build textual cohesion, for instance sentence adverbs such as speaker-attitude *vielleicht* 'perhaps', *natürlich* 'of course', and logical connectives such as *außerdem* 'moreover', *deshalb/deswegen/daher* 'therefore'. Interestingly though, these 'other adverbials' are significantly more frequent in the pre-field in native German (18 per cent) than in Swedish (6 per cent, Table 1). It is thus perhaps not surprising that our L2 learners underuse such adverbials in the pre-field, as evinced by the fact that when advanced L2 texts were rewritten by native Germans, figures nearly doubled from 8 per cent to 14 per cent (Table 4). Sometimes native speakers move a connective adverbial from post-verbal position to the pre-field, as in (10'), the rewritten version of (10), or simply add a logical connective.

(10)   Man weiß   jetzt, mehr als   früher, daß es nicht selbstklar
        one knows now   more than before   that it not   self-evident
        eine Familie zu haben ist. Ich finde **deswegen**, daß...
        a   family   to have   is   I   think therefore   that
        'Nowadays people know better than before that you don't just have a
        family as a matter of course. Therefore I think that...'

                                                           (advanced L2 essay)

(10')   [...]. **Deswegen** finde ich, daß...
                 therefore   think I   that   (rewritten by native speaker)

Native judges also repeatedly characterize a lack of adverbials in clause-initial position as un-German: 'Adverbiale am Satzanfang fehlen' [clauses should more often begin with an adverbial], 'es gibt zu wenig kommentierende Wörter wie *leider, zum Glück* etc. am Satzanfang' [there are not enough commentary words like *leider* 'unfortunately', *zum Glück* 'fortunately', etc. in clause-initial position], 'Der Gebrauch von *Dadurch, Deshalb* etc. würde den Text flüssiger machen' [using *dadurch, deshalb*, etc. would improve textual coherence].

The native German comments and rewritings thus confirm the results from our L1 and L2 analyses. For detailed discussion, see Bohnacker and Rosén (2007, 2008).

19.5 Conclusion

In this chapter, we have used corpus data from two closely related languages, German and Swedish, to shed light on the interaction of syntax and discourse pragmatics concerning the pre-field of V2 declaratives. Our corpora exhibit different frequency distributions of pre-field constituents; for instance, 73 per cent of Swedish declaratives start with a subject, but only 50 per cent do so in German. Rates of clause-initial expletives are substantially higher in Swedish than in German, whilst rates of objects and adjuncts are lower. We traced these distributional differences back to discourse-pragmatic differences in the functions of V2 declaratives: German has a stronger preference for new/rhematic information in clause-initial position compared to Swedish, where new information is realized further to the right in the clause ('rheme later'). To achieve this, Swedish native speakers tend to fill the pre-field position with elements of no informational value such as expletives or with elements of low informational value, such as an informationally given subject or object pronoun. German too allows these options, but also places rhematic subjects as well as phonologically heavier objects and adverbials in the pre-field, including morphologically complex pronominal adverbs and a range of connective and sentence adverbials.

We also looked at the interaction of syntax and discourse pragmatics in L2 acquisition. When investigating Swedish-speaking learners of German as a foreign language, we found that they employ V2 already after a few months of exposure—years before they put that syntax to appropriate discursive use. Early mastery of V2 suggests syntactic transfer from L1 Swedish. However, an analysis of the learner corpora also indicates that transfer of this syntactic property goes hand in hand with discourse-pragmatic transfer at beginning, intermediate, and advanced level. In Swedish, there are stricter constraints on what can (or does) occur in the pre-field than in German, and this difference has repercussions for L2 acquisition. The learners use the pre-field mainly for informationally given elements and expletives, thereby underusing the position from a German perspective. In support of these findings, we reported on a rewriting experiment where native informants commented on and rewrote advanced L2 texts 'to make them sound more German'. The results illustrated that the L2 usage, despite fully grammatical V2, comes across as non-native. L1 constraints on information structure are not relaxed even though they are too restrictive for the L2, resulting in texts that are unidiomatic and not fully cohesive from the perspective of a native speaker. Like much of the research in this relatively new area of L2 interface phenomena, our results suggest that mastery of 'pure' syntax is well in advance of mastery of appropriate discourse-pragmatic use of that syntax.

Do these findings tell us anything about the architecture of grammar and the interfaces involved? One could certainly describe our results with a 'discourse-free' theory of syntax, where V2 is identical across languages, but where discourse-pragmatic differences between Swedish and German and ensuing L2 problems are treated as *pragmatic* and outside of grammar and located at an external interface with the conceptual-intentional system (cf. Prince 1998; White 2009). Or one could try to capture the results with a cartographic approach to syntax, where discourse-pragmatic differences and

L2 problems would be treated as essentially *syntactic* and *grammar-internal* and located inside the computational system (e.g. Belletti and Leonini 1994). We will refrain from doing either here. We have illustrated cross-linguistic differences concerning the relationship between word order and discourse pragmatics in V2 declaratives in Swedish and German and shown that learners— subtly but persistently—transfer information-structural patterns from their L1 into the L2. In our view, this evidence for transfer can and should stand independently of any particular theoretical slant.

Processing (In)alienable Possessions at the Syntax-Semantics Interface

CHIEN-JER CHARLES LIN

20.1 Introduction

Possession is an important predicative function commonly expressed in human languages. It is expressed in the form of verbs such as *have* and *be* as in *John has a car* in English and *C'est livre est de Charles* 'This book is of Charles (literal translation)' in French, and in the nominal domain, via possessive noun phrases such as *John's mother* and *the mother of John*. In this chapter, we focus on the construction and interpretation of possessive relations in sentences. In particular, we discuss the special syntactic and semantic properties of relational nouns in contrast with those of non-relational nouns. We show that alienable and inalienable nouns have distinct linguistic behaviours and they induce distinguishable processing patterns in online sentence comprehension.

Possession is used here as a cover term for a wide range of relations held between nominal entities. The phrase *the girl's professor*, for example, can be interpreted in multiple ways, some of which are listed in (1).

(1) the girl's professor:
   a. the person who teaches the girl as a professor in college
   b. the professor that the girl assisted
   c. the professor that the girl is investigating
   d. the professor that the girl writes about

Possessive constructions serve to associate two noun phrases while not specifying precisely how this association should be interpreted. Nevertheless, certain interpretations seem to dominate over others. For instance, within a neutral context, *the girl's professor* is preferably interpreted as the professor of the girl in college in (1a), rather than the professor that the girl writes about in (1d). In (2)–(4), the interpretations in the (a)s are preferred in comparison with those in the (b)s. That is, relations such as kinships terms, ownership, part/whole, and agentivity, are the preferred interpretations in comparison with other pragmatically motivated interpretations.

(2) the boy's mother:
   a. the woman who is the female parent of the boy
   b. the mother who the boy was painting a portrait of

(3) the boy's hand:
   a. the hand on the arm of the boy
   b. the hand of a sculpture that the boy was sketching

(4) the boy's essay:
   a. the essay that the boy wrote
   b. the essay by E. B. White that the boy will talk about in class

Due to the range of plausible interpretations in these possessive phrases, how to reach an appropriate interpretation based on the syntactic, semantic, and discourse information available becomes a critical issue. In this chapter, we look at a specific group of nouns—the inalienable nouns (e.g., kinship terms and body parts)—which are inherently relational. These nouns are not derived from verbs, so their relational nature cannot have been a result of the argument structure of verbs. They are relational in the sense that they create a relation between the noun itself and another entity, which is usually interpreted as the possessor of the noun. Interpretations of these possessive relations lie at the interface of syntax, semantics, and pragmatics as these interpretations can be felicitous or infelicitous due to violations in these different aspects.

20.2 Alienable and Inalienable Nouns: An Initial Differentiation

In some languages, inalienable nouns appear differently than alienable nouns inside noun phrases. Chatino—an Otomangean language of the Zapotecan family, for instance, places possessor NPs immediately after relational nouns that denote 'body parts, body pain and body fluids, family members, and certain concrete possessions like houses and clothes, as well as certain abstract posses-sions like language and memory' (Carleton and Waksler 2000: 392). Alienable nouns require the adposition *ji?i* to appear between the noun being possessed and the possessor. The following Chatino examples (Carleton and Waksler ibid) illustrate this difference. Examples (5) and (6) are both noun phrases with relational nouns, while (7) is a noun phrase with an alienable noun.[1]

---

[1] One of the reviewers suggested that, in languages such as Vietnamese, the preposition in noun phrases with alienable nouns such as (7) tends to be omitted when the possessive relation between the

(5) yane kuna?a
     neck woman
     'woman's neck'

(6) ike ni?i
     head house
     'the house's roof'

(7) xolo? ji?i Jua
     knife of Juan
     'Juan's knife'

In many other languages (e.g., Chinese, English, Japanese, Korean, French), even though alienable and inalienable nouns are not overtly distinguishable, there remain unique semantic and syntactic properties associated with these nouns. Patterns of sentence comprehension, which we report in section 20.4, provide evidence that corroborates this distinction.

These alienable and inalienable nouns have been given distinct semantic representations. In Barker's (1995) treatment of possessive descriptions, nouns are distinguished into those that express intrinsic possessive relations (e.g., *child*) and those that construct possessive relations extrinsically (e.g., *human*). The denotation of *child* presupposes the existence of a person that takes this child as an offspring. It is, therefore, a two-place predicate, relating a possessor argument and a person that is possessed as a child. A *human*, on the other hand, composes a one-place predicate; it is itself argument-complete. This distinction is characterized by the contrastive grammaticality in (8–9; cf. Barker 1995: 76):

(8) Lexical possession:
     a. a child of John
     b. John's child

(9) Extrinsic possession:
     a. a human (*of John)
     b. John's human

Postnominal possessives (8a and 9a) in English can only be used with relational nouns since the nominal head is obligatorily supplied with an internal argument. Given that *human* does not take an internal argument,

two nouns is unambiguous. The appearance of the preposition between the nouns may have to do with the potential ambiguity that exists between the noun phrases. When the relation is unambiguous, the preposition tends to be omitted.

a human of John in (9a) is ill-formed. Prenominal possessives like (8b) and (9b) take both intrinsic and extrinsic possessive arguments depending on at which level the possession is formed. In prenominal possessions, therefore, the two nominal arguments hold an ambiguous relation—both lexical and extrinsic possessions are possible. Lexical possession is formed at the level internal to the noun phrase, creating an inherent inalienable relation only in (8b). Extrinsic possession is obtained by coercing a relation between the possessee and the possessor based on the pragmatic context, which is possible in both (8b) and (9b). Thus, while *John's child* can mean either 'the offspring of John (i.e., lexical possession)' or 'the child (of someone else) that John is taking care of (i.e., extrinsic possession with the internal argument suppressed),' *John's human* exclusively denotes a human that is not possessed by John but is related to John in some way based on the context (i.e., extrinsic possession). For instance, this human can be a sketch of a human body that John just created.

Barker (1995: 54) represents the meaning of lexical possession as (10), and that of extrinsic possession as (11). R stands for a two-place predicate, while P stands for a one-place relation. π stands for the extrinsic possessive relation, which is interpreted based on the context.

(10)   Lexical possession: $\lambda R[R]$

(11)   Extrinsic possession: $\lambda P \lambda x \lambda y [\pi(x, y) \wedge P(y)]$

The notion of relational nouns is often discussed under the rubric of *inalienable possessions.* Vergnaud and Zubizarreta (1992: 596) referred to inalienable nouns as 'inherently defined in terms of another object, of which it is a part' and involving '*argument dependency in lexical representations* [italics original].' Accordingly, inalienable nouns take semantic arguments at the lexical level, assigning the role of POSSESSOR to these obligatory arguments that they take. Body-part terms are the 'inherent, universal' inalienable nouns, with the extended categories including 'nouns for clothes, kinship terms, picture nouns, and still others' (Vergnaud and Zubizarreta 1992: 597). In this chapter, we focus on kinship terms.[2]

---

[2] It is worth noting that inalienable possessions, though seemingly conceptually based, are not direct reflections of people's encyclopedic knowledge about such relations. The distinction between inalienable and alienable possessives is at least partially idiosyncratic and grammatical. Barker (1995: 59) exemplified this point by stating that the concept of *human*, though presupposing the existence of a person and the existence of his parents and grandparents, does not encode such relations as part of the lexical knowledge. The term *child*, as a lexical possessive, would emphasize the possessive relation between a human being and his parents.

Based on argument saturation at the lexical level and the additional discourse-linked operator π for interpreting extrinsic possessions, the asymmetry presented in (2)–(4) has a representational explanation. For inalienable nouns such as *mother* and *hand*, a genitive construction naturally takes the available argument as the possessor, satiating the possessor argument requirement at the lexical level of possession. The secondary discourse-motivated interpretations can be construed when the required possessor argument is suppressed and when a discourse-bound operator π is coerced into existence.[3]

20.3 Alienability and Syntactic Alternations

As discussed so far, inalienable nouns subcategorize for an internal possessor argument at the lexical level of the representation. Based on this subcategorizational difference, inalienable and alienable nouns also diverge in syntax (Alexiadou 2003; Castillo 2001; Español-Echevarria 1997). In (12), where a part-whole relation has to exist between the external argument position (*John*) and the secondary predicate, for instance, only inalienable nouns such as body parts can appear in these secondary predicates, not alienable nouns.[4] In (13), the inalienable noun *son* has to be licensed by a possessor argument. When the possessor of this kinship term cannot be identified, the sentence (e.g., 13b) is ungrammatical.[5]

(12) a. Mary kicked John on the *leg*.
      b. *Mary kicked John on the *door*.

(13) a. A *man* came into the room.
      b. *A *son* came into the room.
      c. Mary's *son* came into the room.
      d. Mary has a son.

Previous syntactic literature on alienability (e.g., see review in Antrim 1996) generally agrees that inalienable nouns take arguments. This argument has to be bound by an antecedent at a higher level—either in the same sentence or in the discourse. In (13), the possessor appears at the specifier position of the possessive DP in (13c), and at the specifier of the sentential CP in (13d).

---

[3] Barker (2008: 7) analyses this process as applying a detransitivizing type shifter Ex and then applying the 'pragmatically-controlled relational variable' π.

[4] Note that this structure is limited to part-whole relations and does not extend to the kinship relations. That is, it is ungrammatical to say *Mary kicked John on the father*, even though *the father* here is an inalienable noun.

[5] Given enough contextual information about the possessor, however, this sentence can become more acceptable as in *A son came into the room to look for his mother*.

Notably, what is crucial in these sentences with inalienable nouns is that a c-commanding relation has to exist between a possessor argument and the noun itself, not just the linear precedence of the possessor relative to the inalienable noun. In Lin (2006), I demonstrated that in Mandarin possessive relative clauses, where the relative clauses are followed by their head nouns, a kinship term that appears at the sentence-initial position as in (14a) can linearly precede its possessor argument (i.e., the head of the relative clause). This sentence is nevertheless grammatical because the inalienable noun is c-commanded by the head-noun. (14b), however, is ungrammatical because the possessor argument of the inalienable noun is not bound by any c-commanding antecedent.

(14) a. 女兒被卡車撞死的那位校長感到痛心。[6]

     nyuer   bei   kache zhuangsi de   nawei xiaozhang gandao
     daughter BEI truck hit-dead REL that   president feel
     tongxin
     heartbroken
     'The president whose daughter was hit dead by a truck was heartbroken.'

    b. *女兒被卡車撞死。

     nyuer   bei   kache zhuangsi
     daughter BEI truck hit-dead
     'Daughter was hit dead by a truck.'

Binding relations can be satiated not only within the same sentence by a c-commanding relation but also within the immediate discourse whereby who the possessor is can be inferred. Therefore, (14b) can become acceptable if the context provides sufficient information to license the possessor argument (i.e., the parent(s)) subcategorized for by *daughter*.

One consequence of the analysis that an inalienable noun takes a syntactic argument is that the possessor argument is subcategorized for and receives its theta role at the lower base-generated position close to the inalienable noun. Syntactic derivations associated with this implicit possessor argument have been accounted for using *possessor extraction* or *possessor raising*, which occur across predicate boundaries such as those of secondary predicates.[7] In the

---

[6] Abbreviations used in the transliteration: ACC: accusative case; BEI: passive marker in Mandarin; CL: classifier; DEC: declarative marker; GEN: genitive case; NOM: nominative case; PST: past tense; REL: relativizer.

[7] See Castillo (2001) for a typological review of possessor raising across languages. An alternative account resorts to binding relations between the higher possessor argument and the empty possessive pronoun. The fact that a possessive pronoun can sometimes appear at the possessor argument

following, we provide examples where secondary predications involving alienable and inalienable nouns have distinct syntactic realizations in three languages—Japanese, Korean, and Chinese. These languages demonstrate the existence of a possessor argument position that needs to be licensed by a possessor operator.

In Japanese, the alienability of a noun phrase is related to whether it can compose a secondary predicate. Inalienable nouns form argument-taking predicates while alienable nouns do not. This can be shown by contrasting (15a–b) and (15c–d) (Ogawa 2001: 13).

(15) a. Taroo ga   Hanako no   syasin o   mita.
          Taroo NOM Hanako GEN picture ACC saw
          'Taroo saw Hanako's picture.'

      b. Taroo ga   Hanako o   syasin-de mita.
          Taroo NOM Hanako ACC picture-in saw
          'Taroo saw Hanako in a picture.'

      c. Taroo ga   Hanako no   kuruma o   mita.
          Taroo NOM Hanako GEN car   ACC saw
          'Taroo saw Hanako's car.'

      d. *Taroo ga   Hanako o   kuruma-de mita.
          Taroo NOM Hanako ACC car-in   saw
          'Taroo saw Hanako in a car.'

Like *John's child* in (8b), *Hanako no syasin* 'Hanako's picture' in (15a) is ambiguous. In the inalienable sense, Hanako is the person whose picture has been taken; in the alienable sense, Hanako can be the person who took the picture or just a person who owns the picture (in which someone else appears). Only the inalienable sense is possible with (15b), where the inalienable noun forms a stage-level predicate that appears in a secondary predicate. The possessor position is licensed by *Hanako*, a possessor argument that has been raised to receive the accusative case. In (15c), where *kuruma* 'car' is an alienable noun, a secondary predicate like (15d) is unlicensed as there is no possessor position inside the secondary predicate to be bound by the possessor, *Hanako*.

Analogous examples are drawn from the 'multiple object construction' in Korean (Choe 1987: 101, cited in Ogawa 2001: 6), in which only body parts are allowed to appear in secondary predicates:

position in some languages suggests that the empty position can be a pronoun bound by the possessor. Therefore, even though we adopt a raising analysis for most of the data discussed below, the possibility of a pronoun analysis is not excluded.

(16) a. Chelsoo ka   Yenghilul   noon lul   po-at-ta.
          Chelsoo NOM Yenghi-ACC eye   ACC   see-PST-DEC
          'Chelsoo saw Yenghi's eye.'

      b. *Chelsoo ka   Yenghilul   kwaja lul   mek-et-ta.
          Chelsoo NOM Yenghi-ACC cookie ACC eat-PST-DEC
          'Chelsoo ate Yenghi's cookie.'

Similar patterns can be found in Mandarin Chinese. In the following, we focus on sentences with secondary predicates embedded in Mandarin BA constructions. As in Japanese and Korean, these secondary predicates can only be licensed when they are headed by an inalienable noun with an empty possessive pronoun being c-commanded by a possessor argument. Mandarin BA construction has the linear structure of (17). Semantically, DP1 denotes the do-er; DP2 the do-ee. The VP within the BA-phrase contains a secondary predicate, out of which DP2 moves.[8]

(17)   DP1 BA DP2 V t_{DP2}

The examples in (18) show that when the alienable and inalienable nouns appear inside a possessive phrase headed by the genitive marker *de* in Mandarin (similar to *'s* in English and *no* in Japanese denoting both internal and external possessions), all three DPs—his two legs, his drumstick, and his lecture—can appear as DP2. That is, (18a–c) are well-formed both semantically and syntactically. However, only (18a), in which the noun is inalienable, has a grammatical counterpart in (19).

(18) a. 我 把 他 的   雙   腿 打斷。
          wo ba ta de   shuang tui daduan
          I BA he GEN two   leg break
          'I broke his two legs.'

      b. 我 把 他 的   鼓棒   打斷。
          wo ba ta de   gubang   daduan
          I BA he GEN drumstick break
          'I broke his drumstick.'

      c. 我 把 他 的   演講   打斷。
          wo ba ta de   yanjiang daduan
          I BA he GEN lecture   break
          'I broke (disrupted) his lecture.'

---

[8] See Li (2006) for a comprehensive review of the syntax of Mandarin BA.

(19) a. 我 把 他 打斷 雙   腿。
       wo ba ta daduan shuang tui
       I BA he break two   leg
       'I broke his two legs. (lit. I broke him two legs.)'

    b. *我 把 他 打斷   鼓棒。
       wo ba ta daduan gubang
       I BA he break   drumstick
       'I broke his drumsticks.'

    c. *我 把 他 打斷   演講。
       wo ba ta daduan yanjiang
       I BA he break   lecture
       'I broke (disrupted) his lecture.'

Such contrasts in grammaticality can be accounted for by postulating a possessor argument subcategorized for by *shuangtui* 'the two legs' in the secondary predicate of (19a). This argument position holds a dependency with the possessor *ta* 'he' (i.e., DP2), which has been raised to the specifier position above the VP to receive case. The lack of this possessor argument in (19b) and (19c) broaches the dependency between DP2 and a trace inside the VP, thus leading to the ungrammaticality.[9]

Putting together evidence from the syntax and semantics associated with alienable and inalienable nouns, we propose the structure in (20). Inalienable nouns take an argument at the specifier position, composing a narrow inalienable possessive interpretation.[10]

(20) Structure of inalienable noun phrases

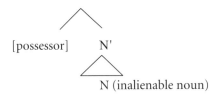

[possessor]   N'

            N (inalienable noun)

---

[9] The grammaticality judgements in this article are based on Mandarin Chinese spoken in Taiwan. Similar judgements were also provided by Cheng and Ritter (1987).

[10] Similarly, adopting the distinction between S-syntax and L-syntax of Hale and Keyser (1991), it has been proposed that inalienable possessions are at the level of L-syntax, and alienable possessions at S-syntax. Suzuki (1997), for instance, proposed a structure where *y* is a relational head that takes the possessor at the specifier position and the possessees (i.e., the inalienable noun itself) as the complement.

Alienable possessive phrases are constructed as a functional phrase taking the alienable noun as the complement and another DP at the specifier position as the external possessor. This functional phrase is headed by a relational variable π, which is interpreted based on the context. The proposed syntactic representation for alienable possessive phrases is provided in (21). In the next section, we examine the processing consequences of these different representations.

(21)   Structure of alienable noun phrases

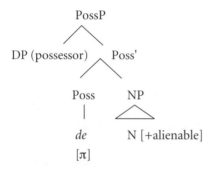

20.4 Processing Alienable and Inalienable Possessions: A Self-paced Reading Experiment

A sentence-comprehension experiment was conducted to investigate the processing of possessive relations. We hypothesize that inalienable noun phrases such as kinship terms subcategorize for a possessor argument. This argument position facilitates the integration of a possessor argument in a sentence as the possessor noun can tightly integrate with the thematic grid created by the inalienable noun. Possessive relations involving alienable nouns, on the other hand, would require additional integration costs because the possessive relation is not readily coded within these alienable noun phrases and an additional functional phrase needs to be coerced, with the operator heading the functional phrase (π) being licensed by a dominant relation in the context.

The distinctive processing of inalienable and alienable possessions mirrors processing differences between arguments and adjuncts in the sentence-processing literature. Much research on sentence comprehension investigated whether the theta role of a gap position is assigned immediately or left unspecified until the verb is reached (Altmann 1999; Aoshima, Phillips, and Weinberg 2004; Boland, Tanenhaus, Garnsey, and Carlson 1995; Stowe, Tanenhaus, and Carlson 1991). With regard to arguments and adjuncts, it is generally agreed that the arguments of a verb are more readily integrated into the sentence than its adjuncts (Ahrens 2003; Boland *et al.* 1995; Schütze and Gibson 1999; Speer and Clifton 1998). Speer and Clifton (1998), for instance, found that participants read preposition phrases faster when they are arguments of a verb than when they are adjuncts. Preposition phrases that can serve as either arguments or adjuncts also tend to be understood as arguments (Schütze and Gibson 1999).

In summary, the nominal entities associated with a verb can be distinguished into arguments and adjuncts. In sentence processing, the arguments of a verb are integrated and understood more easily, while adjuncts take more efforts. We therefore predict that if the possessors of inalienable nouns are indeed arguments, they will be processed faster than the possessors of alienable nouns.[11]

The experiment reported below consisted of self-paced readings of sentences that contain Chinese possessive relative clauses like the following:

(22)   Possessive Relative Clause in Mandarin Chinese
女兒　　打翻　水　　的　那位　先生　　嗓門　　很　大
nyuer   dafan shui   de   nawei xiansheng sangmen hen   da
daughter spill   water REL that   guy   voice   very loud
'The guy whose daughter spilled the water has a loud voice.'

Relative clauses in Chinese are prenominal; that is, the relativized positions are bound by head nouns that follow the relative clauses. In a possessive relative clause like (22), the head noun *xiansheng* 'guy' serves as the possessor of *nyuer* 'daughter' in the relative clause. In accordance with the syntactic and semantic evidence discussed, we hypothesize that the relativized possessor is located at the possessee position.[12] Reading-time data allow us to see whether the alienability of the possessee noun phrase affects how possessive relations are constructed. The following experimental results corroborate the alienable/inalienable distinction in Mandarin nouns.

20.4.1 *Participants*

Twenty-four undergraduate students (six males, eighteen females) from National Cheng-Chi University were paid to participate in the experiment. All participants were native speakers of Mandarin Chinese, who were exposed to Mandarin Chinese since birth. The participants had normal vision, and were naïve to the purpose of the experiment.

---

[11] See also Pylkkänen and McElree (2006: 547–8) for a review on processing differences between arguments and adjuncts.

[12] In Lin (2006) and Lin (2008), I showed that the parser is sensitive to the different structural positions of the possessee in a possessive relative clause, suggesting that a relativized possessor gap does exist at the positions of these possessee noun phrases. When the possessee is at a higher structural position (e.g., the subject) thus being closer to the possessor head, the construction of a possessive dependency is easier than when it is located at a lower position (e.g., the object).

20.4.2 *Materials*

The experimental materials were sentences with passive possessive relative clauses, in which the first noun was a possessee and the head noun of the relative clause served as the possessor.[13] In the inalienable condition, the first noun was an inalienable noun (i.e., a kinship term). In the alienable condition, the first noun was an alienable noun (i.e., a non-kinship personal term). Examples of the materials are provided in (23)–(24):

(23)   Condition A: Inalienable kinship terms
　　　 父親　　被　警察　　抓走　　 的　　總裁　　　顯得　十分
　　　 fuqin　bei　jingcha　zhuazou　de　　zongcai　　 xiande　shifen
　　　 father　BEI　police　take　　 REL　chairperson　appear　very
　　　 慌張。
　　　 huangzhang
　　　 nervous
　　　 'The chairperson whose father was taken by the police appeared very nervous.'

(24)   Condition B: Alienable non-kinship personal terms
　　　 員工　　　　被　警察　　抓走　　 的　　總裁　　　顯得　十分
　　　 yuangong　bei　jingcha　zhuazou　de　　zongcai　　 xiande　shifen
　　　 employee　BEI　police　take　　 REL　chairperson　appear　very
　　　 慌張。
　　　 huangzhang
　　　 nervous
　　　 'The chairperson whose employee was taken by the police appeared very nervous.'

Twenty-four pairs of sentences were created (see Appendix for the paired list of alienable and inalienable nouns used); these pairs of nouns used across conditions were matched on word frequency (based on Sinica Corpus; CKIP, 1995) and online response times on possessive relations.[14] All the target nouns

---

[13] We adopted possessive relative clauses of the passive (BEI) construction in Chinese because, according to Lin (2006) and Lin, Fong, and Bever (2005), possessive relative clauses involving passives (where the possessor gap is located at the subject position) are most comprehensible among the different kinds of possessive relative clauses investigated. That is, the dependency between the possessor head noun and a possessor gap at the subject position is constructed more efficiently than one between the head noun and a possessor gap at a lower position.

[14] The items in this experiment were tested on the decision times of possessive relations. After the self-paced reading experiment, these twenty-four participants were asked to make online decisions on the possibility of possessive relations between nominal pairs (N1 and N3 in (25)). Each trial presented a sentence, which states a possessive relation between two nouns (e.g., *The doctor has a daughter/*

(the alienable and inalienable nouns and the head nouns) appeared only once in the experiment.[15] The materials were arranged by a Latin-Square design, so that each participant only read a sentence once in either condition A or condition B. In addition to the target sentences, 122 filler sentences of various syntactic types were included as distracters.

20.4.3 Procedure

A self-paced reading experiment, with a moving-window presentation, was conducted using Linger 2.94 developed by Doug Rohde at MIT. No spaces were inserted between words or phrases since the standard writing of Chinese does not contain spaces. All materials were presented randomly, with consecutive occurrences of the target items avoided. After the last word of each sentence, the whole sentence disappeared. A comprehension question on the content of that sentence appeared. The comprehension question was either a true/false question or a multiple-choice question.[16] No feedback was given if the participant response was correct. Participants were instructed to read the sentences at a natural rate, and to understand the sentences in order to answer the comprehension questions correctly. Twelve practice trials were presented before the main section started. The reading time for each region, the time taken to answer the comprehension questions, and the responses to the comprehension questions were recorded. Participants took a break every fifty sentences. The whole experiment took twenty to twenty-five minutes to complete.

20.4.4 Results and Discussion

Comprehension accuracy did not differ across conditions (93.06 per cent for sentences with inalienable nouns; 90.63 per cent for sentences with alienable nouns). The average reading times of each region were compared across conditions. Only reading times of the sentences that were correctly understood were analysed. The regions in the experimental sentences were coded as in (25).

---

patient; the chairperson has a(n) father/employee), on the computer screen. The participants determined if such relations were possible. The results showed no significant differences on response times between inalienable nouns (kinship terms) and alienable nouns (non-kinship personal terms), suggesting that the possibility of possessive relations was not an interfering factor in this experiment.

[15] In Mandarin, multiple terms sometimes refer to the same kinship relationship. In this study, *husband* appeared twice as (老公 *laogong* and as 丈夫 *zhangfu*), and *father* appeared twice (as 父親 *fuqing* and as 老爸 *laoba*). All other kinship relations only appeared once.

[16] For example, the comprehension question for (23) was: *Was the nervous person a beggar?* The question for (24) was: *Who was nervous? The employee or the chairperson?*

(25)   N1   BEI N2   V1   DE   N3
        父親 / 員工   被 警察   抓走   的   總裁
        fuqin/yuangong bei jingcha zhuazou de   zongcai
        father/employee BEI police   take   REL chairperson
        V2
        顯得十分慌張。
        xiande-shifen-huangzhang
        appear-very-nervous
        'The chairperson whose father/employee was taken by the police
        appeared very nervous.'

By-region RTs are presented in Figure 1. Paired-sample *t*-tests were performed
on the by-region reading times of the two conditions. Alienability had a
significant effect on N3 (the head noun) both by subject analysis (t(23) =
3.33, $p < .01$) and by item analysis (t(23) = 2.28, $p < .05$). No other regions
showed significant differences (*t*s < 1.62, *p*s > 0.12). These results supported
the effect of inalienability on processing. Sentences with inalienable nouns
were read faster on the head noun, i.e., the possessor region, than sentences
with alienable nouns.

Notably, the RT difference was not found directly on the alienable and
inalienable nouns (N1), indicating that alienable and inalienable nouns did
not differ in reading times by themselves. The significant difference was found
on the head-noun region (N3), where the integration effect on relativization
takes place. N3 is also where the possessor argument of N1 is located and

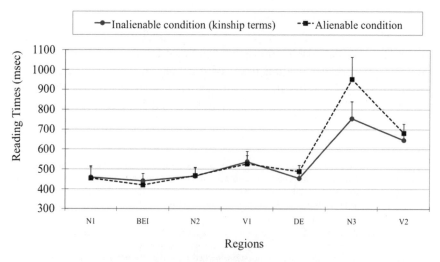

FIGURE 1. Reading times of sentences differing on the alienability of N1.

where the possessive relation between N1 and N3 gets constructed. Since the N3s in both inalienable and alienable conditions are identical, the reading-time difference on this region should be due to the differences in integrating these nouns with the alienable/inalienable nouns (N1s).

These experimental results were consistent with the syntactic and semantic analyses provided in previous sections, that possessive relations involving inalienable nouns are more easily constructed since the possessor noun phrase directly saturates the argument requirement of the relational noun. Possessions involving alienable nouns are more consuming to construct because an additional functional phrase needs to be inserted, and a context-dependent variable (π) needs to be postulated at the possessive head for semantic interpretation.

20.5 Concluding Remarks

In this chapter, we provided linguistic and processing evidence for the existence of thematic relations between inalienable nouns and their possessors. Inalienable nouns can appear in secondary predicates where an implicit possessor position located at the inalienable noun is licensed by a higher possessor argument. The lack of such a position in the secondary predicate keeps alienable nouns from being c-commanded by a possessor argument in these constructions. Semantically, an inalienable noun assigns the thematic role of (inherent) possessor to its argument, while an alienable possessive relation is constructed by coercing a context-dependent relation between the external possessor and the alienable noun. A sentence comprehension experiment demonstrated that inalienable nouns are indeed processed differently from alienable nouns. The parser is more efficient in associating an inalienable noun with its possessor argument than constructing a possessive relation between an alienable noun and an external possessor. Both the linguistic and processing evidence, therefore, suggests that inalienable nouns are inherently relational, subcategorizing for an internal possessor argument. This relational property of an inalienable noun can account for its syntactic patterns, the dominant semantic interpretations, and the processing efficiencies that are distinct from those of alienable nouns.

Acknowledgements

I thank Mike Silverstein and San Duanmu for directing my attention to the issue of possessive (in)alienability in relative-clause processing. The two anonymous reviewers have made very helpful suggestions, which significantly benefited the revision of this chapter. I also thank the Ministry of Education in Taiwan, the Fulbright Foundation, and SBSRI at the University of Arizona for indirectly sponsoring this research. The experiments were conducted in National Cheng-Chi University with assistance from One-Soon Her and Hui-Ling Tzeng. All errors, are, nevertheless, my own responsibility.

Appendix: N1(inalienable)/N1(alienable)-N2-N3(head noun) in the experiment

1. 女兒(daughter)/病人(patient)-歹徒(gangster)-醫生(doctor)
2. 外甥(son of sister)/球友(ballgame mate)-流氓(mob)-男子(guy)
3. 父親(father)/員工(employee)-警察(police)-總裁(chairperson)
4. 孫子(grandson)/同伴(friend)-經理(manager)-婦人(woman)
5. 老婆(wife)/團員(tour mate)-壞人(bad guy)-導遊(tour guide)
6. 父母(parents)/同學(school mate)-鄰居(neighbour)-工讀生(part-time student worker)
7. 外公(mother's father)/保母(nanny)-恐怖份子(terrorist)-小朋友(kid)
8. 祖父(father's father)/雇主(employer)-大學生(college student)
9. 兒子(son)/主任(section manager)-地下錢莊(illegal loaner)-行員 (banker)
10. 老公(husband)/班長(class leader)-卡車(truck)-女老師(female teacher)
11. 孩子(child)/ 學生(student)-濃煙(smoke)-研究員(researcher)
12. 丈夫(husband)/-顧客(customer)-海浪(sea wave)-老闆娘(female boss)
13. 妻子(wife)/ 讀者(reader)-癌症(cancer)-作家(writer)
14. 姊姊(eldersister)/秘書(secretary)-仰慕者(admirer)-董事長(business president)
15. 舅舅(mother's brother)/歌迷(fan)-警衛(security guard)-明星(showbiz celebrity)
16. 表弟(younger male cousin on mother's side)/保鏢(bodyguard)-法官 (judge)-國代(senator)
17. 媳婦(daughter in law)/長官(supervisor)-記者(reporter)-隊長(captain)
18. 妹夫(brother in law)/士官(Sergeant Major)-貨車(cargo truck)-連長 (lieutenant)
19. 姑姑(aunt on father's side)/廚師(chef)-火(fire)-飯店經理(hotel manager)
20. 外婆(maternal grandmother)/藝人(performer)-蜜蜂(bee)-製作人 (producer)
21. 堂哥(elder male cousin on father's side)/貴賓(guest of honour)-香蕉 (banana)-小開(rich kid)

22. 兄長(elder brother)/幹事(administrative secretary)-敵人(enemy)-議員
    (legislative representative)
23. 外孫(daughter's son)/僕人(servant)-洪水(flood)-富豪(rich man)
24. 老爸(father)/工友(janitor)-不良少年(teenage gangsters)-校長
    (principal)

21

Picturing the Syntax-Semantics Interface: Online Interpretation of Pronouns and Reflexives in Picture NPs*

ELSI KAISER, JEFFREY T. RUNNER, RACHEL
S. SUSSMAN, AND MICHAEL K. TANENHAUS

21.1 Introduction

The Binding Theory—the set of structural conditions partially determining the referential possibilities for pronouns and reflexives—lies directly at the syntax-semantics interface, since it defines the syntactic constraints on the (semantic) interpretation of NPs. In this chapter, we investigate the processing of pronouns and reflexives in picture NPs (PNPs), in order to examine how syntactic and semantic information is integrated during real-time language comprehension. We discuss the results of two eye-tracking experiments (Kaiser, Runner, Sussman, and Tanenhaus 2009; see also Kaiser *et al.* 2008) showing that the interpretation of pronouns and reflexives is influenced by both syntactic and semantic constraints, and explore the implications of this finding for our view of the syntax/semantics interface. Our findings indicate that there are no systematic differences between the effects of structural and semantic constraints on the final interpretation of pronouns or reflexives, either in terms of their relative strength or in their timing during real-time processing. Our results suggest a complex interaction between structural and semantic constraints for both reflexives and pronouns.

* Special thanks to Rebekka Puderbaugh for help with the experiments. Many thanks to Roumyana Pancheva as well as audiences at NELS 2006, CUNY 2007, and CLS 2007, where earlier versions of some aspects of this work were presented. Needless to say, any remaining errors are our own. This research was partially supported by NSF grants BCS-010776 and BCS-0518842, and NIH grant HD-27206.

In addition, we examine the possibility that syntactic constraints are typically 'hard constraints', with categorical effects, while semantic constraints are 'softer', with more gradient effects. Our results support a view in which both syntactic and semantic constraints can have gradient effects, during both online processing and the final interpretation of pronouns and reflexives. These results have important implications for the syntax-semantics interface, which we discuss in section 21.7.

21.2 Effects of Structural Information

The observation that pronominal and reflexive noun phrases in English have a nearly complementary distribution has played a central role in syntactic theory. As illustrated in (1), the pronoun *him* cannot refer to the subject of the clause containing the pronoun, whereas the reflexive *himself* must be bound by the subject:

(1)   Jack$_j$ claims that [Jake$_i$ admires him$_{*i/j}$/himself$_{i/*j}$]

Conditions A and B of classic Binding Theory aim to provide a structural account of this complementarity (e.g. Chomsky 1981). Condition A constrains the distribution of reflexives and Condition B applies to pronouns. According to Condition A, a reflexive needs to be bound by a c-commanding antecedent in its local domain. Condition B, conversely, requires a pronoun to be free in its local domain.[1] In example (1), the relevant local domain is the embedded clause, as indicated by the square brackets. The reflexive *himself* needs to be bound in its local domain and thus must be interpreted as referring to the local subject *Jake*. In contrast, the pronoun *him* needs to be locally free and thus cannot refer to *Jake*. However, *him* can refer to the non-local subject *Jack*, because that is outside of its local domain.

Let us now consider the predictions that Conditions A and B make for reflexives and pronouns in possessorless PNPs. In example (2a), Condition A requires that the reflexive *himself* be bound by the local subject *Peter*. Similar to the object-position reflexive in example (1), the reflexive in the possessorless PNP in (2a) cannot be bound by the matrix subject *Andy*, due to the matrix subject being outside the reflexive's local domain. In contrast, According to classic Condition B, the pronoun *him* cannot be bound by the local subject *Peter*, but can refer to the matrix subject *Andy*. Thus, reflexives

---

[1] Simplifying somewhat, the local domain is typically the minimal clause or possessed NP (see below).

and pronouns in possessorless PNPs are predicted to be in complementary distribution.[2]

(2a)   Andy$_i$ said that [Peter$_j$ saw the picture of himself$_{*i/j}$/him$_{i/*j}$].

possessorless PNP

(2b)   Mary$_i$ saw [Lisa$_j$'s picture of her$_{i/*j}$/herself$_{*i/j}$].   *possessed PNP*

Classic Binding Theory predicts a similar complementarity for pronouns and reflexives in possessed PNPs (ex. (2b)). In possessed picture NPs, the presence of a possessor limits the local domain to the picture NP itself. Since reflexives need to be bound by a local antecedent (Condition A), this means that the reflexive *herself* must be bound by the possessor *Lisa*. Because pronouns need to be free in the local domain (Condition B), the pronoun *her* cannot refer to the possessor but is free to refer to the subject of the sentence (*Mary*).[3]

However, although the principles of the Binding Theory capture the distribution of pronouns and reflexives in a wide range of syntactic contexts, it was noticed early on that the referential possibilities shown in (2a–b) do not fully reflect people's interpretations, in particular for PNPs without possessors. Many researchers, including Jackendoff (1972), Chomsky (1986), Williams (1987), Reinhart and Reuland (1993), Keller and Asudeh (2001), and Tenny (2004, 2003), have pointed out that pronouns in possessorless PNPs are not excluded from being coreferential with the subject. They noted that both reflexives and pronouns can be interpreted as referring to the local subject (e.g. *Peter* in example (2a)), contrary to the predictions of Condition B.

The referential properties of pronouns and reflexives in *possessed PNPs* have also been shown to be problematic for classic Binding Theory. Keller and Asudeh (2001) and Runner, Sussman, and Tanenhaus (2003, 2006) investigated the interpretation of pronouns and reflexives in possessed PNPs using magnitude estimation and visual-world eye-tracking respectively. They found that not only pronouns but also reflexives can refer to the subject of the sentence (e.g. *Mary* in example (2b)), contrary to the predictions of Condition A (see also Jaeger 2004).[4]

In sum, although classic Binding Theory predicts that pronouns and reflexives cannot refer to the same antecedent (i.e., are in complementary

---

[2] See below for discussion of later augmentations of classic BT (e.g. Chomsky 1986) that do predict a lack of complementarity here.

[3] We use the terms 'subject', 'possessor', and 'object' as theory-neutral structural terms which can also be understood in theory-specific terms such as e.g., 'DP in Spec,TP'.

[4] In particular, Runner *et al.* (2006) found that (i) with a reflexive in a possessed PNP, participants chose Mary (ex. 2b) as the antecedent of the reflexive on around 25% of trials, and (ii) with a pronoun in a possessed PNP, participants chose Mary as the antecedent of the pronoun on about 95% of trials.

distribution), this complementarity appears to break down in both possessor-less and possessed PNPs.

21.3 Effects of Semantic Information

Many researchers have suggested that in domains where the complementarity of pronouns and reflexives breaks down, their use and interpretation are influenced or determined by semantic and discourse constraints[5] (e.g., Cantrall 1974; Kuno 1987; Zribi-Hertz 1989; Pollard and Sag 1992; Reinhart and Reuland 1993; Tenny 1996, 2003).

The interpretation of reflexives in possessorless PNPs has been argued to be influenced by factors such as the potential antecedents' point of view, degree of awareness and semantic role (e.g. Pollard and Sag 1992; Kuno 1987). For example, it appears that reflexives in PNPs sound better when they refer to the person whose point of view is being represented (e.g. *John$_i$ was going to get even with Mary. That picture of himself$_i$ in the paper would really annoy her, as would the other stunts he had planned*, where the narrative is being told from John's perspective, sounds better than a narrative where we are assuming Mary's perspective: *Mary was quite taken aback by the publicity John$_i$ was receiving. That picture of himself$_i$ in the paper had really annoyed her, and there was not much she could do about it*, Pollard and Sag 1992). Furthermore, Kuno (1987) noted that when the entity in subject position is unaware that the PNP refers to him/her, the sentence is degraded (e.g. *John$_i$ still doesn't know that there is a picture of himself$_i$ in the morning paper* sounds worse than *John$_i$ knows that there is a picture of himself$_i$ in the morning paper*, Kuno 1987: 164).

In this paper, we explore the effects of another factor that has been suggested to be relevant, namely the notion of 'source of information'. Kuno (1987) suggests that in a sentence like (3a), the reflexive *herself* can be interpreted as coreferential with *Mary* because she is the one who John receives the information from, i.e., she is the source of information. This contrasts with example (3b), where Mary is not the source of information. In our experimental work, we tested the hypothesis in (4) for reflexives. (Our use of the term 'source' draws on Sells's (1987) definition of *source* as the one who is the intentional agent of the communication.[6])

---

[5] We use 'constraint' as theory-neutral term referring to 'a principle or rule of grammar that can be either satisfied or violated in a given linguistic structure' (Sorace and Keller 2005: 1503).

[6] According to this view, PNP reflexives may possess one of the characteristics of logophoric pronouns (see e.g. Reinhart and Reuland 1993). We leave for future work exploring the full range of logophoric properties in PNP reflexives.

(3a)   John heard from Mary about a damaging rumour about herself that was going around. (Kuno 1987: 175)

(3b)   John told Mary about a damaging rumour about [??]herself that was going around.

(4)   *Source constraint:*
Reflexives in PNPs prefer antecedents that are sources of information.

One of the reasons why we are interested in testing the source constraint in particular is because an interesting converse claim has been made regarding the interpretation of pronouns in possessorless PNPs. Tenny (2003) claims that pronouns have a preference for antecedents that are perceivers of information, and notes that 'verbs that provide a sentient, perceiving antecedent are especially conducive' to local binding (Tenny 2003: 14).[7] Examples (5a,b), from Reinhart and Reuland (1993: 685), illustrate the effects of perceiver status. Example (5a) has a perceiving subject and sounds better than (5b) which has a source subject. In our experimental work, we tested the hypothesis in (6) for pronouns.

(5a) Max_i heard the story about him_i.

(5b)   *Max_i told the story about him_i.

(6)   *Perceiver constraint:*
Pronouns in PNPs prefer antecedents that are perceivers of information.

Chomsky (1986: 167) discussed examples similar to those in (5), suggesting that with *tell*, a null PRO possessor optionally appears in the 'story' NP, obligatorily bound by the subject NP. The presence of the null PRO delimits the 'story' NP as the domain in which the pronoun must be free, thus accounting for the contrast in (5). However, this PRO-in-NP approach has been criticized in the literature as both empirically and theoretically inadequate (e.g., Williams 1982, 1985, 1987; Runner, Sussman, and Tanenhaus 2006; see also Grimshaw 1990; Bhatt and Pancheva 2006). In addition, in our own work where we investigated experimentally the interpretation of prenominal possessive pronouns in sentences with *heard* and *told*, we found no clear support for the PRO-in-NP hypothesis (Kaiser, Runner, Sussman, and Tanenhaus 2007). For these reasons, we focus on the version of Binding Theory that does not assume a null PRO to be present in PNPs.[8]

---

[7] Tenny proposes point-of-view/sentience-based binding domains and argues that pronouns must be free in their local point-of-view domains (e.g. Tenny 2003).

[8] Also, Chomsky's account depended on the claim that it is more likely that in (5), Max would be telling his own stories (rather than someone else's), motivating the obligatory binding between the subject and a null possessor. In our examples, with picture NPs, no such preference is apparent. In an

By investigating two closely related hypotheses—the perceiver constraint for pronouns and the source constraint for reflexives—we can begin to gain insights into whether and how pronouns and reflexives differ in how sensitive they are to semantic constraints, relative to structural constraints. It is worth noting that, when discussing the effects of non-structural factors on the interpretation of pronouns and reflexives, we refer to them as 'semantic' constraints, for ease of exposition. We leave open the question of whether the source/perceiver distinction that we focus on in this paper should be regarded as a semantic, thematic role manipulation or a discourse-level/pragmatic manipulation (e.g., having to do with perspective-taking).

21.4 On the Relationship between Syntactic and Semantic Information

In this section we focus on the relationship between syntactic and semantic information, and how one might expect them to differ from (or resemble) each other. In particular, we discuss debates concerning the traits that have been attributed to syntactic information and semantic information, as well as disagreements regarding the ways in which structural and non-structural information are used during real-time language comprehension. Investigating anaphor resolution in PNPs has potentially interesting implications for these questions.

21.4.1 *Traits of Syntactic and Semantic Constraints*

A common assumption is that syntactic constraints are more 'robust' than non-syntactic constraints and that violating syntactic rules has more severe consequences than violating other principles. For example, Keller's (2000) optimality-theoretic syntax approach divides constraints into hard and soft constraints. He claims that a violation of a hard constraint results in strong unacceptability, whereas violating a soft constraint results in milder unacceptability (see also Belletti and Rizzi 1988). More recently, Sorace and Keller (2005) hypothesized that syntactic constraints (such as constraints involving subject-auxiliary inversion and subject-verb agreement) are hard constraints; whereas soft constraints are semantic or pragmatic in nature, such as constraints on extraction having to do with definiteness marking and

---

example like, 'Peter told Greg about the picture of him,' it does not seem to be the case that the picture must belong to Peter in order to limit the binding domain to the PNP. However, in both our examples and the ones Chomsky discusses (like (5)), the perceiver preference holds.

the referential/non-referential distinction. They further hypothesize that soft constraints are more susceptible to cross-linguistic variation.

The claim that violating a syntactic constraint leads to severe unacceptability whereas violating a semantic constraint results in only mild unacceptability seems to be at least indirectly related to the idea that syntactic constraints are categorical/deterministic whereas semantic constraints or discourse constraints are more gradient (see also Erteschik-Shir 2006). In recent years, some have argued that gradience is a property of core grammar, specifically syntax (e.g., Fanselow, Féry, Schlesewsky and Vogel 2006; Sorace and Keller 2005; Gahl and Garnsey 2006; Bybee 2006), whereas others argue that syntax is deterministic/categorical (e.g. Newmeyer 2003; Reuland 2006) and that any apparent gradience may be due to other factors such as the nature of the processing system or extra-syntactic contextual effects. In sum, both the distinction between soft vs hard constraints and the gradience debate have to do with the question of whether syntax patterns differently from other kinds of information.

21.4.2 *Timing of Syntactic and Semantic Information during Processing*

The idea that syntactic information has a special status in comparison to other kinds of information also occurs in the psycholinguistic sentence-processing literature. Two opposing views regarding the relation between syntax and semantics have been proposed: a modular view and an inter-active view. According to modular, two-stage models of sentence processing (e.g., Frazier and Fodor 1978), the initial stage of processing is guided only by syntactic information, and other kinds of information (semantic, pragmatic, frequency information, etc.) guide parsing only during a second stage of processing. In contrast, constraint-based models (e.g. MacDonald, Pearlmutter, and Seidenberg 1994; Trueswell, Tanenhaus, and Garnsey 1994, *inter alia*) regard processing as guided by multiple sources of information from the very beginning. On this view, multiple weighted constraints guide processing and result in different possible parses receiving different amounts of activation. The multiple-constraints view does not treat syntax and semantics as temporally modular subsystems.

Existing psycholinguistic work on binding theory, focusing primarily on the time-course of processing direct-object pronouns and reflexives, has led to conflicting conclusions. Some researchers (e.g., Nicol and Swinney 1989, Clifton, Kennison, and Albrecht 1997; Sturt 2003) argue for a two-stage model with an initial syntax-only stage during which only structural Binding constraints guide processing. In contrast, Badecker and Straub (2002) argue for an interactive constraint model, where multiple weighted constraints simultaneously influence reference resolution from the first moments onwards (see also Runner *et al.* 2006). In sum, in psycholinguistics, as in the theoretical domain, it has been argued that syntactic information is fundamentally distinct from other kinds of information in specific ways, but this view has also been challenged.

21.5 Experimentation at the Syntax-Semantics Interface

In this paper, we aim to contribute to the discussion regarding the nature of syntactic constraints and their relation to other information by investigating the contribution of syntactic and semantic information to the real-time processing of pronouns and reflexives in PNPs. We summarize the results of two experiments we conducted, testing the hypothesized source/perceiver preferences of pronouns and reflexives which allow us to comment on (i) the role that syntactic and semantic constraints play in determining participants' final interpretations as well as on (ii) the timing and nature of the impact that syntactic and semantic constraints exert on the real-time processing of pronouns and reflexives. We focus on what our results can (and cannot) tell us about the nature of the syntax-semantics interface.

In these studies, participants wore a lightweight headmounted eye-tracker (ISCAN EC-501) while listening to sentences and viewing scenes presented on a computer screen. The scenes consisted of the characters mentioned in the sentence and a picture of each character (see example (7), Figure 1). Participants were told to use the computer mouse to click on the picture mentioned in the sentence. Thus, with this method we obtained information about participants' final interpretations, as well as time-course information about what referents they considered as potential antecedents. Existing research demonstrates that eye-movements to objects in a display are closely time-locked to potential referents that a listener considers as language unfolds over time (Cooper 1974; Tanenhaus, Spivey-Knowlton, Eberhard and Sedivy 1995). Thus we can use looks to pictures to shed light on what participants consider as potential referents for pronouns and reflexives as the sentence unfolds in real time.

21.6 Eye-tracking Experiments

21.6.1 *Experiment 1: Possessorless PNPs*

This experiment investigated pronouns and reflexives in PNPs without possessors. Participants heard sentences with possessorless PNPs while viewing scenes similar to Figure 1, and we recorded participants' picture choices and

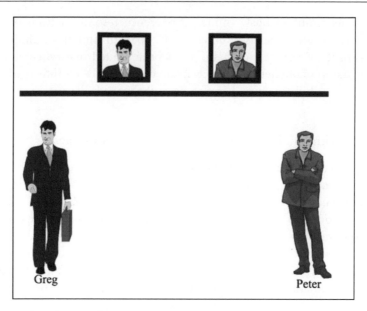

FIGURE 1. Sample scene from Experiment 1.

eye-movements.[9] To investigate effects of source and perceiver status on the interpretation of pronouns and reflexives, we looked at sentences with *heard* and *told* (ex. 7). With *tell,* the subject is the source and the object is the perceiver, and with *hear,* the object is the source and the subject is the perceiver.

(7)   Greg *told/heard from* Peter about the picture of *him/himself* on the wall.

Predictions: The classic Binding Theory predicts that the verb manipulation should not affect reference resolution in possessorless PNPs: reflexives should prefer the subject equally strongly in (7a) and (7b); and pronouns should prefer the object equally strongly in (7a) and (7b). However, the theoretical syntax literature is not entirely clear on what the structurally licensed antecedent for reflexives and pronouns is predicted to be in a sentence like (7). One possibility is that *heard from* (which contains an additional preposition that is not present with *told*) might reduce the syntactic prominence of the object— leading to the prediction that the object Andrew is less capable of binding a reflexive inside a PNP when the verb is *heard* ('... heard from Andrew...') than when the verb is *told* ('... told Andrew...'). However, Pollard and Sag (1992)

---

[9] Five female and five male characters were used. Participants were familiarized with the characters' names beforehand. The names were shown below the characters on all scenes.

TABLE 1. Possessorless PNPs: Percentage of subject and object picture choices.

	Pronouns		Reflexives	
	told	*heard*	*told*	*heard*
Subject picture choices	16.7%	62.5%	93.8%	87.5%
Object picture choices	83.3%	37.5%	6.3%	12.5%

and Jackendoff (1990b) argued that the structural binding possibilities for the subject and the object should not be sensitive to the presence of the preposition, and hence should not differ by verb (see also Runner 1998); and in our own earlier work using a scene-verification task we found that reflexives show an overall preference for subjects and pronouns an overall preference for objects (or a dispreference for subjects, Kaiser *et al.* 2009). We will refer to these basic structural preferences as the *subject constraint* (reflexives) and *anti-subject constraint* (pronouns).

If semantic and syntactic constraints both play a role, the predictions are that (i) in the pronoun conditions, there will be more subject interpretations with *heard* than *told* (*perceiver constraint*, (6)) and that (ii) in the reflexive conditions, there will be more object interpretations with *heard* than *told* (*source constraint*, (4)), despite the presence of the preposition *from* in the *heard* conditions (see above).

As for the time course of processing, a purely structural view predicts no effects of semantic information at any point: pronouns and reflexives should exhibit an early and persistent syntactically driven referential interpretation— which should furthermore be categorical, if syntactic constraints are non-gradient. If both syntactic and semantic constraints do play a role in processing, then according to the two-stage model, semantic effects should only surface after an initial syntax-only processing stage. In contrast, an interactive multiple-constraints model predicts early, probabilistic effects of both structural and semantic information.

Results—picture choices: In the reflexive conditions, there was an overall subject preference, as can be seen in Table 1. However, the number of object choices was slightly higher with *heard* (12.5 per cent, where the object is the source) than *told* (6.3 per cent where the object is the perceiver)—though this difference was not statistically significant. In contrast, the pronoun conditions showed a significant verb effect: more subject interpretations with *heard* than *told* (62.5 per cent vs 16.7 per cent), as predicted by the perceiver hypothesis. Our results suggest that the structural subject constraint for reflexives is strong—though not absolute (approx. 9 per cent violations overall). However, the anti-subject constraint for pronouns does not appear to be as strong: the semantic preference for perceiver modulates the structural constraint. These results represent participants' final interpretations and are comparable to judgements of preferred interpretations of these sentences. In addition, if the extra preposition in the *heard* sentences had made the object less prominent, we would have expected more object choices for pronouns and fewer object choices for reflexives (compared to *told* sentences), exactly of what occurred. Thus, our results cannot be derived from the presence/absence of the preposition. (For more detailed picture-choice results, eye-movement patterns from 200ms before anaphor onset to 1800ms after anaphor onset, and full statistical analyses for Experiments 1 and 2, please see Kaiser *et al.* 2009.)

Results—eye movements: The eye-tracking results, which can tell us when and how the structural constraints interact with the semantic constraints, show that both pronouns and reflexives were influenced by semantic constraints early during processing. With pronouns, eye movements revealed a significant *perceiver preference* emerging 200ms post-pronoun-onset, which is the earliest point at which one can expect to see input-driven eye movements (Matin, Shao, and Boff 1993). In the time period from 200ms to 600ms after pronoun onset, in the *told* conditions the average proportion of looks to the object picture (perceiver) was 0.42, whereas with *heard*, the average proportion of looks to the object picture (source) was only 0.25 (see Table 2). With reflexives, eye movements showed that the strong subject preference observed in the offline picture choice data is not absolute: there is an early, subtle but significant sensitivity to source. Starting 200ms post-onset, participants looked more at the object-picture when it was the source (with *heard*) than when it was the perceiver (with *told*). In the time period from 200ms to 600ms after reflexive onset, in the *heard* conditions the average proportion of looks to the object picture (source) was 0.3, whereas with *told*, the average proportion of looks to the object picture (perceiver) was only 0.18. Thus, the eye-movement patterns indicate that reflexives' subject preference is modulated by a *source preference*. And again, it is worth noting that the pattern of results we observed cannot be attributed to the presence of an extra preposition in the *heard* conditions. This is because the results are the opposite of what would be expected if the preposition were creating additional structure affecting the antecedent availability of the object NP in the *heard* conditions.

On the basis of the eye-tracking data, we can conclude that both pronouns and reflexives are immediately sensitive to both semantic and syntactic information. Reflexives' overall subject-preference indicates the syntactic

TABLE 2. Possessorless PNPs: Proportion of looks to the subject picture and the object picture, in the 200ms to 600ms time period after the onset of the referring expression.

	Pronouns		Reflexives	
	told	*heard*	*told*	*heard*
Proportion of looks to subject picture	0.3	0.44	0.49	0.44
Proportion of looks to object picture	0.42	0.25	0.18	0.3

subject constraint is weighted more heavily than the semantic source constraint; with pronouns the relative weights of the syntactic and semantic constraints (anti-subject constraint, perceiver constraint) appear more evenly matched.

These findings suggest that during real-time processing, syntax and semantics are both contributing during the same temporal phase, and both pronouns and reflexives are susceptible to both syntactic and semantic constraints. The data are compatible with an interactive constraint-based model, and do not support an initial encapsulated syntax-only stage or a purely structural approach that fails to acknowledge semantic constraints. The gradient nature of the data patterns raises the question of whether gradience is a property of the core grammar or whether it stems from the processing system or another source. We discuss this issue in section 21.7.

21.6.2 *Experiment 2: Possessed PNPs*

Experiment 2 aims to further our understanding of the relation between structural and semantic constraints. The presence of the possessor means that pronouns and reflexives in possessed PNPs are guided by further structural constraints (see below). By investigating the processing of PNPs with possessors, we can investigate the relative strengths of different structural constraints and compare their impact to that of semantic constraints. The results of Experiment 1 showed that in the reflexive conditions, the structural subject constraint outweighs the semantic source constraint, and that in the pronoun conditions, the structural anti-subject constraint and semantic perceiver constraint compete more evenly. Does this asymmetry between pronouns and reflexives extend to possessed PNPs?

Similar to Experiment 1, participants listened to sentences while looking at scenes containing the three mentioned characters (ex. (8)) and a picture of each one. Before the start of the experiment, it was made clear to participants that one character (the possessor) owns all three pictures (e.g. Peter in ex.(8)). To minimize potential confusion, the possessor character was always located in the middle, between the other two characters. Participants' task was to click on the mentioned picture. Verb type (*heard/told*) and anaphoric form (*pronoun/ reflexive*) were manipulated. Participants' picture choices and eye movements were recorded.

(8)   Greg *told/heard from* John about Peter's picture of *him/himself.*

Predictions: A reflexive in a possessed PNP should be bound by the possessor, according to classic Binding Theory. We call this the *possessor constraint.* A pronoun in a possessed PNP must not be bound by the possessor but is free to refer to the subject or the object. We call this the *anti-possessor constraint.* From a purely structural standpoint, the verb manipulation should have no effect on the referential preferences of reflexives or pronouns. Reflexives should consistently opt for the possessor, and pronouns for either the subject or the object.

Moreover, the subject constraint that played a role for reflexives in posses-sorless PNPs is now irrelevant, according to Binding Theory. However, a multiple-constraint approach that assumes that *both* the subject constraint and the possessor constraint influence the interpretation of reflexives in possessed PNPs predicts that participants' choices may be split between the subject and the possessor and the degree to which they favour one or the other will depend on the relative strengths of the two structural constraints. More-over, if reflexives in possessed PNPs are influenced by the semantic source constraint, one might expect more object choices with *hear* and more subject choices with *tell.*

For pronouns, Binding Theory rules out coreference with the possessor but is silent on the choice between the subject vs the object: both are equally available. This leaves the door open for the perceiver constraint to emerge, which should result in more object choices with *told* and more subject choices with *heard.* However, as with the reflexives, we can ask about the status of the anti-subject constraint: is it now entirely irrelevant? If *both* the structural anti-possessor constraint and the anti-subject constraint are equally influential in guiding interpretation, with *told* pronouns may prefer the object (the per-ceiver) over the subject (due to the anti-subject constraint) or the possessor (due to the anti-possessor constraint). With *heard*, the pronouns would prefer the subject (the perceiver, but goes against anti-subject constraint) or the object (fits with anti-subject constraint, but not the perceiver) over the possessor (goes against anti-possessor constraint, and is not the perceiver). Alternatively, structural constraints may not pattern as a 'block', and the

TABLE 3. Possessed PNPs: Percentage of subject, object, and possessor picture choices.

	Pronouns		Reflexives	
	told	*heard*	*told*	*heard*
Subject picture choices	20.8%	79.7%	9.8%	7.8%
Object picture choices	76.9%	18.8%	0.4%	0.0%
Possessor picture choices	2.3%	1.6%	89.8%	92.2%

effects of the anti-possessor constraint may be stronger or weaker than discussed above. Experiment 2 enables us to test this possibility. The logic of the predictions regarding the time course of structural and semantic constraints is similar as for possessorless PNPs.

Results: Participants' picture choices showed a strong perceiver preference in the pronoun conditions (see Table 3). With *heard*, the subject (perceiver) was chosen 79.7 per cent of the time. With *told*, participants tended to choose the object (76.9 per cent object choices). There were very few possessor choices in both verb conditions (around 2 per cent). In the reflexive conditions, in contrast, no verb effect emerged. The possessor was usually chosen regardless of verb (89.8 per cent possessor choices with *told* and 92.2 per cent with *heard*). Participants hardly ever chose the object, but there were 7.8 per cent subject choices with *heard* and 9.8 per cent with *told*. This experiment showed again that, for reflexives, the possessor constraint effects were strong but not absolute (approx. 9 per cent violations). However, for pronouns the anti-possessor constraint was extremely strong (only approx. 2 per cent violations), and the choice of subject over object was strongly influenced by the perceiver constraint.

The eye-tracking data support the conclusions drawn on the basis of the picture-choice data. Reflexives were guided by a strong possessor preference and showed no clear indication of a verb effect, whereas pronouns were sensitive to the verb and exhibited a perceiver preference. Interestingly, in the pronoun conditions in Experiment 2 it took somewhat longer for the perceiver preference to emerge than in Experiment 1, perhaps as a result of the greater visual and referential complexity of the display.

The pattern of results is compatible with a constraint weighting which assumes that, for pronouns, the anti-possessor constraint is weighted more heavily than the perceiver constraint and the anti-subject constraint. So, even though Experiment 1 may have led one to believe that pronouns are sensitive to both structural and semantic constraints at fairly equal levels, Experiment 2 shows the structural anti-possessor constraint in fact outweighs the other two. For reflexives, the overarching possessor preference in Experiment 2 suggests that the possessor constraint outweighs the source constraint and the subject constraint. However, the low but nevertheless detectable rate of subject interpretations hints at a weak structural constraint pushing the reflexive towards the subject, regardless of semantic role. We are not the first to observe that reflexives in possessed PNPs are not restricted to the possessor (Keller and Asudeh 2001; Jaeger 2004; Runner *et al.* 2003, 2006). Our results support the earlier findings, and further suggest that the subject interpretations in possessed PNPs stem from something other than the source preference of reflexives in PNPs without possessors.

21.7 Discussion and Conclusions

This chapter investigated the nature and interaction of structural and non-structural constraints on pronouns and reflexives, with the aim of clarifying this important area of the syntax-semantics interface. Our results suggest that at least for the constraints we examined, there are no systematic differences between the effects of structural constraints and semantic constraints on the final interpretation of pronouns or reflexives, either in terms of their relative strength or in the timing of their use during real-time processing. If we rank the constraints according to their strength, we observe a complex interaction between structural and semantic constraints for both reflexives and pronouns. More specifically, our results suggest that the interpretation of pronouns is guided by two fairly evenly weighted constraints, namely the perceiver constraint and the anti-subject constraint, as well as a powerful anti-possessor constraint. The interpretation of reflexives is sensitive to a strong subject constraint and, when applicable, a strong possessor constraint. We also found significant source preference effects with reflexives.

The complementary semantic preferences that we found for pronouns and reflexives raise the question of *why* pronouns should show a preference for perceivers of information while reflexives prefer sources of information. Although we cannot offer a full answer to this question here, we have begun to investigate this question in recent cross-linguistic work on pronouns and reflexives in Dutch and German (Kaiser and Runner 2008). In particular, our findings for Dutch suggest that the source/perceiver distinction may be separable from the reflexive/pronoun distinction and that the source preference may be related to a more general preference for prominent antecedents. We hope that future work can further our understanding of these issues, and also shed light on the question of how the source/perceiver distinction relates to the other factors that have been found to influence the interpretation and/or acceptability of reflexives and pronouns in PNPs.

Our eye-tracking data show that both pronouns and reflexives exhibit an early sensitivity to both structural and semantic constraints. We assume that the nature of real-time processing has implications for the syntax-semantics interface, and thus our results suggest that the mechanism responsible for anaphor resolution—standardly assumed to be part of syntax—is capable of accessing information that is outside of 'syntax proper', namely source/perceiver information. The finding that structural and non-structural information guide processing from the earliest moments suggests that the syntax-semantics interface is continuously 'active', mediating between syntax and semantics, and that it is able to access (or 'read') information as fine-grained as the source/perceiver distinction.[10] Our findings are contrary to the predictions of a two-stage syntax-first processing theory which claims that any connection between syntax and semantics is only possible after an initial syntax-only component has completed its processing, i.e., that the interface between syntax and semantics is dependent on the output of purely syntactic computation.

A striking property of our data is their gradient nature, which raises questions regarding the source of the gradience. One possibility is that the core grammar is non-gradient (e.g. Reuland 2006; see also Newmeyer 2003) and that the appearance of gradience derives from properties of the processing system, a system that operates under time pressure with limited memory and attentional resources. Alternatively, gradience could be a characteristic of the core grammar (Sorace and Keller 2005; Gahl and Garnsey 2006). Space does not permit a full discussion of these issues, but the former analysis would presumably require a set of 'binding' conditions to hold in the processing system, which also applies different constraints to pronouns and reflexives. We leave for future work the question of how these patterns could be derived without creating a secondary, potentially redundant 'binding theory' for the processing system.

Finally, let us turn briefly to the question of whether PNPs constitute an environment that is exempt from Binding Theory (see e.g. Pollard and Sag 1992) in which reflexives are not true syntactic reflexives but rather logophors, sensitive primarily to discourse information. Given that we observed fairly strong effects of seemingly syntactic constraints on reflexives in both possessed and possessorless PNPs, our results seem to suggest that both syntactic and semantic constraints guide anaphor resolution with PNPs.

---

[10] The processing models discussed in the psycholinguistic literature have not explicitly focused on the question of 'legibility' (see, e.g. Reinhart 2000, 2002 who argues that only a restricted set of features can be 'read' by the computational system (narrow syntax)).

References

Abramson, A. and Erickson, D. (1992). 'Tone splits and voicing shifts in Thai: phonetic plausibility'. *Haskins Laboratories Status Report on Speech Research*, SR-109/110: 255–62.

—— and Lisker, L. (1985). 'Relative power of cues: F_0 shift versus voice timing', in V. Fromkin (ed.), *Phonetic Linguistics: Essays in Honor of Peter Ladefoged*. San Diego: Academic Press, 25–33.

Ackema, P. (1995). *Syntax below Zero*. Utrecht: LED.

—— and Neeleman, A. (1998). 'Conflict resolution in passive formation', *Lingua* 104: 13–29.

—— —— (2004). *Beyond Morphology*. Oxford: Oxford University Press.

Adger, D. (2003). *Core Syntax*. Oxford: Oxford University Press.

—— and Ramchand, G. (2005). 'Merge and move: Wh-dependencies revisited', *Linguistic Inquiry* 36 (2): 161–93.

Ahn, H. (1999). 'Post-Release Phonatory Processes in English and Korean: Acoustic Correlates and Implications for Korean Phonology'. Ph.D. dissertation, University of Texas at Austin.

Ahn, S.-C. and Iverson, G. (2004). 'Dimensions in Korean laryngeal phonology', *Journal of East Asian Linguistics* 13: 345–79.

—— and Lee, J. (2008). 'Laryngeal contrasts in loanword phonology: a case study from Korean and Thai', *Studies in Phonetics, Phonology, and Morphology* 14(1): 107–20. [Written in Korean].

Ahrens, K. (2003). 'Verbal integration: the interaction of participant roles and sentential argument structure', *Journal of Psycholinguistic Research* 32 (5): 497–516.

Aissen, J. (1997). 'On the syntax of obviation', *Language* 73: 705–30.

Aksu-Koç, A. and Slobin, D. I. (1985). 'The acquisition of Turkish', in D. I. Slobin (ed.), *Cross-linguistic Studies on Language Acquisition, Vol. 1*. Mahwah, NJ: Lawrence Erlbaum Associates.

Alboiu, G. (2005). 'When CP-domains are pro-Case'. Paper presented at the CLA Conference, UWO.

—— (2007). 'Null Expletives and pro: the View from Romance'. Paper presented at the 37th LSRL conference.

Alexiadou, A. (1996). 'Aspectual restrictions on word order', *Folia Linguistica* 30: 36–46.

—— (1998). 'Parametrizing AGR: word-order, V-movement and EPP-checking', *Natural Language and Linguistic Theory* 16: 491–539.

—— (1999). 'Tests for unaccusativity in a language without tests for unaccusativity', in *Proceedings of the 3rd International Conference on Greek Linguistics*. Athens: Ellinika Grammata, 23–31.

—— (2004). 'Voice morphology in the causative-inchoative alternation: evidence for a non-unified structural analysis of unaccusatives', in A. Alexiadou, E. Anagnostopoulou, and M. Everaert (eds.) *The Unaccusativity Puzzle: Explorations of the Syntax-Lexicon Interface*. Oxford: Oxford University Press, 115–36.

—— (2000). 'Some remarks on word order and information structure in Romance and Greek', *ZASPIL* 20: 119–36.

—— (2003). 'Some Notes on the Structure of Alienable and Inalienable Possessors', in M. Coenem and Y. D'hulst (eds.), *From NP to DP: The Expression of Possession in Noun Phrases*. Amsterdam: John Benjamins, 167–88.

—— and Anagnostopoulou, E. (1998). 'Unaccusativity mismatches in Greek', Paper presented at the 8th CGG in Palmela.

—— —— and Schäfer, F. (2006). 'The properties of anticausatives crosslinguistically', in M. Frascarelli (ed.), *Phases of Interpretation*. Berlin: Mouton, 187–211.

—— and Schäfer, F. (2009). 'There down in Spec,vP: an argument'. Paper presented at the GGS Meeting in Leipzig.

Altmann, G. T. M. (1999). 'Thematic role assignment in context', *Journal of Memory and Language* 41: 124–45.

Alves, M. J. (1999). 'What's so Chinese about Vietnamese?', in G. Thurgood (ed.), *Papers from the Ninth Annual Meeting of the Southeast Asian Linguistics Society*, 221–42.

Ammann, H. (1928). *Die Menschliche Rede. Sprachphilosophische Untersuchungen 2. Teil: Der Satz*. Darmstadt: Wissenschaftliche Buchgesellschaft.

Anagnostopoulou, E. (1994). 'Clitic dependencies in Modern Greek'. Ph.D. dissertation, University of Salzburg.

—— (2003). *The Syntax of Ditransitives: Evidence from Clitics*. Berlin: Mouton de Gruyter.

Antrim, N. M. (1996). 'On the status of possessives'. Unpublished dissertation, University of Southern California.

Aoshima, S., Phillips, C., and Weinberg, A. (2004). 'Processing filler-gap dependencies in a head-final language', *Journal of Memory and Language* 51: 23–54.

Aoun, J., Choueiri, L., and Hornstein, N. (2001). 'Resumption, movement, and derivational economy', *Linguistic Inquiry* 32 (3): 371–403.

Arad, M. (1998). 'VP Structure and the Syntax-Lexicon Interface'. Ph.D. dissertation, University College London.

—— (2003). 'Locality constraints on the interpretation of roots: the case of Hebrew denominal verbs', *Natural Language and Linguistic Theory* 21: 737–78.

Arnold, J. E., Losongco, A., Wasow, T., and Ginstrom, R. (2000). 'Heaviness vs. newness: the effects of structural complexity and discourse structure on constituent ordering', *Language* 76: 28–55.

Asher, N. (1993). *Reference to Abstract Objects in Discourse*. Dordrecht: Kluwer.

Avery, P. and Idsardi, W. (2001). 'Laryngeal dimensions, completion and enhancement', in T. Alan Hall (ed.), *Distinctive Feature Theory*. Berlin, New York: de Gruyter, 41–70.

Babby, L. (1980). *Existential Sentences and Negation in Russian*. Ann Arbor, MI: Karoma Publishers.

—— (2001). 'The Genitive of Negation: a Unified Analysis', in S. Franks *et al.* (eds.), *Proceedings of FASL 9*. Ann Arbor, MI: Michigan Slavic Publications, 1–35.

Babyonyshev, M. (forthcoming). 'Genitive of Negation in Russian', in A. Przepior-kowski and S. Brown (eds.), *Negation in Slavic*. Slavica Publishers.

Badecker, W. and Straub, K. (2002). 'The processing role of structural constraints on the interpretation of pronouns and anaphors', *Journal of Experimental Psychology: Learning, Memory and Cognition* 28: 748–69.

Baker, M. C. (1985). 'The Mirror Principle and morphosyntactic explanation', *Linguistic Inquiry* 16: 373–415.

—— (1988). *Incorporation: A Theory of Grammatical Function Changing*. Chicago: University of Chicago Press.

—— (1997). 'Thematic roles and syntactic structure', in L. Haegeman, *Elements of Grammar*. Dordrecht: Kluwer, 137–78.

—— (2002). 'Building and merging, not checking: the non existence of (Aux)-S-V-O languages', *Linguistic Inquiry* 33: 321–8.

—— (2003). *Lexical Categories: Verbs, Nouns and Adjectives*. Cambridge: Cambridge University Press.

Baldwin, D., Baird, J., Saylor, M., and Clark, A. (2001). 'Infants parse dynamic action', *Child Development* 72: 708–17.

Baltin, M. (1987). 'Do antecedent-contained deletions exist?', *Linguistic Inquiry* 18 (4): 579–96.

Barbiers, S. and Rooryck, J. (1998). 'On the interpretation of "there" in existentials', in K. Shahin., S. Blake., and E.-S. Kim (eds.), *Proceedings of WCCFL 17, UBC*. Stanford: CLSI, 59–73.

Bard, E. G., Robertson, D., and Sorace, A. (1996). 'Magnitude Estimation of Linguistic Acceptability', *Language* 72(1): 32–68.

Barker, C. (1995). *Possessive Descriptions*. Stanford, CA: CSLI.

—— (2008). 'Possessives and relational nouns', in C. Maienborn, K. V. Heusinger, and P. Portner (eds.), *Semantics: An International Handbook of Natural Language Meaning*. Berlin: Mouton de Gruyter.

Barragan, L. M. (2003). 'Movement and allomorphy in the Cupeño verb construction', in L. M. Barragan and J. D. Haugen (eds.), *Studies in Uto-Aztecan: MITELF 5*. Cambridge, MA: MIT Working Papers in Linguistics.

Barss, A. (1986). 'Chains and anaphoric dependence: on reconstruction and its implications'. Ph.D. dissertation, MIT, Cambridge, MA.

—— and Lasnik, H. (1986). 'A note on anaphora and double objects', *Linguistic Inquiry* 17: 347–54.

Bartels, C. (2004). 'Acoustic correlates of "second occurrence" focus: towards an experimental investigation', in H. Kamp and B. Partee (eds.), *Context-Dependence in the Analysis of Linguistic Meaning*. Amsterdam: Elsevier, 354–61.

Barwise, J. and Cooper, R. (1981). 'Generalized quantifiers and natural language', *Linguistics and Philosophy* 4: 159–219.

Bayer, J. (1999). 'Final complementizers in hybrid languages', *Journal of Linguistics* 35: 233–71.

Bayer, J. (2004). 'Was Beschränkt die Extraktion?', in F. J. D'Avis (ed.), *Deutsche Syntax: Empirie und Theorie*. Gothenburg: Acta Universitatis Gothoburgensis, 233–57.

Beaver, D. and Clark, B. (2008). *Sense and Sensitivity: How Focus Determines Meaning*. Malden, MA: Blackwell.

—— —— Flemming, E., Jaeger, F., and Wolters, M. (2007). 'When semantics meets phonetics: acoustical studies of second occurrence focus', *Language* 83: 245–76.

Beavers, J. (2008). 'Scalar complexity and the structure of events', in J. Dölling, T. Heyde-Zybatow, and M. Schäfer (eds.), *Event Structures in Linguistic Form and Interpretation*. Berlin: Mouton de Gruyter, 245–65.

—— Levin, Beth, and Wei, Tham Shiao (2004). 'A morphosyntactic basis for variation in the encoding of motion events'. Paper presented at the conference on Diversity and Universals in Language: Consequences of Variation. Stanford University.

Beck, S. (2006). 'Intervention effects follow from focus interpretation', *Natural Language Semantics* 14: 1–56.

—— and Johnson, K. (2004). 'Double objects again', *Linguistic Inquiry* 35: 97–124.

—— and Kim, S.-S. (1997). 'On Wh-operator scope in Korean', *Journal of East Asian Linguistics* 6: 339–84, Dordrecht: Kluwer.

—— and Snyder, W. (2001). 'Complex predicates and goal PPs: evidence for a semantic parameter', in A. H.-J. Do, L. Dominguez, and A. Johansen (eds.), *Proceedings of the 25th Annual Boston University Conference on Language Development*. Somerville, MA: Cascadilla Press, 114–22.

Beckman, M. and Pierrehumbert, J. (1986). 'Intonational structure in English and Japanese', *Phonology Yearbook* 3: 255–310.

Beghelli, F. (1993). 'A Minimalist approach to quantifier scope', in A. J. Schafer (ed.), *Proceedings of the North East Linguistic Society* 23. University of Ottawa: Graduate Linguistic Student Association, 65–80.

—— (1995). 'The Phrase Structure of Quantifier Scope'. Ph.D. dissertation, UCLA, Los Angeles.

Belletti, A. (1988). 'The case of unaccusatives', *Linguistic Inquiry* 19: 1–34.

—— and Rizzi, L. (1988). Psych-verbs and (theta)-theory. *Natural Language and Linguistic Theory*, 6(3), 291–352.

—— (2004). 'Aspects of the low IP area', in L. Rizzi (ed.), *The Structure of CP and IP. The Cartography of Syntactic Structures*, Vol. 2. New York: Oxford University Press, 16–51.

—— and Leonini, C. (2004). 'Subject inversion in L2 Italian', in S. Foster-Cohen, M. Sharwood Smith, A. Sorace, and M. Ota (eds.), *Eurosla Yearbook* 4. Amsterdam: John Benjamins, 95–118.

Beghelli, F., and Rizzi, L (1988). 'Psych verbs and Theta Theory', *Natural Language and Linguistic Theory* 6: 291–352.

Benedicto, E. (1997). *The Syntax and Semantics of non-canonical NP Positions.* Ph.D. dissertation, University of Massachusetts, Amherst.

Beneš, E. (1971). 'Die Besetzung der ersten Position im deutschen Aussagesatz', *Fragen der Strukturellen Syntax und der Kontrastiven Grammatik. Sprache der Gegenwart* 17. Düsseldorf: Schwann, 160–82.

Benincà, P. (1988). 'L'ordine Degli Elementi Della Frase e le Costruzioni Marcate', in L. Renzi and G. Salvi (eds.), *Grande Grammatica Italiana di Consultazione.* Bologna: Il Mulino, 115–19.

—— and Poletto, C. (2004). 'Topic, focus, and V2: defining the CP sublayers', in Luigi Rizzi (ed.), *The Structure of CP and IP: The Cartography of Syntactic Structures*, Vol. 2. Oxford: Oxford University Press, 52–75.

Benmamoun, E. (2000). *The Feature Structure of Functional Categories: A Comparative Study of Arabic Dialects.* Oxford: Oxford University Press.

Bennis, H. (1986). *Gaps and Dummies.* Dordrecht: Foris.

Bentley, D. (2004). 'Ne-cliticization and split intransitivity', *Journal of Linguistics* 40: 219–62.

—— (2006). 'Existentials and locatives'. Ms. University of Manchester.

Berman, S. (1987). 'Situation-based semantics for adverbs of quantification', in J. Blevins and A. Vainikka (eds.), *University of Massachusetts Occasional Papers*, vol. 12. University of Massachusetts at Amherst, 8–23.

Besten, H. den (1985). 'The Ergative Hypothesis and free word order in Dutch and German', in J. Toman (ed.), *Studies in German Grammar.* Dordrecht: Foris, 23–65.

Bezooijen, R. van (2005). 'Approximant /r/ in Dutch: routes and feelings', *Speech Communication* 47 (1–2): 15–31.

Bhat, D. N. S. (1994). *The Adjectival Category: Criteria for Differentiation and Identification.* Amsterdam: John Benjamins.

Bhatt, R. and Pancheva, R. (2006). 'Implicit arguments', in *The Blackwell Companion to Syntax*, vol. II. Oxford: Blackwell Publishers, 554–84.

Bianchi, V. (2006). 'On the syntax of personal arguments', *Lingua* 116: 2023–67.

Birner, B. (1994). 'Information structure and English inversion', *Language* 70: 233–59.

Bishop, J. (2008). 'The effect of position on the realization of second occurrence focus'. *Proceedings of Interspeech 2008.*

Bittner, M. (1999). 'Concealed causatives', *Natural Language Semantics* 7: 1–78.

Boas, H. C. (2003). *Resultative Constructions in English and German.* Stanford: CSLI Publications.

—— (2005). 'Determining the productivity of resultatives: a reply to Goldberg and Jackendoff', *Language* 81 (2): 448–64.

Bobaljik, J. (1994). 'What does adjacency do?' *MIT Working Papers in Linguistics* 22 :1–32

Boeckx, C. (2003). '(In)direct binding', *Syntax* 6 (3): 213–36.

Boersma, P. (1998). 'Functional Phonology'. Ph.D. dissertation, University of Amsterdam. The Hague: Holland Academic Graphics.

—— and Weeknink, D. (2008). 'Praat: Doing Phonetics by Computer (Version 4.2.29)' [Computer program].

Bohnacker, U. (2005). 'Nonnative acquisition of verb second: on the empirical underpinnings of universal L2 claims', in M. den Dikken and C. Tortora (eds.), *The Function of Function Words and Functional Categories*. Amsterdam and Philadelphia: John Benjamins, 41–77.

—— (2006). 'When Swedes begin to learn German: from V2 to V2', *Second Language Research* 22: 1–44.

—— (2010). 'The clause-initial position in L2 Swedish declaratives: Word order variation and discourse pragmatics', *Nordic Journal of Linguistics* 33.2.

—— and Rosén, C. (2007). 'How to start a declarative V2 clause: transfer of syntax or information structure in L2 German', in M. Anderssen and M. Westergaard (eds.), *Nordlyd 34.3*. Tromsø: CASTL, 29–56.

—— —— (2008). 'The clause-initial position in L2 German declaratives: transfer of information structure', *Studies in Second Language Acquisition* 30(4): 511–38.

Boland, J., Tanenhaus, M. K., Garnsey, S. M., and Carlson, G. N. (1995). 'Verb argument structure in parsing and interpretation: evidence from Wh-questions', *Journal of Memory and Language* 34: 774–806.

Borer, H. (1980). 'Empty subjects in Modern Hebrew and Constraints on Thematic Relations'. *Proceedings of NELS 10*.

—— (1991). 'The causative-alternation: a case study in parallel morphology', *The Linguistic Review* 8: 119–58

—— (1995). 'The ups and downs of Hebrew verb movement', *Natural Language and Linguistic Theory* 13: 527–606.

—— (2005a). *Structuring Sense: An Exo-Skeletal Trilogy*. New York: Oxford University Press.

—— (2005b). *Structuring Sense. Volume 2: The Normal Course of Events*. Oxford: Oxford University Press.

—— (2006). 'Locales'. Talk given at the opening colloquium of the SFB 732, Universität Stuttgart, Nov. 2006.

—— and Grodzinsky, Y. (1986). 'Syntactic cliticization and lexical cliticization, the case of Hebrew dative clitics', in H. Borer (ed.), *The Syntax of Pronominal Clitics*. Syntax and Semantics 19. San Diego: Academic Press.

Borik, O. (2002). 'Aspect and reference time'. Ph.D. dissertation, Utrecht: Utrecht Institute of Linguistics OTS.

Bošković, Ž. (1997). 'Superiority effects with multiple Wh-fronting in Serbo-Croatian', *Lingua* 102: 1–20.

—— (2000). 'On multiple feature-checking: multiple Wh-fronting and multiple head-movement', in S. Epstein and N. Hornstein (eds.), *Working Minimalism*, Cambridge, MA: MIT Press, 159–87.

Bowers, J. (1997). 'A binary analysis of resultatives', in R. C. Blight and M. J. Moosally (eds.), *Proceedings of the Texas Linguistics Society*, vol. 38. Austin: University of Texas, 43–58.

Branigan, P. (1992). 'Subjects and Complementizers'. Ph.D. dissertation, MIT, Cambridge, MA.

Bresnan, J. (1977). 'Variables in the theory of transformations', in P. Culicover, T. Wasow, and A. Akmajian (eds.), *Formal Syntax*. New York: Academic Press, 157–96.

—— (1982). 'Control and complementation', in Joan Bresnan (ed.), *The Mental Representation of Grammatical Relations*. Cambridge, MA: MIT Press, 282–390.

—— (1993). 'Locative inversion and the architecture of UG'. Ms. Stanford.

—— and Kanerva, J. (1989). 'Locative inversion in Chichewa', *Linguistic Inquiry* 20: 1–50.

Broccias, C. (2008). 'Towards a history of English resultative constructions: the case of adjectival resultative constructions', *English Language & Linguistics* 12: 27–54.

Brody, M. (1990). 'Some remarks on the focus field in Hungarian', *UCL Working Papers in Linguistics*, 201–25.

Broekhuis, H. (2006). 'Extraction from subjects', in H. Broekhuis, N. Corver, R. Huybregts, U. Kleinhenz, and J. Koster (eds.), *Organizing Grammar*. Berlin: Mouton de Gruyter, 59–68.

Browman, C. P. and Goldstein, L. M. (1989). 'Articulatory gestures as phonological units', *Phonology* 6: 201–51.

—— —— (1992). 'Articulatory phonology: an overview', *Phonetica* 49: 155–80.

Bruce, G. (1998). 'Allmän och Svensk prosodi', *Praktisk Linguistik*, vol. 16. Institutionen för Lingvistik, Lunds Universitet.

Bruening, B. (2001). 'Syntax at the edge'. Ph.D. dissertation, MIT, Cambridge, MA.

Bruhn-Garavito, J. (2000). 'The syntax of Spanish multi-functional clitics and near-native competence'. Ph.D. dissertation, McGill University, Montreal.

Büring, D. (1997). *The Meaning of Topic and Focus: The 59th Street Bridge Accent*. London: Routledge.

—— (2003). 'On D-trees, beans, and B-Accents', *Linguistics & Philosophy* 26 (5): 511–45.

—— (2008). 'Been there, marked that – a tentative theory of second occurrence focus'. Ms. UCLA.

Burzio, L. (1981). 'Intransitive verbs and Italian auxiliaries'. Ph.D. dissertation, MIT, Cambridge, MA.

—— (1986). *Italian Syntax: A Government-Binding Approach*. Dordrecht: Reidel and Dordrecht: Kluwer.

Butler, J. (2004). 'Phase structure, phrase structure, and quantification'. Ph.D. dissertation, University of York.

Bybee, J. L. (1985). *Morphology: A Study of the Relation between Meaning and Form*. Amsterdam: John Benjamins.

—— (2006). 'From usage to grammar: the mind's response to repetition', *Language* 82: 529–51.

Cagri, I. M. (2005). 'Minimality and Turkish relative clauses'. Ph.D dissertation, University of Maryland College Park.

Campbell, N. and Beckman, M. (1997). 'Stress, prominence, and spectral tilt', in A. Botinis *et al.* (ed.), *Intonation: Theory, Models and Applications (Proceedings of an ESCA Workshop*, Athens, 18–20 September 1997). ESCA and University of Athens Department of Informatics.

Cantrall, W. (1974). *Viewpoint, Reflexives, and the Nature of Noun Phrases.* The Hague: Mouton.

Cardinaletti, A. (2004). 'Toward a cartography of subject positions', in L. Rizzi (ed.), *The Structure of CP and IP: The Cartography of Syntactic Structures.* Oxford: Oxford University Press, 115–66.

Carleton, T. and Waksler, R. (2000). 'Pronominal markers in Zenzontepec Chatino', *International Journal of American Linguistics* 66: 383–418.

Carnie, A. (2006). *Syntax: A Generative Introduction.* Malden: Wiley-Blackwell.

Carrier, J. and Randall, J. H. (1992). 'The argument structure and syntactic structure of resultatives', *Linguistic Inquiry* 23: 173–234.

Castillo, J. C. (2001). 'Thematic relations between nouns'. Unpublished dissertation, University of Maryland at College Park.

Chafe, W. (1987). 'Cognitive constraints on information flow', in R. Tomlin (ed.), *Coherence and Grounding in Discourse.* Amsterdam: John Benjamins, 21–55.

Cheng, C. D. and Hsin-yi, C. H. (2006). 'Is it difficult to acquire subjacency and the ECP?', *Taiwan Journal of Linguistics* 4: 89–130.

Cheng, L. (1991). 'On the typology of WH-questions'. Ph.D. dissertation, MIT, Cambridge, MA.

—— and Ritter, E. (1987). 'A small clause analysis of inalienable possession in Mandarin and French', *Proceedings of NELS* 18: 65–78.

Cheng, L. L.-S., Huang, C.-T. J., and Tang C.-C. J. (1997). 'Negative particle questions: a dialectal comparison', in J. Black and V. Motapanyane (eds.), *Micro-Parametric Syntax: Dialectal Variation in Syntax.* Philadelphia: John Benjamins, 41–74.

Chila-Markopoulou, D. and Mozer, A. (2001). 'Telicity and referentiality in the VP of Modern Greek: aspect and determiner', (Telikotita kai anaforikotita sti rimatiki frasi tis NE: Pion energias kai arthro), in Y. Agouraki *et al.* (eds.), *Proceedings of the 4th International Conference on Greek Linguistics.* Nicosia: University Studio Press, 138–45.

Chinese Knowledge Information Processing Group (CKIP). (1995). *Character Frequency of Modern Chinese* (No. Technical report 95–01). Taipei: Institute of Information Science, Academia Sinica.

Cho, T. and Ladefoged, P. (1999). 'Variation and universals in VOT: evidence from 18 languages', *Journal of Phonetics* 27: 207–29.

Choe, H. S. (1987). 'Syntactic adjunction, A-Chain and the ECP–multiple identical case construction in Korean', *North Eastern Linguistic Society* 17: 100–21.

Choi, J.-W. (1985). 'Pitch-accent and q/wh words in Korean', in S Kuno, J. Whitman, I.-H. Lee, and Y.-S. Kang, (eds.), *Harvard Studies in Korean Linguistics.* Seoul: Hanshin, 113–23.

Chomsky, N. (1957). *Syntactic Structures.* The Hague: Mouton

—— (1965). *Aspects of the Theory of Syntax.* Cambridge, MA: MIT Press.

—— (1970). 'Remarks on nominatization', in R. Jacobs and P. Rosenbaum (eds.). *Readings in English Transformational Grammar.* Waltham, MA: Ginn, 184–221.

—— (1971). 'Deep structure, surface structure and semantic interpretation', in D. Steinberg and L. Jakobovits (eds.), *Semantics: An Interdisciplinary Reader in Philosophy. Linguistics and Psychology.* Cambridge: Cambridge University Press, 232–96.

Chomsky, N. (1981). *Lectures on Government and Binding*. Dordrecht: Foris.

—— (1986). *Knowledge of Language*. New York: Praeger.

—— (1989). 'Some notes on economy of derivation and representation', in I. Laka and A. Mahajan (eds.), *MIT Working Papers in Linguistics #10*. MIT, 43–74.

—— (1993). 'A Minimalist Program for linguistic theory', in K. Hale and J. Keyser (eds.), *The View from Building 20*. Cambridge, MA: MIT Press, 1–52.

Chomsky, N. (1995a). 'Bare phrase structure', in G. Webelhuth (ed.), *Government Binding Theory and the Minimalist Program*. Oxford: Oxford University Press, 383–439.

—— (1995b). *Minimalist Program*. Cambridge, MA: MIT Press.

—— (2000). 'Minimalist inquiries: the framework', in R. Martin, D. Michaels, and J. Uriagereka (eds.), *Step by Step: Essays on Minimalist Syntax in Honor of Howard Lasnik*. Cambridge, MA: MIT Press, 89–155.

—— (2001). 'Derivation by phase', in Michael Kenstowicz (ed.), *Ken Hale: A Life in Language*. Cambridge, MA: MIT Press, 1–52.

—— (2008). 'On phases', in R. Freidin, C. Otero, and M.-L. Zubizarreta (eds.), *Foundational Issues in Linguistic Theory*. Cambridge, MA: MIT Press, 133–66.

—— and Halle, M. (1968). *The Sound Pattern of English*. New York: Harper and Row.

—— and Lasnik, H. (1977). 'Filters and Control', *Linguistic Inquiry* 8: 425–504.

Chung, D. (2000). 'On the representation and operation of WH-questions', *Seoul International Conference on Language and Computation*.

Cinque, G. (1999). *Adverbs and Functional Heads: A Cross-Linguistic Perspective*. Oxford: Oxford University Press.

—— (2005). 'Deriving Greenberg's Universal 20 and its exceptions', *Linguistic Inquiry* 36: 315–32.

Citko, B. (2005). 'On the nature of Merge: External Merge, Internal Merge, and Parallel Merge', *Linguistic Inquiry* 36 (4): 475–96.

Clahsen, H. and Muysken, P. (1986). 'The availability of Universal Grammar to adult and child learners: a study of the acquisition of German word order', *Second Language Research* 2: 93–119.

Clancy, P. (1980). 'Referential choice in English and Japanese narrative discourse', in Wallace L. Chafe (ed.), *The Pear Stories: Cognitive, Cultural, and Linguistic Aspects of Narrative Production*. Norwood, NJ: Ablex, 127–202.

Clements, G. N. (1980). *Vowel Harmony in Nonlinear Generative Phonology: An Autosegmental Model*. Bloomington, IN: Indiana University Linguistics Club.

Clifton, C., Jr, Kennison, S., and Albrecht, J. (1997). 'Reading the words her, his, him: implications for parsing principles based on frequency and structure', *Journal of Memory and Language*, 36: 276–292.

Cohen, A. and Erteschik-Shir, N. (2002). 'Topic, focus and the interpretation of bare plurals', *Natural Language Semantics* 10.

Cohn, A. (2006). 'Is there Gradient Phonology?', in G. Fanselow, C. Féry, R. Vogel, and M. Schlesewsky (eds.), *Gradience in Grammar: Generative Perspectives*. Oxford: Oxford University Press, 25–44.

Cole, P. and Hermon, G. (1994). 'Is there LF Wh-movement?', *Linguistic Inquiry* 25: 239–62.

—— —— (1998). 'The typology of wh-movement: wh-questions in Malay', *Syntax* 1–3: 221–58.

Collins, B. and Mees, I. (1996). *The Phonetics of English and Dutch.* 3rd edn. Leiden: E. J. Brill.

Collins, C. (1997). *Local Economy.* Cambridge, MA: MIT Press.

Comrie, B. (1976). *Aspect.* Cambridge: Cambridge University Press.

—— (1981). *Language Universals and Linguistic Typology.* Chicago: University of Chicago Press.

Cooper, R. (1974). 'The control of eye fixation by the meaning of spoken language', *Cognitive Psychology* 6: 84–107.

—— (1979). 'The interpretation of pronouns', in F. Heny and H. Schnelle (eds.), *Syntax and Semantics 10: Selections from the Third Groningen Round Table.* New York: Academic Press, 61–92.

Crain, S., Conway, L., and Ni, W. (1994). 'Learning, parsing, and modularity', in C. Clifton, L. Frazier, and K. Rayner (eds.), *Perspectives on Sentence Processing.* Hillsdale, NJ: Lawrence Erlbaum Associate, 443–67.

Croft, W. (1991). *Syntactic Categories and Grammatical Relations.* Chicago: Chicago University Press.

Cuervo, C. (2003). 'Datives at Large'. Ph.D. dissertation, MIT, Cambridge, MA.

Culicover, P. (1993). 'Evidence against ECP accounts of the that-trace effect', *Linguistic Inquiry* 24: 557–61.

—— and Jackendoff, R. (1995). '*Something Else* for the Binding Theory', *Linguistic Inquiry* 26: 249–75.

Daneš, F. (1970). 'Zur linguistischen Analyse der Textstruktur', *Folia Linguistica* 4: 72–9.

Davidson, D. (1967). 'The logical form of action sentences', in N. Rescher (ed.), *The Logic of Decision and Action.* Pittsburgh, PA: University of Pittsburgh Press, 81–95.

Dayal, V. (1996). *Locality in Wh-quantification.* Dordrecht: Kluwer.

—— (2002). 'Single-pair versus Multiple-pair answers: *Wh*-in-situ and scope', *Linguistic Inquiry* 33: 512–20.

Deal, A. R. (2009). 'The origin and content of expletives: evidence from "selection"', to appear in *Syntax.*

Déchaine, R.-M. (1993). 'Predicates Across Categories'. Ph.D. dissertation, University of Massachusetts, Amherst, MA.

Deguchi, M. and Kitagawa, Y. (2002). 'Prosody and Wh-questions', in Masako Hirotani (ed.), *Proceedings of the North East Linguistics Society,* vol. 1. City University of New York and New York University, Amherst, MA: GLSA, University of Massachusetts, Amherst, 73–92.

Delattre, P. and Freeman, D. C. (1968). 'A dialect study of American r's by x–ray motion picture', *Linguistics* 44: 29–68.

Demirdache, H. and Uribe-Etxebarria, M. (2000). 'The primitives of temporal relations', in R. Martin, D. Michaels, and J. Uriagereka (eds.), *Step by Step: Essays on Minimalist Syntax in Honor of Howard Lasnik.* Cambridge, MA: MIT Press, 157–86.

Dentler, S. (2000). 'Deutsch und Englisch – das gibt immer Krieg!', in S. Dentler, B. Hufeisen, and B. Lindemann (eds.), *Tertiär- und Drittsprachen: Projekte und Empirische Untersuchungen.* Tübingen: Stauffenburg, 77–97.

Dikken, M. den (1995). *Particles: On the Syntax of Verb-Particle, Triadic and Causative Constructions.* New York: Oxford University Press.

Dikken, M. den (2003a). 'Lexical integrity, checking and the mirror: a checking approach to syntactic word-formation', *Journal of Comparative Germanic Linguistics* 6: 169–225.

Dikken, M. den (2003b). 'On the morphosyntax of Wh-movement', in C. Boeckx and K. Grohmann (eds.), *Multiple Wh-Fronting. Linguistics Today,* 64. Amsterdam: John Benjamins, 77–98.

Di Sciullo, A.-M. and Williams, E. (1987). *On the Definition of Word.* Cambridge, MA: MIT Press.

Dixon, R. M. W. (1982). *Where Have all the Adjectives Gone?* Berlin: de Gruyter.

Dobler, E., Newell, H., Piggott, G., Skinner, T., Sugimura, M., and Travis, L. (2009). 'Narrow syntactic movement after Spell-Out'. Paper presented at Minimalist Approaches to Syntactic Locality, Budapest.

Dobrovie-Sorin, C. and Laka, B. (1996). 'Generic Bare NPs'. Ms. University Paris 7 and University of Strasburg.

Docherty, G. J. (1992). *The Timing of Voicing in British English Obstruents.* New York and Berlin: Foris.

Doron, E. (1986). 'The pronominal copula as agreement clitic', in H. Borer (ed.), *The Syntax of Pronominal Clitics.* Syntax and Semantics 19. New York: Academic Press, 313–32.

Dowty, D. (1979). *Word Meaning and Montague Grammar: The Semantics of Verbs and Times in Generative Semantics and Montague's PTQ.* Dordrecht and London: Reidel.

Dryer, M. (1994). 'The pragmatics of association with only'. Paper presented at the 1994 Winter Meeting of the LSA. Boston, Massachusetts.

Duffield, N. (1999). 'Final modals, adverbs and antisymmetry in Vietnamese', *Revue québécoise de linguistique* 27: 92–129.

—— (2005). 'Flying squirrels and dancing girls: events, inadvertent cause and unaccusativity in English', in L. Bateman and C. Ussery (eds.), *Proceedings of NELS 35.* Booksurge Publishing, 154–75.

—— (2007a). 'Interesting facts? Events, inadvertent cause, and unaccusativity in English present participles'. Paper presented at *Forces in Grammatical Theory Conference,* Paris.

—— (2007b). 'Aspects of Vietnamese clause structure: separating tense from assertion', *Linguistics* 45: 765–814.

Duffield, N. (ed.) (2009). *Vietnamese Online Grammar Project,* < http://www.vietnamese-grammar.group.shef.ac.uk > .

Duffield, N. (in prep.). 'Close to perfect: particles and projections in Vietnamese syntax'. Ms. University of Sheffield.

—— (submitted a). 'Illusory islands?: A note on "Wh-islands in Vietnamese" (Bruening & Tran 2006)', *Journal of East Asian Linguistics*.

—— (submitted b). 'Complementizers, Q-markers and Yes-No questions in Vietnamese: implications for parameter-setting', *Natural Language and Linguistic Theory*.

—— and Phan, T. (in prep.). 'Temporal Relations in Vietnamese'. Ms, University of Sheffield.

Dupoux, E., Kaheki, K., Hirose, Y., Pallier, C., and Mehler, J. (1999). 'Epenthetic vowels in Japanese: a perceptual illusion?', *Journal of Experimental Psychology* 25: 1568–78.

Eid, M. (1983). 'The copula function of pronouns', *Lingua* 59: 197–207.

—— (1991). 'The copula pronoun in Arabic and Hebrew', in B. Comrie and M. Eid (eds.), *Perspectives on Arabic Linguistics III*. Amsterdam & Philadelphia: John Benjamins, 31–61.

Elbourne, P. D. (2005). *Situations and Individuals*. Cambridge, MA: MIT Press.

Embick, D. (2000). 'Features, syntax, and categories in the Latin Perfective', *Linguistic Inquiry* 31: 185–230.

Embick, D. (2007). 'Linearization and local dislocation: derivational mechanics and interactions', *Linguistic Analysis* 33: 303–36.

—— and Noyer, R. (2001). 'Movement operations after syntax', *Linguistic Inquiry* 32 (4): 555–95.

Emonds, J. E. (1976). *A Transformational Approach to English Syntax*. New York: Academic Press.

Endo, Y. (2007). *Locality and Information Structure*. Amsterdam: John Benjamins.

Epstein, S. D. and Seely, T. D. (2002). 'Rule applications as cycles in a level-free syntax', in S. D. Epstein and T. D. Seely (eds.), *Derivation and Explanation in the Minimalist Program*. Malden, MA: Blackwell, 65–89.

Erteschik-Shir, N. (1973). 'On the nature of island constraints'. Ph.D. dissertation, MIT, Cambridge, MA.

—— (2006). 'What's what?', in G. Fanselow, C. Féry, M. Schlesewsky, and R. Vogel (eds.), *Gradience in Grammar*. Oxford: Oxford University Press.

Español-Echevarría, M. (1997). 'Inalienable possession in copulative contexts and the DP-structure', *Lingua* 101: 211–44.

Espinal, M. T. (1991). 'The representation of disjunct constituents', *Language* 67: 726–63.

Evans, G. (1977). 'Pronouns, quantifiers, and relative clauses', *Canadian Journal of Philosophy* 7: 467–536.

Ewen, C. J. and Hulst, van der H. (2001). *The Phonological Structure of Words*. Cambridge: Cambridge University Press.

Fabricius-Hansen, C. and Solfjeld, K. (1994). 'Deutsche und norwegische Sachprosa im Vergleich', *Arbeitsberichte des Germanistischen Instituts der Universität Oslo* 6.

Fanselow, G. (2007). 'The restricted access of information structure to syntax: a minority report', in C. Féry, G. Fanselow and M. Krifka (eds.), *Interdisciplinary Studies on Information Structure* 6. Potsdam: Universitätsverlag Potsdam, 205–220.

Fanselow, G., Féry, C., Schlesewsky, M., and Vogel, R., (2006). 'Introduction', in G. Fanselow, C. Féry, M. Schlesewsky, and R. Vogel (eds.), *Gradience in Grammar*. Oxford: Oxford University Press.

Fassi Fehri, A. (1993). *Issues in the Structure of Arabic Clauses and Words*. Dordrecht: Kluwer.

Féry, C. (2007). 'Information structural notions and the fallacy of invariant correlates', in C. Féry, G. Fanselow, and M. Krifka (eds.), *Interdisciplinary Studies on Information Structure* 6. Potsdam: Universitätsverlag Potsdam, 161–84.

—— and Samek-Lodovici, V. (2006). 'Focus projection and prosodic prominence in nested foci', *Language* 82: 131–50.

—— and Shinichiro, I. (2009). 'The Phonology of Second Occurrence Focus', *Journal of Linguistics* 45: 285–313.

Fiengo, R. and May, R. (1994). *Indices and Identity*. Cambridge, MA: MIT Press.

—— and McClure, W. (2002). 'On How to Use –*Wa*', *Journal of East Asian Linguistics* 11: 5–41.

Fintel, K. von (1994). 'Restrictions on quantifier domains'. Ph.D. dissertation: University of Massachussets, Amherst, MA.

Fitzpatrick, J. and Groat, E. (2005). 'The timing of syntactic operations: phases, c-command, remerger, and Lebeaux effects'. Paper presented at ECO5, March 2005.

Flemming, E. (1995). 'Auditory Representations in Phonology'. Ph.D. dissertation, UCLA.

Fodor, J. A. (1970). 'Three reasons for not deriving "kill" from "cause to die"', *Linguistic Inquiry* 1: 429–38.

Folli, R. and Ramchand, G. (2005). 'Prepositions and results in Italian and English: an analysis from event decomposition', in H. Verkyul, H. van Hout, and H. de Swartz (eds.), *Perspectives on Aspect*. Dordrecht: Springer, 81–105.

Foulkes, P. and Docherty, G. J. (2000). 'Another chapter in the story of /r/: "labiodental" variants in British English', *Journal of Sociolinguistics* 4: 30–59.

Fox, D. (1999). 'Reconstruction, Binding Theory, and the interpretation of chains', *Linguistic Inquiry* 30 (2): 157–96.

—— (2002). 'Antecedent-contained deletion and the copy theory of movement', *Linguistic Inquiry* 33 (1): 63–96.

—— (2003). 'On logical form', in R. Hendrick (ed.), *Minimalist Syntax*. Oxford: Blackwell, 82–123.

—— and Nissenbaum, J. (1999). 'Extraposition and scope: a case for overt QR', in S. Bird, A. Carnie, J. D. Haugen, and P. Norquest (eds.), *Proceedings of the West Coast Conference on Formal Linguistics* 18. Somerville, MA: Cascadilla Press, 132–44.

—— —— (2004). 'Condition A and scope reconstruction', *Linguistic Inquiry* 35 (3): 475–85.

—— and Pesetsky, D. (2004). 'Cyclic linearization of syntactic structure', *Theoretical Linguistics* 31 (1–2): 1–46.

Frampton, J. (2004). Copies, traces, occurrences, and all that: evidence from Bulgarian multiple Wh-phenomena. Ms. Northeastern University.

—— and Gutmann, S. (2000). 'Crash-proof syntax'. Ms. Northeastern University.

Frascarelli, M. and Hinterhölzl, R. (2007). 'Types of topic in German and Italian', in K. Schwabe and S. Winkler (eds.), *On Information structure, Meaning and Form*. Amsterdam: John Benjamins, 87–116.

Frazier, L. and Fodor, J. D. (1978). 'The sausage machine: a new two-stage parsing model', *Cognition* 6: 291–325.

Freeze, R. (1992). 'Existentials and other locatives', *Language* 68: 553–95.

Freidin, R. (1986). 'Fundamental issues in the theory of Binding', in B. Lust (ed.), *Studies in the Acquisition of Anaphora*, Vol. 1. Dordrecht: Reidel, 151–88.

Fujita, K. (1996). 'Double objects, causatives and derivational economy', *Linguistic Inquiry* 27: 146–73.

Gahl, S. and Garnsey, S. (2006). 'Knowledge of grammar includes knowledge of syntactic probabilities', *Language* 82: 405–10.

Gallego, Á. and Uriagereka, J. (2006). 'Sub-extraction from subjects: A Phase Theory account', in J. Camacho, N. Flores-Ferrán, L. Sánchez, V. Déprez, and M. J. Cabrera (eds.), *Romance Linguistics 2006*. Amsterdam: John Benjamins, 149–62.

Geach, P. (1962). *Reference and Generality*. New York, Ithaca: Cornell University Press.

Gennari, S. and MacDonald, M. (2005/6). 'Acquisition of negation and quantification: insights from adult production and comprehension', *Language Acquisition* 13: 125–68.

Gergely, G. and Csibra, G. (2003). 'Teleological reasoning in infancy: the naïve theory of rational action', *Trends in Cognitive Sciences* 7: 287–92.

Geuder, W. (2000). 'Oriented adverbs: issues in the lexical semantics of event adverbs', Ph.D. dissertation, Universität Tübingen.

Geurts, B. (1998). 'Presuppositions and anaphors in attitude contexts', *Linguistics and Philosophy* 21: 545–601.

—— and van der Sandt, R. (2004). 'Interpreting focus', *Theoretical Linguistics* 30: 1–44.

Giannakidou, A. and Merchant, J. (1998). 'Aspectual effects on donkey anaphora', *Studies in Greek Linguistics* 18: 141–54.

—— —— (2002). Modularity in the Minimalist Program. Paper presented at the Maryland Mayfest.

Gick, B., Campbell, F. Oh, S., and Tamburri–Watt, L. (2006). 'Toward universals in the gestural organization of syllables: a cross–linguistic study of liquids', *Journal of Phonetics* 34: 49–72.

Givón, T. (1983). 'Introduction', in T. Givón (ed.), *Topic Continvity in Discourse*. Amsterdam and Philadelphia: John Benjamins, 5–41.

—— (1984). *Syntax: A Functional-Typological Introduction*. Amsterdam: John Benjamins.

Gleitman, L. (1990). 'The structural sources of verb meanings', *Language Acquisition* 1: 3–55.

Glenberg, A., Robertson, D., Jansen, J., and Johnson-Glenberg, M. (1999). 'Not propositions', *Journal of Cognitive Science Systems Research* 1: 19–33.

Goad, H. and Travis, L. (in preparation). 'Navajo verbal morphology and the syntax/phonology interface'. Ms. McGill University, Montreal.

Godjevac, S. (2004). *Focus Projection in Serbo-Croatian*. Stanford: CSLI.

Goldberg, A. E. (1995). *Constructions: A Construction Grammar Approach to Argument Structure*. Chicago: Chicago University Press.

—— and Jackendoff, R. (2004). 'The resultative as a family of constructions', *Language* 80: 532–68.

—— —— (2005). 'The end result(ative)', *Language* 81 (2): 474–7.

Goldberg, L. (2005). 'Verb-Stranding VP Ellipsis: A Cross-Linguistic Study'. Ph.D. dissertation, McGill University.

Goldsmith, J. (1990). *Autosegmental and Metrical Phonology*. Oxford: Blackwell.

Green, G. M. (1972). 'Some observations on the syntax and semantics of instrumental verbs', *Chicago Linguistic Society* 8: 83–97.

Grewendorf, G. (2005). 'The discourse configurationality of scrambling', in J. Sabel and M. Saito (eds.), *The Free Word Order Phenomenon: Its Syntactic Sources and Diversity*. Berlin: Mouton de Gruyter, 75–135.

Grice, P. (1975). 'Logic and conversation', in P. Cole and J. Morgan, (eds.), *Syntax and Semantics*. New York: Academic Press, 41–58.

Grimshaw, J. (1990). *Argument Structure*. Cambridge, MA: MIT Press.

—— (1991). 'Extended projection'. Unpublished manuscript, Brandeis University.

Gualmini, A. (2003). 'The Ups and Downs of Child Language'. Ph.D. dissertation, College Park: University of Maryland.

—— (2004a). *The Ups and Downs of Child Language*. New York: Routledge.

—— (2004b). 'Some knowledge children don't lack', *Linguistics* 42: 957–82.

—— Hulsey, S., Hacquard, V., and Fox, D. (2008). 'The Question-Answer requirement and scope assignment', *Natural Language Semantics* 16: 205–37.

—— and Schwarz, B. (2009). 'Solving learnability problems in the acquisition of semantics', *Journal of Semantics* 26: 185–215.

Guasti, M. T., Chierchia, G., Crain, S., Foppolo, F., Gualmini, A., and Meroni, L. (2005). 'Why children and adults sometimes (but not always) compute implicatures', *Language and Cognitive Processes* 20: 667–96.

Guenther, F. H., Espy–Wilson, C. Y., Boyce, S. E., Matthies, M. L., Zandipour, M., and Perkell, J. S. (1999). 'Articulatory tradeoffs reduce acoustic variability during American English /r/ production', *Journal of the Acoustical Society of America* 105: 2854–65.

Gussenhoven, C. (1983). 'Testing the reality of focus domains', *Language and Speech* 26: 61–80.

Haan, G. de (1994). 'Inflection and cliticization in Frisian: *-sto, -ste, -st*', *NOWELE* 23: 75–90.

Haegeman, L. (1988). 'Parenthetical Adverbials: The Radical Orphanage Approach', in S. Chiba (ed.), *Aspects of Modern Linguistics*. Tokyo: Kaitakushi, 232–254.

Haegeman, L. (1992). 'Negation in West Flemish and the Neg Criterion', *Proceedings of the North Eastern Linguistics Society (NELS) 22*. Amherst: University of Massachussetts, GLSA.

Haegeman, L. (1995). *The Syntax of Negation*. Cambridge: Cambridge University Press.

Haegeman, L., and Zanuttini, R. (1991). 'Negative Heads and the Neg Criterion', *The Linguistic Review* 8: 233–52.

Hagstrom, P. (1998). 'Phrasal Movement in Korean Negation'. *Proceedings of SCIL* 9.

Haider, H. (2005). 'Mittelfeld Phenomena', in M. Everaert and H. van Riemsdijk (eds.), *The Blackwell Companion to Syntax* vol.3. Oxford: Basil Blackwell, 204–274.

Hajičová, E., Partee, B. H., and Sgall, P. (1998). *Topic-Focus Articulation, Tripartite Structures, and Semantic Content*. Dordrecht: Kluwer.

Håkansson, G. (1997). 'Barnets väg till svensk Syntax', in R. Söderbergh (ed.), *Från Joller till Läsning och Skrivning*. Malmö: Gleerups, 47–60.

Hale, K. (1980). 'Remarks on Japanese phrase structure: comments on papers on Japanese syntax'. *MIT Working Papers in Linguistics* 2. Cambridge, MA: MIT, 185–203.

—— (2000). 'There-insertion unaccusatives'. Ms. MIT.

—— (2001). 'Navajo verb stem position and the bipartite structure of the Navajo conjunct sector', *Linguistic Inquiry* 32 (4): 678–93.

—— (2004). 'On the significance of Eloise Jelinek's pronominal argument hypothesis', in A. Carnie, H. Harley, and M. Willie (eds.), *Formal Approaches to Functional Phenomena*. Amsterdam: John Benjamins, 11–43.

Hale, K. and Keyser, J. (1991). 'On the syntax of argument structure', in *Lexicon Project Working Paper #34*. MIT Center for Cognitive Science.

—— —— (1993). 'On argument structure and the lexical expression of syntactic relations', in K. Hale and S. J. Keyser (eds.), *The View from Building 20: Essays in Honor of Sylvain Bromberger*. Cambridge, MA: MIT Press, 53–109.

—— —— (2002). *Prolegomenon to a Theory of Argument Structure*. Cambridge, MA: MIT Press.

Halle, M. and Marantz, A. (1993). 'Distributed morphology and the pieces of inflection', in K. Hale and S. J. Keyser (eds.), *The View from Building 20: Essays in Honor of Sylvain Bromberger*. Cambridge, MA: MIT Press, 111–76.

Halliday, M. and Hasan, R. (1976). *Cohesion in English*. London: Longman.

Halliday, M. A. K. (1967). 'Notes on transitivity and theme in English, Part I', *Journal of Linguistics* 3: 37–81.

Hallman, P. (2000). 'The structure of predicates: interactions of derivation, case and quantification'. Ph.D. dissertation, University of California, Los Angeles.

Hameed, J. (1985). 'Lexical phonology and morphology of Modern Standard Turkish', *Cahiers Linguistiques d'Ottawa* 14: 71–95.

Han, J.-Im. (1996). 'The phonetics and phonology of "tense" and "plain" consonants in Korean'. Ph.D. dissertation, Cornell University.

Hara, Y. (2006). 'Grammar of knowledge representation: Japanese discourse items at interfaces'. Ph.D. dissertation. University of Delaware.

Harley, H. (1995.) 'Subjects, events and licensing', Ph.D. dissertation, MIT, Cambridge, MA.

—— (1996). 'Sase bizarre: the Japanese causative and structural case', in P. Koskinen (ed.), *Canadian Linguistics Association (CLA 1995)*, University of Toronto Working Papers in Linguistics, 225–35.

Harley, H. (2004). 'Merge, conflation and head movement: the First Sister Principle revisited,' in K. Moulton, (ed.), *Proceedings of NELS 34*, University of Massachusetts Amherst: GSLA, 239–54.

—— (2007a). 'External arguments: on the independence of Voice° and v°'. Paper presented at the 30th GLOW meeting, University of Tromsø, Norway, 12–14 April 2007.

—— (2007b). 'The bipartite structure of verbs cross-linguistically, or why Mary can't exhibit John her paintings'. Write-up of a talk given at the 2007 ABRALIN Congres in Belo Horizonte, Brazil.

—— (2008). 'On the causative construction', in S. Miyagawa and M. Saito (eds.), *The Oxford Handbook of Japanese Linguistics*. Oxford: Oxford University Press, 20–53.

Harves, S. (2002). 'Unaccusative Syntax in Russian'. Ph.D. dissertation. Princeton University.

Haspelmath, M. (1993). 'More on the typology of inchoative/causative verb alternations', in B. Comrie and M. Polinsky (eds.), *Causatives and Transitivity*. Amsterdam: John Benjamins, 87–120.

Hayashishita, J.-R. (2008). 'On the nature of inverse scope readings'. Ms. University of Otago.

Hayes, B. (1984). 'The phonology of rhythm in English', *Linguistic Inquiry* 15: 33–74.

—— and Lahiri, A. (1991). 'Bengali intonational phonology', *Natural Language and Linguistic Theory* 9: 47–96.

Hazout, I. (1991). 'Verbal nouns: theta-theoretic studies in Hebrew and Arabic'. Ph.D. dissertation, University of Massachusetts, Amherst, MA.

—— (1995). 'Actions nominalization and the lexicalist hypothesis', *Natural Language and Linguistic Theory* 13: 355–404.

Heim, I. (1990). 'E-type pronouns and donkey anaphora', *Linguistics and Philosophy* 13 (2): 137–78.

—— and Kratzer, A. (1998). *Semantics in Generative Grammar*. Malden, MA: Blackwell.

Hengeveld, K. (1992). *Non-Verbal Predication: Theory, Typology, Diachrony*. Berlin: Mouton de Gruyter.

Hertel, T. J. (2003). 'Lexical and discourse factors in the second language acquisition of Spanish word order', *Second Language Research* 19: 273–304.

Heuvel, H. van den and Cucchiarini, C. (2001). 'r–Deletion in Dutch. Rumours or reality', in H. Van de Velde and R. van Hout (eds.), *'r–atics: Sociolinguistic, Phonetic and Phonological Characteristics of /r/*. Brussels: Etudes & Travaux – ILVP/ULB. No 4, 185–98.

Heycock, C. (1993). 'Focus projection in Japanese', in M. González (ed.), *Proceedings of NELS* 24: 157–71.

—— (2008). 'Japanese -*wa*, -*ga*, and information structure', in M. Saito and S. Miyagawa (ed.), *The Oxford Handbook of Japanese Linguistics*. Oxford: Oxford University Press, 54–83.

Higginbotham, J. (1983). 'The logic of perceptual reports: an extensional alternative to situation semantics', *The Journal of Philosophy* 80 (2): 100–27.

—— (1985). 'On Semantics', *Linguistic Inquiry* 16: 547–93.

—— (1999). 'Accomplishments', *Proceedings of the Nanzan GLOW: the second GLOW meeting in Asia*. Nagoya: Nanzan University, 131–9.

—— and Ramchand, G. (1997). 'The stage level/individual level distinction and the mapping hypothesis', *Oxford Working Papers in Linguistics, Philology and Phonetics* 2: 53–83.

Hill, J. (2005). *A Grammar of Cupeño*. Berkeley: University of California Press.

Hirotani, M. (2003). 'Prosodic effect on the comprehension of Japanese Wh-question'. Poster Presentation at the *Sixteenth Annual CUNY Conference on Human Sentence Processing*, 27–9 May.

Hockett, F. (1942). 'A system of descriptive phonology', *Language* 18: 3–21.

Hoekstra, T. (1988). 'Small clause results', *Lingua* 74: 101–39.

—— and Mulder, R. (1990). 'Unergatives as copular verbs: locational and existential predication', *The Linguistic Review* 7: 1–79.

Hoji, H. (1985). 'Logical form constraints and configurational structures in Japanese'. Ph.D. dissertation, University of Washington.

Honcoop, M. (1998). 'Dynamic excursions on weak islands', Ph.D. dissertation, University of Leiden.

Honma, Y. (1981). 'Durational relationship between Japanese stops and vowels', *Journal of Phonetics* 9: 273–81.

Hopper, P. and Thompson, S. (1984). 'The discourse basis for lexical categories in Universal Grammar', *Language* 60: 703–52.

Horn, L. R. (1989). *A Natural History of Negation*. Chicago: University of Chicago Press.

Hornstein, N. (2009). *A Theory of Syntax*. Cambridge: Cambridge University Press.

Horrocks, G. and Stavrou, M. (2003). 'Actions and their results in Greek and English: the complementarity of morphologically encoded aspect and syntactic resultative predication', *Journal of Semantics* 20: 297–327.

Horvath, J. (1986). *Focus in the Theory of Grammar and the Syntax of Hungarian*. Dordrecht: Foris.

—— (1995). 'Structural Focus, Structural Case, and the Notion of Feature-assignment', in K. Kiss (ed.), 1995a, 28–64.

House, A. and Fairbanks, G. (1953). 'The influence of consonant environment upon the secondary acoustical characteristics of vowels', *Journal of the Acoustical Society of America* 25: 105–13.

Hsiao, F. (2002). 'Tonal domains are stress domains in Taiwanese: evidence from focus', *MIT Working Papers in Linguistics* 42: 109–40.

Hulsey, S., Hacquard, V., Fox, D., and Gualmini, A. (2004). 'The Question-Answer requirement and scope assignment', in A. Csirmaz, A. Gualmini, and A. Nevins (eds.), *Plato's Problem: Problems in Language Acquisition*. Cambridge, MA: MITWPL, 71–90.

Hulst, H., van der and Weijer, J. van de (1991). 'Topics in Turkish Phonology', in H. Boeschoten and L. Verhoeven (eds.), *Turkish Linguistics Today*. Leiden: Brill, 11–59.

Hulst, H., van der and Weijer, J. van de (1995). 'Vowel Harmony', in J. A. Goldsmith (ed.), *The Handbook of Phonological Theory*. Oxford: Blackwell, 495–534.

Huss, V. (1978). 'English word stress in the postnuclear position', *Phonetica* 35: 86–105.

Inkelas, S. (1999). 'The exceptional stress-attracting suffixes in Turkish: representations versus the grammar', in R. Kager, H. van der Hulst, and W. Zonnerveld (eds.), *The Prosody-Morphology Interface*. Cambridge: Cambridge University Press, 134–87.

Inkelas, S. and Orgun, C. O. (1995). 'Level ordering and economy in the lexical phonology of Turkish', *Language* 71: 763–93.

—— —— (1998). 'Level (non)ordering in recursive morphology: evidence from Turkish', in S. G. Lapointe, D. K. Brentari, and P. M. Farrel (eds.), *Morphology and its Relation to Phonology and Syntax*. Stanford: CSLI, 360–410.

—— —— (2003). 'Turkish Stress', *Phonology* 20: 139–61.

Ishihara, S. (2001). 'Stress, focus, and scrambling in Japanese', in *MIT Working Paper in Linguistics 39: A Few from Building E39*: 142–75

—— (2003). 'Intonation and interface conditions'. Ph.D. dissertation, MIT, Cambridge, MA.

—— (2007). 'Major phrase, focus intonation, multiple Spell-Out', *The Linguistic Review* 24: 137–67.

Ishii, T. (2004). 'The Phase Impenetrability Condition, the Vacuous Movement Hypothesis, and *that*-t effects', *Lingua* 114: 183–215.

Ito, C., Kang, Y., and Kenstowicz, M. (2006). 'The adaptation of Japanese loanwords into Korean', *MIT Working Papers in Linguistics* 52: 65–104.

Iverson, G. K. and Salmons, J. C. (1995). 'Aspiration and laryngeal representation in Germanic', *Phonology* 12: 369–96.

Iwata, S. (2006). 'Argument resultatives and adjunct resultatives in a lexical constructional account: the case of resultatives with adjectival result phrases', *Language Sciences* 28 (5): 449–96.

—— (2008). 'A door that swings noiselessly open may creak shut: internal motion and concurrent changes of state', *Linguistics* 46 (6): 1049–108.

Jackendoff, R. (1972). *Semantic Interpretation in Generative Grammar*. Cambridge, MA: MIT Press.

—— (1977). *X-bar Syntax*. Cambridge, MA: MIT Press.

—— (1990a). *Semantic Structures*. Cambridge, MA: MIT Press.

—— (1990b). 'On Larson's treatment of the double object construction', *Linguistic Inquiry* 21: 427–56.

—— (1992). 'Mme. Tussaud meets the Binding Theory', *Natural Language and Linguistic Theory* 10: 1–31.

—— (2002). *Foundations of Language: Brain, Meaning, Grammar, Evolution*. New York: Oxford University Press.

—— (2007). *Language, Culture, Consciousness: Essays on Mental Structure*. Cambridge, MA: MIT Press.

Jacobs, J. (1991). 'Focus ambiguities', *Journal of Semantics* 8: 1–36.

Jaeger, F. (2005). 'Only always associates audibly. Even if only is repeated. The prosodic properties of second occurrence focus in English'. Stanford University. Ms.

Jaeger, T. F. (2004). 'Binding in picture NPs revisited: evidence for a semantic principle of extended argumenthood', in *Proceedings of the LFG04 Conference*. Stanford: CSLI Publications.

Jones, M. (2009). 'Patterns of variability in apical trills: an acoustic study of data from 19 languages'. Unpublished ms.

Jörgensen, N. (1976). *Meningsbyggnaden i talad svenska*. Lund: Studentlitteratur.

Joseph, A., Hornstein, N., Lightfoot, D., and Weinberg, A. (1987). 'Two types of locality', *Linguistic Inquiry* 18: 537–77.

Jun, S.-A. and Oh, M.-R. (1996). 'A prosodic analysis of three types of Wh-phrase in Korean', *Language and Speech* 39 (1): 37–61

Kabak, B. and Vogel, I. (2001). 'The phonological word and stress assignment in Turkish', *Phonology* 18: 315–60.

Kadmon, N. (2001). *Formal Pragmatics*. Oxford: Blackwell.

Kageyama, T. (1989). 'The place of morphology in the grammar: verb-verb compounds in Japanese', *Yearbook of Morphology* 2: 73–94.

Kahnemuyipour, A. (2001). 'On Wh-questions in Persian', *Canadian Journal of Linguistics* 46 (1/2): 41–61.

—— (2003). 'Syntactic categories and Persian stress', *Natural Language and Linguistic Theory* 21(2): 333–79.

—— (2004). 'The Syntax of Sentential Stress'. Ph.D. dissertation, University of Toronto.

—— (2005). 'Escaping sentential stress'. Talk given at the CUNY Graduate Center, Syntax Supper series.

—— (2009). *The Syntax of Sentential Stress*. Oxford: Oxford University Press.

—— and Massam, D. (2006). 'Patterns of phrasal movement: the Niuean DP', in H.-M. Gärtner, P. Law, and J. Sabel (eds.), *Clause Structure and Adjuncts in Austronesian Languages*. Berlin: Mouton de Gruyter, 125–49.

Kaiser, E. and Runner, J. T. (2008). 'Intensifiers in German and Dutch anaphor resolution', in N. Abner and J. Bishop (eds.), *Proceedings of the 27th West Coast Conference on Formal Linguistics*. Somerville, MA: Cascadilla Proceedings Project, 265–73.

—— —— Sussman, R. S., and Tanenhaus, M. K. (2007). 'Pronouns as reflexives? A look at prenominal possessive pronouns'. Presentation at the Linguistic Society of American Annual Meeting, Anaheim, January 2007.

—— —— —— —— (2008). 'The real-time interpretation of pronouns and reflexives: structural and semantic information', in E. Efner and M.Walkow (eds.), *Proceedings of 37th Annual Meeting of the North East Linguistics Society (NELS)*. University of Massachusetts: GLSA, 73–85.

—— —— —— —— (2009). 'Structural and semantic constraints on the resolution of pronouns and reflexives', *Cognition* 112: 55–80.

Kaisse, E. (1985). 'Some theoretical consequences of stress rules in Turkish', *CLS* 21(1). 199–209.

—— (1986). 'Toward a lexical phonology of Turkish', in M. Brame, H. Contreras, and F. Newmeyer (eds.), *A Festschrift for Sol Saporta*. Seattle: Noit Amrofer, 231–40.

Kamali, B. and Samuels, B. (2008). 'The syntax of Turkish pre-stressing suffixes'. Presentation at TIE3, Lisbon.

Kamp, H. (1979). 'Events, instants and temporal reference', in R. Bäuerle, U. Egli, and A. von Stechow (eds.), *Semantics from Different Points of View*. Berlin: Springer, 376–417.

—— (1981a). 'Some remarks on the logic of change, Part I', in C. Rohrer (ed.), *Time, Tense, and Quantifiers: Proceedings of the Stuttgart Conference on the Logic of Tense and Quantification*. Tübingen: Max Niemeyer, 135–79.

—— (1981b). 'A theory of truth and semantic representation', in J. Groenendijk, T. Janssen, and M. Stokhof (eds.), *Formal Methods in the Study of Language*. Amsterdam: Mathematisch Centrum, 277–322.

—— and Reyle, U. (1993). *From Discourse to Logic: Introduction to Modeltheoretic Semantics of Natural Language, Formal Logic and Discourse Representation Theory*. Dordrecht: Kluwer.

Kandybowicz, J. (2006). '*Comp-Trace* effects explained away'. Paper presented at WCCFL 25.

Kari, J. (1975). 'The disjunct boundary in the Navajo and Tanaina verb prefix complexes', *International Journal of American Linguistics* 41: 330–45.

Karttunen, L. (1973). 'Presuppositions of compound sentences', *Linguistic Inquiry* 4: 169–93.

Kawahara, S. (2005). 'Voicing and geminacy in Japanese: an acoustic and perceptual study', in K. Flack and S. Kawahara (eds.), *University of Massachusetts Occasional Papers in Linguistics* 31: 87–120.

Kawamura, T. (2004). 'A feature-checking analysis of Japanese scrambling', *Journal of Linguistics* 40: 45–68.

Kayne, R. (1984). *Connectedness and Binary Branching*. Dordrecht: Foris.

—— (1985). 'Principles of particle constructions', in J. Guéron, H.-G. Obenauer, and J.-Y. Pollock (eds.), *Grammatical Representation*. Dordrecht: Foris.

—— (1994). *The Antisymmetry of Syntax*. Cambridge, MA: MIT Press.

—— (2008). 'Expletives, datives and the tension between morphology and syntax', in T. Biberauer (ed.), *The Limits of Syntactic Variation*. Amsterdam: John Benjamins, 175–217.

Kean, M.-L. (ed.), *Juncture*. Saratoga, CA: Anma Libri, 107–29.

Keller, F. (2000). 'Gradience in grammar: experimental and computational aspects of degrees of grammaticality'. Ph.D. dissertation. University of Edinburgh.

—— and Asudeh, A. (2001). 'Constraints on linguistic coreference: structural vs. pragmatic factors', in J. Moore and K. Stenning (eds.), *Proceedings of 23rd Annual Conference of the Cognitive Science Society*. Mahwah: L. Erlbaum, 483–88.

Kenstowicz, M. and Suchato, A. (2006). 'Issues in loanword adaptation: a case study from Thai', *Lingua* 116: 921–49.

Ketrez, F. N. (2005). 'Children's Scope of Indefinite Objects'. Ph.D. dissertation, University of Southern California.

Kim, C.-W. (1965). 'On the autonomy of the tensity features in stop identification (with special reference to Korean stops)', *Word* 21: 339–59.

Kim, H. (2006). 'A feature-driven non-native percept in the loanword adaptation between Japanese and Korean'. Paper presented at the Phonology Forum 2006, Tokyo.

Kim, S.-S. (2002). 'Focus matters: two types of intervention effect'. Paper presented at WCCFL 21, Santa Cruz.

Kiparsky, P. and Kiparsky, C. (1970). 'Fact', in M. Bierwisch and K. Heidolph (eds.), *Progress in Linguistics*. The Hague: Mouton, 143–73.

Kishimoto, H. (2006). 'Japanese as a topic-movement language', *Scientific Approaches to Language* 5: 85–105

Kiss, K. (1995a). *Discourse Configurational Languages*. New York: Oxford University Press.

—— (1995b). 'NP movement, operator movement, and scrambling in Hungarian', in K. Kiss (ed.), *Discourse Configurational Languages*. New York: Oxford University Press. 207–43.

Kitagawa, Y. and Fodor, J. D. (2003). 'Default prosody explains neglected syntactic analysis in Japanese', in W. McClure (ed.), *Japanese/Korean Linguistics,* vol. 12. Stanford: CSLI Publications, 267–79.

—— and Tomioka, S. (2003). 'Masked island effects in Japanese'. Talk presented at *Workshop on Altaic Formal Linguistics (WAFL),* held at MIT, May.

Klatt, D. H. (1976). 'Linguistic uses of segmental duration in English: acoustic and perceptual evidence', *Journal of the Acoustical Society of America* 59: 1208–21.

Klein, W. (1994). *Time in Language*. London and New York: Routledge.

—— (1995). 'A time-relational analysis of Russian aspect', *Language* 71: 669–95.

—— (n.d.). 'On times and arguments'. Ms. Nijmegen: Max Planck Institute for Psycholinguistics.

Klima, J. (1964). 'Negation in English', in J. Fodor and J. Katz (eds.), *The Structure of Languages*. New Jersey: Prentice-Hall, 246–323.

Ko, H.-J. (2005). 'Syntax of Why-in-situ: Merge into [Spec,CP] in the overt syntax', *Natural Language & Linguistic Theory* 23 (4): 867–916.

Koizumi, M. (1993). 'Object agreement phrases and the Split VP Hypothesis', *MIT Working Papers in Linguistics: Papers on Case and Agreement* 18: 99–148.

—— (1995). 'Phrase Structure in Minimalist Syntax'. Ph.D. dissertation, MIT, Cambridge, MA.

Koopman, H. and Szabolcsi, A. (2000). *Verbal complexes*. Cambridge, MA: MIT Press.

Koot, H., van de and Mathieu, E. (2003). 'What's in an island?'. *UCL Working Papers in Linguistics* 15: 277–313.

Koppen, M. van (2005). *One Probe – Two Goals: Aspects of Agreement in Dutch Dialects*. Utrecht: LOT.

Kornfilt, J. (1993). 'Infinitival WH-Constructions and complementation in Turkish', in K. Börjars and N. Vincent (eds.), *Eurotyp Working Papers: Group 3: Subordination and Complementation*, vol. 4. Strasbourg and Manchester: European Science Foundation, 66–83.

—— (1996). 'On some copular clitics in Turkish', in A. Alexiadou *et al.* (eds.), *ZAS Papers in Linguistics*, vol. 6. Berlin: ZAS, 96–114.

Köskinen, P. (2000). 'Children's acquisition of negation: Turkish evidence', in A. Göksel and C. Kerslake (eds.), *Studies on Turkish and Turkic Languages*. Turcologica 46. Wiesbaden: Harrassowitz Verlag, 299–306.

Krämer, I. (2000). 'Interpreting Indefinites'. Ph.D. dissertation, Max Planck Institute for Psycholinguistics, Nijmegen.

Kratzer, A. (1989). 'An Investigation of the Lumps of Thought', *Linguistics and Philosophy* 12 (5): 607–53.

—— (1990). 'Uniqueness', *Linguistics and Philosophy* 13: 273–324.

—— (1994). 'The event argument and the semantics of voice'. Ms. University of Massachusetts, Amherst.

—— (1996). 'Severing the external argument from its verb', in J. Rooryck and L. A. Zaring (eds.), *Phrase Structure and the Lexicon*. Studies in Natural Language and Linguistic Theory, 33. Dordrecht and Boston: Kluwer, 109–37.

—— (2002). 'Facts: particulars or information units?', *Linguistics and Philosophy* 25 (5): 655–70.

—— (2005a). 'Indefinites and the operators they depend on: from Japanese to Salish', in G. N. Carlson and F. J. Pelletier (eds.), *Reference and Quantification: The Partee Effect*. Stanford: CSLI Publications, 113–42

—— (2005b). 'Building resultatives', in C. Maienborn and A. Wöllstein (eds.), *Event Arguments: Foundations and Applications*. Tübingen: Max Niemeyer, 177–212.

—— (forthcoming). 'Situations in natural language semantics', in *The Stanford Encyclopedia of Philosophy*.

—— and Selkirk, L. (2007). 'Phase theory and prosodic spellout: the case of verbs', *The Linguistic Review* 24: 93–135.

Krifka, M. (1991). 'A compositional semantics for multiple focus constructions', in S. Moore and A. Z. Wyner (eds.), *Proceedings of Semantics and Linguistic Theory 1*. Cornell University: CLC Publications, 127–58.

—— (2001). 'Quantifying into question acts', *Natural Language Semantics* 9: 1–40.

—— (2004). 'Focus and/or context: a second look at second occurrence focus', in H. Kamp and B. Partee (eds.), *Context-Dependence in the Analysis of Linguistic Meaning*. Amsterdam: Elsevier, 187–207.

—— (2007). 'Basic notions of information structure', in C. Féry, G. Fanselow, and M. Krifka (eds.), *Interdisciplinary Studies on Information Structure* 6. Potsdam: Universitätsverlag Potsdam, 13–55.

Kucerova, I. (2009). 'T-extension and null-subject licensing', in S. Lima, K. Mullin, and B. Smith (eds.), *Proceedings of NELS 39* (forthcoming).

Kuno, S. (1973). *The Structure of the Japanese Language*. Cambridge, MA: MIT Press.

Kuno, S. (1987). *Functional Syntax: Anaphora, Discourse, and Empathy*. Chicago: University of Chicago Press.

Kuroda, S.-Y. (1965). 'Generative grammatical studies in the Japanese language'. Ph.D. dissertation, MIT.

—— (1988). 'Whether we agree or not: a comparative syntax of English and Japanese', in W. J. Poser (ed.), *Papers from the Second International Workshop on Japanese Syntax*. Stanford: CSLI, 103–43.

—— (2005). 'Focusing on the matter of topic: a study of *wa* and *ga* in Japanese', *Journal of East Asian Linguistics* 14:1–58.

Kuwabara, K. (1998). 'Overt Wh-movement and scope-fixing scrambling: a preliminary study', in K. Inoue (ed.), *Researching and Verifying an Advanced Theory of Human Language*. Kanda University of International Studies, 115–27.

Kwon, N. (2004). 'A semantic and syntactic analysis of Vietnamese causatives'. Paper presented at Western Conference on Linguistics, UC, San Diego.

LaCharité, D. and Paradis, C. (2005). 'Category preservation and proximity versus phonetic approximation in loanwords adaptation', *Linguistic Inquiry* 36 (2): 223–58.

Ladefoged, Peter (2001). *Vowels and Consonants: An Introduction to the Sounds of Language*. Oxford: Blackwell.

Ladusaw, W. (1979). 'Polarity sensitivity as inherent scope relations'. Ph.D. dissertation, Austin: University of Texas.

Laka, I. (1990). 'Negation in syntax: on the nature of functional categories and projections'. Ph.D. dissertation, MIT.

Lakoff, G. (1970). *Irregularity in Syntax*. New York: Holt, Rinehart and Winston.

—— and J. Ross. (1979). 'A note on anaphoric islands and causatives', *Linguistic Inquiry* 3: 121–5.

Lambrecht, K. (1994). *Information Structure and Sentence Form: Topic, Focus and the Mental Representations of Discourse Referents*. Cambridge: Cambridge University Press.

—— (2000). 'When subjects behave like objects: an analysis of the merging of S and O in sentence focus constructions across languages', *Studies in Language* 24: 611–82.

Landau, I. (2009). *The Locative Syntax of Experiencers*. Cambridge, MA: MIT Press.

Langendoen, D. T. and Savin, H. (1971). 'The projection problem for presuppositions', in C. Fillmore and D. T. Langendoen (eds.), *Studies in Linguistic Semantics*. New York: Holt, Rinehart and Winston, 54–60.

Larson, R. K. (1988). 'On the double object construction', *Linguistic Inquiry* 19: 335–91.

—— (1991). 'Some issues in verb serialization', in C. Lefebvre (ed.), *Serial Verbs*. Philadelphia: John Benjamins, 185–210.

Lasnik, H. and Saito, M. (1992). *Move Alpha*. Cambridge, MA: MIT Press.

Lawson, E., Stuart-Smith, J., and Scobbie, J.M. (2008). 'Articulatory insights into language variation and change: preliminary findings from an ultrasound study of derhoticisation in Scottish English' in K. German (ed.), *U. Penn. Working Papers in Linguistics 14.2: Papers from NWAV 36*, 102–10.

Lebeaux, D. (1988). 'Language acquisition and the form of the grammar'. Ph.D. dissertation, University of Massachusetts, Amherst.

—— (1991). 'Relative clauses, licensing, and the nature of the derivation', in S. Rothstein (ed.), *Perspectives on Phrase Structure: Heads and Licensing*. San Diego: Academic Press, 209–39.

Lee, H.-W. (2002). *Thai Grammar* [Written in Korean]. Seoul: HUFS Press.

Lee, K.-S., and Tomioka, S. (2001). 'LF blocking effects are topic effects: Wh-questions in Japanese and Korean'. Unpublished ms. University of Delaware.

Lee, M.-H., and Chung, S.-W. (1999). 'Focus projection in Korean'. Forthcoming.

Lees, R. B. (1961). *The Phonology of Modern Standard Turkish*. Uralic and Altaic Series 6. Bloomington: Indiana University.

—— (1962). 'A compact analysis for the Turkish personal morphemes', in N. Poppe (ed.), *American Studies in Altaic Linguistics*, Indiana University Uralic and Altaic Series 13, Bloomington: Indiana University & The Hague: Mouton, 141–76.

Leeuw, E. de (2009). *An Acoustic Analysis of Bi–Directional Interference in German–English Bilinguals*. Ph.D. dissertation, Queen Margaret University, Edinburgh.

Lehiste, I. (1980). 'Phonetic manifestation of syntactic structure in English', *Annual Bulletin of the Research Institute of Logopaedics and Phoniatrics* 14: 1–27.

—— and Peterson, G. (1961). 'Some basic considerations in the analysis of intonation', *Journal of the Acoustic Society of America* 33: 419–23.

Levin, B. (1993). *English Verb Classes and Alternations: a Preliminary Investigation*. Chicago: University of Chicago Press.

—— (1999). 'Two structures for compositionally derived events', in *Proceedings of SALT 9.* Ithaca, NY: Cornell Linguistics Circle, 199–233.

—— and Rappaport-Hovav, M. (1994). 'A preliminary analysis of causative verbs in English', *Lingua* 92: 35–77.

—— —— (1995). *Unaccusativity at the Syntax-Lexical Semantics Interface*. Cambridge, MA: MIT Press.

Lewis, D. (1973). 'Causation', *Journal of Philosophy* 70: 556–67.

Li, Y.-H. A. (2006). 'Chinese Ba', in M. Everaert and H. V. Riemsdijk (eds.), *The Blackwell Companion to Syntax: Volume 1*. Malden, MA: Blackwell, 374–468.

Liberman, M. (1979). *The Intonational System of English*. New York: Garland.

—— and Prince, A. (1977). 'On stress and linguistic rhythm', *Linguistic Inquiry* 8: 249–336.

Lidz, J. and Musolino, J. (2005/6). 'On the quantificational status of indefinites: the view from child language', *Language Acquisition* 13: 73–102.

—— and Williams, A. (2002). 'Reflexivity and resultatives', in L. Mikkelsen and C. Potts (eds.), *WCCFL 21 Proceedings*. Somerville, MA: Cascadilla Proceedings Project, 250–63.

Lieber, R. (1992). *Deconstructing Morphology: Word Formation in Syntactic Theory*. Chicago: University of Chicago Press.

Lin, C.-J. C. (2006). 'Grammar and parsing: a typological investigation of relative-clause processing'. Unpublished dissertation, University of Arizona, Tucson.

—— (2008). 'The processing foundation of head-final relative clauses', *Language and Linguistics* 9: 813–38.

—— Fong, S., and Bever, T. G. (2005). 'Left-edge advantage of gap searching in Chinese possessor relativization'. Paper presented at the 2005 Conference on Architectures and Mechanisms for Language Processing (AMLaP-2005), Ghent University, Ghent, Belgium.

Lindau M. (1985). 'The story of /r/', in V. Fromkin V (ed.), *Phonetic Linguistics: Essays in Honor of Peter Ladefoged*. Orlanda: Academic Press, 157–68.

Lisker, L. and Abramson, A. (1964). 'A cross language study of voicing in initial stops', *Word* 20: 384–422.

Lonzi, L. (1986). 'Pertinenza della struttura tema-rema per l'analisi sintattica' [The relevance of theme-rheme structure for syntactic analysis], in H. Stammerjohann (ed.), *Theme-Rheme in Italian*. Tübingen: Narr, 99–120.

Lozano, Cristobal (2006). 'Focus and split-intransitivity: the acquisition of word order alternations in non-native Spanish', *Second Language Research* 22: 145–87.

—— and Mendikoetxea, A. (2005). 'Postverbal subjects at the interfaces in Spanish and Italian learners of L2 English: a corpus analysis'. Paper presented at the 4th International Contrastive Linguistics Conference, Universidad de Santiago de Compostela, Spain, 19 September 2005.

MacDonald, M. C., Pearlmutter, N. J., and Seidenberg, M. S. (1994). 'The lexical nature of syntactic ambiguity resolution', *Psychological Review* 101: 676–703.

Mahajan, A. (2000). 'Towards a unified treatment of WH-expletives in Hindi and German', in U. Lutz, G. Müller, and A. von Stechow (eds.), *Wh-scope Marking*. Amsterdam: John Benjamins, 317–22.

Manzini, R. M. and Savoia, L. (2002). 'Parameters of subject inflection in Italian dialects', in P. Svenonius (ed.), *Subjects, Expletives and the EPP*. Oxford: Oxford University Press, 157–200.

Marandin, J. M. (2001). 'Unaccusative inversion in French'. Ms. Paris 7.

Marantz, A. (1984). *On the Nature of Grammatical Relations*. Cambridge, MA: MIT Press.

—— (1997). 'No escape from syntax. Don't try morphological analysis in the privacy of your own lexicon', in A. Dimitriadis, L. Siege, C. Surek-Clark, and A. Williams (eds.), *Proceedings of the 21st Annual Penn Linguistics Colloquium. UPenn Working Papers in Linguistics* 4 (2): 201–25.

Martí, L. (2003). 'Contextual variables'. Ph.D. dissertation: University of Connecticut.

Massam, D. (2003). 'Questions and the left periphery in Niuean', in A. Riehl and Th. Savella (eds.), *Proceedings of the Ninth Annual Meeting of the Austronesian Formal Linguistics Association (AFLA 9)*. Cornell Working Papers in Linguistics 19, 94–106.

Mateu, J. (2005). 'Arguing our way to the direct object restriction on English resultatives', *Journal of Comparative Germanic Linguistics* 8: 55–82.

—— (2002). 'A Minimalist account of conflation processes: parametric variation at the lexicon-syntax interface', in A. Alexiadou (ed.), *Theoretical Approaches to Universals*. Amsterdam: John Benjamins, 211–36.

Mateu, J. and Rigau, G. (2001). 'A syntactic approach to illusive event type-shiftings', Technical report, Universitat Autonoma de Barcelona, Bellaterra. GGT research report 01–3.

Matin, E., Shao, K. C., and Boff, K. R. (1993). 'Saccadic overhead: information processing time with and without Saccades', *Perception & Psychophysics* 53 (4): 372–80.

Matthewson, L. (2001). 'Quantification and the nature of cross-linguistic variation', *Natural Language Semantics* 9 (2): 145–89.

Matushansky, O. (2006). 'Head-movement in linguistic theory', *Linguistic Inquiry* 37.1.

May, R. (1985). *Logical Form, its Structure and Derivation*. Cambridge, MA: MIT Press.

McCawley, J. (1968a). 'Lexical insertion in a transformational grammar without deep structure', in B. Darden, C.-J. Bailey, and A. Davison (eds.), *Papers from the Fourth Regional Meeting, Chicago Linguistic Society, April 19–20, 1968*. Chicago, IL: University of Chicago, 71–80.

—— (1968b). 'The Role of Semantics in a Grammar', in E. Bach and R. Harms (eds.), *Universals in Linguistic Theory*. New York: Hold, Rinehart and Winston, 124–69.

—— (1971). 'Prelexical syntax', *Georgetown Monograph Series on Language and Linguistics* 24: 19–33.

McCloskey, J. (1996). 'On the scope of verb-movement in Irish', *Natural Language and Linguistic Theory* 14: 47–104.

—— (2001a). 'On the distribution of subject properties in Irish', in W. Davies and S. Dubinsky (eds.), *Objects and Other Subjects*. Dordrecht and Boston: Kluwer, 157–92.

—— (2001b). 'The morphosyntax of Wh-extraction in Irish', *Journal of Linguistics* 37: 67–100.

McDonough, J. (2000). 'Incorporating onsets in Navajo: the D-Effect', in A. Carnie, E. Jelinek, and M. A. Willie (eds.), *Papers in Honor of Ken Hale*. Cambridge, MA: MIT Working Papers in Linguistics, 177–88.

—— (2003). *The Navajo Sound System*. Dordrecht: Kluwer.

McIntyre, A. (2004). 'Event paths, conflation, argument structure, and VP shells', *Linguistics* 42 (3): 523–71.

Melchiors, M. (2007). 'Die Syntaktische Analyse des Deutschen Dativs – ein Komplizierter Fall'. Ph.D. dissertation, University of Tübingen.

Mendikoetxea, A. (2006). 'Unergatives that "become" unaccusatives in English locative inversion: a lexical-syntactic approach', in C. Copy and L. Gournay (eds.), *Points de vue sur l'inversion. Cahiers de recherche en grammaire anglaise de l'énonciation*. Tome 9. Paris: Editions Orphys, 133–55.

—— (forthcoming). *Some Notes on the Syntactic, Semantic and Pragmatic Properties of Locative Inversion in English*. Ms. Universidad Autónoma de Madrid.

Merchant, J. (2001). *The Syntax of Silence*. Oxford: Oxford University Press.

Mielke, J., Baker, A., and Archangeli, D. (forthcoming). 'Variability and homogeneity in American English /ɹ/ Allophony and /s/ Retraction', in C. Fougeron and M. D'Imperio (eds.), *Variation, Detail, and Representation*, Laboratory Phonology 10. Berlin: Mouton de Gruyter.

Miller, G., Galanter, E., and Pribram, K. (1960). *Plans and the Structure of Behavior.* New York: Holt.

Miyagawa, S. (1994). '(S)ase as an Elsewhere Causative', *Program of the Conference on Theoretical Linguistics and Japanese Language Teaching.* Tsuda University, Tokyo, 61–76.

—— (1998). '(S)ase as an elsewhere causative and the syntactic nature of words', *Journal of Japanese Linguistics* 16: 67–110.

—— (2001). 'The nature of weak islands', In the *4th KGGC Summer School Lecture Collection,* 53–64.

Morgan, Jerry. (1969). 'On arguing about semantics', *Papers in Linguistics* 1: 49–70.

Moro, A. (1997). *The Raising of Predicates. Predicative Noun Phrases and the Theory of Clause Structure.* Cambridge: Cambridge University Press.

Morzycki, M. (2005). 'Mediated modification: functional structure and the interpretation of modifier position'. Ph.D. dissertation. University of Massachusetts, Amherst.

Müller, G. (2008). 'On deriving CED effects from the PIC'. Ms. University of Leipzig.

Musolino, J. (1998). 'Universal Grammar and the acquisition of semantic knowledge'. Ph.D. dissertation. College Park: University of Maryland.

—— (2006a). 'Structure and meaning in the acquisition of scope', in V. van Geenhoven (ed.), *Semantics in Acquisition.* New York: Springer, 141–66.

—— (2006b). 'On the semantics of the subset principle', *Language Learning and Development* 2: 195–218.

—— Crain, S., and Thornton, R. (2000). 'Navigating negative quantificational space', *Linguistics* 38: 1–32.

—— and Lidz, J. (2002). 'Preschool logic: truth and felicity in the acquisition of quantification', in *Proceedings of the Boston University Conference of Language Acquisition* 26: 406–16.

—— —— (2003). 'The scope of Isomorphism: turning adults into children', *Language Acquisition* 11: 277–91.

—— —— (2006). 'Why children aren't universally successful with quantification', *Linguistics* 44: 817–52.

Nagahara, H. (1994). 'Phonological phrasing in Japanese'. Ph.D. dissertation, UCLA.

Nakanishi, K. (2001). 'Prosody and information structure in Japanese: a case study of topic marker *wa*', *Japanese / Korean Linguistics*10: 434–47.

—— (2007). 'Prosody and scope interpretations of the topic marker *wa* in Japanese', in C. Lee, M. Gordon, and D. Büring (eds.) *Topic and Focus: Cross-linguistic Perspectives on Meaning and Intonation.* Dordrecht: Springer, 177–93.

Ndayiragije, J. (1999). 'Checking economy', *Linguistic Inquiry* 30: 399–444.

Neeleman, A., and Koot, H. van de (2008). 'Dutch scrambling and the nature of discourse templates', *Journal of Comparative Germanic Linguistics* 11: 137–89.

—— —— Titov, H. E., and Vermeulen, R. (2009). 'A syntactic typology of topic, focus and contrast', in J. van Craenenbroeck (ed.), *Alternatives to Cartography.* Berlin: Mouton de Gruyter, 15–51.

Neeleman, A. and Reinhart, T. (1998). 'Scrambling and the PF interface' in M. Butt and W. Gueder (eds.), *The Projection of Arguments*. Stanford: CSLI, 309–53.

Nespor, M. (1999). 'Stress domains', in H. van der Hulst (ed.), *Word Prosodic Systems in the Languages of Europe*. Berlin: Mouton de Gruyter, 117–59.

—— and Vogel, I. (1982). 'Prosodic domains of external sandhi rules', in H. van der Hulst and N. Smith, (eds.), *The Structure of Phonological Representations*, Part I, Dordrecht: Foris, 225–55.

—— —— (1986). *Prosodic Phonology*. Dordrecht and Riverton, NJ: Foris.

Newell, H. (2004a). 'A late adjunction solution to bracketing paradoxes', in L. Bateman and C. Ussery (eds.), *Proceedings of the 25th Meeting of the Northeastern Linguistics Society* (NELS 35), 451–62.

—— (2004b). 'The phonological phase'. Ms. McGill University, Montreal.

—— (2005). 'Bracketing paradoxes and particle verbs: a late adjunction analysis', in S. Blaho, L. Vicente, and E. Schoorlemmer (eds.), *Proceedings of Console XIII*. Leiden: University of Leiden, 249–72.

—— (2008). 'Aspects of the morphology and phonology of phases'. Ph.D. dissertation, McGill University, Montreal.

—— and Piggott, G. (2006a). 'Syllabification, stress and derivation by phase in Ojibwa', *McGill Working Papers in Linguistics* 20.

—— —— (2006b). 'The morphological control of phonology within Ojibwe lexical categories', *Papers of the 37th Algonquian Conference*. University of Manitoba, 269–89

Newman, S. (1946). 'On the stress system of English', *Word* 2: 171–87.

Newmeyer, F. (1998). *Language Form and Language Function*. Cambridge, MA: MIT Press.

Newmeyer, F. (2003). 'Grammar is grammar and usage is usage,' *Language* 78: 682–707.

Nichols, L. (2001). 'The syntactic basis of referential hierarchy phenomena: clues from languages with and without morphological case', *Lingua* 111: 515–37.

Nicol, J. and Swinney, D. (1989). 'The role of structure in coreference assignment during sentence comprehension', *Journal of Psycholinguistic Research* 18: 5–20.

Nishigauchi, T. (1990). *Quantification in the Theory of Grammar*. Dordrecht: Kluwer.

Nissenbaum, J. (2000). 'Investigations of covert phrase movement'. Ph.D. dissertation, MIT, Cambridge, MA.

Nozawa, T., Katayama, M., Sasaki, M., and Ishihara, Y. (2000). 'On the perception and production of Japanese stops by native speakers of Korean', *Journal of the Acoustical Society of America* 108 (5): 2652.

Nunes, J. (1995). 'The copy theory of movement and linearization of chains in the Minimalist Program'. Ph.D. dissertation, University of Maryland.

—— (1996). 'On why traces cannot be phonetically realized', in K. Kusumoto (ed.), *Proceedings of North East Linguistic Society*. Harvard University and MIT: Graduate Linguistic Student Association, 211–26.

—— (1999). 'Linearization of chains and phonetic realization of chain links', in S. Epstein and N. Hornstein (eds.), *Working Minimalism*. Cambridge, MA: MIT Press, 217–49

—— (2001). 'Sideward movement', *Linguistic Inquiry* 32 (2): 303–44.

—— (2004). 'Linearization of chains and sideward movement', *Linguistic Inquiry Monographs*. Cambridge, MA: MIT Press.

Ogawa, Y. (2001). 'The stage/individual distinction and (in)alienable possession', *Language* 77: 1–25.

O'Grady, W. (1998). 'The Syntax of Idioms', *Natural Language and Linguistic Theory* 16: 279–312.

O'Leary, C. and Crain, S. (1994). 'Negative polarity items (a positive result) positive polarity items (a negative result)'. Paper presented at the *Boston University Conference on Language Development*.

Ortega-Santos, I. (2005). 'On Locative Inversion and the EPP in Spanish', *Actas del VIII Encuentro Internacional de Lingüística del Noroeste de la Universidad de Sonora* (México).

O'Shaughnessy, D. (1981). 'A study of French vowel and consonant durations', *Journal of Phonetics* 9: 385–406.

Oshima, D. (2008). 'Morphological vs. phonological contrastive topic marking', in *Proceedings of CLS*, 41(1): 371–84.

Ouhalla, J. (1988). 'The Syntax of Head Movement'. Ph.D. dissertation, University College London.

—— (1990). 'Sentential negation, relativized minimality and the aspectual status of auxiliaries', *The Linguistic Review* 7: 183–231.

—— (1991). *Functional Categories and Parametric Variation*. London: Routledge.

—— (1993). 'Subject-extraction, negation and the anti-agreement effect', *Natural Language and Linguistic Theory* 11: 477–518.

—— (2002). 'Negative sentences in Arabic', in J. Ouhalla and U. Shlonsky (eds.), *Themes in Arabic and Hebrew Syntax*. Dordrecht: Kluwer, 299–320.

—— (2005). 'Agreement features, agreement and antiagreement', *Natural Language and Linguistic Theory* 23: 655–86.

Paradis, C. and LaCharité, D. (1997). 'Preservation and minimality in loanword adaptation', *Journal of Linguistics* 33: 379–430.

Parsons, T. (1990a). 'Events in the semantics of English: a study in subatomic semantics', in *Current Studies in Linguistics Series, 19*. Cambridge, MA: MIT Press, 334.

—— (1990b). *Events in the Semantics of English: A Study in Subatomic Semantics*. Cambridge, MA: MIT Press.

Partee, B. (1991). 'Topic, focus and quantification', in S. Moore and A. Z. Wyner (eds.), *Proceedings of Semantics and Linguistic Theory 1*. Cornell University: CLC Publications, 159–87.

—— (1999). 'Focus, quantification, and semantics-pragmatics issues', in P. Bosch and R. van der Sandt (eds.), *Focus: Linguistic, Cognitive, and Computational Perspectives*. Cambridge: Cambridge University Press, 213–31.

Partee, B. and Borschev, V. (2005). 'Genitive of negation, scope of negation in Russian existential sentences', *Proceedings of FASL* 10. Ann Arbor, MI: Michigan Slavic Publications, 120–9.

Peperkamp, S. and Dupoux, E. (2003). 'Reinterpreting loanword adaptation: the role of perception', in *Proceedings of the 15th International Congress of Phonetic Sciences*, 367–70.

Perlmutter, D. (1972). 'Evidence for Shadow Pronouns in French', in P. M. Perantueau, J. N. Levi, and G. C. Phares (eds.), *The Chicago Which Hunt*. Chicago: Chicago Linguistic Society 73–105.

—— (1978). ' Impersonal passives and the Unaccusativity Hypothesis', in *Proceedings of the Fourth Annual Meeting of the Berkeley Linguistic Society*. Berkeley: Berkeley Linguistic Society, 157–89.

Pesetsky, D. (1982). 'Paths and categories'. Ph.D. dissertation, MIT, Cambridge, MA.

—— (1995). *Zero Syntax*. Cambridge, MA: MIT Press.

—— (2000). 'Phrasal movements and its kin'. Cambridge, MA: MIT Press.

Pickering, M. and Barry, G. (1991). 'Sentence processing without empty categories', *Language and Cognitive Processes* 8: 147–61.

Pierrehumbert, J. (1980). 'The phonology and phonetics of English intonation'. Ph.D. dissertation: MIT.

—— (2002). 'Word–specific phonetics', in C. Gussenhoven and N. Warner (eds.), *Laboratory Phonology* 7. Berlin: Mouton de Gruyter, 101–39.

—— Beckman, M., and Ladd, D. R. (2000). 'Conceptual foundations of phonology as a laboratory science', in N. Burton–Roberts, P. Carr, and G. Docherty (eds.), *Phonological Knowledge*. Oxford: Oxford University Press, 273–303.

Pinker, S. (1984). *Language Learnability and Language Development*. Cambridge, MA: Harvard University Press.

Pinto, M. (1997). 'Licensing and Interpretation of Inverted Subjects in Italian'. Ph.D. dissertation, Utrecht.

Plug, L. and Ogden, R. (2003). 'A parametric approach to the phonetics of postvocalic /r/ in Dutch', *Phonetica* 60: 159–86.

Polinsky, M. and Kluender, R. (2007). 'Linguistic typology and theory construction: common challenges ahead', *Linguistic Typology* 11: 273–83.

Pollard, C. and Sag, I. (1992). 'Anaphors in English and the scope of Binding Theory', *Linguistic Inquiry* 23: 261–303.

Pollock, J.-Y. (1989). 'Verb-movement, UG and the structure of IP', *Linguistic Inquiry* 20: 365–424.

Port, R. F. and Leary, A. P. (2005). 'Against formal phonology', *Language* 81: 927–64.

Poser, W. (1984). 'The phonetics and phonology of tone and intonation in Japanese'. Ph.D. dissertation, MIT, Cambridge, MA.

Postal, P. M. (1969). 'On so-called pronouns in English', in D. Reibel and S. Schane (eds.), *Modern Studies in English*. Englewood Cliffs, NJ: Prentice-Hall, 201–44.

Potts, C. (2002). 'The syntax and semantics of *As*-parentheticals', *Natural Language and Linguistic Theory* 20: 623–89.

Prince, E. (1981). 'Toward a taxonomy of given-new information', in P. Cole (ed.), *Radical Pragmatics*. New York: Academic Press, 249–64.

—— (1992). 'The ZPG letter: subjects, definiteness and information stats', in S. Thompson and W. Mann (eds.), *Discourse-Description. Diverse Analyses of a Fundraising Text*. Amsterdam: John Benjamins, 295–325.

—— (1998). 'On the limits of syntax, with reference to left dislocation and topicalization', in P. Culicover and L. McNally (eds.), *Syntax and Semantics. Vol. 39. The Limits of Syntax*. New York: Academic Press, 281–302.

Progovac, L. (1988). 'A binding approach to polarity sensitivity'. Ph.D. dissertation, University of Southern California.

—— (1991). 'Polarity in Serbo-Croatian: anaphoric NPIs and pronominal PPIs', *Linguistic Inquiry* 22: 567–72.

Pustejovsky, J. (1991). 'The syntax of event structure', *Cognition* 41: 47–81.

Pylkkänen, L. and McElree, B. (2006). 'The syntax-semantics interface: on-line composition of sentence meaning', in M. J. Traxler and M. A. Gernsbacher (eds.), *Handbook of Psycholinguistics*, 2nd edn. Amsterdam: Elsevier.

R Development Core Team. (2008). *R: A Language and Environment for Statistical Computing*. R Foundation for Statistical Computing. Vienna, Austria.

Rackowski, A. and Travis, L. (2000). 'V-Initial Languages: X or XP Movement and Adverb Placement', in A. Carnie and E. Guilfoyle (eds.), *The Syntax of Verb-Initial Languages*. Oxford: Oxford University Press, 117–142.

Ramchand, G. C. (1997). *Aspect and Predication: the Semantics of Argument Structure*. Oxford: Clarendon/Oxford University Press.

—— (2008). *Verb Meaning and the Lexicon: A First Phase Syntax*. Cambridge and New York: Cambridge University Press.

Rapoport, T. R. (1999). 'Structure, Aspect, and the Predicate', *Language* 75 (4): 653–77.

Rapp, I. and A. von Stechow. (1999). 'Fast "almost" and the visibility parameter for functional adverbs', *Journal of Semantics* 16: 149–204.

Rappaport Hovav, M., and Levin, B. (2001). 'An event structure account of English resultatives', *Language* 77 (4): 766–97.

Reenen, Pieter van (1994). 'Driemaal R in de Nedeslandse dialecten', *Taal & Tongval Themanvmmer* (special issue) 7: 54–72.

Reinhart, T. (1981). 'Pragmatics and linguistics: an analysis of sentence topics', *Philosophica* 27: 53–94.

—— (1982). 'Pragmatics and linguistics: an analysis of sentence topic', Bloomington: Indiana University Linguistics Club, 1–38.

—— (1998). '*Wh*-in-situ in the framework of the Minimalist Program', *Natural Language Semantics* 6: 29–56.

—— (2000). *The Theta System: Syntactic Realization of Verbal Concepts*. OTS Working Papers in Linguistics, University of Utrecht.

—— (2002). 'The Theta System - an overview', *Theoretical Linguistics*, 28 (3): 229–90.

—— and Reuland, E. (1993). 'Reflexivity', *Linguistic Inquiry* 24: 657–720.

Reis, M. (1980). 'On justifying topological frames: "positional field" and the order of nonverbal constituents in German', *Documentation et Recherche en Linguistique Allemande Contemporaine* 22/23: 59–85.

Reuland, R. (2006). 'Gradedness: interpretive dependencies and beyond', in G. Fanselow, C. Féry, M. Schlesewsky, and R. Vogel (eds.), *Gradience in Grammar*. Oxford: Oxford University Press, 45–69.

Rezac, M. (2004). 'Elements of cyclic syntax: Agree and Merge'. Ph.D. dissertation, University of Toronto.

Rice, K. (2000). *Morpheme Order and Semantic Scope: Word Formation in the Athapaskan Verb*. Cambridge: Cambridge University Press.

Richards, M. (2007). 'On object shift, phases, and transitive expletive constructions in Germanic', in P. Pica *et al.* (eds.), *Linguistic Variation Yearbook* 6. Amsterdam and New York: John Benjamins, 139–59.

—— and Biberauer, T. (2005). 'Explaining *Expl*', in M. den Dikken and C. Tortora (eds.), *The Function of Function Words and Functional Categories*. Amsterdam and New York: John Benjamins, 115–53.

Richards, N. (1997a). 'Subjacency forever!', in V. Samiian (ed.), *Proceedings of WECOL 1996*. Fresno: California State University, 243–55.

—— (1997b). 'What moves where when in which language'. Ph.D. dissertation, MIT

—— (2001). *Movement in Language: Interactions and Architectures*. New York: Oxford University Press.

Rigau, G. (1997). 'Locative sentences and related constructions in Catalan', in A. Mendikoetxea and M. Uribe-Etxebarroa (eds.), *Theoretical Issues at the Morphology-Syntax Interface*. Bilbao/Donostia: UPV, 395–421.

Rizzi, L. (1982). *Issues in Italian Syntax*. Dordrecht: Foris.

—— (1990). *Relativized Minimality*. Cambridge, MA: MIT Press.

—— (1996). 'Residual verb second and the Wh-criterion', in A. Belletti and L. Rizzi (eds.), *Parameters and Functional Heads*. New York: Oxford University Press, (2) 63–90.

—— (1997). 'The fine structure of the left periphery', in L. Haegeman, (ed.), *Elements of Grammar: Handbook in Generative Syntax*. Dordrecht: Kluwer, 281–337.

—— (2004a). 'Locality and left periphery', in A. Belletti (ed.), *Structures and Beyond*. Oxford: Oxford University Press, 104–31.

—— (2004b). *The Structure of CP and IP: The Cartography of Syntactic Structures*. Oxford: Oxford University Press.

—— (2006). 'On the form of chains: criterial positions and ECP effects', in L. Cheng and N. Corver (eds.), *Wh-Movement:Moving On*. Cambridge, MA: MIT Press, 97–133.

—— and Shlonksy, U. (2007). 'Strategies of subject extraction', in H. M. Gartner and U. Sauerland (eds.), *Interfaces + Recursion = Language? Chomsky's Minimalism and the View from Syntax-Semantics*. Berlin: Mouton de Gruyter, 115–60.

Roberts, C. (1996). 'Information structure in discourse: towards an integrated formal theory of pragmatics', *OSU Working Papers in Linguistics* 49. *Papers in Semantics*.

Rochemont, M. (1986). *Focus in Generative Grammar*. Amsterdam: John Benjamins.

Rohrbacher, B. (1994). 'The Germanic languages and the full paradigm: a theory of V to I raising'. Ph.D. dissertation, University of Massachusetts, Amherst, MA.

Romaine, S. (1979). 'Postvocalic /r/ in Scottish English: sound change in progress?', in P. Trudgill (ed.), *Sociolinguistic Patterns in British English*. London: Edward Arnold, 145–57.

Rooth, M. (1985). 'Association with focus'. Ph.D. dissertation, University of Massachusetts, Amherst, MA.

—— (1992). 'A theory of focus interpretation', *Natural Language Semantics* 1: 75–116.

—— (1996). 'On the interface principles for intonational focus', in T. Galloway and J. Spence (eds.), *Proceedings of SALT VI*. Ithaca, NY: Cornell University, 202–26.

—— (2004). 'Comments on Krifka's paper', in H. Kamp and B. Partee (eds.), *Context-Dependence in the Analysis of Linguistic Meaning*. Amsterdam: Elsevier, 475–87

—— (2009). 'Second occurrence focus and relativized stress F', in M. Zimmerman and C. Féry (eds.), *Information Structure: Theoretical, Typological, and Experimental Perspectives*. Oxford: Oxford University Press, 15–35.

Rosén, C. (2006). *Warum klingt das nicht deutsch? Probleme der Informationsstrukturierung in deutschen Texten schwedischer Schüler und Studenten*. Stockholm: Almqvist & Wiksell.

Ross, J. R. (1967). 'Constraints on variables in syntax'. Ph.D. dissertation, MIT, Cambridge, MA.

—— (1983). 'Inner islands'. *BLS* 10, 258–65.

Rothstein, S. (2004). *Structuring Events*. Oxford: Blackwell.

Roussou, A. and Tsimpli, I. (1993). 'On the interaction of case and definiteness in Modern Greek', in I. Philippaki-Warburton, K. Nikolaidis, and M. Sifianou (eds.), *Themes in Greek Linguistics*. Amsterdam: John Benjamins, 69–76.

Runner, J. T. (1998). *Noun Phrase Licensing*. New York: Garland Publications.

—— Sussman, R., and Tanenhaus, M. (2003). 'Assignment of reference to reflexives and pronouns in picture noun phrases: evidence from eye movements', *Cognition* 89: B1-B13.

—— —— —— (2006). 'Assigning reference to reflexives and pronouns in picture noun phrases', *Cognitive Science* 30: 1–49.

Sabel, J. (2000). 'Expletives as features', in R. Billerey *et al.* (eds.), *WCCFL 19 Proceedings*. Somerville, MA: Cascadilla Press, 411–24.

Saito, M. (1985). 'Some asymmetries in Japanese and their theoretical implications'. Ph.D. dissertation, MIT, Cambridge, MA.

Sakai, H. (1994). 'Complex NP constraint and case conversion in Japanese', in M. Nakamura (ed.), *Current Topics in English and Japanese: Proceedings of the Second English/Japanese Comparative Syntax Workshop*. Tokyo: Hituzi Syoboo, 179–203.

Saksena, A. (1982). *Topics in the Analysis of Causatives with an Account of Hindi Paradigms*. Los Angeles, CA: University of California Press.

Sauerland, U. (1998). 'The meaning of chains'. Ph.D. dissertation, MIT, Cambridge, MA.

Sauerland, U. (2004). 'The interpretation of traces', *Natural Language Semantics* 12: 63–127.

Schachter, P. (1985). 'Parts-of-speech systems', in T. Shopen (ed.), *Language Typology and Syntactic Description*. Cambridge: Cambridge University Press, 3–61.

Schank, R. and Abelson, R. (1977). *Scripts, Plans, Goals, and Understanding: An Inquiry into Human Knowledge Structures*. Hillsdale, NJ: Lawrence Erlbaum.

Schein, B. (1993). *Plurals and Events*. Cambridge, MA: MIT Press.

Schmid, M. (1999). *Translating the Elusive: Marked Word Order and Subjectivity in English-German Translation*. Amsterdam and Philadelphia: John Benjamins.

Schütze, C. and Gibson, E. (1999). 'Argumenthood and English prepositional phrase Attachment', *Journal of Memory and Language* 40: 409–31.

Schwartz, B. D. and Sprouse, R. (1996). 'L2 cognitive states and the full transfer/full access model', *Second Language Research* 12: 40–72.

Schwarzschild, R. (1997). 'Why some foci must associate'. Ms. Rutgers University.

—— (1999). 'Givenness, Avoid F and other constraints on the placement of accent', *Natural Language Semantics* 7: 141–77.

Scobbie, J. M. (1997). *Autosegmental Representation in a Declarative Constraint–based Framework*. New York: Garland.

—— (2005). 'Interspeaker variation among Shetland islanders as the long-term outcome of dialectally varied input: speech production evidence for fine-grained linguistic plasticity'. *QMUC Speech Science Research Centre Working Paper WP2*.

—— (2006a). '(r) as a variable', in K. Brown (editor–in–chief), *The Encyclopaedia of Language and Linguistics. 2nd Edition*, vol. 10. Oxford: Elsevier, 337–44.

—— (2006b). 'Flexibility in the face of incompatible English VOT systems', in L. Goldstein, D. H. Whalen, and C. T. Best (eds.), *Laboratory Phonology 8. Varieties of Phonological Competence*. Berlin: Mouton de Gruyter, 367–92.

—— (2007). 'Interface and overlap in phonetics and phonology', in G. Ramchand and C. Reiss (eds.), *The Oxford Handbook of Linguistic Interfaces*. Oxford: Oxford University Press, 17–52.

—— and Pouplier, M. (2010). The role of syllable structure in external sandhi: an EPG study of vocalisation and retraction in word-final English /l/. *Journal of Phonetics* 38: 240–59.

—— Sebregts, K., and Stuart-Smith, J. (2009). *Dutch Rhotic Allophony, Coda Weakening, and the Phonetics-Phonology Interface*. QMU Speech Science Research Centre Working Papers, WP-18.

—— and Stuart–Smith, J. (2008). 'Quasi–phonemic contrast and the fuzzy inventory: examples from Scottish English', in P. Avery, E. B. Dresher, and K. Rice (eds.), *Contrast: Perception and Acquisition: Selected Papers from the Second International Conference on Contrast in Phonology*. Berlin: Mouton de Gruyter, 87–113.

—— —— and Lawson, E. (2008). *Looking Variation and Change in the Mouth: Developing the Sociolinguistic Potential of Ultrasound Tongue Imaging*. Final Report for ESRC Project RES–000–22–2032.

Sebba, M. (1987). *The Syntax of Serial Verbs*. Amsterdam: John Benjamins.

Sebregts, K. and Scobbie, J. M. (2005) 'From facts to phonology: an empirical study of rhotic allophony'. Oral paper presented at the 13th Manchester Phonology Meeting, Manchester.

Sebregts, K., Tops, E., Bezooijen, R. van, Van de Velde, H., Hout, R. van, Willemyns, R., and Zonneveld, W. (2003). 'Sociogeografische, Fonetische en Fonologische Variatie in /r/. Een Onderzoek in Nederlandse en Vlaamse Grote Steden', in T. Koole, J. Nortier, and B. Tahitu (eds.), *Bijdragen aan de 4e Sociolinguistische Conferentie*. Delft: Eburon, 375–85.

Selkirk, E. (1980a). 'Prosodic domains in phonology: Sanskrit revisited', in M. Aronof and M.-L. Kean (eds.), *Juncture*. Saratoga, CA: Anma Libri, 107–29.

—— (1980b). 'The role of prosodic categories in English word stress', *Linguistic Inquiry* 11: 563–605.

—— (1984). *Phonology and Syntax: The Relation between Sound and Structure*. Cambridge, MA: MIT Press.

—— (1986). 'On derived domains in sentence phonology', *Phonology Yearbook* 3: 371–405.

Selkirk, E. (2008). 'Contrastive focus, givenness and the unmarked status of "discourse-new"', *Acta Linguistica Hungarica* 55: 331–46.

Sells, P. (1987). 'Aspects of Logophoricity', *Linguistic Inquiry* 18 (3): 445–79.

Shibatani, M. (1973). 'Semantics of Japanese causativization', *Foundations of Language* 9: 327–73.

—— (1976). 'The grammar of causative constructions: a conspectus', in M. Shibatani (ed.), *Syntax and Semantics 6: The Grammar of Causative Constructions*. New York: Academic Press, 1–40.

Shimizu, K. (1999). 'A study on phonetic characteristics of voicing of stop consonants in Japanese and English' [Written in Japanese], *Journal of the Phonetic Society of Japan* 3 (2): 4–10.

Shinohara, S. (1997). *Analyse Phonologique de L'adaptation Japonaise de Mots Etrangers*. Thèse pour le doctorat, Universite de la Sorbonne Nouvelle.

—— (2006). 'Perceptual effects in segments in loanword phonology', *Lingua* 116: 1046–78.

Shlonsky, U. (1987). 'Null and displaced subjects'. Ph.D. dissertation, MIT, Cambridge, MA.

—— (1997). *Clause Structure and Word Order in Hebrew and Arabic*. New York and Oxford: Oxford University Press.

Siloni, T. (1997). *Noun Phrases and Nominalizations*. Dordrecht: Kluwer.

Silva, D. J. (2006). 'Acoustic evidence for the emergence of tonal contrast in contemporary Korean', *Phonology* 23: 287–308.

Silverman, D. (1992). 'Multiple scansions in loanword phonology: evidence from Cantonese', *Phonology* 9: 289–328.

Simpson, A. (2009). 'Vietnamese and the typology of passive constructions'. Paper presented at *Workshop on Linguistics of Vietnamese*, University of Stuttgart, July 2009.

Simpson, A. P. (1999). 'Fundamental problems in comparative phonetics and phonology. Does UPSID help to solve them?', in *Proceedings of the XIVth ICPhS*, vol. 1, 349–52.

Simpson, J. (1983). 'Resultatives', in L. Levin, M. Rappaport, and A. Zaenen (eds.), *Papers in Lexical-Functional Grammar.* Bloomington: Indiana University Linguistics Club, 143–57.

Sioupi, A. (2002). 'Morphological and telicity aspect with accomplishment VPs in Greek', in B. Hollebrandse, A. van Hout, and C. Vet (eds.), *Crosslinguistic Views on Tense, Aspect and Modality.* Amsterdam and New York: Rodopi, 131–44.

Skinner, T. (2009). 'Investigations of Downward Movement'. Ph.D. dissertation, McGill University, Montreal.

Sluijter, A. and Heuven, V. van (1996). 'Spectral balance as acoustic correlate of linguistic stress', *Journal of the Acoustical Society of America* 100: 2471–85.

Smith, C. (1991). *The Parameter of Aspect.* Dordrecht: Kluwer.

Snyder, W. (1995). 'Language acquisition and language variation. The role of morphology'. Ms, MIT, Cambridge, MA.

—— (2001). 'On the nature of syntactic variation: evidence from complex predicates and complex word-formation', *Language* 77: 324–42.

Sohn, H.-M. (1999). *The Korean Language.* Cambridge: Cambridge University Press.

Sohn, K.-W. (1995). 'Negative polarity items, scope and economy'. Ph.D. dissertation, University of Connecticut, Storrs, CT, distributed by MIT Working Papers in Linguistics, Cambridge, MA.

Son, M. (2006). 'Directed motion and non-predicative PathP in Korean', in P. Svenonius (ed.), *Nordlyd 34.2: Special Issue on Adpositions.* Tromsø: University of Tromsø, 176–99.

—— (2007). 'Directionality and resultativity: the cross-linguistic correlation revisited', in M. Bašić *et al.* (eds.), *Tromsø Working Papers on Language and Linguistics: Nordlyd 34.2, Special Issue on Space, Motion, and Result.* Tromsø: University of Tromsø, 126–64.

—— and Svenonius, P. (2008). 'Microparameters of cross-linguistic variation: directed motion and resultatives', in N. Abner and J. Bishop (eds.), *Proceedings of the 27th West Coast Conference on Formal Linguistics.* Somerville, MA: Cascadilla Proceedings Project, 388–96.

Sorace, A. and Keller, F. (2005). 'Gradience in linguistic data', *Lingua* 115 (11): 1497–1524.

Sorenson, J. M., Cooper, W. E., and Paccia, J. M. (1978). 'Speech timing of grammatical categories', *Cognition* 6: 135–53.

Speas, M. (1990). *Phrase Structure and Natural Language.* Dordrecht: Kluwer.

Speas, M. (1991). 'Functional heads and the Mirror Principle', *Lingua* 84: 181–214.

Speer, S. R. and Clifton, C. J. (1998). 'Plausibility and argument structure in sentence comprehension', *Memory and Cognition* 26: 965–78.

Sportiche, D. (2003). 'Reconstruction, Binding and Scope'. Ms, University of California, Los Angeles.

Starke, M. (2001). 'Move dissolves into Merge: a theory of locality'. Ph.D. dissertation, University of Geneva.

Stechow A. von (1991). 'Focusing and backgrounding operators', in A. Werner (ed.), *Discourse Particles: Descriptive and Theoretical Investigations on the Logical, Syntactic and Pragmatic Properties of Discourse Particles in German*. Amsterdam: John Benjamins, 37–84.

—— (1995). 'The different readings of *wieder* "again": a structural account', *Journal of Semantics* 13: 87–138.

Stepanov, A. (2002). 'Late adjunction and Minimalist phrase structure', *Syntax* 4: 94–125.

Steriade, D. (2001). 'The phonology of perceptibility effects: the P-map and its consequences for constraint organization'. Ms. UCLA.

Stevens, K. (1998). *Acoustic Phonetics*. Cambridge, MA: MIT Press.

Stjepanović, S. (1999). 'What do second position cliticization, scrambling, and multiple wh-fronting have in common?' Ph.D. dissertation, University of Connecticut, Storrs.

Stone, M. (1997). 'Laboratory techniques for investigating speech articulation', in W. J. Hardcastle and J. Laver (eds.), *Handbook of Phonetic Sciences*. Oxford: Blackwell, 11–32.

Stowe, L. A., Tanenhaus, M. K., and Carlson, G. N. (1991). 'Filling gaps on-line: use of lexical and semantic information in sentence processing', *Language and Speech,* 34: 319–40.

Stuart–Smith, J. (2007). 'A sociophonetic investigation of postvocalic /r/ in Glaswegian adolescents', *Proceedings of the 16th International Congress of Phonetic Sciences*: 1449–52.

Sturt, P. (2003). 'The time-course of the application of binding constraints in reference resolution', *Journal of Memory and Language* 48: 542–62.

Stutterheim, C. von (1997). *Einige Prinzipien der Textproduktion: Empirische Untersuchungen zur Produktion Mündlicher Texte*. Tübingen: Max Niemeyer.

Suzuki, T. (1997). 'A theory of lexical functions: light heads in the lexicon and the syntax'. Unpublished dissertation, University of British Columbia.

Szabolcsi, A. (1997). *Ways of Scope-Taking*. Dordrecht, Boston, and London: Kluwer.

Tada, H. (1992). 'Nominative objects in Japanese', *Journal of Japanese Linguistics* 14: 91–108.

Takahashi, S. (2006). 'Decompositionality and identity'. Ph.D. dissertation, MIT, Cambridge, MA. Massachusetts Institute of Technology.

Talmy, L. (1976). 'Semantic causative types', in M. Shibatani (ed.), *Syntax and Semantics 6: The Grammar of Causative Constructions*. New York: Academic Press, 43–116.

—— (1988). 'Force dynamics in language and cognition', *Cognitive Science* 12: 49–100.

Tanenhaus, M. K., Spivey-Knowlton, M. J., Eberhard, K. M., and Sedivy, J. E. (1995). 'Integration of visual and linguistic information in spoken language comprehension', *Science* 268: 1632–4.

Teleman, U., Hellberg, S., and Andersson, E. (1999). *Svenska Akademiens Grammatik. Vol. 4. Satser och Meningar.* Stockholm: Nordstedts Ordbok.

Tenny, C. (1994). *Aspectual Roles and the Syntax-Semantics Interface.* Dordrecht: Kluwer.

—— (1996). 'Short distance pronouns and locational deixis'. LinguistList online conference.

—— (2003). *Short Distance Pronouns in Representational Noun Phrases and a Grammar of Sentience.* Ms.

—— (2004). 'Pronoun binding and the grammar of sentience'. Talk presented at the Workshop on Semantic Approaches to Binding Theory, held at the 16th European Summer School in Logic, Language, and Information, Nancy, France.

Thomas, M. (1988). 'Submissive passives in Vietnamese', in L. McLeod, G. Larson, and D. Brentani (eds.), *Proceedings of the 24th Regional Meeting of the Chicago Linguistic Society.* Chicago: CLS.

Tiedeman, R. (1995). 'Some remarks on antecedent contained deletion', in S. Haraguchi and M. Funaki (eds.), *Minimalism and Linguistic Theory.* Hituzi Syobo: Tokyo, 67–103.

Tokizaki, H. (1999). 'Prosodic phrasing and bare phrase structure', in P. Tamanji, M. Hirotami, and N. Hall (eds.), *Proceedings of NELS 29.* Amherst: GLSA, 381–95.

Tomioka, N. (2006). 'The interaction between restructuring and causative morphology in Japanese'. *Proceedings of the 2005 Annual Meeting of the CLA.*

—— (2007). 'The distribution and interpretation of adjunct locative PPs', in A. Asbury, J. Dotlacil, B. Gehrke, and R. Nouwen (eds.), *Syntax and Semantics of Spatial P.* Amsterdam: John Benjamins.

Tomioka, S. (2009). 'Contrastive topics operate on speech acts', in M. Zimmermann and C. Féry (eds.), *Information Structure: Theoretical, Typological, and Experimental Perspectives.* Oxford: Oxford University Press, 115–38.

—— (forthcoming). 'Resultatives and the typology of causative predicate', in N. Ono (ed.), *Kekka Koubun Kenkyuu no Shin Shiten [New Perspectives: Research on Resultative Constructions.]* Tokyo: Hitsuji Shobo.

Tomioka, S. (2007). 'The Japanese existential possession: a case study of pragmatic disambiguation', *Lingua* 117: 881–902.

Torrego, E. (1989). 'Unergative-unaccusative alternations in Spanish', MIT Working Papers 10.

Tortora, C. (2001). 'Evidence for a null locative in Italian', in G. Cinque and G. Salvi (eds.), *Current Studies in Italian Syntax: Essays offered to L. Renzi.* Amsterdam: Elsevier, 313–26.

Travis, L. D. (1991). 'Derived objects, inner aspect, and the structure of VP'. Paper presented at the 22nd Annual Meeting of the North East Linguistics Society (NELS 22), University of Delaware.

—— (1992a). 'Inner aspect and the structure of VP', *Cahiers Linguistique de l'UQAM* 1: 130–46.

—— (1992b). 'Two quirks of structure: non-projecting heads and the Mirror Image Principle', *Journal of Linguistics* 28: 469–84.

—— (1994). 'Event phrase and a theory of functional categories', in P. Koskinen (ed.), *Proceedings of the Canadian Linguistics Association.* Toronto: CLA, 559–70.

—— (2000a). 'Event structure in syntax', in C. Tenny and J. Pustejovsky (eds.), *Events as Grammatical Objects: The Converging Perspectives of Lexical Semantics and Syntax.* Stanford, CA: CSLI Publications, 145–85.

—— (2000b). 'The L-Syntax/S-Syntax boundary: evidence from Austronesian', in I. Paul, V. Phillips, and L. Travis (eds.), *Formal Issues in Austronesian Linguistics.* Dordrecht: Kluwer, 167–94.

—— (2010). *Inner Aspect: The Articulation of VP.* Dordrecht: Springer Publishers.

Truckenbrodt, H. (1995). 'Phonological phrases: their relation to syntax, focus and prominence'. Ph.D. dissertation, MIT, Cambridge, MA.

Trueswell, J., Sekerina, I., Hill, N., and Logrip, M. (1999). 'The kindergarten-path effect: studying on-line sentence processing in young children', *Cognition* 73: 89–134.

—— Tanenhaus, M., and Garnsey, S. M. (1994). 'Semantic influences on parsing: use of thematic role information in syntactic disambiguation', *Journal of Memory and Language* 33: 285–318.

Truswell, R. (2007). 'Locality of Wh-Movement and the Individuation of Events'. Ph.D. dissertation, University College London.

Tsimpli, I. M. (1995). 'Focusing in Modern Greek', in K. Kiss (ed.), *Discourse Configurational Languages.* Oxford: Oxford University Press.

Unsworth, S. (2005). 'Child L2, Adult L2, Child L1: Differences and similarities. A study on the acquisition of direct object scrambling in Dutch'. Ph.D. dissertation, Utrecht University.

—— Gualmini, A., and Helder, C. (2008). 'Children's interpretation of indefinites in sentences containing negation: a reassessment of the cross-linguistic picture', *Language Acquisition* 15: 315–28

Vallduví, E. (1990). '"Only" and focus', *The Penn Review of Linguistics* 14: 143–56.

—— (1992). *The Informational Component.* New York: Garland.

—— and Engdahl, E. (1996). 'The linguistic realization of information packaging', *Linguistics* 34: 459–519.

Van de Velde, H. (1996). 'Variatie en Verandering in het Gesproken Standaardnederlands'. Ph.D. dissertation, KUN Nijmegen.

—— and Hout, R. van (1999). 'The Pronunciation of (r) in Standard Dutch', in R. van Bezooijen and R. Kager (eds.), *Linguistics in the Netherlands 1999.* Amsterdam and Philadephia: John Benjamins, 177–88.

—— —— (2001). *R–atics: Sociolinguistic, Phonetic and Phonological Characteristics of /r/.* Etudes & Travaux 4. Brussels: Institut des Langues Vivantes et de Phonétique, Université Libre de Bruxelles.

Van der Sandt, R. (1992). 'Presupposition Projection as Anaphora Resolution', *Journal of Semantics* 9: 333–77.

Van Valin, R. D. Jr (1990). 'Semantic Parameters of Split Intransitivity', *Language* 66 (2): 221–60.

Vazquez Alvarez, Y. and Hewlett, N. (2007). 'The "trough effect": an ultrasound study', *Phonetica* 64: 105–21.

Vendler, Z. (1957). 'Verbs and times', *Philosophical Review* 66: 143–60.

—— (1967). *Linguistics in Philosophy*. Ithaca: Cornell University Press.

Verkuyl, H. (1993). *A Theory of Aspectuality: The Interaction Between Temporal and Atemporal Structure*. Cambridge: Cambridge University Press.

—— (1999). *Aspectual Issues: Studies on Time and Quantity*. Stanford: CSLI Publications.

Vergnand, J. R. and Zubizarreta, M. L. (1992). 'The definite determiner and the inalienable constructions in French and in English', *Linguistic Inquiry* 23: 595–652.

Vermeulen, R. (2009b). 'The syntax of topics in Japanese'. Ms. Ghent University.

—— (2009). 'Contrast, topic and contrastive topics in Japanese', in *MIT Working Papers in Linguistics: Proceedings of Workshop on Altaic Formal Linguistics* 5: 361–72.

Verspoor, C. M. (1997). 'Contextually-dependent lexical semantics'. Ph.D. dissertation, University of Edinburgh.

Vichit-Vadakan, R. (1976). 'The concept of inadvertence in Thai periphrastic causative constructions,' in M. Shibatani (ed.), *Syntax and Semantics*. New York: Academic Press, 459–76.

Vieregge, W. H. and Broeders, A. P. A. (1993). 'Intra– and Interspeaker Variation of /r/ in Dutch', *Eurospeech* 93: 267–70.

Vikner, S. (1997). 'V-to-I movement and inflection for person in all tenses', in L. Haegeman (ed.), *The New Comparative Syntax*. London and New York: Longman, 189–213.

Voortman, B. (1994). *Regionale Variatie in het Taalgebruik Van Notabelen. Een Sociolinguïstisch Onderzoek in Middelburg, Roermond en Zutphen*. Universiteit van Amsterdam. Amsterdam: IFOTT

Wagner, M. (2005). 'Prosody and recursion'. Ph.D. dissertation, MIT, Cambridge, MA.

Ward, G. and Birner, B. (1995). 'Definiteness and the English existential', *Language* 71: 722–42.

Wason, P. (1965). 'The context of plausible denial', *Journal of Verbal Learning and Verbal Behavior* 4: 7–11.

—— (1972). 'In real life negatives are false', *Logique et Analyse* 15: 17–38.

Watanabe, A. (1992). 'Subjacency and S-structure movement of WH-in-situ', *Journal of East Asian Linguistics* 1: 255–91.

—— (2003). 'Wh and operator constructions in Japanese', *Lingua* 11: 519–58.

Wayland, R. (2000). 'Perceptual assimilation and categorical discrimination of Korean stop consonants by native Thai speakers', *The Journal of the Acoustical Society of America* 108 (5): 2652.

Wechsler, S. (1997). 'Resultative predicates and control', in R. C. Blight and M. J. Moosally (eds.), *Proceedings of the Texas Linguistics Society*, vol. 38. Austin: University of Texas, 307–21.

—— (2005a). 'Resultatives under the 'event-argument homomorphism' model of telicity', in N. Erteschik-Shir and T. Rapoport (eds.), *The Syntax of Aspect: Deriving Thematic and Aspectual Interpretation*. Oxford: Oxford University Press, 255–73.

—— (2005b). 'Weighing in on scales: a reply to Goldberg and Jackendoff', *Language* 81 (2): 465–73.

Westman, M. (1974). *Bruksprosa*. Lund: Liber/Gleerups.

Whelpton, M. (2006). 'Resultatives in Icelandic – a preliminary investigation', < *http://ling.auf.net/lingBuzz/000292* > .

—— (2007). 'Building Resultatives in Icelandic', in E. Bainbridge and B. Agbayani (eds.), *Proceedings of 34th Western Conference on Linguistics (WECOL 2006)*, vol. 17. Fresno, CA: California State University, 478–86.

White, L. (2009). 'Grammatical theory: interfaces and L2 knowledge', in W. C. Ritchie and T. K. Bhatia (eds.), *The New Handbook of Second Language Acquisition*. Leeds: Emerald, 49–68.

Whitman, J. (2001). 'Kayne 1994: p.143, fn.3', in G. Alexandrova (ed.), *The Minimalist Parameter*. Amsterdam: John Benjamins, 77–100.

Wilkins, W. (1988). 'Thematic structure and reflexivization', in W. Wilkins (ed.), *Syntax and Semantics 21: Thematic Relations*. San Diego: Academic Press, 191–213.

Williams, A. (2005). 'Complex causatives and verbal valence', Ph.D. dissertation, University of Pennsylvania.

—— (2008). 'Word order in resultatives', in C. Chang and H. Haynie (eds.), *WCCFL 26 Proceedings*. Somerville, MA: Cascadilla Proceedings Project, 507–15.

Williams, E. (1980). 'Predication', *Linguistic Inquiry* 11: 203–38.

—— (1981). 'Argument structure and morphology', *The Linguistic Review* 1: 81–114.

—— (1982). 'The NP cycle', *Linguistic Inquiry* 13 (2): 277–95.

—— (1983). 'Against small clauses', *Linguistic Inquiry* 14: 287–308.

—— (1985). 'PRO and the subject of NP', *Natural Language and Linguistic Theory* 3: 297–315.

—— (1986). 'A reassignment of the functions of LF', *Linguistic Inquiry* 17 (2): 264–300.

—— (1987). 'Implicit arguments, the Binding Theory and control', *Natural Language and Linguistic Theory* 5: 151–80.

—— (1988). 'Is LF distinct from S-Structure? a reply to May', *Linguistic Inquiry* 19 (1): 135–46.

Wolff, P. (2003). 'Direct causation in the linguistic coding and individuation of causal events', *Cognition* 88: 1–48.

Wurmbrand, S. (2000). *Infinitives*. Berlin: Mouton de Gruyter.

—— (2001). *Infinitives: Restructuring and Clause Structure*. Berlin and New York: Mouton de Gruyter.

Yip, M. (1993). 'Cantonese loanword phonology and Optimality Theory', *Journal of East Asian Linguistics* 2: 261–91.

Young, R. W. (2000). *The Navajo Verb System*. Albuquerque: University of New Mexico Press.

Young, R. W. and Morgan, W. (1987). *The Navajo Language: A Grammar and Collo-quial Dictionary.* Albuquerque: University of New Mexico Press.

Zacks, J. and Tversky, B. (2001). 'Event structure in perception and conception', *Psychological Bulletin* 127: 3–21.

Zifonun, G., Hoffmann, L., and Strecker, B. (1997). *Grammatik der Deutschen Sprache. Schriften des Instituts für Deutsche Sprache*, Vol. 2. Berlin and New York: Walter de Gruyter.

Zribi-Hertz, A. (1989). 'Anaphor binding and narrative point of view - English reflexive pronouns in sentence and discourse,' *Language* 65 (4): 695–727.

Zubizarreta, M. L. (1992). 'The lexical encoding of scope relations among arguments', in T. Stowell and E. Wehrli (eds.), *Syntax and Semantics 26: Syntax and the Lexicon.* San Diego: Academic Press,

—— (1998). *Prosody, Focus and Word Order.* Cambridge, MA: MIT Press.

Zwart, J.-W. (1997). *Morphosyntax of Verb Movement.* Dordrecht: Kluwer.

Index

Note: Page numbers followed by 'n' denote references in the footnotes.

OXFORD STUDIES IN THEORETICAL LINGUISTICS